The changing rules on the
of force in international l

Melland Schill Studies in International Law
Series editor Professor Dominic McGoldrick

The Melland Schill name has a long-established reputation for high standards of scholarship. Each volume in the series addresses major public international law issues and current developments. Many of the Melland Schill volumes have become standard works of reference. Interdisciplinary and accessible, the contributions are vital reading for students, scholars and practitioners of public international law, international organisations, international relations, international politics, international economics and international development.

The changing rules on the use of force in international law

Tarcisio Gazzini

Manchester University Press

Published by Manchester University Press
Oxford Road, Manchester M13 9NR, UK
www.manchesteruniversitypress.co.uk

British Library Cataloguing-in-Publication Data
A catalogue record for this book is available from the British Library

ISBN 0 7190 7324 3 *hardback*
EAN 978 0 7190 7324 3
ISBN 0 7190 7325 1 *paperback*
EAN 978 0 7190 7325 0

First published in the USA and its Dependencies, Philippines and Canada
by Juris Publishing, Inc.
71 New Street, Huntingdon, New York 11743
www.jurispub.com

Library of Congress Cataloging-in-Publication Data applied for

ISBN 1 929446 75 6 *hardback*
ISBN 1 929446 74 8 *paperback*

First published 2005

14 13 12 11 10 09 08 07 06 05 10 9 8 7 6 5 4 3 2 1

Typeset in 10/12pt Times
by Northern Phototypesetting Co Ltd, Bolton
Printed in Great Britain
by Bell & Bain Ltd, Glasgow

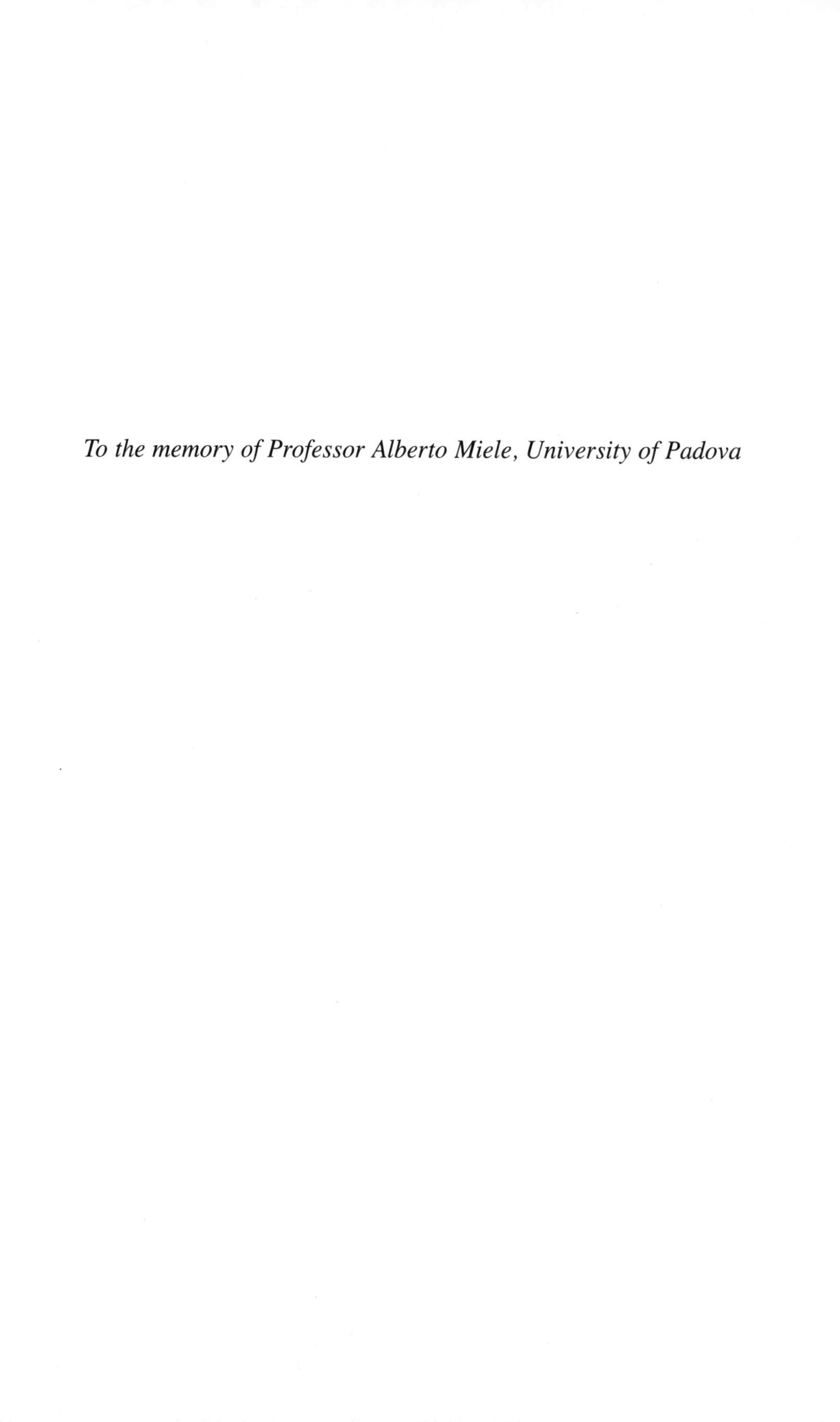

To the memory of Professor Alberto Miele, University of Padova

Contents

Abbreviations

AASL	Annals of Air and Space Law
AFDI	Annuaire français de droit international
AIDI	Annuaire de l'Institut de droit international
AJICL	African Journal of International and Comparative Law
AJIL	American Journal of International Law
AJPIL	Austrian Journal of Public International Law
ASDI	Annuaire suisse de droit international
ASIL Proceedings	Proceedings of the American Society of International law
AUILR	American University International Law Review
AULR	American University Law Review
BFSP	British and Foreign State Papers
BJIL	Brooklyn Journal of International Law
BYIL	British Yearbook of International Law
CWRILJ	Case Western Reserve International Law Journal
CI	Comunità internazionale
CILJ	Cornell International Law Journal
CJTL	Columbia Journal of Transnational Law
CLP	Current Legal Problems
CYIL	Canadian Yearbook International Law
DAI	Documents d'actualité internationale
EG	Enciclopedia giuridica
EJIL	European Journal of International Law
ETS	European Treaty Series
EuGRZ	Europäische Grundrechte-Zeitung
FA	Foreign Affairs
FILJ	Fordham International Law Journal
GJIL	Georgia Journal of International Law
GS	Transactions of the Grotius Society
GYIL	German Yearbook of International law
HJIL	Harvard Journal of International Law
IA	International Affairs
ICJ Rep.	Reports of Judgments, Advisory Opinions and Orders of the International Court of Justice

ICJR	International Commission of Jurists Review
ICLQ	International and Comparative Law Quarterly
IJIL	Indian Journal International Law
IL	International Lawyer
ILJ	International Law Journal
ILM	International Legal Materials
ILR	International Law Reports
ILS	International Law Studies
IO	International Organisations
IR	International Relations
IS	International Spectator
Isr. LR	Israel Law Review
IYHR	Israel Yearbook on Human Rights
IYIL	Italian Yearbook of International Law
JAIL	Japanese Annual of International Law
JALC	Journal of Air Law and Commerce
JCSL	Journal of Conflict and Security Law
JDI	Journal du droit international
LJ	Law Journal
LJIL	Leiden Journal of International Law
LNOJ	League of the Nations Official Journal
LNTS	League of Nations Treaty Series
LR	Law Review
Mich. LR	Michigan Law Review
MJIL	Michigan Journal of International Law
Mil. LR	Military Law Review
MLR	Modern Law Review
MPYUNL	Max Plank Yearbook United Nations Law
Nat. Int.	National Interest
NILR	Netherlands International Law Review
NLR	Naval Law Review
NWCR	Naval War College Review
LNTS	League of the Nations Treaty Series
NYIL	Netherlands Yearbook of International Law
NYUJILP	New York University Journal of International Law & Politics
ÖZöRV	Österreichisches Zeitschrift für öffentliches und Völkerrecht
RBDI	Revue belge de droit international
RdC	Recueil des cours de l'Académie de droit international de La Haye
RDI	Rivista di diritto internazionale
RDMDG	Revue de droit militaire et droit de guerre
RFDAS	Revue française de droit aérien et spatial
RGDIP	Revue générale de droit international

RHDI	Revue hellénique de droit international
RICJ	Review of the International Commission of Jurists
RIDT	Revue international de théorie du droit
RIIA	Reports of International Arbitral Awards
SDLR	San Diego Law Review
TIAS	United States Treaties and Other International Agreements
TJIL	Texas Journal of International Law
TLCP	Transnational Law and Contemporary Problems
UCLR	University of Chicago Law Review
UNCIO	United Nations Conference on International Organisation
UNTS	United Nations Treaty Series
VJIL	Virginia Journal of International Law
VJTL	Vanderbilt Journal of Transnational Law
WCPD	Weekly Compilation of Presidential Documents (United States)
YBILC	Year Book International Law Commission
YBWA	Year Book of World Affairs
YJIL	Yale Journal of International Law
ZaöRV	Zeitschrift für ausländischer öffentliches Recht und Völkerrecht

Introduction

Recent State practice on humanitarian intervention, repression of international terrorism and enforcement of disarmament obligations poses a serious challenge to the current legal regulation of the use of force. States are divided on several issues that lie at the heart of the structure and organisation of the international community. These issues include the prerogatives and role of the Security Council in the maintenance of international peace and security as well as the admissibility of pre-emptive self-defence and military enforcement measures not authorised by the United Nations.

Using the collective system envisaged in the UN Charter as a paradigm, this study aims to provide a systematic view of the rules governing the use of force in international law. It assesses whether existing legal categories on the regulation of force have been disrupted by the new threats to international peace and security caused by terrorism and weapons of mass destruction,[1] or whether they may still be adequate, with certain adjustments where necessary, to govern the use of force in international law.[2]

The study rejects a static vision of the Charter in favour of a more flexible and mainly inductive approach[3] based on the analysis of the practice of States 'in and extra United Nations'[4] and of the Organisation itself as an international legal subject. Largely developed from the perspective of the sources of international law, this approach pays particular attention to the normative powers of the Security Council, the interaction between the Charter and customary international law, and the processes of desuetude and informal modification of treaties.

In this perspective, the content of the rules governing the use of force in international law are not to be construed on the basis of postulates established through the inclusion of these rules in the Charter and their reiteration in subsequent

[1] See A. Cassese, 'Terrorism is also Disrupting Some Crucial Legal Categories of International Law', 12 *EJIL* (2001) 993.

[2] See. G. Abi-Saab, 'There is No Need to Reinvent the Law', posted at www.crimesofwar.org.

[3] G. Schwarzenberger, *The Inductive Approach to International Law* (London: Stevens, 1965).

[4] The expression is borrowed from G. Arangio-Ruiz, *infra* note I-25, p. 45.

documents. Rather, it has to be determined through the analysis of the practice regarding the interpretation and application of these norms by the subjects to which these are addressed. Hence, the formation and evolution of international law have accurately been described as

> a process of continuous interaction, of continuous demand and response, in which the decision-makers of particular nations states unilaterally put forwards claims of the most diverse and conflicting character . . . and in which other decision-makers . . . weight and appraise these competing claims in terms of the interests of the world community and of the rival claimant, and ultimately accept or reject them.[5]

The rules on the use of force, including Art. 2(4) of the United Nations Charter, are exposed – as is any other rule of international law – to such a process. They evolve in accordance with the needs of the international community as expressed by the claims put forward by some States and accepted, or at least acquiesced in, by the majority of the other States. Even qualifying these rules as peremptory norms does not mean that their content has been perpetually shaped, although a larger critical mass may be required in order to bring about a normative change. In any case, ascertaining whether and when such an incremental process has led to a normative change is a difficult task that implies a careful assessment of the behaviour of the subjects of the international legal system.

Part 1 is dedicated to the collective use of force within the framework of the Charter, whose ambitious project is based on the premise that armed force can be resorted to exclusively in the common interest. Chapter I has an introductory character and describes the collective security system as envisaged in the Charter. It begins with a short discussion of the powers granted to the Security Council for the discharge of its primary responsibility for the maintenance of international peace and security, and the conditions under which these powers may be exercised. The discussion touches upon the Security Council's powers related to measures not involving the use of force in order to better appreciate the normative role of the Security Council and the legal effects of its resolutions. An examination of the legal and political limits to the Security Council's powers and the possible remedies available to Member States concludes the chapter.

Chapter II explores the extent to which the collective security system has functioned since the end of the Cold War in spite of the non-implementation of Arts. 43 *et seq*. of the Charter that were intended to put at the disposal of the Security Council the armed forces necessary to discharge its responsibilities. On one occasion, during the Somali crisis, the Security Council directly took military coercive measures. The operations were conducted by the armed forces, previously engaged in a peace-keeping operations, provided by some States on the basis of *ad hoc* agreements.

[5] M. S. McDougal, 'The Hydrogen Bomb Tests and the International Law of Sea', 49 *AJIL* (1955) 353, p. 354.

In all the other crises in which the Security Council was involved, it limited itself to authorising member States to use military force. With the possible exception of NATO coercive military operations conducted in Bosnia-Herzegovina until August 1995, the operations were carried out by Member States without any effective control by the Security Council. It is argued that the legal basis of the operations is to be found in a customary rule that emerged throughout the 1990s as a result of a uniform practice supported by an adequate *opinio juris*, and that eventually informally modified the Charter. The so-called authorisation practice has enabled the collective security system to function, albeit in a rather selective manner and with a limited centralised control over the use of force. Its functioning, however, depends on the lasting agreement among the permanent members of the Security Council. As soon as such an agreement fades away, the system becomes ineffective.

Chapter III is dedicated to the recent main instances of use of force that have provoked controversy between the Member States of the Security Council and more generally of the United Nations. The final act of the Bosnian conflict, the military coercive activities carried out in the aftermath of the Gulf crisis (1991–1999), and the Kosovo crisis marked a period of unilateralism that culminated with the recent massive intervention in Iraq.

The United States, supported by its NATO allies, or at least some of them, openly challenged the authority of the Security Council and attempted to downgrade its authorisation from a legal requirement to a matter of political convenience. The claim was steadily resisted by the overwhelming majority of States. Bearing in mind that the evolution of international law is the result of the claims, reactions and counter-claims of States, an attempt is made to assess the impact of these cases on the collective security system and the perspectives ahead.

Part 2 deals with the use of force by States either individually or jointly. The shortcomings and failures of the collective security system certainly have an impact on the rules governing the use of force and on their evolution. Nonetheless, the general prohibition on the use of force does not hinge upon the effective functioning of the collective security system. The continuing existence of the ban on the use of force is not openly questioned by States, nor even by those more inclined to resort to military force. Yet, the debate concerns the limits of the prohibition on using force rather the existence of the prohibition itself.

In this perspective, Chapter IV and V are based on, and ultimately aim to verify, the assumption that the prohibition on the use of force is still binding upon States, as systematically confirmed by the International Court of Justice.

The content of such a prohibition is defined in general terms in Chapter IV through the analysis of its exceptions. Through the lenses of the interaction between the Charter and customary international law, this chapter considers the evolution of the right to self-defence – the only exception expressly provided for in the Charter – and the possible (re-)emergence of other exceptions.

With regard to self-defence, it is submitted that, contrary to the view held by the International Court of Justice and the majority of authors, any hostile military activities may trigger a forceful reaction, without the trespassing of a threshold of gravity being required. The limits of the use of force in self-defence are considered, with particular attention to the lawfulness of defensive action aimed at intercepting an offensive activity before it reaches its target. Bearing in mind the normative powers of the Security Council, the research also deals with the international control over self-defence claims. Finally, the chapter discusses the alleged (re-)emergence of new exceptions to the general ban on the use of force, namely armed countermeasures, rescue of nationals abroad, and intervention on humanitarian grounds.

Considering the magnitude of recent developments, the use of force in the related fields of international terrorism and weapons of mass destruction has been dealt with separately in Chapter V. The inquiry purports to verify whether the notion of self-defence, intended as defensive military action against hostile military activities conducted by subjects of international law, is adequate to govern the use of force to curb international terrorism and counter the proliferation of weapons of mass destruction. The question is two-fold. On the one hand, it is necessary to verify whether terrorist activities can be qualified as armed attacks for the purpose of Art. 51. On the other hand, the attribution of these activities to States or other entities is rather complex, as demonstrated by the relationship between the Taliban government and Al Qaeda.

The most difficult problems related to self-defence concern the limits to which the notion of interceptive self-defence can be stretched and ultimately the admissibility of pre-emptive military measures deliberately directed at eliminating threats that are potential but not yet immediate and concrete.

When States cannot be held responsible for the terrorist activities and the military reaction implies an encroachment on the sovereignty of other States, the State using force may be tempted to justify its action as armed reprisals or under the doctrine of state of necessity, depending on the prior violation by the target State of its international obligations concerning the prevention and repression of terrorism.

The second part of the chapter is devoted to the unilateral or joint use of force in relation to the possession, threat and use of weapons of mass destruction. It focuses in particular on the controversial question concerning the legality of the threat or use of nuclear weapons in self-defence and of the pre-emptive military action against threats posed by these weapons. Often referring to the recent Iraqi crisis, it further deals with the collective and unilateral means at the disposal of the United Nations and its members to enforce disarmament obligations and tackle the proliferation of weapons of mass destruction.

Part 1

The collective use of force

I

The collective security system established by the Charter

This Chapter describes the collective security system as envisaged in the United Nations Charter. It deals with the legal basis of the Security Council's powers and the conditions under which such powers can be exercised. These powers are then analysed following the two-fold distinction between non-military and military measures. Particular focus is laid on the legal effects of the Security Council's resolutions. A discussion on the limits to the Security Council's powers and the remedies against their violations concludes the chapter.

The pivotal role of Art. 39 of the Charter

It is appropriate to begin the analysis of the collective security system established by the Charter with some basic considerations on the pivotal role of Art. 39. A determination under Art. 39 on the existence of a threat to peace, breach of peace or act of aggression paves the way for the Security Council to indicate provisional measures under Art. 40 or to impose, authorise or recommend economic or military measures under Arts. 41 and 42.[1] The Security Council's practice reveals a clear preference for a general reference to Chapter VII rather than to Art. 39.[2]

[1] Such a determination is generally considered as necessary before the Security Council decides upon enforcement measures: see R. Higgins, *The New United Nations: Appearance and Reality* (Hull: University of Hull Press, 1993), p. 10; V. Gowlland-Debbas, 'Security Council Enforcement Action and Issues of State Responsibility', 43 *ICLQ* (1994) 55, p. 61; F. L. Kirgis, 'The Security Council's First Fifty Years', 89 *AJIL* (1995) 506, p. 512; J. A. Frowein and N. Krisch, 'Article 39', in B. Simma (ed.), *The Charter of the United Nations*, 2nd ed. (Oxford: Oxford University Press, 2002) p. 717. Relying in particular on res. 678 (1990) and res. 833 (1993), however, H. Freudenschuß, 'Article 39 of the UN Charter Revisited: Threats to the Peace and the Recent Practice of the UN Security Council', 46 *AJPIL* (1993) 1, observes that 'Security Council members no longer pay much attention to the presence or absence of a reference to such a threat'.

[2] Among the rare references to Art. 39, see Res. 598 (1987) concerning the Iran–Iraq conflict and Res. 660 (1990) concerning the Iraqi invasion of Kuwait. On both occasions the Security Council determined the existence of a breach to peace and indicated provisional measures under Art. 40.

A formal reference to Art. 39 or to Chapter VII, however, does not appear to be necessary, provided that the language used in the resolution denotes sufficiently clearly that the Security Council intends to avail itself of, or at least to reserve, the possibility of exercising Chapter VII powers. In the event of follow-up, such an intention may also be inferred from previous resolutions.

The finding of a violation of international law is not an indispensable prerequisite for the Security Council's resort to enforcement measures, although such a finding has, on a number of occasions, been linked with the determination under Art. 39.[3] The notion of threat to peace is wider than the general prohibition to threat or use of force incorporated in Art. 2(4). This reflects the intention of the contracting parties not to confine the Security Council's reaction to a response to internationally wrongful acts.[4] Hence, 'The purpose of enforcement action under Art. 39 is not to maintain or restore law, but to maintain and restore peace, which is not necessarily identical with the law'.[5] Being functional to the maintenance of international peace and security, enforcement measures do not necessarily coincide with measures directed at sanctioning breaches of international law.[6]

This has been demonstrated by the events relating to the maintenance of the arms embargo imposed by Security Council Resolutions 713 (1991) and 727 (1992) against Bosnia-Herzegovina. The legality of these enforcement measures was not challenged, either before the International Court of Justice[7] or elsewhere,

[3] V. Gowlland-Debbas, *supra* note 1, pp. 63 *et seq*.

[4] The choice of a neutral term such as 'measures' in Arts. 41 and 42 further supports this view. The use in Art. 39 and Art. 2(4) of the same expression, however, would have better defined the legal obligations of Member States: see H. Kelsen, *The Law of the United Nations* (London: Stevens, 1951), p. 737.

[5] See H. Kelsen, *supra* note 4, p. 736. Accordingly, Kelsen prefers to qualify such measures as political, although it does not rule out the possibility of considering them as legal sanctions on the assumption that Member States are obliged to refrain from any conduct the Security Council may subsequently declare to be a threat to international peace. This view, however, hardly matches the importance given by Kelsen to the unambiguous definition of any obligation (pp. 709–710) and the discretion enjoyed by the Security Council under Art. 39, *infra* note 19. See also J. Kunz, 'Sanctions in International Law', 54 *AJIL* (1960) 324, pp. 329–30; J. Combacau, 'The Exception of Self-Defence in U.N. Practice', in A. Cassese (ed.), *The Current Legal Regulation of the Use of Force* (Dordrecht: Nijhoff, 1986) p. 9 *et seq*., pp. 16.

[6] G. Cohen-Jonathan, 'Article 39', in J. P. Cot and A. Pellet (eds.), *La Charte des Nations Unies* (Paris: Economica, 1991), p. 648, notes that the Charter is based upon 'un imperatif essentiellement politique'. See also R. Higgins, 'The Place of International Law in the Settlement of Dispute by the Security Council', 64 *AJIL* (1970) 1, p. 16; M. L. Forlati Picchio, *La sanzione nel diritto internazionale* (Padova: CEDAM, 1974), pp. 128 *et seq*. and 183 *et seq*.; G. Gaja, 'Réflexions sur le rôle du Conseil de Sécurité dans le nouvel ordre mondial. A propos des rapports entre maintien de la paix et crimes internationaux des Etats', 97 *RGDIP* (1993) 297, p. 300.

[7] *Application of the Convention on Prevention and Punishment of the Crime of Genocide*, Provisional Measures, Order of 16 April, *ICJ Reports 1993*, pp. 3 *et seq*.; Order of 13 September 1993, *ibid*., pp. 325 *et seq*.

on the ground that no prior breach of international law by Bosnia-Herzegovina had been alleged or established.[8]

The determination under Art. 39 normally constitutes the first step of the decision-making process leading to enforcement measures. Being a decision under Chapter VII, it is exempted from the domestic jurisdiction clause included in Art. 2(7) of the Charter.[9] Having established the existence of one of the situations listed in Art. 39, the Security Council is called upon to assess – from a costs–benefits perspective – whether, and eventually which kind of enforcement measures are appropriate.[10]

The determination under Art. 39 is a mere prerequisite for the decision to resort to enforcement measures that should follow only as *extrema ratio* and provided that the remedy is no worse than the evil (so-called 'ethic of responsibility'), especially when these measures have a military nature.[11] This excludes that a determination under Art. 39 entails any obligation to adopt enforcement measures.[12] As maintained by the International Court of Justice, the provisions contained in Chapter VII 'speak of *situations* as well as disputes, and it must lie within the powers of the Security Council to police a situation, even though it does not resort to enforcement action against a State'.[13] Even before that, any positive obligation to decide enforcement measures is inconceivable in a system like the one established by the Charter, because of the absence of sanctions[14] or remedies[15] in the event of inactivity of any organ.

[8] For another example, see *infra*, text corresponding to note II-21.

[9] On this point, N. D. White, *Keeping the Peace*, 2nd ed. (Manchester: Manchester University Press, 1997), p. 56.

[10] In the *Report to the President on the results of the San Francisco Conference*, 26 June, 1945, Dept. of State Pub. No. 2349, p. 91, it is maintained that Art. 39 'leaves a wide latitude to the discretion of the Security Council, which decides whether a threat to peace, breach of peace, or act of aggression exists, and having so decided is free to choose whether to make recommendations to the disputing parties or to proceed with sanctions or to do both'.

[11] N. Bobbio, *Una guerra giusta? Sul conflitto del Golfo* (Venezia: Marsilio, 1991), pp. 41 *et seq.*; M. L. Picchio Forlati, 'Introduzione', in M. L. Forlati Picchio (ed.), *Le Nazioni Unite* (Torino: Giappichelli, 1998), p. 15.

[12] Security Council practice confirms this conclusion. In Res. 598 (1987), for instance, the Security Council determined that there existed a breach of the peace and adopted certain provisional measures under Art. 40 of the Charter. More recently, in Res. 1072, the Security Council determined that the continued deterioration of the security and humanitarian situation in Burundi amounted to a threat to the region of the Great Lakes, but did not resort to any economic or military enforcement measures.

[13] *Certain Expenses of the United Nations (Article 17, paragraph 2 of the Charter)*, Advisory Opinion, *ICJ Reports 1962*, pp. 151 *et seq.*, p. 167. The verb 'to police' has been translated into French as 'prendre en main'.

[14] H. Kelsen, *supra* note 4, p. 154.

[15] B. Conforti, *The Law and Practice of the United Nations*, 2nd ed. (The Hague: Kluwer, 2000), p. 36.

Reluctant to use the expressions 'breach of peace'[16] and 'act of aggression',[17] the Security Council has widely resorted to that of 'threat to peace'. This expression can hardly be defined in legal terms[18] and leaves an extremely wide discretion to the Security Council, which is generally accepted[19] and certainly was the intention of the contracting parties.[20] The Security Council has fully exploited such a discretion, in some cases even beyond any reasonable limits[21] or in a rather suspicious selective manner.[22]

[16] The precedents concern the following crises: Korea (Res. 82, 25 June 1950); Falkland/Malvinas (Res. 502, 3 April 1982); Iran–Iraq (Res. 598, 20 June 1987); Iraq–Kuwait (Res. 660, 2 August 1990).

[17] In a few cases, the Security Council qualified limited military actions as 'act of armed aggression' (see, for instance, Res. 573 (1985) condemning the Israeli raid against PLO headquarters in Tunisia) or as 'acts of aggression' (see, for instance, Res. 577 (1985) and Res. 611 (1988)). In general, see N. D. White, *supra* note 9, pp. 50 *et seq.*; J. A. Frowein, *supra* note 1. The discretion enjoyed by the Security Council to determine on a case-by-case basis the existence of an aggression is not affected by General Assembly Res. 3314 (XXIX), adopted on 14 December 1974 (see, in particular, Arts. 2 and 4).

[18] In *Prosecutor* v. *Tadic* (Establishment of the International Tribunal), 20 October 1995, in 35 *ILM* (1996) 32, para. 29, the ICTFY observed that whereas 'the act of aggression is more amenable to a legal determination, the threat to peace is more a political concept'. Similarly, see *Prosecutor* v. *Kanyabashi*, International Criminal Tribunal for Rwanda, Decision on Jurisdiction, Case ICTIL 96-15-T, 18 June 1997. L. Henkin, 'Conceptualizing Violence: Present and Future Developments in International Law', 60 *Albany LR* (1997) 571, p. 575 notes that 'the threat to international peace and security . . . is not capable of legal definition, but only of political determination by a political body'.

[19] According to H. Kelsen, *supra* note 4, p. 727, 'it is completely within the discretion of the Security Council to decide what constitutes a threat to peace'. In his dissenting opinion in the *Genocide case*, *supra* note 7, p. 439, E. Lauterpacht observes that it is not for the Court 'to substitute its discretion for that of the Security Council in determining the existence of a threat to peace, a breach of peace or an act of aggression, or the political steps to be taken following such a determination'. See also the twin dissenting opinions of M. Weeramantry in the *Questions of Interpretation and Application of the 1971 Montreal Convention arising from the Aerial Incident at Lockerbie*, Provisional Measures, *ICJ Reports 1992*, pp. 3 and 114, at pp. 66 and 176; the twin separate opinions of P. H. Kooijmans and dissenting opinions of S. M. Schwebel, in *Lockerbie cases*, *supra*, Preliminary Objections, Judgment, *ICJ Reports 1998*, p. 9 (Libya v. United Kingdom) and p. 115 (Libya v. United States), respectively pp. 59, 149, and 80, 171; the dissenting opinion of R. Y. Jennings in the *Lockerbie* case concerning the United Kingdom, Preliminary Objections, p. 110. For a more prudent approach, see M. Bedjaoui, dissenting opinion in *Lockerbie* cases, Preliminary Measures, *supra*, pp. 42–3 and 152–3. In *The New World Order and the Security Council. Testing the Legality of its Acts* (Dordrecht:, Nijhoff, 1994), pp. 52–3, the same author seems to limit the control of legality to the concrete action carried out following a determination under Art. 39.

[20] See *Report of the Rapporteur of Committee III/3 to Commission III on Chapter VIII*, Doc. 881, 12 *UNCIO*, pp. 502 *et seq.*, p. 505.

[21] See, for instance, the critical remarks on the *Lockerbie* case made by G. Arangio-Ruiz, 'On the Security Council's "Law-Making" ', 83 *RDI* (2000) 609, pp. 702 *et seq.*

[22] See, in particular, the considerations made by I. Brownlie, 'The Decisions of the Political Organs of the United Nations and the Rule of Law', in S. St Macdonald (ed.), *Essays in Honour of Wang Tieya* (Dordrecht: Nijhoff, 1993), p. 91; and *The Rule of Law in International Affairs* (The Hague: Nijhoff, 1998), pp. 217 *et seq.*

The legal basis of the Security Council's powers

Without prejudice to the processes of formal and informal modification, the Charter is a virtually universally accepted multilateral treaty intended first and foremost to regulate, on a lasting but still contractual basis, the relationship between Member States, and between them and the Organisation. As pointed out by France: 'Les Etats Membres des Nations Unies ont souscrit, qu'ils soient Membres originaires ou non, aux engagements de la Charte, mais rien de plus. La Charte est un traité par lequel les Etats n'ont aliéné leur compétence que dans la stricte mesure ils ont consenti.'[23]

Neither the so-called implied powers theory nor the so-called general powers theory can lead to an enlargement of the Security Council's powers.

The so-called implied powers theory is to be understood in the context of treaty interpretation. Indeed, in the *Reparation case*[24] the International Court of Justice relied heavily on implied provisions of the Charter,[25] whereas in the *Administrative Tribunal case*, the power of the General Assembly to establish an administrative tribunal was affirmed through the interpretation of Arts. 7, 22 and 101(1) of the Charter.[26] What is not admissible is to invoke the implied powers theory,[27] the principle of effectiveness or mere considerations of necessity[28] to

[23] *Certain Expenses case*, *supra* note 13, *Pleadings*, p. 133.

[24] In *Reparation for Injuries Suffered in the Service of the United Nations*, Advisory Opinion, *ICJ Reports 1949*, pp. 174 *et seq*., p. 182, the Court maintained that 'the Organisation must be deemed to have those powers which, though not expressly provided in the Charter, are conferred upon it by necessary implication as being essential to the performance of its duties'. At p. 179, the Court conceded that the Charter needs to be interpreted and applied in such a way to allow the Organisation to *effectively* discharge its functions.

[25] G. Arangio-Ruiz, *The United Nations Declaration on Friendly Relations and the System of the Sources of International Law* (Alpheen aan Rijn: Sijthoff & Noordhoff, 1979), p. 280.

[26] *Effect of Awards of Compensation made by the U.N. Administrative Tribunal*, Advisory Opinion of 13 August 1954, *ICJ Reports 1954*, pp. 47 *et seq*., p. 58.

[27] In the dissenting opinion to the *Administrative Tribunal* case, *supra* note 26, p. 80, G. H. Hackworth correctly pointed out: 'The doctrine of implied powers is designed to implement within reasonable limitations, and not to supplant or vary, expressed powers'. In general, see M. Rama-Montaldo, 'International Legal Personality and Implied Powers of International Organizations', 44 *BYIL* (1970) 111; K. Skubiszewski, 'Implied Powers of International Organizations', in Y. Dinstein (ed.), *International Law at a Time of Perplexity, Essays Rosenne* (Dordrecht: Nijhoff, 1989), p. 855.

[28] In the dissenting opinion to *Legal consequences for States of the Continued Presence of South Africa in Namibia (South West Africa) notwithstanding Security Council Resolution 276 (1970)*, Advisory Opinion, *ICJ Reports 1971*, pp. 16 *et seq*., p. 339, A. Gros warned that 'To say that a power is necessary, that it logically results from a certain situation, is to admit the non-existence of any legal justification. Necessity knows no law, it is said; and indeed to invoke necessity is to step outside the law'. According to D. W. Bowett, *The Law of International Institutions*, 4th ed. (London: Stevens, 1982), p. 338, in the *Certain Expenses case*, the Court 'showed no inclination to ask whether the establishment of UNEF was *necessary*'.

modify or expand the powers of the United Nations political organs under the Charter.[29]

Through the so-called general or residual powers of the Security Council, nonetheless, the Court attempted to read Art. 24(2) of the Charter as presupposing the existence of general or residual powers beside the specific powers conferred upon the Security Council under Chapters VI, VII, VIII and XII.[30] Such an interpretation is far from satisfactory.[31] For the purpose of this study, suffice it to note that this reading of the Charter would lead to the unacceptable result that the Security Council could resort to enforcement powers outside the framework of action needed to tackle threats to peace, breaches of peace, or acts of aggression, thus evading the conditions established in Chapter VII.[32]

The enquiry into the powers bestowed on the Security Council by Member States logically proceeds with the law-making power. In discharging its responsibilities to maintain international peace and strictly within this functional limit,[33] the Security Council 'may create new law for the concrete case'[34] when it consid-

[29] P. Spender, sep. op. in *Certain Expenses*, *supra* note 13, p. 197, reminded the Court that the right to interpret the Charter gives no power to alter it.

[30] *Namibia case*, *supra* note 28, pp. 52 *et seq*. The Court relied on a Secretary-General's Statement concerning the Statute of Trieste, according to which 'the members of the United Nations have conferred upon the Security Council powers commensurate with the responsibility for the maintenance of peace and security. The only limitations are the fundamental principles and purposes found in Chapter I of the Charter', S/PV. 91, 10 January 1947, pp. 44–5. In this sense, see R. Higgins, 'The Advisory Opinion on Namibia: Which UN Resolutions are Binding under Article 25 of the Charter?', 21 *ICLQ* (1972) 270; J. Delbrück, 'Article 24', in B. Simma (ed.), *supra* note 1, pp. 442 *et seq*.; T. D. Gill, 'Legal and Some Political Limitations on the Power of the UN Security Council to Exercise its Enforcement Power Under Chapter VII of the Charter', 26 *NYIL* (1995) 33.

[31] See the separate opinion of S. Petren and the dissenting opinions of G. Fitzmaurice and A. Gros in the *Namibia case*, *supra* note 28, respectively pp. 136, 293 and 340. For the latter judge, the Court's reading of Art. 24(2) amounted to 'another attempt to modify the principles of the Charter as regards the powers vested by States in the organs they instituted'.

[32] G. Gaja, *supra* note 6, p. 311, observes that 'on arriverait en effet à admettre que sur la base du chapitre VII – même en présence d'un acte d'agression – les pouvoirs du Conseil seraient plus limités que ceux qui sont lui conférés dans les domaines où la Charte ne lui a attribué aucun rôle d'une manière expresse'. See also H. Kelsen, *supra* note 4, p. 284; J. Dugard, 'Namibia (South Ouest Africa): The Court's Opinion, South Africa's Response, and the Prospects for the Future', 11 *CJTL* (1972) 1; B. Conforti, *supra* note 15, pp. 205 *et seq*.; G. Arangio-Ruiz, *supra* note 21, p. 654.

[33] G. Arangio-Ruiz, *supra* note 21, especially pp. 627 *et seq*. and 697 *et seq*.

[34] H. Kelsen, *supra* note 4, p. 295. Kelsen's views have been endorsed, if not paraphrased, in *Joint Declaration of Judges Evensen, Tarassov, Guillaume and Aguilar Mawdsley*, *Lockerbie cases*, Provisional Measures, *supra* note 19, pp. 24–5 and 136–7. After noting that under no conventional or customary international norm was Libya obliged to surrender the two individuals the judges observed that the Security Council, considering the existing situation as unsatisfactory, resorted to the Chapter VII powers. Libya was thereby deprived from the right to choose between prosecuting or extraditing the two suspects, as established by Art. 7 of the 1971 Montreal Convention.

ers existing law to be unsatisfactory.[35] As to the legal foundation of the Security Council's law-making, it was pointed out that

> [i]l est normal d'admettre que les sources formelles puissent dériver l'une de l'autre: ainsi beaucoup d'auteurs considèrent-ils que les règles relatives à la force obligatoire des traités sont d'origine coutumière: il n'y a donc aucun inconvénient à reconnaître que la force obligatoire de la législation internationale découle de traités; mais cette législation constitue une source distincte car elle se manifeste selon des procédés qui sont différents des actes conventionnels.[36]

This law-making process is based on the consent expressed by Member States when ratifying the Charter and thus accepting Arts. 25, 41 and 103.[37] It has been defined as 'of third degree' to underline its nature, which differs from the traditional sources of international law, namely treaties and custom.[38]

The consensual basis of the Security Council's law-making power is confirmed by the fact that even the States which have been more heavily targeted by the Security Council's decisions have limited themselves to challenging on both political and legal grounds the lawfulness and legitimacy of the underlying decisions; they have neither contested in principle the exercise of Chapter VII powers by that organ, nor have they abandoned the Organisation. At the same time, Member States other than the target of the enforcement measures have systematically conformed their conduct to the Security Council's mandatory resolutions, even when such conduct would have been otherwise contrary to international law or has prevented them from enjoying their subjective rights.[39]

[35] On the law-making power in relation to the authorisation to use force and the exercise of the right to self-defence, see respectively, *infra* pp. 54 *et seq.* and pp. 153 *et seq.*

[36] P. Reuter, 'Organisations internationales et évolution du droit', in *L'évolution du droit public. Etudes offertes à Achille Mestre* (Paris, Sirey, 1956), pp. 447 *et seq.*, pp. 452–3.

[37] In this regard, the view taken by the ICJ in the *Lockerbie* cases, Preliminary measures, *supra* note 19, pp. 15 and 126, namely that Libya's rights under the Montreal Convention had been forfeit by virtue of Arts. 25 and 103, overlooks the crucial importance of Art. 41.

[38] G. Morelli, *Nozioni di diritto internazionale*, 7th ed. (Padova: CEDAM, 1967), p. 38. In the *Restatement of the Law (Third). The Foreign Relations of the United States*, St Paul: American Law Institute, 1987, vol. I, § 102, comment (g) and note 3, binding resolutions are referred to as 'secondary source'. With regard to the proposal put forward – but eventually withdrawn – at the 1946 World Health Conference which would have granted the Assembly the power to enact regulations immediately binding upon Member States, J. Kunz, 'Revolutionary Creation of Norms of International Law', 41 *AJIL* (1947) p. 121, footnote 8, points out that 'legally such a norm, created by the treaty procedure, with the consent and ratification of the contracting parties, and binding only upon Member States, would not be revolutionary at all'.

[39] Among many examples, see the attitude of the States parties to the 1948 Danube Convention in relation to the implementation of the economic enforcement measures imposed by Res. 757 (1992), 787 (1992) and 820 (1993). In the resolution adopted on 28 April 1993, the International Commission of the Danube declared the determination of riparian States 'to fulfil strictly their obligations under the Charter of the United Nations' (S/25808). See also the declaration by Bulgaria, Hungary and Romania, both individually (respectively S/25213, S/25201, S/25189) and jointly (S/25322).

The relationship between the obligations deriving from the Security Council's resolutions and those having a source different from the Charter are governed by Art. 103 of the Charter.[40] As affirmed by the International Court of Justice with regard to Security Council Resolution 748 (1992),[41] the obligations stemming from binding Security Council resolutions prevail over other obligations. The fact that all Member States have not only consistently complied with Security Council's mandatory resolutions (*usus*), but also perceived such conduct as part of their obligations deriving from the Organisation membership (*opinio juris*), supports the Court's view.

Rather than introducing a hierarchy of norms in a formal sense, Art. 103 sets up a mechanism accepted by Member States as necessary for the correct functioning of the Organisation and the effectiveness of the Security Council's action. It ensures, between Member States,[42] the *primacy* of the Charter's obligations – including those imposed by binding Security Council resolutions – over obligations stemming from other sources, without affecting the validity of conflicting

[40] It has further been observed that since treaties usually derogate from customary law, there is no reason not to extend the Charter primacy to customary law, provided this does not amount to a violation of *jus cogens*: see L. Condorelli, 'La Corte internazionale di giustizia e gli organi politici delle Nazioni Unite', 77 *RDI* (1994) 897, pp. 909–10. Similarly, C. Dominicé, 'L'Article 103 de la Charte des Nations Unies et le droit international humanitaire', in L. Condorelli, A. M. La Rosa and S. Scherrer (eds.), *The United Nations and International Humanitarian Law* (Paris: Pédone, 1996), pp. 177 *et seq.*; M. H. Mendelson, 'The *Nicaragua Case* and Customary International Law', in W. E. Butler (ed.), *The Non-Use of force in International Law* (Dordrecht: Nijhoff, 1989), p. 85 *et seq.*, p. 86. *Contra* M. Bedjaoui, dissenting opinion in *Lockerbie* cases, Provisional Measures, *supra* note 19, pp. 47 and 157, who concludes that Art. 103 'does not cover such rights as may have other than conventional sources and be derived from general international law'. In the same sense, see J. Combacau, *Le pouvoir de sanction de l'ONU: étude théorique de la coercition non militaire* (Paris: Pédone, 1974), p. 282; D. W. Bowett, 'Judicial and Political Functions of the Security Council and the International Court of Justice', in H. Fox (ed.), *The Changing Constitution of the United Nations* (London: BIICL, 1997), p. 81.

[41] *Lockerbie* cases, Provisional Measures, *supra* note 19, respectively pp. 15 and 126. See also the separate opinion of M. Shahabudden, *ibid.*, pp. 28 and 140, and the dissenting opinion of C. G. Weeramantry, *ibid.*, pp. 61 and 171. This view finds support in the *travaux préparatoires*, see *Report of Committee IV/2*, Doc. 933, 13 *UNCIO*, pp. 703 *et seq.*, p. 708. In literature, see L. Kopelmanas, *L'Organisation des Nations Unies* (Paris: Sirey, 1949), pp. 172 *et seq.*; G. Fitzmaurice, *The Law and Procedure of the International Court of Justice* (Cambridge: Grotius, 1986), vol. II, p. 431; E. Roucounas, 'Engagements parallèles et contradictoires', 206 *RdC* (1987–VI) 9, p. 67. *Contra*, D. W. Bowett, *supra* note 40, p. 81. G. Arangio-Ruiz, 'Article 39 of the ILC First-Reading Draft Articles on State Responsibility', 83 *RDI* (2000) 747, p. 752 remains rather sceptical on the extension of Art. 103 primacy to Security Council resolutions.

[42] H. Kelsen, *supra* note 4, pp. 117–18. J. Combacau, *supra* note 40, p. 287, considers Art. 103 as a 'mécanisme à usage interne, s'adressant aux seuls Etats membres'. See also, G. Fitzmaurice, *3rd Report on the Law of Treaties*, 10 *YBILC* (1958–II), p. 45; H. Waldock, *3rd Report on the Law of Treaties*, 16 *YBILC* (1964–II), p. 74; G. Kojanec, *Trattati e Stati terzi* (Padova: CEDAM, 1961), pp. 227 *et seq.* The question is today to a large extent obsolete because of the virtually universal membership of the Organisation.

treaties, when applicable.[43] Member States are therefore prevented from invoking their legal relationships established outside the Charter in order to escape compliance with the Charter obligations.

The economic enforcement measures

The Charter sets up a centralised procedure for the adoption of enforcement measures not involving the use of force. The departure from Art. 16 of the Covenant is quite striking. Under that provision, States were obliged immediately to adopt a series of predetermined measures against any member which, according to their own unilateral judgement, had resorted to war in disregard of Arts. 12, 13 or 15. Under the Charter, the Security Council is called upon to decide, following a determination under Art. 39, whether and which kind of economic enforcement measures are needed to restore or maintain international peace and security. Within this functional limit, the Security Council may recommend or impose the adoption of enforcement economic measures with regard to certain States or other subjects of international law. In so doing, it exercises extensive normative powers directed at regulating the Member States' contribution to the collective action.

In addition to imposing upon the target State the obligation to adopt a certain conduct, regardless of whether such conduct is compulsory or merely permitted under customary or conventional international law, the Security Council's mandatory resolution may temporarily deprive it of the legal protection of otherwise protected interests. The resolution thus renders lawful the adoption by the other Member States of the economic enforcement measures, to the extent that such measures could not be justified under other rules of conventional or customary international law (permissive effect).

Such a permissive effect may be attributed also to resolutions recommending economic enforcement measures.[44] The power to impose the adoption of economic enforcement measures necessarily presupposes the power to make these measures permitted, had they been otherwise contrary to international law. Since

[43] G. Fitzmaurice, *3rd Report on the Law of Treaties*, 10 *YBILC* (1958–II), p. 44; H. Waldock, *2nd Report on the Law of Treaties*, 15 *YBILC* (1963–II), p. 55; E. Sciso, 'On Article 103 of the Charter of the United Nations in the Light of the Vienna Convention on the Law of Treaties', 38 *ÖZöRV* (1987) 161; T. Flory, 'Article 103', in J. P. Cot and A. Pellet (eds.), *supra* note 6, p. 1374. *Contra* R. Bernhardt, 'Article 103', in B. Simma (ed.), *supra* note 1, pp. 1292 *et seq*.

[44] Although not expressly foreseen in Art. 41, the power to recommend enforcement measures is undisputed. However, the Security Council seems to have abandoned this practice. For the precedents of initially voluntary, and subsequently mandatory, economic enforcement measures, see: V. Gowlland-Debbas, *Collective Response to Illegal Acts in International Law: United Nations Action in the Question of Southern Rhodesia* (Dordrecht: Nijhoff, 1990); L. Sohn, *Rights in Conflict: The United Nations and South Africa* (New York: Transnational Publishers, 1994).

nothing prevents the Security Council from restraining itself to exercising only the latter power, it must be admitted that hortatory resolutions may render lawful conduct otherwise amounting to an international wrongful act, thus precluding the international responsibility of the concerned States.[45]

Mandatory resolutions also impose upon all Member States the obligation to take, within their respective jurisdiction, all necessary measures to implement the economic enforcement measures, even if this implies non-compliance with pre-existing obligations owed to the target State or non-enjoyment of their own subjective rights (mandatory effect). Under Art. 48(1), the Security Council may opt for a selective imposition of the obligation to take economic enforcement measures. This provision constitutes no autonomous legal basis for any obligation; it exclusively concerns the limitation of the addressees of obligations deriving from other articles of the Charter, and in particular from Art. 41.

The international normative phase is then followed by the operative activities, that may be coupled with the adoption of the required regulations and administrative acts, carried out by national authorities within each Member State's legal system.[46]

Suspension or withdrawal of economic enforcement measures may raise complex problems. The exclusive competence of the Security Council was challenged in the 1970s by the United Kingdom and the United States, which maintained that Member States could unilaterally lift the economic embargo against Southern Rhodesia upon their own appreciation on the attainment of the objectives pursued by the relevant Security Council resolutions. A significant number of Member States, and in particular the Soviet Union and the African States, strongly protested against the failure effectively to implement the relevant resolutions as required by Art. 25 of the Charter.[47]

During the Gulf crisis, the United Kingdom and the United States apparently abandoned their controversial position and declared that only the Security Council could decide upon the lifting of the enforcement measures adopted against Iraq.[48] It remains to be seen whether this change in attitude was directed at strengthening the Security Council's authority, or rather at affirming the right of any permanent members to maintain indefinitely the economic enforcement measures in force. In any case, the so-called right to last resort permits the striking of a balance between the corporate will of the Organisation and the right of

[45] On this point see M. L. Forlati Picchio, *supra* note 6, pp. 227 *et seq*. Such an effect, on the contrary, must be ruled out with regard resolutions adopted by the Security Council under Chapter VI or by the General Assembly.

[46] The sanctions imposed against Iraq by Res. 661 (1990) are an example among many. See *Questionnaire Concerning National Measures adopted in Implementation of Security Council Resolution 661 (1991)*, in M. Weller, *The Kuwait Crisis: Sanctions and their Economic Consequences* (Cambridge: Cambridge University Press), 1991, pp. 516 *et seq*.

[47] On the question, see D. D. Caron, 'The Legitimacy of the Collective Authority of the Security Council', 87 *AJIL* (1993) 552, pp. 578 *et seq*.

[48] UN Doc. S/PV.2977, 23 February 1991, respectively pp. 301 and 313.

Member States not to be compelled to comply with decisions they perceive as unlawful.[49]

The most remarkable development of recent Security Council practice is the adoption of Resolutions 1373 and 1540. Instead of imposing certain measures in order to solve a given crisis, the resolutions imposed on Member States a comprehensive set of obligations respectively directed at preventing the commission of terrorist acts and depriving terrorist groups of any form of support, and at curbing the proliferation and trafficking of weapons of mass destruction by non-State actors. The unprecedented latitude and general character of these obligations and the lack of any spatial or temporal limits make the resolutions comparable in good substance to international treaties.[50]

The attitude of Member States remains the crucial element in assessing the power of the Security Council to enact general legislation. No State has challenged the lawfulness of the first resolution and very few have expressed concern with regard to the second one. Virtually all States have complied with the obligations stemming from both resolutions, including the submission of periodical reports.[51] The resolutions may constitute a valuable precedent for further legislative activities by the Security Council which – is unchallenged – may in due time pave the way to an unexpected enlargement of that organ normative powers.[52]

Alternatively, the resolutions could be considered as treaties concluded in simplified – and indeed highly atypical – form. Given the absolute freedom enjoyed by States as to the form in which they conclude international treaties, it may be argued that the unanimous attitude of Member States amounts to the expression of their consent to assume the international obligations embodied in the resolutions.

The military enforcement measures

The core of the collective security system established by the Charter lies in Arts. 42 *et seq*. In contrast to economic enforcement measures, in the case of military enforcement measures, the Security Council was meant to take *directly*, with the advice and assistance of the Military Staff Committee, such military action by air, sea and land as might be necessary to maintain or restore international peace and

[49] See *infra* text corresponding to notes 113 *et seq*.

[50] L. Condorelli, 'Les attentats du 11 septembre et leur suites: où va le droit international?', 105 *RGDIP* (2001) 829, p. 835, has compared it to 'une convention musclée destinée à régir toute lutte contre toute sorte de terrorisme d'aujourd'hui ou de demain'. See also P. C. Szasz, 'The Security Council Starts Legislating', 96 *AJIL* (2002) 901.

[51] Speaking in the name of the European Union, the Italian representative declared before the Security Council that 'the European Union considers . . . Res. 1373 (2001) to be the cornerstone of the international community's co-operation strategy and it is firmly committed to its implementation', S/PV. 4845 (Res. I), 16 October 2003, p. 15. As declared by the US representative on the same occasion, all 191 Member States of the United Nations had submitted the periodical report to the Committee (*ibid.*, p. 9).

[52] See also *infra* notes 122 and 123.

security.[53] The creation of armed forces at the disposal of the Security Council was thus envisaged through the conclusion of special agreements between Member States and the Security Council.[54]

The qualitative improvement with respect to the Covenant of the League of Nations is remarkable. Under the Covenant, the Council could merely advise Member States on the measures to tackle potential or actual aggressions,[55] or recommend to them military action to contribute to 'protect the Covenant of the League'[56] against the resort to war in disregard of Arts. 12, 13 and 15.[57] Both Arts. 10 and 16 were ambiguously drafted and raised problems of interpretation.[58] Even admitting the binding character of these articles,[59] the obligations relating to individual or collective military reaction were seriously undermined by the undisputed freedom which Member States enjoyed as to the degree, form and entity of their participation.[60]

Under Art. 11, which may be seen as the precursor to Art. 39 of the Charter, the League of the Nations was called upon to take any action deemed wise and effectual to safeguard international peace, regardless of any violations of the Covenant. The maintenance of international peace was simultaneously considered as the

[53] Art. 42 of the Charter.

[54] Art. 43 of the Charter.

[55] Art. 10 of the Covenant.

[56] For H. Kelsen, 'Sanctions in International Law under the Charter of the United Nations', 31 *Iowa LR* (1946) 499, p. 514, 'The use of armed force as an enforcement measure is expressly destined for the protection of the Covenant, that is for the defence of the particular law of the League'.

[57] Art. 16.

[58] See also the so-called Lodge reservation to the Covenant which would have excluded any obligation under Art. 10 and preserved the exclusive competence of the Congress with regard to deployment of American armed forces. See L. Gross, 'The Charter of the United Nations and the Lodge Reservation', 41 *AJIL* (1947) 531.

[59] According to M. L. Forlati Picchio, *supra* note 6, pp. 137–8, Arts. 10 and 16 imposed on States the obligation to provide *uti singuli* assistance to the State victim of aggression – or possibly, in the case of Art. 16, to participate in the associated reaction – but left them free to choice the form of such an assistance or participation. However, she admits that the interpretation supported by the Anglo–Saxon and Nordic States that the articles had a mere recommendatory nature eventually prevailed: see *Questions Relating to Art. 16 of the Covenant*, Doc. C.444.M.287.1938.VII, p. 15. On the non-binding nature of Art. 16, see *Reports and Resolutions on the Subject of Art. 16 of the Covenant*, Doc. A.14.1927, V, p. 43. I. Brownlie, *The Use of Force by States in International Law* (Oxford: Clarendon Press, 1963), p. 229, observes that Art. 10 'implied an obligation to aid the victim of aggression but it was interpreted in such a way that such aid was permitted rather than obligatory'. H. Kelsen, *supra* note 4, pp. 274 and 985 considered that this article was not legally binding but had only moral or political importance.

[60] According to the interpretation given by the Assembly on 24 September 1923 – but not adopted because of the opposition of Persia – 'it was for the constitutional authorities of each member to decide . . . in what degree the member is bound to assume the execution of these obligations by employment of its military forces'. See also the resolution adopted on 9–10 August 1923 by the International Law Institute, and J. B. Scott, 'Interpretation of Article X of the Covenant of the League of Nations', 18 *AJIL* (1924) 108.

most prominent objective of the Organisation, and an interest common to all its members.[61] This may justify the attribution of a permissive effect to the recommendations adopted by the Council under Art. 11. By virtue of the special nature of Art. 11, these recommendations – although deprived of binding effect[62] – amounted to a circumstance precluding wrongfulness with regard to the recommended conduct.[63]

Yet, the Covenant introduced the notion of *bellum legale*, which was meant to replace that of *bellum justum*.[64] It did not abolish war but made its legality depend on the respect of certain procedural requirements, rather than on the intrinsic justice of its cause.[65] Under Art. 15, in particular, Member States reserved their right to resort to force to the extent that they considered necessary for the maintenance of rights and justice when: (i) the other party had not complied within three months with the decision of an arbitral tribunal or with the report adopted by the Council or the Assembly (respectively unanimously and by qualified majority); (ii) the Council or the Assembly were unable to adopt a report by the required majority.

The progress made by the Covenant was significant insofar as resort to force was conditional upon the pronouncement of an arbitral tribunal or one of the main political organs of the Organisation. The system was nonetheless unsatisfactory. Had the Council or the Assembly been unable to adopt a binding report, resort to force was subject only to the cooling-off period provision.[66] Additionally, no compulsory judicial settlement of dispute mechanism was put in place, as Art. 13 was limited to the disputes all parties considered as suitable for adjudication. Even when it was possible for the Council or the Assembly to adopt a binding report or for the arbitral tribunal to deliver a judgment, the evaluation of compliance with

[61] Under Art. XI, any war or threat to war, 'whether immediately affecting any of the members of the League or not' (the French text reads: 'qu'elle affecte directement ou non l'un des Membres de la Société'), was considered as a matter of concern to the whole Organisation. Q. Wright, 'Permissive Sanctions Against Aggression', 37 *AJIL* (1942) 103, p. 104, points out: 'Recognition of the general interest in war, wherever it occurs, accorded in Art. 11 of the League of Nations Covenant as well as in the Pact of Paris, provided the juridical basis for permissive sanctions'.

[62] On 3 March 1932, the President of the Council observed that Art. 11 'est tout entier de prévention, de conciliation, comme il ressort de son texte, qui ne permet au Conseil de prendre une décision valable qu'avec l'accord des parties elles-mêmes'. *Contra* J. Kunz, 'L'article 11 du Pacte de la Société des Nations', 39 *RdC* (1932) 683, p. 786, for whom Art. 11 'oblige les membres, non directement intéressés au conflit en question, à aider la Société dans les mesures qu'elle a prises. Mais il oblige également les Membres, partis en cause, à accepter les mesures prises par la Société'.

[63] M. L. Forlati Picchio, *supra* note 6, p. 154 *et seq*.

[64] J. Kunz, '*Bellum Justum* and *Bellum Legale*', 45 *AJIL* (1951) 528.

[65] On the 'just war' doctrine, see J. Von Elbe, 'The Evolution of the Concept of Just War in International Law', 33 *AJIL* (1939) 786; A. Nussbaum, 'Just War. A Legal Concept?', 42 *Mich. LR* (1043) 453; S. Chesterman, *'Just War or Just Peace? Humanitarian Intervention and International Law'*, (Oxford: Oxford University Press, 2001), pp. 7 *et seq*.; N. K. Tsagourias, 'Jurisprudence of International Law. The Humanitarian Dimension', (Manchester: Manchester University Press, 2001), pp. 5 *et seq*.

[66] Art. 12.

the report or the decision was left to Member States. As a result, the *bellum legale* notion under the Covenant was to a large extent exposed to the same objections raised against the *bellum justum* doctrine.

From this perspective, the 1924 Geneva Protocol[67] – which was never ratified – would have represented a remarkable step towards a more effective centralised control of the use of force. Under Art. 2, military measures would have been lawful only when taken to resist acts of aggression or acting in agreement with the Council or the Assembly. In the second case, the positive pronouncement of the Council or the Assembly – and no longer the failure to adopt a binding report or the unilateral judgment on non-compliance – was elevated to a necessary requirement for lawful resort to force. The Council or the Assembly's act supporting the use of force would have had a permissive effect by making lawful conduct otherwise contrary to the rules on the use of force established under the Covenant and the Protocol.[68] The Protocol may therefore be seen as the ancestor of the so-called authorisation practice.[69]

The Charter further developed the *bellum legale* notion and attempted to overcome the main gaps of the Covenant. Apart from the case of self-defence, no threat or use of force would have been lawful without a decision of the Security Council under Chapter VII or VIII. Equally important, Art. 2(4) prohibits not only the use of force – which in itself would have already been a remarkable improvement compared with the Covenant[70] – but also the threat to use force.[71]

The obligations stemming from Art. 2(4) possess an *erga omnes* character. The essence of *erga omnes* obligations, which are aimed at protecting interests common to all Member States,[72] is their legal indivisibility.[73] Compliance with

[67] 19 *AJIL Suppl.* (1925) 9.

[68] This excluded international adjudication with regard to resort to force in agreement with the Council or the Assembly see M. L. Forlati Picchio, *supra* note 6, pp. 171 *et seq.*, who quotes the following part of the *Rapport Bénès–Politis* on the Protocol, p. 10: 'Il ne serait pas, en effet, admissible que l'arbitrage obligatoire fût, entre le mains de l'ennemi de la communauté, une arme pour entraver la liberté d'action de ceux qui, au nom de l'intérêt général, cherchent à lui imposer le respect de ses engagements'. A permissive effect must equally be recognised to Art. 2, para 2(3) of the Treaty of Mutual Guarantee between Germany, Belgium, France, Great Britain and Italy, 16 October 1925, 54 *LNTS* 290.

[69] See *infra* pp. 43 *et seq.*

[70] See I. Brownlie, *supra* note 59, pp. 59–60.

[71] In general, see R. Sadurska, 'Threats to Force', 82 *AJIL* (1988) 239.

[72] During the San Francisco conference it had been emphasised that 'The use of force is left possible only in the common interest. As long as we have an Organisation, the Organisation only is competent to see the common interest and to use force in supporting it': Report of Rapporteur of Committee I to Commission I, Doc. 994, 13 June 1945, 6 *UNCIO* p. 446, at p. 451. In *Reservations to the Convention on the Prevention and Punishment of the Crime of Genocide*, Advisory Opinion, *ICJ* Reports *1951*, p. 15, at p. 23, the ICJ observed that: 'the contracting States do not have any interest of their own; they merely have, one and all, a common interest, namely in the accomplishment of those high purposes which are the *raison d'être* of the convention'.

[73] See G. Arangio-Ruiz, *4th Report on State Responsibility*, 44 *YBILC* (1992–II), part 2, pp. 33 *et seq.*

these obligations satisfies simultaneously and inseparably the legally protected interests shared by all States, in the case of Art. 2(4) the maintenance of international peace through the renunciation of military force as a means of settling international disputes.

The legal relationships deriving therefrom cannot be split, as it is normally possible with multilateral treaties, into a bunch of bilateral relationships, which permits each State to comply with the obligations imposed by the treaty in relation to some contracting parties and disregard them in relation to others. Selective compliance with an *erga omnes* obligation is impossible: either a given State respects them with regard to all other States or commits a violation affecting the subjective rights of all of them. For each Member State, therefore, there exists a 'unique legal situation'[74] *vis-à-vis* all other addressees of the norm.

As it is the case for human rights or humanitarian law treaties,[75] contracting parties accepted Art. 2(4) on the assumption that each of them possesses a legal right to obtain its respect and to react to its violations, regardless of whether such violations are directed against the reacting State itself.[76] Except in case of self-defence, however, the *inademplenti non est adimplendum* principle is not applicable to Art. 2(4) because of the indivisible nature of the obligation and the consequent impossibility of isolating the relationship between the breaching and the reacting States.[77] If non-compliance with Art. 2(4) could in principle be justifiable *vis-à-vis* the State responsible for the violation, it would unavoidably amount to an international wrongful act *vis-à-vis* all other States. The unilateral or joint reaction, accordingly, can not take the form of a military action contrary to Art. 2(4), unless all States express their consent to suspending the validity of this provision with regard to the State accused of having breached it.

Hence, the great innovation of the Charter remains the decision of Member States to entrust the Security Council with the power to deprive a State of the legal protection it enjoys under Art. 2(4) against the threat or use of force. The Security Council's decision expresses the will of the whole membership temporarily to exclude the concerned State from such a legal protection and to activate the

[74] G. Morelli, *A proposito di norme internazionali cogenti*, 51 *RDI* (1968) 108, p. 115.

[75] L. Condorelli and L. Boisson de Chazournes, 'Quelques remarques à propos de l'obligation des Etats de "respecter et faire respecter" le droit humanitaire "en toutes circonstances"', in C. Swinarski., *Studies and Essays on international Humanitarian Law and Red Cross Principles in Honour of J. Pictet* (Geneva: ICRC, 1984), pp. 17 *et seq*.

[76] As noted by G. Arangio Ruiz, *supra* note 73, p. 43, 'A State can thus be injured by a breach of an *erga omnes* obligation even if it did not suffer any damage other than the infringement of its right'. See also ICTY, *Prosecutor* v. *Furundzija*, 10 December 1998, in 37 *ILM* (1998) 317, para 151. The concept was already present in Art. XI of the Covenant, *supra* note 61.

[77] In *Responsabilité de l'Allemagne à raison des dommages causés dans les colonies portugaises du Sud d'Afrique* (*Naulilaa case*), 2 *UNRIAA* p. 1011, p. 1025 it has been stated that a countermeasure 'a pour effet de suspendre momentanément, dans le rapport des deux Etats, l'observance de telle ou telle règle du droit de gens'.

collective security mechanism.[78] As emphasised by Art. 1(1) of the Charter, the whole collective security system is built around the notion of collective effective measures aimed at protecting the interest common to all members of preventing further armed violence.

This does not mean at all that the use of force could be permitted where no governmental authority exists within the internationally recognised borders of a State. Without prejudice to the question of humanitarian intervention, the deployment of troops in a so-called failed State by Member States remains unlawful without a Security Council Chapter VII resolution. The argument that the use of force does not violate the sovereignty of any State must be rejected if it is accepted that the obligation not to resort to military force, being based on a an interest common to all States, is legally indivisible.[79] In other words, all States possess a legal right in the respect of the prohibition on using military force, even when concerning a territory where no effective government is functioning.

The use of force was hence put under strict and complete control of the Security Council.[80] Apart from self-defence, resort to force was permitted only if taken by the Security Council itself under Art. 42, or by regional organisations in accordance with Art. 53. Whereas under the Covenant the inaction of, or the disagreement within, the Council would have paved the way to unilateral resort to force, under the Charter no measures of military self-help have been made available to Member States to settle their disputes, enforce international judgments, or more generally to react to violations of international law, not even those involving use of force but not justifying the exercise of self-defence.[81]

There is more. Even assuming that armed forces were made available to the Security Council through the conclusion of Art. 43 special agreements, or in other forms,[82] there would have been no guarantee of functioning of the collective

[78] The *Report of Committee I to Commission I*, 6 *UNCIO* p. 459, unequivocally states that 'The use of force remains legitimate only to back up decisions of the Organisation'. Alternatively, the consent of all States would be required.

[79] Additionally, as noted by G. Tesauro, *Il finanziamento delle organizzazioni internazionali* (Napoli: Jovene, 1967), p. 129, it is not necessary that the action is directed *against* a State to qualify it as enforcement: it is sufficient that its objective is to restore the peace.

[80] I. Brownlie, *supra* note 59, p. 273, observes: 'The whole subject of the Charter was to render unilateral use of force, even in self-defence, subject to the control of the Organisation'.

[81] H. Kelsen, 'Collective Security and Collective Self-Defense under the Charter of the United Nations', 42 *AJIL* (1948) 783, p. 787 notes that 'the Charter does not at all exclude the possibility of unsettled disputes. An unsettled dispute means that a member whose rights has been violated by another state, has neither the legal power to protect itself, nor is protected by a centralised action of the community'. See also: H. Kelsen, *supra* note 4, p. 269. R. W. Tucker, 'The Interpretation of War under Present International Law', 4 *ILQ* (1951) 11, p. 26; J. Kunz, *supra* note 64, p. 533. Such a conclusion is rejected as absurd by M. Reisman, *Nullity and Revision. The Review and Enforcement of International Judgments and Awards* (New Haven: Yale University Press, 1971), pp. 847 *et seq*.

[82] See *infra* pp. 35 *et seq*.

security system. First, the Security Council could have been paralysed, as indeed happened for decades. Second, it could have decided not to resort to its Chapter VII powers either because the situation did not qualify as a threat to international peace or because military reaction was not considered as necessary and effective. Finally, Security Council action could have been simply unsuccessful. In all these instances, Member States respectful of the general prohibition of use of force must still refrain from resort to force for non-strictly defensive purposes.[83]

The United Nations was never meant to be a super-State. Rather, it was set up as an association of sovereign States built on the basis of the wartime military alliance.[84] The attempt to go beyond an alliance system[85] evolved around the provisions embodied in Chapter VII, whose objective was 'to concentrate authority in one body and give that body the power and the means to assert its authority'.[86] The restricted Council membership and the unequal voting rights merely reflect the power distribution at the time of the conclusion of the Charter.[87] Since the functioning of the organisation presupposed a lasting agreement between the Great Powers,[88] the difference between the formation of a permanent alliance among the Great Powers, and the establishment of the United Nations on the basis of the sovereign equality of its members (the two options then available, according to the United States Government) was immediately perceived as more apparent than real.[89]

[83] Additionally, as observed by T. Franck, 'Of Gnats and Camels: Is There a Double Standard at the United Nations?', 78 *AJIL* (1984) 811, p. 833, under the Charter 'There is no commitment to equal protection'.

[84] See *Report to the President*, *supra* note 10, p. 100. See also *Reparation case*, *supra* note 24, p. 179; G. Fitzmaurice, dissenting opinion in *Namibia case*, *supra* note 28, p. 241. In literature, see, in particular, L. Gross, *supra* note 58, p. 550; G. Arangio-Ruiz, *supra* note 25, pp. 252 *et seq*.

[85] According to L. Goodrich, A. P. Simon, *The United Nations and the Maintenance of International Peace and Security* (Washington: Brookings Institution, 1945), p. 452, 'the decision was taken to go one step beyond a simple alliance system and provide for national contingents to be placed at the disposal and under the direction of an international organ, the Security Council'.

[86] See *Report to the President*, *supra* note 10, p. 100. 'Authority' has been defined by E. B. Haas, *When Knowledge is Power: Three Models of Change in International Organizations* (Berkeley: University California Press), 1990, p. 87 as 'the ability of the organisation to have its decisions implemented irrespective of the goodwill of the member concerned'.

[87] *Report to the President*, *supra* note 10, p. 41.

[88] R. Ago, 'Le quarantième anniversaire des Nations Unies', in D. Bardonnet (ed.), *The Adaptation of Structures and Methods at the United Nations* (Dordrecht: Nijhoff, 1986), pp. 25 *et seq*., p. 26, observes that 'tout le système reposait sur le postulat de l'existence et du maintien d'une volonté de coopération entre les Etats qui n'étaient, par ailleurs, pas disposés à renoncer à leur souveraineté et à accepter l'autorité d'une organisation supranationale'.

[89] H. Kelsen, *supra* note 4, footnote 7, pp. 270–1. R. W. Tucker, *supra* note 81, p. 28, concludes that 'in many important respects the Charter resembles a political alliance rather than the constitution of an international community, and that the primary aim seems to have

Reductive as this interpretation may be, the Charter developed the victor States alliance and institutionalised its unequal nature. The voting system was dictated not only by the consciousness that no collective enforcement measures would ever be effective without overwhelming military power coupled with a sufficiently large political support,[90] but also by the need to avoid the risks related to a military action not supported by all the Great Powers.[91]

Nevertheless, the so-called veto power must not be demonised. It certainly prevents the Security Council from acting against any permanent member or its allies, but at the same time it represents the most effective institutional guarantee of the legality of the organs activities.[92] Yet, the stricter the voting procedure, the easier it is to prevent the organ from abusing its powers.

The limits to the Security Council's powers

The extensive powers embodied in Chapter VII of the Charter could induce the conclusion that 'To enter the United Nations differs profoundly from accepting a treaty of the usual type . . . A State which becomes a member of the world organisation . . . agrees to change status under international law [and] gives blanket powers to the Security Council'.[93] The second part of this statement is not necessarily true. The existence of limits to the Security Council's Chapter VII powers

---

been the establishment of a security system designed to serve rather limited purposes'. L. Gross, *supra* note 58, p. 550, reminds that 'The price for the entry of certain of the Great Powers into an international security organisation, now as then, is the elimination of what is widely believed to be the basic notion of collective security [namely the compulsory character of the collective reaction] from its constitution'. According to G. Arangio-Ruiz, 'The "Federal Analogy" and UN Charter Interpretation: A Crucial Issue', 8 *EJIL* (1997) 1, p. 11, 'the system does not go far beyond the vesting of some states with rights, faculties or obligations, which appear to be quite similar, in good legal substance, to those embodied or implied in an *unequal alliance* treaty'.

[90] With regard to the Security Council enforcement powers, the *Report to the President*, *supra* note 10, p. 93, points out that 'in the view of the requirement of unanimity of the permanent members and of the representative character especially of the elective members, any positive action by it may be counted upon to reflect the wishes of the majority of the Assembly'.

[91] A. Ross, *The United Nations: Peace and Progress* (Totowa: Bedminster, 1966), p. 198, points out that the Organisation is based on the assumption that 'it is possible to organize peace only when the Great Powers, in unity, lead the way'.

[92] M. W. Reisman, 'The Constitutional Crisis in the United Nations', 87 *AJIL* (1993) 83, p. 95 rightly observes: 'As a victors' creation, the only control [over Security Council action] was the veto assigned to the permanent members of the Council'. See also M. N. Schmitt, 'Preemptive Strategies in International Law', 24 *MJIL* (2003) 515, p. 547. See also *infra* notes IV-233, IV-259, V-69 and V-120.

[93] C. Tomuschat, 'Obligations Arising for Member States Without or Against their Will', 241 *RdC* (1993–IV) 195, p. 249. See also R. Lillich, 'Humanitarian Intervention through the United Nations: towards the Development of Criteria', 53 *ZaöRV* (1993) 557, p. 564.

is undisputed, however difficult it is to define them and to ensure their effective respect. In the *Certain Expenses case*, the Court firmly stated that 'the purposes of the Organisation are broad indeed, but neither they nor the powers conferred to effectuate them are unlimited'.[94]

A full inquiry on the limits of Security Council powers goes beyond the purpose of this study.[95] Suffice it to note that it is generally accepted that when discharging its responsibilities under Chapter VII of the Charter, the Security Council must respect the peremptory norms and *all* the Charter provisions.[96] Besides, the proportionality and necessity principles, which may be included among the principles underpinning the Charter itself,[97] must guide the Security Council's action,[98] especially when the enforcement measures have a military nature.[99]

[94] *Supra* note 13, p. 168. See also *Conditions of Admission of a State to Membership in the United Nations (Charter, Art. 4)*, Advisory Opinion, *ICJ Reports 1947/1948*, pp. 57 *et seq*., p. 64 and G. Fitzmaurice, dissenting opinion in *Namibia case*, *supra* note 28, p. 293. The very fact that there is a presumption of legality (see *infra* text corresponding to note 108) clearly implies the existence of limits. In *Prosecutor* v. *Tadic* (Jurisdiction), Trial Chamber, 10 August 1995, Case No. IT-94-I-T, the ICTY concludes that the Security Council 'is thus subjected to certain constitutional limitation, and neither the text nor the spirit of the Charter conceives of the Security Council as unbound by law'. See also: M. Bedjaoui, *The New World Order*, *supra* note 19; V. Gowlland-Debbas, 'The Relationship between the International Court of Justice and the Security Council in the Light of the Lockerbie Case', 88 *AJIL* (1994) 643; K. Zemanek, 'Is the Security Council the Sole Judge of its own Legality?', in E. Yapko and T. Boumedra (eds.), *Liber Amicorum Judge M. Bedjaoui* (The Hague: Kluwer, 1999), pp. 629 *et seq*.; B. Martenczuk, 'The Security Council, the International Court and Judicial Review: What Lesson from Lockerbie?', 10 *EJIL* (1999) 517.

[95] On this question, see, in particular: T. D. Gill, *supra* note 30; P. Puoti, 'Limiti giuridici all'azione del Consiglio di sicurezza delle Nazioni Unite nel settore del mantenimento della pace', 108 *Studi Senesi* (1996) 287. S. Lamb, 'Legal Limits to United Nations Security Council Powers', in G. S. Goodwin-Gill and S. Talmon (eds.), *The Reality of International Law. Essays Brownlie* (Oxford: Clarendon Press, 1999), p. 361.

[96] G. Fitzmaurice, dissenting opinion in *Namibia case*, *supra* note 28, p. 226; L. Condorelli, *supra* note 40 p. 912; G. Arangio-Ruiz, *supra* note 21; M. W. Reisman, *supra* note 90, p. 92, vaguely affirms that the Security Council must respect some of the rules of the Charter. Entirely unconvincing is the position of the Secretary General held in 1947, *supra* note 30. An involuntary violation of peremptory norms was prospected in *Genocide Convention case*, Order of 13 September 1993, *supra* note I-7, by E. Lauterpacht, dissenting opinion, p. 441.

[97] L. Condorelli, *supra* note 40. See also J. G. Gardam, 'Proportionality and Force in International Law', 87 *AJIL* (1993) 391; M. Bothe, 'Les limites des pouvoirs du Conseil de Sécurité', in R. J. Dupuy (ed.), *The Development of the Role of the Security Council* (Dordrecht: Nijhoff, 1993), pp. 67 *et seq*., p. 78.

[98] See also *Accountability of International Organisations*, *ILA Report of the 69th Conference*, London, 2000, pp. 875 *et seq*.

[99] J. G. Gardam, 'Legal Restraint on Security Military Enforcement Action', 17 *MJIL* (1996) 285.

The very existence of limits implies the possibility of infringements of these limits, which would make the Security Council's action unlawful.[100] A clear confirmation may be found in Art. 25 of the Charter, imposing upon Member States a duty to carry out all decisions of the Security Council taken in accordance with the Charter.[101] Much has been written on the admissibility of judicial review of such acts by the International Court of Justice,[102] but the question is still far from being settled. The Court has demonstrated great prudence on the issue,[103] whereas some influential Member States have strongly expressed their reluctance to see the Court as the guardian of the United Nations' legality.[104] If such a control were to be admitted, the Court could pronounce itself on the lawfulness of the Security Council's acts, either in the form of an advisory opinion, requested by the General Assembly or any other authorised body, or within the context of inter-States disputes. The effectiveness of such a control, nonetheless, must be weighted against – respectively – the non-binding character of advisory opinions and the fact that the effects of the Court's findings in contentious cases are limited to the parties to the dispute. It must be noted that in a recent contentious case, the Court refused to established whether Security Council Resolution 713, in part concerning the maintenance of an arms embargo against Bosnia-Herzegovina, was incompatible with the right to self-defence of that State, since, in so doing, it would have

[100] On some of the most controversial recent decisions of the Security Council, see M. Weller, 'The Lockerbie Case: A Premature End of the "New World Order"', 3 *AJICL* (1992) 319; B. Graefrath, 'Iraqi compensation and the Security Council', 55 *ZaöRV* (1995) 1; G. Arangio-Ruiz, 'The Establishment of the International Criminal Tribunal for the Former Territory of Yugoslavia and the Doctrine of Implied Powers of the United Nations', in F. Lattanzi and E. Sciso (eds.), *Dai tribunali penali internazionali* ad hoc *a una corte permanente* (Napoli: Ed. Scientifica, 1996), pp. 31 *et seq.*

[101] See H. Kelsen, *supra* note 4, p. 95; G. Fitzmaurice, diss. op. in *Namibia case*, *supra* note 28, p. 281; D. W. Bowett, 'The Impact of Security Council Decisions on Dispute Settlement Procedures', 5 *EJIL* (1994) 89, p. 92. In this sense, J. Combacau, *supra* note 40, p. 287, and G. Arangio-Ruiz, *supra* note 21, p. 709, speak, respectively, of 'résolutions incontestables' and 'valid resolutions'.

[102] Among the many studies devoted to this issue, see T. M. Frank, 'The "Power of Appreciation": Who is the Ultimate Guardian of UN Legality?', 86 *AJIL* (1992) 519; W. M. Reisman, *supra* note 90; G. R. Watson, 'Constitutionalism, Judicial Review, and the World Court', 34 *HILJ* (1993) 1; L. Condorelli, *supra* note 40; J. E. Alvarez, 'Judging the Security Council', 90 *AJIL* (1996) 1.

[103] *Lockerbie* cases, Preliminary Objections, *supra* note 19, p. 9 and p. 115. See also K. Skubiszewski, dissenting opinion in *Case Concerning East Timor (Portugal* v. *Australia)*, *ICJ Reports*, 1995, p. 251.

[104] See the position of the United Kingdom in the *Lockerbie case*, Preliminary Objections, *supra* note 19, CR 97/17, par. 5.43 to 5.52. This attitude was particularly evident with regard to the work of the International Law Commission on State responsibility when in 1996 the *Special rapporteur* proposed a judicial control over the determination concerning international crimes made by the main political organs of the Organisation: see G. Arangio-Ruiz, *7th Report on State Responsibility*, A/CN.4/469, 9 May 1995, pp. 33 *et seq.*

clarified the legal situation for the entire international community in violation of Art. 41 of the Court Statute.[105]

The non-existence of an institutional redress against *ultra vires* acts makes unsound any analogy with administrative law in national legal systems. It has been argued that in these circumstances, the concept of voidability cannot be applied to the acts of the United Nations; these acts are consequently either fully valid or absolutely null *ab initio*.[106] Until the alleged violation has not been established by a competent body, the acts of the United Nations produce their effects, including the permissive and mandatory effects described above with regard to Security Council mandatory resolutions.[107] Accordingly, as the Court has maintained on several occasions, the acts of the United Nations are presumed to be *intra vires*.[108] In the *Expenses case*, in particular, the Court made a distinction between acts exceeding the powers of the Organisation as a whole, and acts carried out in disregard of the internal division of competence. Although the Court did not elaborate on that point, the distinction reinforces the presumption of lawfulness of the second class of acts.[109]

As with any presumption, this one can also be rebutted. Leaving aside the controversial judicial review by the International Court of Justice, neither the self-limitation of the Security Council,[110] nor the faithful cooperation between the two organs[111] offers adequate guarantees. Consequently, Member States retain the right unilaterally to pass judgement on the lawfulness of the Security Council's acts and to refuse compliance with them.[112]

105 *Genocide Convention case*, Order of 13 September 1993, *supra* note I-7, p. 345.

106 G. Morelli, sep. op. *Certain Expenses case*, *supra* note 13, pp. 222–3. See also E. Lauterpacht, 'The Legal Effects of Illegal Acts of International Organizations', in R. Y. Jennings *et al.* (eds.), *Cambridge Essays in International Law* (London: Stevens, 1956), pp. 88 *et seq.*, p. 115.

107 In *Certain Expenses case*, *supra* note 13, *Pleadings*, p. 322 *et seq.*, p. 332, the Italian government argued that 'la non-validité de l'acte ne devient effective qu'après avoir été constatée par l'organe compétente. Par conséquent, l'acte nul, pour autant qu'il n'est pas déclaré non valable, déploie ses effets'. In the same sense, see the position of the US government: *ibid.*, pp. 413 et *seq.*, pp. 415–16. See also E. Osieke, 'The Legal Validity of *Ultra Vires* Decisions of International Organizations', 77 *AJIL* (1983) 239.

108 *Certain Expenses case*, *supra* note 13, p. 168; *Namibia Case*, *supra* note 28, p. 22; *Lockerbie cases*, Preliminary Measures, *supra* note 19, pp. 15 and 126.

109 According to G. Morelli, *supra* note 106, only serious violations, such as manifest *excès de pouvoir*, would be sanctioned with nullity, at the exclusion of violations of rules governing the competences within the Organisation. See also D. Ciobanu, *Preliminary Objections Relating to the Jurisdiction of the United Nations Political Organs* (The Hague: Nijhoff, 1975), esp. pp. 67 *et seq.*

110 I. Brownlie, *The Rule of Law*, *supra* note 22, p. 226.

111 E. Lauterpacht, dissenting opinion in *Genocide Convention case*, *supra* note 7, p. 442 concludes that 'the Court has identified a source of doubt regarding the validity of the embargo resolution which, though not directly operative by itself, requires that the Security Council give the matter further consideration'.

112 See, for instance, G. Fitzmaurice, *4th* Report on the Law of Treaties, 11 *YBILC* (1959–II), p. 50; A. J. P. Tammes, 'Decisions of International Organs as a Source of International Law', 94 *RdC* (1958–II) 265, p. 352.

Apart from the voting procedure, the only real guarantee against unlawful acts of the Security Council remains indeed the so-called right of last resort.[113] A Member State could challenge the lawfulness of the act and refuse to comply with the obligations deriving therefrom, if any,[114] provided that legal justification is offered[115] during the deliberations of the organ, or as soon as a State has the opportunity to manifest its dissent.[116] Not differently from what normally occurs in international law, in particular with regard to countermeasures, the attitude of each State is based on its own unilateral judgement. The risk inherent in each State being *judex in re sua* can only be mitigated but certainly not eliminated with the limitation of the right to last resort to cases of manifest violations.[117]

For the States represented in the Security Council, the opposition must take the form of a negative vote justified not on political considerations, such as ineffec-

[113] See dissenting opinions of B. Winiarski and J. L. Bustamante, in *Certain Expenses case*, *supra* 13, respectively pp. 232 and 305. P. Spender, *ibid.*, p. 196, further states that withdrawal from the Organisation is not an acceptable solution for dissenting States who have the right to remain in the Organisation (but see G. Fitzmaurice, *ibid.*, p. 212); A. Gros, sep. op., in *Interpretation of the Agreement of 25 March 1951 between the WHO and Egypt*, Advisory Opinion, *ICJ Reports 1980*, pp. 73 *et seq.*, p. 104; M. Bedjaoui, *Lockerbie cases*, Preliminary Measures, *supra* note 19, pp. 43 and 153; A. S. El Kosheri, *ibid.*, pp. 102 *et seq.* and 204 *et seq.* In literature, see *Report on Reference to the International Court of Justice of Questions of United Nations Competence*, 44 *ASIL* (1950) 256, p. 267; B. Conforti, 'Le rôle de l'accord dans le système des Nations Unies', 142 *RdC* (1974–II) 203, pp. 253 *et seq.*; J. A. Frowein, 'Reaction by Non-Directly Affected States to Breaches of Public International Law', 248 *RdC* (1994–IV) 349, p. 385. With regard to the alleged unlawfulness of the maintenance of arms embargo against Bosnia-Herzegovina, the Islamic Conference Organisation declared that Res. 713 'neither legally nor morally applies to Bosnia and Herzegovina' (Declaration dated 18 May 1995, S/1995/422) and affirmed that the Organisation and United Nations Member States could provide the means of self-defence to Bosnia and Herzegovina (Resolution adopted on 4 August 1994, S/1994/949 Annex) and urged a unilateral response by the members of the international community (S/1994/1121). In August 1995, the US Congress passed a law – immediately vetoed by the President – aiming at disregarding Res. 713 in respect to Bosnia-Herzegovina; see *Statement Vetoing Legislation to Lift the Arms Embargo Against Bosnia*, August 11, 1995, in *Papers of the Presidents of the US*, 1995, vol. II, p. 1253.

[114] With regard to financial contribution, E. Zoller, 'The "Corporate Will" of the United Nations and the Rights of the Minority', 81 *AJIL* (1987) 610, p. 632 argues that the power to withdraw assessment for UN action is not left to unfettered discretion but nonetheless 'derives from, and is necessary implied by, the UN legal order'.

[115] N. Angelet, 'Protest against Security Council Decisions', in K. Wellens (ed.), *International Law: Theory and Practice, Essays E. Suy* (The Hague: Nijhoff, 1998), pp. 277 *et seq.*, p. 281.

[116] B. Conforti, *supra* note 113, pp. 237 *et seq.* H. Lauterpacht, sep. op., *Genocide Convention,* Order of 13 September 1993, *supra* note 7, p. 441, apparently does not rule out that the resolution could become unlawful after its adoption and ceases to be valid and binding at a later stage.

[117] See, in particular, G. Fitzmaurice, sep. op. *Certain Expenses case*, *supra* note 13, pp. 204–5. See also the position of the U.K. and the U.S. government in *Certain Expenses case*, *supra* note 13, *Pleadings*, respectively pp. 337 and 413.

tiveness of the measures decided upon, but on the alleged unlawfulness of the act. Admitting that abstaining States could also challenge the lawfulness of the resolution, provided that they have adequately motivated their vote, would undermine the effectiveness of the Organisations action and the certainty of its acts. Abstention should rather be assimilated to acknowledgement, or at least acquiescence that the act has been taken in accordance with, or is merely permitted by, the Charter, but in any case is not contrary thereto[118]. Although recent practice offers at least another example (see the position of Cuba in regard to Resolution 665), contesting the lawfulness of a resolution and not voting against its adoption is simply contradictory.

A fortiori, the right to challenge the lawfulness of the resolution does not belong to States casting a positive vote. Should they link the resolution to a given interpretation, what may be subsequently challenged is the correct interpretation and application of the act, and not its lawfulness.[119] In this regard, resolutions allegedly authorising Member States to use military force have been the subject of different interpretation, both at the time of their adoption[120] and afterwards.[121]

Furthermore, admitting that a State may abstain from or even vote in favour of a resolution it deems unlawful will seriously undermine the function of guarantee attributed to the so-called veto right. The privileged position of permanent members involves the responsibility to prevent the Security Council from adopting unlawful acts. The same is true for non-permanent members, although in that case their opposition may not impede the adoption of the act.

Member States who have failed to manifest their dissent on legal grounds – through a negative vote if represented in the Security Council, or through an appropriate declaration or concluding behaviour at the earliest possible moment –

[118] L. Gross, 'Expenses of the United Nations for Peace-Keeping Operations', 17 *IO* (1963) 11, p. 33. For G. Fitzmaurice, dissenting opinion in *Certain Expenses case*, *supra* 13, p. 210, abstention with regard to non-mandatory resolutions indicates 'approval of, or at any rate tacit acquiescence in, its being carried out by those Member States which are ready to do so'. *Contra*, B. Conforti, *supra* note 113, pp. 241 *et seq*. who bases his view on several examples – all relevant but rather old – of practice within the Security Council.

[119] *Contra* B. Conforti, *supra* note 113, pp. 245 *et seq*.

[120] A case in point is Security Council Res. 988, 16 June 1995 (13–0–2), regarding the establishment of the Rapid Reaction Force in Bosnia-Herzegovina. The resolution was adopted upon a proposal of France, Great Britain and the Netherlands (S/1995/470, Annex), according to which the Force intended to provide UNPROFOR with effective protection and would have operated under the existing chain of command and rules of engagement. Interestingly, it was stated that a further Security Council resolution was requested to expand the authorised level of force. Some States welcomed the resolution as a stronger approach to the enforcement of the existing UNPROFOR mandate (see in particular the observations made by the United Kingdom and France: S/PV. 3543, 16 June 1995, respectively pp. 18–19, and pp.19–20); others criticised it as implying a creeping abandonment of the peacekeeping principles (see the position of China, *ibid*., p. 14; and the Russian Federation, *ibid*., pp. 9 *et seq*.

[121] On Res. 687, concerning the implementation of the conditions imposed on Iraq at the end of the Gulf conflict, see *infra* pp. 60 *et seq*. and 79 *et seq*.

cannot elude the obligations, if any, deriving therefrom. In the case of hortatory resolutions, they are prevented from contesting the lawfulness of the recommended or authorised conduct of other Member States.

These considerations are somehow balanced by the fact that the absence of any effective control of legality leaves much room for the application of the rules of general international law. Member States' acquiescence of acts of the Organisation, even when the acts are manifestly ill founded,[122] could signify, for all practical purposes, that the acts produce their effects. It can not be ruled out that these acts might be equated to international agreements concluded in simplified form, nor that general and uniform acceptance of these resolutions could be considered as concluding evidence in the perspective of an informal change of the Charter through subsequent practice.[123]

The Security Council's powers are functionally limited to reacting to acts of aggression, breaches of the peace and threats to peace, the latter not necessarily implying any violation of international law. These powers have voluntarily been conferred onto the Security Council by the members States through the acceptance of the Charter. The decision to resort to non-military measures is centralised, whereas the execution is left to the Member States. The Security Council Resolution adopted under Art. 41 may have a permissive effect in the sense that it renders lawful conduct otherwise contrary to international law. Under Art. 42, in contrast, the Security Council was meant to undertake directly the military measures to maintain international peace and security through the forces put at its disposal by Member States. Whereas the existence of limits to the Security Council's powers is undisputed, the question of control over the Council acts is far from settled. The so-called right to veto and the so-called right of last resort are the most effective – albeit not satisfactory – guarantees against abuses by the Security Council.

[122] B. Conforti, *supra* note 113, pp. 250 *et seq.*

[123] G. Schwarzenberger, *supra* Introduction note 3, p. 113, goes even further when stating that 'By acquiescence and, ultimately, estoppel on the part of members entitled to protest against the usurpation of functions of decision-making, the General Assembly or any other international organ may . . . successfully arrogate to itself functions and powers beyond those allocated to it in its constitution'.

II

The collective security system in practice

This chapter discusses the extent to which the collective security system established in the Charter could function in the 1990s in spite of the non-implementation of Arts. 43 *et seq*. of the Charter. Alongside the dilatation of the notion of threat to peace, the frequent authorisation of the use of force granted to Member States is certainly the main feature of the recent practice of the Security Council. The question of the control exercised by the Security Council over the operations is crucial to identify the legal basis of the use of force authorised by the Security Council and to understand the evolution – or indeed the involution – of the collective security system.

The enlargement of the notion of threat to peace

The enlargement of the notion of threat to international peace, already noticeable in 1992,[1] is one of the most striking features of the Security Council's recent practice.[2] For several reasons, however, the relevant practice is not sufficiently uniform and coherent to define a catalogue of threats to peace. The Security Council determination is frequently based on a combination of circumstances, such as regional military and political instability, massive human rights violations,

[1] See the Security Council declaration dated 31 January 1992, S/23500, in 31 *ILM* (1992) 758. In the declaration issued on 23 February 1993, it noted with concern 'the incidence of humanitarian crises, including mass displacement of population, becoming or aggravating threats to international peace and security' (S/25344).

[2] J. M. Sorel, 'L'élargissement de la notion de menace contre la paix', *in SFDI, Le Chapitre VII de la Charte des Nations Unies* (Paris: Pédone, 1996), p. 3; P. H. Koojimans, 'The Enlargement of the Concept Threat to Peace', in R. J. Dupuy (ed.), *supra* note I-97, p. 111; B. Conforti, 'Le pouvoir discrétionnaire du Conseil de sécurité en matière de constatation d'une menace contre la paix, d'une rupture ou d'un acte d'agression', *ibid*., p. 51; I. Österdahl, *Threat to the Peace: an Interpretation by the Security Council of Article 39 of the Charter* (Uppsala: Iusus, 1998); M. Zambelli, *La constatation des situations de l'article 39 de la Charte des Nations Unies par le Conseil de sécurité* (Genève: Helbing & Lichtenhahn, 2002).

humanitarian crises, flow of displaced persons or refugees[3] or accompanied by statements by Member States precluding any value as precedent,[4] or declarations emphasising the unique character of the situation.[5]

The most consistent developments are those regarding civil wars, humanitarian crises, international terrorism and proliferation of weapons of mass destruction. On a number of occasions, including the crises in Somalia, the former Yugoslavia, Liberia, Haiti, Albania, Sierra Leone and Kosovo, the Security Council did not consider that the internal character of the conflict prevented it from determining the existence of a threat to peace. In certain instances, it went even further and condemned the behaviour of non-State entities as threatening international peace, and imposed economic enforcement measures against them.[6] In *Prosecutor* v. *Tadic*, the ICTY observed that 'there is a common understanding, manifested by the subsequent practice of the member of the United Nations at large, that the threat to peace of Art. 39 may include, as one of its species, internal armed conflicts'.[7]

This conclusion, however, should be endorsed with caution. Firstly, the question of the qualification of most conflicts the Security Council dealt with was far from settled, mainly because of the uncertain international legal status of some of the belligerent parties, and the involvement of foreign governments.[8] Besides, on some occasions, the Secretary General, or some members of the Security

[3] The case of Haiti is illustrative since the threat to international peace was linked to the humanitarian crisis, human rights violations, non-compliance with the Governor Island agreement, lack of democracy, all combined with the request from the legitimate, but non-effective, Aristide government. Concern over the qualification of the situation as a threat to international peace had been expressed by several States, including Mexico, Cuba, Uruguay and Brazil: see S/PV.3413, respectively pp. 4, 5, 7 and 9.

[4] For instance, while voting in favour of Res. 875 (1993) concerning Haiti, China declared: 'The measures authorized . . . are special action taken under the unique and exceptional circumstances in Haiti, and they should not establish a precedent', S/PV.3293, 16 October 1993, p. 18. Similarly, see the position of Brazil: *ibid.*, pp. 23–4.

[5] See in particular, some declarations related to Res. 794 (1992), concerning Somalia; Res. 841 (1993), Res. 875 (1993) and Res. 940 (1994), concerning Haiti; Res. 929 (1994), concerning Rwanda.

[6] See, in particular, Res. 864 (1993), concerning UNITA; and Res. 942 (1994), concerning the self-proclaimed Serb Republic in Bosnia–Herzegovina.

[7] In *Prosecutor* v. *Tadic*, *supra* note I-18, para 30.

[8] The case of the qualification of the conflict in former Yugoslavia is quite significant. See the *Interim Report of the Commission of Experts Established Pursuant to Security Council Resolution 780 (1993)*, S/25174, Annex I. The ICTY declared itself 'empowered to adjudicate crimes perpetrated in the course of both inter-State wars and internal strife' (*Report of the ICTY*, S/1994/1007, p. 13), but experienced serious difficulties in qualifying the different conflicts that had taken place in the former Yugoslavia, as is witnessed by the decisions and the dissenting opinions related to *Prosecutor* v. *Tadic*, *supra* note I-18 and *supra* note I-94.

Council, stressed the lack of any governmental authority,[9] or relied on the consent expressed by the recognised – albeit not effective – government[10] or by certain concerned parties.[11] Finally, the Security Council attributed, almost systematically, a certain importance to the transnational effects or the regional dimensions of the crisis.

The evolution of the notion of threat to international peace has to be appreciated also from the standpoint of human rights. Following the path of the resolutions adopted in 1966 and 1977 in the Southern Rhodesian and South African crises,[12] the Security Council considered that massive violations of human rights and serious humanitarian crises could threaten international peace.[13] This attitude was confronted with the conservative stand of several Member States, which insisted on the transboundary consequences of the situation, such as flow of refugees, to overcome the domestic jurisdiction limit, and expressed concern over the Security Council's involvement in situations that would have been more appropriately handled by UN humanitarian agencies operating, where possible, with the consent of the territorial government.

Furthermore, in a string of resolutions regarding Libya,[14] Sudan,[15] Afghanistan[16] and, more recently, passed in the aftermath of the terrorist attacks against the United States,[17] the Security Council without hesitation declared international terrorism a threat to international peace. The refusal to extradite alleged terrorists,[18] the toleration or *a fortiori* the incitement to or support of terrorist activities directed against other States may certainly amount to violations of international law and pave the way to the victim State's resort to available remedies under

[9] A case in point could be the situation in Somalia in 1992; see the Secretary General's report dated 24 April 1992 (S/24868, p. 3). It is plausible, however, to treat the different factions as entities *superiorem non recognoscentes* and therefore qualify the conflict as international; see A. Pietrobon, *Il sinallagma negli accordi internazionali* (Padova: CEDAM, 1999), pp. 87 *et seq*.

[10] See the case of Haiti, *supra* note 3.

[11] This was probably the case, in particular, in the crises in Somalia and Liberia.

[12] See Res. 232 (1966) and Res. 418 (1977). With regard to the Rhodesian crisis, compare G. Fenwick, 'When is There a Threat to Peace. Rhodesia', 61 *AJIL* (1967) 753; with M. S. McDougal and M. W. Reisman, 'Rhodesia and the United Nations: The Lawfulness of International Concern', 62 *AJIL* (1968) 1. According to T. Franck, 'Fairness in the International Legal and Institutional System', 240 *RdC* (1993–III) 9, p. 204, the two resolutions established the principle that a threat to the peace 'can be created by the conduct of a Government towards its own citizens which grossly and persistently violates firmly established international law'.

[13] The Security Council attached great importance to humanitarian considerations, for instance in Res. 688 (1991), Res. 794 (1992), Res. 929 (1994) and Res. 1078 (1996), concerning Iraq, Somalia, Rwanda and Zaire respectively.

[14] Res. 731 (1991) and Res. 748 (1991).

[15] Res. 1054 (1996)

[16] See, in particular, Res. 1070 (1996), Res. 1267 (1999) and Res. 1333 (2000).

[17] See, in particular, Res. 1368 (2001) and Res. 1373 (2001).

[18] Provided there is a valid extradition treaty or the State is bound by the *aut dedere aut judicare* rule and does not intend to prosecute the alleged terrorists.

conventional or customary international law. However, this does not necessarily imply, nor is it indispensable for, the determination of the existence of a threat to international peace under Art. 39. Such a determination presupposes a situation in which the terrorist activities may cause a concrete and actual risk of military confrontation, an unacceptable level of instability in the region or, on a wider scale, the escalation of the hostile military activities against other States. In the case of the terrorist attacks against the United States on 11 September 2001, the existence of a threat to international peace is self-evident. It is interesting to note that in the preamble of Resolution 1373, the Security Council declared that *any* act of terrorism represented a threat to international peace and security.[19] Building on such a finding, he imposed a comprehensive set of obligations upon Member States.

Finally, the Security Council has declared that the proliferation of weapons of mass destruction and their means of delivery, to which the illicit trafficking had added a new dimension, amount to a threat to international peace and security.[20] In this perspective, in particular, it could resort to enforcement measures in order to induce a State to desist from developing a nuclear programme deemed to cause such a threat, regardless of the commission of any violation of international law by the concerned State.[21] Analogous measures could be taken against a State that is involved in or tolerating trafficking of weapons of mass destruction with non-State actors as defined in Resolution 1540.

The Security Council enjoys no unfettered discretion, however difficult it is to define the limits within which it can make a determination under Art. 39.[22] Some authors suggested construing the discretionary power as a matter of margin of appreciation.[23] Such a view, however, overlooks the fact that the margin of appreciation theory presupposes the existence of judicial bodies competent to elaborate the pertinent criteria and review all decisions invoking such a doctrine. Since the possibility of a review of the Security Council's decision under Art. 39 by an independent judicial body still appears remote, the limits to the discretion of that organ

[19] In the preamble to the Draft Comprehensive Convention on International Terrorism the contracting parties affirmed that 'the suppression of acts of terrorism . . . is an essential element in the maintenance of international peace and security' (A/C.6/551, 28 August 2000).

[20] See, most recently, Res. 1540, adopted on 28 April 2004.

[21] Not being party to the NPT, the concerned State may have committed no breach of its international obligations. See *infra* text notes V-189/190.

[22] In the *Certain Expenses case*, *supra* note I-13, p. 293, G. Fitzmaurice noted that Art. 24 of the Charter 'does not limit the occasions on which the Security Council can act in the preservation of international peace and security, provided that the threat said to be involved is not a figment or pretext'. But R. Lillich, *supra* note I-93, paraphrasing Justice Hughes on the role of the US Supreme Court in interpreting the Constitution, concludes that a threat to peace is 'what the Security Council says it is'. Similarly, see J. Combacau, *supra* note I-40, p. 100.

[23] See M. Bothe, *supra* note I-97, p. 70.

are essentially political.[24] Their respect may, in the first place, be secured from inside, through self-limitation[25] complemented by a genuine effort to define, judiciously and publicly, what amounts to a threat to peace[26] and, perhaps more importantly, through the voting procedure, which prescribes not only a qualified majority, but also the absence of opposition from permanent members.[27]

A more effective form of guarantee may be assured from outside the organ, as all Member States could protest against the Security Council's determination under Art. 39 and even refuse to comply with mandatory economic enforcement measures, or decline to carry out military or non-mandatory economic enforcement measures, when the situation is not perceived as representing a genuine threat to international peace and security.

The consequences of the non-implementation of Articles 43 *et seq.*

Since the establishment of the Organisation, the question whether Art. 42 could function independently from the conclusion of special agreements under Art. 43 has been the object of diverging positions both in State practice[28] and in literature. One view considers Art. 42 as entirely conditional on the conclusion of special agreements, on the basis of the *travaux préparatoires*[29] and of a systematic interpretation of Art. 43 with Art. 106.[30] Although supported in the past by the Secretary General,[31] this view is now rather marginal.[32]

The prevailing and more convincing view admits that the Security Council may overcome the non-implementation of Art. 43 through the conclusion of *ad*

[24] L. Henkin, *supra* note 18, further observes that 'limits on the Security Council's discretion are not judicial, and they cannot be adjudicated in court. The limits on the Security Council's discretion are political. I do not, however, consider those limits as ineffectual'.

[25] I. Brownlie, 'International Law at the Fiftieth Anniversary of the United Nations', 255 *RdC* (1995) 9, p. 226.

[26] F. L. Kirgis, 'The Security Council's First Fifty Years', 89 *AJIL* (1995) 516–17.

[27] On this point, see M. S. McDougal and W. M. Reisman, *supra* note 12, p. 9.

[28] During the Korean crisis, the United Kingdom maintained that without the conclusion of Art. 43 special agreement, the Security Council could not resort to Art. 42, S/PV.476, p. 3, 7 July 1950. In the opposite sense, see the *Memorandum of the U.S.S.R. regarding certain measures to strengthen he effectiveness of the United Nations in maintaining peace and security*, A/AC.121/2, 10 July 1964.

[29] See, in particular, Doc 881, III/3/46, in 12 *UNCIO*, p. 508.

[30] See, in particular: L. Goodrich and A. Simons, *The United Nations and the Maintenance of International Peace and Security* (Washington: Brookings Institution, 1955), pp. 398 *et seq.*

[31] See *United Nations Guard. Report of the Secretary General*, A/656, 28 September 1948, p. 5.

[32] See, for instance, B. H. Weston, 'Security Council Resolution 678 and Persian Gulf Decision Making: Precarious Legitimacy', 85 *AJIL* (1991) 516, p. 519.

hoc agreements with Member States.[33] This view is in line with the flexible approach adopted by the ICJ in the *Expenses cases*, when the Court affirmed that 'nothing in the text of Art. 43 would limit the discretion of the Security Council in negotiating such agreements', and excluded that 'the Charter has left the Security Council impotent in the face of an emergency situation when agreements under Art. 43 have not been concluded'.[34]

Through the conclusion of *ad hoc* agreements, which may be treated as an 'operational alternative' to the *una tantum* agreements envisaged in Art. 43,[35] Member States put at the disposal of the Security Council the armed forces necessary to implement military coercive measures in a given crisis. Such agreements do not need to satisfy any formal requirement and are concluded on a case-by-case and purely voluntary basis. Yet, an obligation to participate in military enforcement measures decided by the Security Council can derive exclusively from special agreements under Art. 43.[36]

In addition to preventing the United Nations from compelling Member States to contribute armed forces or to carry out military enforcement measures, the non-implementation of Art. 43 imposes the reading of Art. 48(1) as concerning exclusively economic enforcement measures. Art. 48(1) confirms and reinforces the general obligation already imposed on Member States by Art. 25 to comply with mandatory decisions found in other articles of the Charter. In this sense, neither Art. 25 nor Art. 48(1) is an autonomous source of obligations. Art. 48(1) merely permits the Security Council to opt for a selective imposition of such obligations, thus exempting part of the membership.[37]

Member States not only decide whether to participate in military enforcement measures, but also negotiate with the United Nations the entity of their contribu-

[33] L. Sohn, 'The Authority of the United Nations to Establish and Maintain a Permanent Force', 52 *AJIL* (1958) 229, p. 230; G. Schwarzenberger, 'Problems of a United Nations Force', 12 *CLP* (1959) 247, p. 254; F. Seyersted, 'United Nations Forces: Some Legal Problems', 36 *BYIL* (1961) 351, pp. 438 *et seq.* and 463 *et seq.*; and *United Nations Forces in the Law of Peace and War* (Leyden: Sijthoff, 1966), p. 400; J. W. Halderman, 'Legal Basis for United Nations Armed Forces', 56 *AJIL* (1962) 971; D. W. Bowett, *United Nations Forces: A Legal Study of United Nations Practice* (London: Stevens, 1964), p. 277; M. L. Picchio Forlati, *supra* note I-6, p. 209; O. Schachter, 'United Nations in the Gulf Conflict', 85 *AJIL* (1991) 452, pp. 463 *et seq.*; R. Higgins, 'The New United Nations and the Former Yugoslavia', 69 *IA* (1993) 465, p. 468; D. Sarooshi, *The United Nations and the Development of Collective Security. The Delegation by the UN Security Council of its Chapter VII Powers* (Oxford: Oxford University Press, 1999), p. 78; S. Chesterman, *supra* note I-65, p. 166.

[34] *Certain Expenses case*, *supra* note I-13, pp. 166 and 167. See also *Statement made during the proceedings by the United States* (Chayes), *ICJ Pleadings*, p. 423.

[35] G. Gaja, 'Use of Force Made or Authorized by the United Nations', in C. Tomuschat (ed.), *The United Nations at Age Fifty* (The Hague: Kluwer, 1995), p. 41.

[36] See *Report to the President*, *supra* note I-10, p. 95. This view is virtually unanimous in the literature on this point; see the authors cited *supra* note 33.

[37] On this point, see O. Schachter, *supra* note 33, p. 463.

tion, the tasks of their forces, and the chain of command under which these forces would operate. Unless otherwise stated in the *ad hoc* agreement, they may also withdraw their forces without having to satisfy any prior notice requirement, especially when, as it happened in Somalia, contrasts emerge on the interpretation of the mandate or on the strategic conduct of the operations. Additionally, contributing States have the right to withdraw their force at any time – even in disregard of provisions on the conditions for withdrawal, if any – when they believe that the operations are carried out in violation of the *ad hoc* agreement,[38] or, *a fortiori*, of the Charter.

Until Member States conclude special agreements, Articles 44 to 46 are deprived of any practical value. Article 44, in particular, establishes that Member States not represented in the Security Council shall participate, without voting rights, in the decisions concerning the employment of their contingents committed to the United Nations through the special agreement concluded under Art. 43. The *ratio* underlining that provision is to provide troops-contributing States with the opportunity to take part in the decision-making process related to the military operations involving their forces made permanently available to the Security Council. Art. 44 does not necessarily apply to cases in which armed forces are provided on a voluntary case-by-case basis.[39] The relationships between Member States and the United Nations are governed by *ad hoc* agreements. Obviously, nothing prevents the inclusion in such agreements of provisions similar to Art. 44 or even offering greater guarantees to States, as it would be the case of a right to be consulted not only at the Security Council level – as envisaged in Art. 44 – but also within the bodies exercising strategic command, presumably the Secretary General or the Military Staff Committee. An inadequate definition by the *ad hoc* agreement of the rights and obligations of contributing States may undermine the unity and effectiveness of the operation, as is amply demonstrated by the Somali crisis.

Peace-enforcement by the United Nations

Nothing prevents the Security Council and Member States from concluding *ad hoc* agreements in the context of ongoing peace-keeping operations, although carrying out coercive military activities would inevitably imply a radical change in the nature of the operation. The main lesson learned from the United Nations' recent practice is that peace-keeping and peace-enforcement are mutually exclusive options. In this regard, the Secretary General has rightly pointed out that 'peace-keeping and the use of force (other than self-defence) should be seen as

[38] This case may be treated as a termination or suspension of treaties because of material breach of the *ad hoc* agreement.

[39] *Contra* D. Sarooshi, *supra* note 33, p. 35.

alternative techniques and not as adjacent points on a *continuum* permitting easy transition from one to the other'.[40]

The crux of the matter is the coercive nature of the operation: when the force imposes its will on one or more concerned parties by military means, or influences the outcome of the conflict, then the operation assumes a hostile character. This would imply 'a fundamental shift from the logic of peace-keeping to the logic of war'.[41] Whether such a shift occurs must be ascertained from a factual standpoint,[42] in the same way as the determination of a state of war between States.[43] As long as military coercive operations are restricted to neutralising unorganised groups,[44] or are tolerated by the concerned parties,[45] the force may continue to carry out a peace-keeping operation. When military enforcement measures are directed against one or more belligerent parties, however, the operation assumes a hostile nature.

The only case in recent practice in which armed forces have been put at the complete disposal of the United Nations for enforcement action has occurred in Somalia, where the Organisation was already actively engaged in a peace-keeping operation.[46] On 26 March 1993, the Security Council, acting under

[40] Report dated 25 January 1995, S/1995/1, p. 9 (known as *Supplement to an Agenda for Peace*). S. Tharoor, 'The Changing Face of Peace-Keeping and Peace-Enforcement', 19 *FILJ* (1995) 408, p. 419, observes that 'peace-keepers have been sent precisely because the world is unable or unwilling to pursue the alternative course: going to war'.

[41] See the Secretary General's report S/1994/1067, 17 November 1994, p. 13. With regard to the possible use of air force to neutralise the Bosnian Serbs' air control system, he pointed out that 'such a pre-emptive action . . . is inevitably considered by the Bosnian Serbs as an hostile act and therefore take UNPROFOR beyond the limits of a peace-keeping operation and quickly make it a party to the conflict'.

[42] See the considerations on the effective coercive and hostile nature of UNOC made by L. M. Moreno Quintana, diss. op. *Certain Expenses case*, *supra* note I-13, p. 246.

[43] See common Art. 2 of the Geneva Conventions, 75 *UNTS* 31, 85, 135 and 287. In literature, see Y. Dinstein, *Aggression and Self-Defence*, 3rd ed. (Cambridge: Cambridge University Press, 2001), pp. 29 *et seq*.

[44] This was the case with UNPROFOR until August 1995. In the report dated 30 May 1995, the Secretary General observes than in the context of a peace-keeping operation 'Military protection serves primarily to dissuade random or unorganised attacks; it cannot substitute for the consent and co-operation of the parties' (S/1995/444, p. 9). Paragraph 4 of Res. 918, adopted on 17 May 1994, allowed UNAMIR to take action if self-defence against *persons or groups* who threaten protected sites, populations and humanitarian personnel.

[45] See, for example, the enforcement of the no-fly zone over Bosnia airspace decided by Security Council Res. 816 (*infra* note 72). The operations were tolerated by the belligerent parties, and in particular by the Bosnian Serbs against whom they were essentially directed. The only combat action took place on 28 February 1994, when four Galeb violating the no-fly zone were shot down near Banja Luka: see 88 *AJIL* (1994) p. 524; 65 *BYIL* (1994) p. 694. The action did not provoke the protest of any of belligerent parties or have negative consequences on the peace-keeping operation.

[46] The Operation in Congo (UNOC) represents an interesting precedent. In the *Certain Expenses case*, *supra* note I-13, the ICJ concluded that ONUC had not been transformed into an enforcement action under Chapter VII of the Charter. This conclusion, which was

Chapter VII, allowed the peace-keeping force (UNOSOM), established by Resolution 751 (1992), to take the military enforcement measures necessary to consolidate, expand and maintain a secure environment throughout Somalia.[47] The mandate was later expanded by Resolution 837 (1993), when UNOSOM II was authorised to take all necessary measures against all those responsible for the armed attacks against it and to establish effective authority throughout Somalia, including arresting those responsible for inciting such attacks.

Through the two resolutions, UNOSOM II assumed a coercive nature. It operated independently from the consent of all concerned parties and, abandoning the restricted use of force to cases of self-defence, resorted to military enforcement measures. Virtually all representatives of the Security Council members described the operation in terms of military enforcement and most of them made an express reference to Chapter VII. Even China declared that UNOSOM II was authorised 'to take enforcement action under Chapter VII in order to implement its mandate' and voted in favour of the resolution.[48] The rules of engagement adopted on May 1993 leave no doubt as to the nature of UNOSOM II.[49] The Secretary General assumed the responsibility for the operation and appointed a Special Representative for Somalia and a Force Commander.[50]

UNOSOM II took military enforcement measures which on several occasions degenerated into serious clashes with local militias.[51] Divergences on the interpretation of the mandate and the overall strategy among the Secretary General, certain States contributing to UNOSOM II and the United States,[52] undermined

---

largely based on the assessment of the nature and intensity of the military activities, was still plausible in June 1962, when the Court delivered its opinion. In the following months, however, ONUC clearly undertook coercive military action incompatible with a peace-keeping operation and was directly involved in the hostilities; see the report sent on 30 January 1963, by the military commander in the field (S/5240, Annex 15).

[47] Res. 814, 26 March 1993 (unanimously). The resolution contains a *renvoi* to the Secretary General's report dated 3 March 1993 (S/25354) that urged the Security Council to endow UNISOM II with enforcement powers under Chapter VII of the Charter and outlined its mandate.

[48] It nonetheless pointed out that the resolution did not set a precedent because of the uniqueness of the situation existing at the time in Somalia (S/PV. 3188, 26 March 1993, p. 22).

[49] The so-called *Frag Order 39*, partly reproduced in F. M. Lorenz, 'Rules of Engagement in Somalia: Were They Effective?', 42 *Naval LR* (1995) 62, p. 66, reads: 'Organized, armed militias, technicals and other crew served weapons are considered a threat to Unisom Force and *may be engaged without provocation*' (emphasis added).

[50] *The United Nations and Somalia*, United Nations Publications, New York, 1996, pp. 42 *et seq*. See also the Secretary General's reports S/26317, 17 August 1993, p. 19; and S/1994/653, 1 June 1994, pp. 28–9 and 45.

[51] For an account of the crisis and the most relevant documents, see *The United Nations and Somalia* , *supra* note 50. See also W. Clarke and J. Herbst (eds.), *Learning from Somalia: Lesson of Armed Humanitarian Intervention* (Boulder: Westview Press, 1997).

[52] Throughout the crisis, United States forces previously engaged in UNITAF or deployed subsequently, operated in support of, but independently from, UNOSOM II. Not

the unity and effectiveness of the operation, and eventually led to the withdrawal of some national contingents, the return to a traditional peace-keeping operation,[53] and the withdrawal of the United Nations from Somalia.

The power of the Security Council to transform a peace-keeping operation into an enforcement one had already been admitted without hesitation by the Secretary General as early as in 1956, in relation to the United Nations Emergency Force (UNEF),[54] and has never been contested since. As for the command and control arrangements, the structure already in place for the peace-keeping operation is normally maintained. The Security Council continues to exercise overall political control whereas the Secretary General assumes the military strategic direction over the enforcement measures. Operational command remains in the hands of the commanders in the field.

The debate on the legal basis for peace-enforcement operations dates back to the Congo crisis. The official United Nations' view, strongly conditioned by the refusal to qualify UNOC as an enforcement operation, invoked Art. 40 as the operation's legal basis. Considering that the Security Council did not invoke Arts. 41 or 42, the Secretary General stated 'that the Council's resolutions could be regarded as implicitly adopted under Art. 40 and had been based on an implicit finding under Art. 39 . . . In the absence of an explicit authorisation to resort to enforcement measures, the Secretary-General could only make use of the diplomatic means at his disposal'.[55]

Reliance on Art. 40 appears to be misplaced. By definition, provisional measures do not prejudice the rights, claims or positions of the concerned parties. Art. 40, therefore, 'only covers invitation addressed by the Security Council to

---

being part of UNOSOM II, they were directed by the competent United States military authorities through chains of command distinct from that established for UNOSOM II. See F. M. Lorenz, *supra* note 49, p. 67; M. Cremasco, 'Il caso Somalia', in N. Ronzitti (ed.), *Comando e controllo nelle forze di pace e nelle coalizioni militari* (Milano: Angeli, 1999), p. 173. Not being covered by the relevant Security Council resolutions, which were directed exclusively at UNOSOM II, the lawfulness of the coercive military activities carried out by the United States force is extremely precarious.

[53] Res. 897, 4 February 1994.

[54] On 6 November 1956, after underlining that UNEF could be stationed and operate only with the consent of the government concerned, he did not exclude 'the possibility that the Security Council could use such a Force within the wider margins provided under Chapter VII' (A/3302, para. 9). With regard to the adoption of coercive measures, he later explained that 'a wide interpretation of the right of self-defence might well blur the distinction between operations of the character discussed in this report and combat operations, which would require a decision under Chapter VII of the Charter, and an explicit, more far-reaching delegation of authority to the Secretary-General' (A/3943, para. 155).

[55] *Annual Report of the Secretary-General on the Work of the Organisation*, 16 June 1960–15 June 1962, pp. 27 and pp. 36. O. Schachter, 'Legal Issues at the United Nations', *Annual Review of the UN Affairs*, 1960–1, p. 142 *et seq*., p. 146, notes that 'the United Nation action was admittedly less than an enforcement measure in the sense of Chapter VII; and yet it was more than a purely technical assistance, contractual operation. It fell between the two and come closest to the provisional measures envisaged in Art. 40'.

parties to a conflict and does not refer to any action, let alone a military action, on the part of the Council'.[56] While still present in the Secretary General's report submitted in 1992,[57] the reference to Art. 40 as the legal basis for enforcement action seems to have been abandoned since.[58]

In the crisis in Somalia, the Security Council refrained from founding its competence on any specific article of the Charter in favour of a general reference to Chapter VII. On that occasion, the competence of the Security Council to establish, under Chapter VII of the Charter, military enforcement measures through the forces made available by Member States and operated under the command and control of the Secretary General and its delegates has been accepted by virtually all Member States.[59] The few reservations raised were in fact confined to the exceptionality of the circumstances in which the operation was to be carried out, and to the political opportunity to embark on such an operation; they did not regard the lawfulness of the enforcement operations as such. Given the complete absence of objections between Member States, this interpretation of Chapter VII of the Charter satisfies even the most stringent construction of the *general acceptability* requirement.[60]

Within Chapter VII, the legal basis of the operation could more precisely be found in Art. 42 functioning independently from the conclusion of special agreements under Art. 43, thanks to the armed forces voluntarily put at the disposal of the Security Council by Member States.[61] Incidentally, Art. 42 was indicated in literature as the most appropriate legal basis of the hostile and non-consensual nature of the operations carried out by UNOC, at least during the military offensive against the Katanganese forces.[62]

[56] G. Gaja, *supra* note 35, p. 53. Also the position of South Africa in the *Certain Expenses* case, *supra* note I-13, *Pleadings*, p. 262.

[57] S/24111, A/47/277, 17 June 1992 (*An Agenda for Peace*).

[58] *Supplement to an Agenda for Peace*, *supra* note 40, pp. 18–19.

[59] For the purpose of establishing the *opinio juris*, it is sufficient that the conduct is perceived as 'lawful or not unlawful under the governing provisions of the constitution'; see C. F. Amerasinge, 'Interpretation of Text of Open International Organizations', 65 *BYIL* (1994) 175, p. 199.

[60] See the document referred to *supra* note I-41, esp. pp. 709 *et seq*. According to J. Castañeda, *Legal Effects of United Nations Resolutions* (New York: Columbia University Press, 1969), p. 123, 'generally acceptable' for the purpose of the interpretation of the Charter means 'acceptable to the majority of the members of the organ in question, in accordance with the voting majority applicable to that organ and the nature of the matter being treated'. Relying on the French text of the document referred to *supra*, which reads 'acceptable à l'ensemble des membres', B. Conforti, *supra* note I-113, footnote 20 p. 227, maintains that the expression requires unanimity. For P. Spender, sep. op. in *Certain Expenses*, *supra* note I-13, pp. 191–2, 'it is not evident on what ground a practice followed by a majority of Member States not in fact accepted by the other Member States could provide any criterion of interpretation'.

[61] G. Gaja, *supra* note 35, p. 53; G. Cellamare, *Le operazioni di* peace-keeping *funzionale* (Torino: Giappichelli, 1999), p. 223.

[62] In this sense, see G. P. Alessi, 'L'evoluzione della prassi delle Nazioni Unite relativa al mantenimento della pace', 47 *RDI* (1964) 556, p. 562; M. Spatafora, 'L'intervento

The only possible deviation from the mechanism established in Arts. 42 *et seq.* is the military role assumed by the Secretary General. Under Art. 47(3), the strategic direction over enforcement operations was assigned to the Military Staff Committee. Unfortunately, the Military Staff Committee has never played any significant role and recent attempts to involve it in the management of international crises had entirely failed.[63] It may be argued that, despite the use of the modal 'shall', Art. 47(3) does not create in favour of the Military Staff Committee an exclusive competence insofar as the strategic direction over enforcement operations is concerned. This provision may be interpreted as permitting the Security Council to charge with such a responsibility not only the Military Staff Committee, but also any other organ or body as is deemed appropriate. The military strategic direction of the forces engaged in coercive operations may be included among the functions the Security Council can entrust to the Secretary General under Art. 98.[64] Such an interpretation is inspired by the principle of effectiveness[65] and finds some support in the flexible approach adopted by the ICJ in the *Certain Expenses case*.[66]

Once accepted that the Member States can put armed forces at the disposal of the Security Council on an *ad hoc* basis, and that the Secretary General and his delegates can exercise strategic command and control over these forces, the operations in Somalia may be considered as an enforcement action carried out by the United Nations, which maintained a firm control over the operations and accord-

militare delle Nazioni Unite in Congo', 51 *RDI* (1968) 517, p. 556; B. Conforti, *La funzione dell'accordo nel sistema della Nazioni Unite* (Padova: CEDAM, 1968), pp. 135 *et seq.* For a more prudent, but substantially similar, view, see R. Y. Jennings, 'The United Nations and the Congo', in *The Listener*, 19 October 1961, p. 612; G. Abi-Saab, *The United Nations Operation in Congo*, (Oxford: Oxford University Press, 1978), pp. 105 *et seq.* See also V. Koretsky, diss. op. *Certain Expenses case, supra* note I-13, p. 275. *Contra*, R. Higgins, *The Development of International Law through the Political Organs of the United Nations* (London: Oxford University Press, 1963), pp. 200 *et seq.*; D.W. Bowett, *supra* note 33, p. 180.

[63] See *infra* notes 87 and 141.

[64] See B. Conforti, *supra* note I-15, p. 200.

[65] On the principle of effectiveness, see, in particular, *Effects of Awards of Compensation made by the U.N. Administrative Tribunal,* Advisory Opinion, *ICJ Reports 1954*, pp. 47 *et seq.*, p. 57; *Certain Expenses case, supra* note I-13, p. 159; *Application for Review of Judgement No. 158 of the United Nations Administrative Tribunal*, Advisory Opinion, *ICJ Reports 1973*, pp. 166 *et seq.*, p. 172–3; *Nuclear Weapons, infra* note V-127, p. 75. See also P. Spender, sep. op. in *Certain Expenses case, supra* note I-13, p. 186, and the position of the International Law Commission, 18 *YBILC* (1966–II), p. 219. On the limits of the principle, see the joint dissenting opinion of P. Spender and G. Fitzmaurice in *South West Africa cases*, Preliminary Objections, Judgment, *ICJ Reports 1962*, p. 3, p. 468; G. Fitzmaurice, '*Vae Victis* or Woe to the Negotiators! Your Treaty or our "Interpretation" of it?', 65 *AJIL* (1971) 358, p. 373.

[66] *Supra* note I-13. See also N. Elaraby, 'The Office of the Secretary-General and the Maintenance of International Peace and Security', in Unitar, *The United Nations and the Maintenance of International Peace and Security* (Dordrecht: Nijhoff, 1987), pp. 183–4.

ingly bore international responsibility with regard to the acts committed by the forces engaged.[67]

The failure of UNOSOM II is to be attributed to several factors, including the lack of an adequate military and political strategy, the divergences between Member States, and ultimately the inability of the United Nations to assume its responsibility for coercive military operations.[68] Welcomed as a historical development, the enforcement actions directly carried out by the United Nations are unlike to be undertaken again in the future. In 1995, the Secretary General admitted that 'neither the Security Council nor the Secretary General at present has the capacity to deploy, direct, command and control operations for this purpose, except perhaps on a very limited scale'.[69] At any rate, international law is not to be blamed for these failures. It provides a sufficiently clear legal framework for military enforcement action accepted by the whole membership and respectful not only of the spirit, but also of the letter, of the Charter.

The so-called authorisation practice

Apart from the isolated case of enforcement military action directly conducted by the United Nations in Somalia, throughout the 1990s the Security Council attempted to overcome the non-implementation of Arts. 43 *et seq.* by authorising Member States to use military force. This occurred, in particular, in the context of

[67] See R. Ago, *3rd Report on State Responsibility*, 23 *YBILC* (1971–II), part I, pp. 267 *et seq.*; ILC, *Report to the General Assembly*, 26 *YBILC* (1974–II), Part. 2, pp. 283 *et seq.* As maintained by P. de Visscher, *Les conditions d'application des lois de la guerre aux opérations militaires de Nations Unies*, 54 *AIDI* (1971), p. 39, 'la responsibilité se situera là où sera placé le contrôle'. It can not be ruled out that contributing member States may bear subsidiary responsibility; on this point see A. Di Blase, 'Sulla responsalibità internazionale per attività delle Nazioni Unite', 57 *RDI* (1974) 250.

[68] *Supplement to an Agenda for Peace*, *supra* note 40, p. 18.

[69] In the context of the situation in eastern Slavonia, Baranja and Sirmium, he concluded that should the Security Council opt for an enforcement operation under Chapter VII 'the deployment and command of the force . . . would best be entrusted to a coalition of member States rather than to the United Nations' (S/1995/1028, p. 8). Eventually the Security Council established a traditional peacekeeping operation: see Res. 1037 (1996).

[70] Res. 665, 25 August 1990 (13–0–2), para. 1, authorising member States co-operating with the government of Kuwait to use 'such measures commensurate to the specific circumstances as may be necessary' to ensure, with regard to all inward and outward maritime shipping, the respect of the economic enforcement measures adopted against Iraq. Res. 678, 28 November 1990 (12–2–1), para. 2, authorising member States co-operating with the Government of Kuwait to use 'all necessary means' to ensure the respect of the resolution so far adopted by the Security Council and to restore international peace and security in the area. The expression 'all necessary means'– which was to become current in subsequent resolutions – was unanimously interpreted as including military measures. This was accepted also by China, which, however, did not share the decision to intervene militarily and abstained from voting (S/PV. 2963, p. 63).

the crisis in the Gulf,[70] Somalia,[71] the former Yugoslavia,[72] Rwanda,[73] Haiti,[74] Albania,[75] East Timor,[76] the Ivory Coast[77] and Congo.[78] The Security Council also authorised the resort to military coercive measures by international forces in the

[71] Res. 794, 3 December 1992 (unanimously), para. 10, authorising the United States – and other member States willing to co-operate under the leadership of that State – 'to use all necessary means to establish as soon as possible a secure environment for humanitarian relief operations'. An enforcement action undertaken by a group of States upon the Security Council authorisation was one of the options suggested by the Secretary General to tackle the situation in Somalia because of the inadequacy of consensual peacekeeping operations; see the report dated 30 November 1992, S/24868, p. 5. In any event, he expressed its preference for an enforcement action under United Nations command and control (p. 6, *idib.*).

[72] See, in particular, the following resolutions: (a) Res. 787, 16 November 1992 (13–0–2), para. 12, authorising member States to undertake naval interdiction operations on the international waters of the Adriatic Sea. Coercive activities were later extended, in accordance with Res. 820, 17 April 1993 (13–0–2), para. 29; (b) Res. 816, 31 March 1993 (14–0–1), para. 4, authorising member States to ensure compliance with the no-fly zone imposed with regard to the Bosnian airspace. See NATO *Press Release* (93) 29, 12 April 1993; (c) Res. 836, 4 June 1993 (13–0–2), para. 10, authorising air power to support UNPROFOR in the performance of its mandate. On NATO activities, see *infra* pp. 109 *et seq.*

[73] Res. 929, 22 June 1994 (10–0–5), paras 2 and 3, authorising France and Senegal to use all necessary means to contribute to the security and protection of displaced persons, refugees and civilian at risk, establish and maintain secure humanitarian areas, provide security and support for humanitarian operations.

[74] Res. 875, 16 October 1993 (unanimously), para. 1, authorising naval interdiction operations necessary to ensure compliance with the economic enforcement measures imposed against Haiti; Res. 940, 31 July 1994 (10–0–2), para. 4, authorising the use of all necessary means to facilitate the departure from Haiti of the military leadership and the restoration of the legitimate authorities and to establish and maintain a secure and stable environment.

[75] Res. 1101, 28 March 1997 (14–0–1), para. 4, authorising the multinational force to facilitate the prompt delivery of humanitarian assistance, to create a secure environment, and to ensure the security and freedom of movement of the personnel of the said multinational force.

[76] Res. 1264, 15 September 1999 (unanimously), para. 3, authorising the multinational force to take all necessary measures to restore peace and security, to protect and support UNAMET in carrying out its mandate, and to facilitate humanitarian assistance. In this case, however, the deployment of the force followed the request by the Indonesian Government.

[77] Res. 1464, 4 February 2003 (unanimously), para. 9, authorising ECOWAS and French forces to guarantee the security and freedom of their forces and to protect the civilians at risk. In para. 1, the Security Council also endorsed the agreement signed by the Ivorian political forces in Linas-Marcoussis on 24 January 2003 (S/2003/99).

[78] Res. 1484, 30 May 2003 (unanimously), para. 1, authorising the deployment of a multinational force charged with stabilising the security conditions and the humanitarian situation in Bunia, ensuring the protection of the airport, the internally displaced persons in the camps of Bunia, and contributing to the safety of civilian population and personnel of international organisations. In the preamble, the Security Council supported the request of the government of the Democratic Republic of Congo and the Ituri parties; see the letter by the Secretary General dated 15 May 2003 (S/2003/574).

context of post-conflicts situations and implementation of peace accords, notably in Bosnia-Herzegovina,[79] Kosovo,[80] Afghanistan[81] and Iraq.[82]

Objections to the lawfulness of the authorisation practice have been rather occasional and have rarely been followed by a negative vote. During the 1990–91 Gulf crisis, in particular, Cuba vigorously contested Resolution 665 – without nonetheless casting a negative vote – and insisted that the forces authorised to take coercive measures should be put under the *direct command* of the Security Council.[83] Successively, Cuba considered Resolution 678 as contrary to the Charter since it would have given the Member States *carte blanche* in total disregard of the procedures established by the Charter.[84] Significantly, it was no longer opposed in principle to the authorisation, but denounced the inadequate involvement of the Security Council.[85] Similarly, Yemen, the other State to abstain from voting on the first resolution and casting a negative vote with regard to the second one, complained about the vagueness of the authorisation and stressed that lack of any effective control by the Security Council over the force engaged in the operations.[86]

The debate within the Security Council, indeed, has focused on the need for an effective system of control, rather than on the admissibility of the authorisation practice as such. Among the permanent members, China was certainly the most reluctant to tackle international crises with military force. Alongside the Soviet Union and the non-aligned members, it insisted on the establishment of a system of accountability to the Security Council.[87] China often abstained from voting on the resolutions authorising the use of force and occasionally stressed

[79] See *infra* note III-50.

[80] See *infra* note III-89.

[81] See *infra* note III-106.

[82] See *infra* note III-123.

[83] According to Cuba, the resolution would have left 'very few paragraphs of Chapter VII inviolated' (S/21529, 15 August 1990, pp. 13–15).

[84] Cuba declared: 'The Council very quickly forgot that in order to authorise the use of military force in accordance with the Charter, there is a specific procedure that must be followed. The Council must also assume authority when that is done and a certain monitoring must take place' (S/PV.2977, 13 January 1991, p. 58). While casting a negative vote with regard to Res. 686, it declared that the Security Council could not authorise member States to resort to force 'without any monitoring, without authority, without supervision of some kind' (S/PV.2978, 3 March, p. 31).

[85] S/PV.2977, 13 January 1991, p. 27.

[86] *Ibid.*, p. 33. It further observed that 'the command of those forces will have nothing to do with the United Nations, although their action will have been authorised by the Security Council' and that 'unclear powers are granted to undertake unspecified actions without a clear definition of the Security Council's role and powers of supervision over those actions' (*ibid.*, pp. 8–10).

[87] China and the Soviet Union stressed the importance of fully utilising the Committee established by Res. 661 (*ibid.*, p. 53) and the Military Staff Committee (*ibid.*, p. 43). Among the non-aligned members, see in particular the position of Malaysia (*ibid.* p. 76). With regard to Res. 794, Zimbabwe stressed the importance of the oversight function of the Secretary General and declared that 'in any enforcement action the United Nations must define the mandate; . . . monitor and supervise its implementation, . . . determine when the

the exceptional character of the situation and denied the value of precedent of the resolution.[88] It must be stressed, though, that on several occasions China concurred in the adoption of the resolution authorising the use of force.[89]

The United States, in turn, supported by the overwhelming majority of the Organisation membership, relied on the uniform and substantially unchallenged practice of authorising Member States since the 1990–91 Gulf crisis, passing through the crises in Somalia, Bosnia-Herzegovina and Rwanda, to affirm the admissibility of the so-called authorisation practice.[90]

When the military coercive operations authorised by the Security Council were carried out by a single State, the armed forces were put under the command and control of that State. For instance, the United Task Force (UNITAF) established in Somalia in accordance with Resolution 794 operated entirely under the United States chain of command and rules of engagement.[91] As admitted by the Secretary General, the United States President 'directed the execution of Operation *Restore Hope* on 4 December 1992. The United States command (USCENTCOM) was given the mission of conducting joint and combined military operations in Somalia, under United Nations auspices'.[92] It was again the United States that defined the mandate of the operation which, contrary to the view held by the Secretary General,[93] did not include the disarmament of local militias.[94]

---

mandate has been fulfilled' (S/PV.3145, 3 December 1992, p. 7). Ecuador added that 'the Security Council is the body that will authorize start-up, continued execution and termination' (*ibid*., p. 13–14). India, in turn, pointed out that 'the United Nations would keep effective political command and control while leaving enough flexibility for the contributing States to retain on the ground the operational autonomy they had requested' (*ibid*., p. 51).

[88] See, in particular, the position expressed when concurring to the adoption of Res. 875 (S/PV.2963, 16 October 1993, p. 18) and abstaining with regard to Res. 940 (S/PV.3413, 31 July 1994, p. 10).

[89] This occurred, in particular, with regard to Resolutions 666 (1990), 794 (1992), 836 (1993), 1264 (1999), 1464 (2003) and 1484 (2003).

[90] See the declaration made on the occasion of the adoption of Res. 875 and Res. 940, respectively (S/PV.3392, 22 June 1994, pp. 6–7, and S/PV.3413, 31 July 1994, p. 13).

[91] See F. M. Lorenz, *supra* note 49, pp. 66–7.

[92] See the letter dated 17 December 1992, S/24976, Annex; and the Secretary General's report dated 19 December 1992.

[93] See the reports dated 19 December 1992, S/24992, p. 2; and 3 March 1993, S/25354, pp. 12–13.

[94] See the United States' letter, *supra* note 92. Discussing whether in legal terms the interpretation of the mandate given by the Secretary General prevails over that of the concerned States (see D. Sarooshi, *supra* note 33, pp. 216–17) does not appear necessary in the case of Somalia. Apart from the fact that the interpretation held by the Secretary General did not reflect that of the majority of the Security Council's members (see H. Freudenschuß, 'Between Unilateralism and Collective Security: Authorizations of the Use of Force by the Security Council', 5 *EJIL* (1994) 492, p. 515), the real point is that neither the Secretary General nor the Security Council can oblige member States to take or continue military enforcement operations beyond those voluntarily agreed upon by these States.

When the intervention is carried out by a multinational force, the establishment of a unified command, normally under the leadership of the most powerful State, is the result of an agreement concluded between participating States. The unified command functions as a common organ of these States, whereas each of these States remains individually responsible on the international plane for the acts committed by their forces.[95] Within the coalition established under Resolution 678, in particular, General Schwarzkopf acted as 'overall commander',[96] whereas contributing countries were involved in the planning phase and accepted the tasks assigned by, and to be performed under the control of, the United States.[97] The decision-making process was firmly in the hands of the United States Government. Acting as commander-in-chief, on 16 January the President ordered the beginning of the military operations.[98] Successively the United States issued an ultimatum on Iraq, put forward the conditions for a cease-fire,[99] launched a massive ground offensive following Iraqi refusal,[100] ordered a suspension of offensive combat operations,[101] and eventually negotiated the cease fire.[102]

When the military coercive operation had been carried out by NATO, in turn, the forces were fully integrated in the Alliance military structure and operated under its rules of engagement and chain of command.[103] The North Atlantic Council (NAC) exercised political control and strategic direction over the

[95] See R. Ago, *supra* note 67, p. 272. With regard to the intervention in Korea, H. Kelsen, *supra* note I-4, p. 940, observes that 'The unification of the armed forces of the Members taking action in compliance with the recommendation of the Security Council is in effect a voluntary agreement of these Members, and the commander of the unified forces is the common organ of these Members'.

[96] The expression is used in *Despatch by Air Chief Marshal Sir Patrick Hine*, 29 June 1991, in M. Weller (ed.), *Iraq and Kuwait: The Hostilities and their Aftermath* (Cambridge: Grotius, 1993), pp. 306 *et seq.*, p. 312. The naval interdiction operations authorised by Res. 665 were carried out without an unified command and under the 'overall co-ordination' of the US (*Interim Report to the Congress, Conduct of the Persian Gulf War*, July 1991, in M. Weller (ed.), *supra*, p. 283).

[97] As for the UK forces, see *Minutes of evidence taken before the Defence Committee*, 8 May 1991, Gen. De La Billiere, in M. Weller (ed.), *supra* note 96, p. 327.

[98] *Letter from the President to the Speaker of the House of Representatives*, 18 January 1991, in M. Weller (ed.), *supra* note 96, p. 280.

[99] The conditions, decided after consultation with Kuwait and the coalition partners, were submitted to Iraq on 22 February. The following day the US informed the Security Council: S/PV.2977, pp. 74–5. The deadline of the ultimatum had been fixed at noon on 23 February.

[100] See the US representative declaration before the Security Council on 26 February 1991 (S/PV.2977, p. 82).

[101] *Letter from the President to the Speaker of the House of Representatives*, 19 March 1991, in M. Weller (ed.), *supra* note 96, p. 283

[102] *Interim Report to the Congress*, *supra* note 96, p. 289.

[103] With regard to the naval interdiction operations on the Adriatic Sea, on 8 June 1993, NATO and Weu approved a combined concept (*Operation Sharp Guard*) and formed the Combined Task Force 440.

operations, while the troops were under the command and control of NATO military authorities.

In general, the Security Council was not involved in the decision-making process concerning the conduction of the military operations. Its role was indeed limited to authorising the use of force, defining the objectives of the operations, and reviewing the reports Member States were supposed to submit to it periodically.[104] It was for the Member States to take any decision concerning the timing and the strategy of the operations.

The military coercive operations carried out by NATO in Bosnia-Herzegovina under Resolution 836 represent a significant exception. The political authority was to be exercised by the NAC in co-ordination with the United Nations. In accordance with the command and control arrangements made between the United Nations and NATO for air strike, nevertheless, the first use of air power was to be requested or authorised by the UN Secretary General (dual-key procedure).[105] Since each single military operation was based on the consent of its Secretary General,[106] the United Nations could maintain effective control over the operations.

The authorisation practice constitutes the Security Council's attempt to overcome the non-implementation of Art. 43 of the Charter as an alternative to enforcement measures put at the disposal of the United Nations by Member States on an *ad hoc* basis. A two-phase decentralised military option was hammered out. In the normative phase, the Security Council, acting under Chapter VII, determines the existence of one of the situations envisaged in Article 39 and makes an evaluation on the effectiveness – from a costs and benefits perspective – of the military intervention.[107] Then, it authorises Member States to take the measures necessary to restore or maintain international peace. In the operative phase, Member States individually or jointly undertake the authorised enforcement action.

[104] C. Ku and H. K. Jacobson, 'Toward a Mixed System of Democratic Accountability', in C. Ku and H. K. Jacobson (eds.), *Democratic Accountability and the Use of Force in International Law* (Cambridge: Cambridge University Press, 2002), pp. 349 *et seq.*, p. 372, note that 'When the United Nations asks individual States or coalition of States to undertake military actions, reporting arrangements are generally extremely loose and the United Nations' ability to influence implementation limited'.

[105] *Decisions taken at the Meeting of the NAC on 9 August 1993*, in *NATO Review*, August 1993, pp. 26 *et seq.* See also *Declaration of the Heads of State and Government*, Brussels, 11 January 1994. For a summary of NATO air strikes, see the UN Secretary General's report dated 17 November 1994 (S/1994/1067, pp. 16–17).

[106] The UN Secretary General further specified that his decision would have been taken on the basis of a request by his Special Representative for the former Yugoslavia, acting on a recommendation by UNPROFOR commander (report dated 18 January 1994, S/1994/50, p. 2).

[107] See *supra* note I-11. In para. 7 of Res. 794, for instance, the Security Council shared the evaluation made by the UN Secretary General that the resort to military measures under Chapter VII was necessary.

The resolution allows – but certainly does not oblige – Member States to take part in the military operations. An obligation in this sense could derive exclusively from special agreements concluded under Article 43. As Member States freely decide whether, how and for how long to participate in the enforcement mechanism),[108] there is no guarantee of functioning. This means that the resolution is bound to become a dead letter unless one or more Member States is ready to undertake the military enforcement measures. The case of Resolution 770, adopted on 13 August 1992, is quite illustrative in this respect.[109] Such an embarrassing situation is avoided when Member States take the initiative through an offer to the Security Council.[110]

It has been argued that once the Member States have accepted participation in the authorised military enforcement action, they cannot withdraw their forces until the objectives of the action have been achieved.[111] This view is not supported by State practice. The decision of the United States partially to withdraw from *Operation Sharp Guard*, in particular, provoked no objections on legal grounds from other Member States or from the international organisations concerned.[112] Besides, it would make little sense to compel a State to continue to take part in an action the objectives or necessity of which if it does not share any more, not to mention if it challenges the lawfulness of the action.

[108] When NATO member States decided to undertake the naval interdiction operation authorised by Security Council Res. 787, by the Security Council, the German government announced that its naval forces already engaged in the monitoring operation would not participate to any activities involving the use of force: see W. Heintschel von Heinegg and H. T. R. Haltern, 'The Decision of the German Federal Constitutional Court of 12 July 1994 in *Re Deployment of the German Armed Forces Out of Areas*', 41 *NILR* (1994) 285, p. 288. When the coercive operations were extended, in accordance with Security Council Res. 820, to the territorial waters of the FRY, the Greek government declared that its forces would not take part in the new operations see H. Vos, 'Co-operation in Peacekeeping and Peace Enforcement', NAA/DSC, 1993 Reports, AK 230, DSC/DC (93), p. 14. See also *infra* note 112.

[109] The Security Council authorised member States to take, nationally or through regional agencies or arrangements, all necessary measures to facilitate the delivery of humanitarian assistance. Since no State was prepared to intervene militarily in the conflict, the Security Council adopted – this time not under Chapter VII of the Charter – Res. 776 which enlarged the peace-keeping operation under way and realised a complete *revirement* in respect of Res. 770. For Zimbabwe, Res. 776 was 'a wise and thoughtful escape route from the provisions of Res. 770' (S/PV.3114, 14 September 1992, p. 4). See also the Indian comment, *ibid.*, p. 7.

[110] This was notably the case in *Operation Restore Hope* (see the offer to intervene made by the United States and challenged to the Security Council through the Secretary General, S/24868, 30 November 1992, p. 5); and in *Opération Turquoise* (see the offer made by France in the letter dated 20 June 1994: S/1994/734).

[111] D. Sarooshi, *supra* note 33, p. 151.

[112] On 11 April 1994, because of growing concern over the legitimacy of the arms embargo with regard to Bosnia–Herzegovina, the US withdrew its participation in the enforcement operations with respect to vessels carrying weapons heading for Bosnia–Herzegovina. The NATO Secretary General immediately declared that the US

In these voluntary terms, the competence of the Security Council to authorise Member States to resort to force has been accepted by virtually the whole membership. As to the legal basis for these operations, the Security Council has systematically invoked Chapter VII generally, whereas only occasionally had Member States referred to Art. 42 of the Charter.[113] It is worth recalling that, during the San Francisco Conference, Norway proposed to insert in the disposition that would have become Art. 42 the possibility of the Security Council authorising Member States to take military enforcement action on behalf of the Organisation.[114] Although the amendment was not accepted, the idea surfaced again in the context of the *Uniting for Peace* resolution,[115] before eventually being accepted in the 1990s as, in the words of the Secretary General, an arrangement that provides the United Nations with 'an enforcement capacity it would not otherwise have and is greatly preferable to the unilateral use of force by Member States without reference to the United Nations'.[116]

Albeit that significant reservations are often formulated as to the vagueness of the legal framework,[117] the risk of marginalising the Security Council,[118] and the unavoidable selectiveness of such types of enforcement mechanism,[119] it is generally accepted that 'the system has evolved a viable alternative, within the terms of its Charter, that permits the Council to authorise states to join in a police force *ad hoc*, instance by instance'.[120]

decision would not prevent NATO and WEU from continuing the enforcement activities: see *Atlantic News*, No. 2670, 16 November 1994. See also WEU Council of Ministers, *Noorddwijk Declaration*, 14 November 1994, para. 24, available at: www.weu.int.

113 In one of these rare cases, Colombia referred to Art. 42 of the Charter as the legal basis for Res. 665: see S/PV.2938, 25 August 1990, p. 21.

114 *Report of Rapporteur of Subcommittee I/1 to Committee I/1*, 6 *UNCIO*, pp. 720–1. The proposal was rejected because of ambiguity on whether the authorisation must be obtained before or after the use of force, and concern about of impairing the right to self-defence.

115 See General Assembly Res. 377. In the *Report on Collective Measures of the Committee*, A/1891 (1951) p. 25, it was expressly envisaged that 'upon the determination to adopt measures involving the use of United Nations armed forces, the Organisation should authorise a State or a group of States to act on its behalf as executive military authority', whereas the Security Council, with the advice and assistance of the Military Staff Committee, would assume the strategic direction of the operations.

116 *Supplement to an Agenda for Peace*, *supra* note 40, pp. 18–19.

117 B. H. Weston, *supra* note 32, p. 522.

118 J. Quigley, 'The "Privatization" of Security Council Enforcement Action: A Threat to Multilateralism', 17 *MJIL* (1996) 249.

119 R. Higgins, 'Peace and Security. Achievements and Failures', 6 *EJIL* (1995) 445, p. 459, notes that 'this technique is not per se unacceptable, but it is also clear that this ensures that enforcement will only take place when there is a perceived national interest in doing so on the part of the major military powers'.

120 T. M. Franck and F. Patel, 'UN Police Action in Lieu of War: "The Old Order Changeth"', 85 *AJIL* (1991) 63, p. 74.

To support this the lawfulness of the authorisation practice, authors rely on Art. 39,[121] Art. 42,[122] possibly read in conjunction with Art. 48[123] or Art. 106,[124] solely on Art. 106,[125] on 'some assumed penumbra of powers available under Chapter VII',[126] on the Security Council's implied powers,[127] on a customary norm which has emerged,[128] or is still taking shape,[129] within the Charter, probably out of political expediency.[130]

Other authors, however, object that, in the legal vacuum resulting from the non-implementation of Article 43, Member States could unilaterally resort to force upon a determination by the Security Council of the existence of a threat to international peace and security.[131] The intervention is consequently governed by general international law, with Member States acting either *uti singuli* on the basis of the state of necessity theory,[132] or *uti universi* to protect the fundamental values of the international community.[133] In this sense, the Security Council authorisation is not directed at removing a legal hurdle[134] – namely the prohibition to resort to armed force – but rather amounts to a procedural guarantee.[135]

[121] See B. Simma, 'Does the UN Charter Provide an Adequate Legal Basis for Individual or Collective Responses to violations of International Obligations *erga omnes*?', in J. Delbrück (ed.), *The Future of International Law Enforcement. New Scenarios – New Law?* (Berlin: Duncker & Humblot, 1993), pp. 125 *et seq.*, pp. 138–9.

[122] See T. M. Franck, F. Patel, *supra* note 120, p. 66.

[123] See M. Weller, 'Peace-Keeping and Peace-Enforcement in the Republic of Bosnia and Herzegovina', 56 *ZaöRV* (1996) 70, p. 175.

[124] See V. Starace, 'Uso della forza nell'ordinamento internazionale', in *EG*, vol. 32 (1994) 1, p. 9.

[125] See A. S. Miller, 'Universal Soldiers: U.N. Standing Armies and the Legal Alternatives', 81 *Georgetown LJ.* (1993) 773.

[126] See B. H. Weston, *supra* note 32, p. 522.

[127] See F. L. Kirgis, 'The Security Council's First Fifty Years', 89 *AJIL* (1995) 506, p. 521

[128] See O. Schachter, *supra* note 33, p. 453; G. Gaja, 'Problemi attuali concernenti l'uso della forza nel sistema delle Nazioni Unite', in SIOI, *L'O.N.U.: Cinquant'anni di attività e prospettive per il futuro* (Roma: Presidenza del Consiglio, 1996), pp. 416 *et seq.*, p. 423.

[129] See B. Conforti, *supra* note I-15, p. 204.

[130] See H. Freudenschuß, *supra* note 94, pp. 526 *et seq.*

[131] See F. Lattanzi, 'Consiglio di sicurezza ed emergenza umanitaria', in SIOI, *supra* note 128, 503 *et seq.*, p. 510.

[132] See F. Lattanzi, *Assistenza umanitaria e intervento di umanità* (Torino: Giappichelli, 1997), p. 97.

[133] See P. Picone, 'Interventi delle Nazioni Unite e obblighi *erga omnes*', in P. Picone (ed.), *Interventi delle Nazioni Unite* (Padova: CEDAM, 1995), pp. 552 *et seq.*; and 'Valori fondamentali della comunità internazionale e Nazioni Unite', 50 *Com. Int.* (1995) 439.

[134] See F. Lattanzi, *supra* note 131.

[135] See P. Picone, 'Interventi delle Nazioni Unite e obblighi *erga omnes*', *supra* note 133, p. 556. On the admissibility of use of force to ensure the respect of mandatory Security Council resolutions, see *infra* paras 15 and 16.

The question of control

Treating all cases of use of force authorised by the Security Council as a unique genre seems unwise: their legal basis depends primarily on the control exercised over the operations by the Security Council. If there is nothing inherently wrong with the practice of authorisation, the crux of the matter remains the degree of control exercised by the Security Council. In order to qualify as effective, such control must necessarily include the power to revise the objectives of the enforcement action, to assess when they are achieved, and ultimately to suspend or terminate the operations.[136]

There is a tendency to overlook the fact that the voting system established by the Charter exposes the Security Council to the risk of being unable to suspend or terminate the operations because of the opposition of one or more permanent members, and in particular the members which are carrying out enforcement measures. The problem concerns most of the cases in which States have been authorised to use force.[137] The question of the so-called *reverse veto* has generally been discussed in the context of suspension or withdrawal of economic enforcement measures.[138] In contrast, in the case of military enforcement measures, the main problem is not to establish whether Member States can unilaterally suspend or terminate the observance of obligations imposed by the Security Council. The resolutions authorising the use of force, in fact, are never mandatory and can produce only a permissive effect. Only the Security Council – or alternatively all Member States – can deprive a State of the legal protection ensured by Art. 2(4) against any threat or use of force. The authorisation thus renders lawful the military coercive measures that otherwise would have been contrary to the general ban on the use of force.

The Security Council voting system ensures that no State can be deprived of such a protection and exposed to the lawful use of force unless (a) all permanent members concur in, or at least do not oppose, the resolution authorising the use of force, and (b) the qualified majority requirement is satisfied. Having obtained the authorisation to use military force, however, the opposition of a single permanent Member State can prevent the revision and withdrawal of the authorisation. Under the circumstances, the resolution continues to produce its effect and in particular to permit Member States to take the authorised enforcement action in spite of the fading away of the agreement within the Security Council.

[136] See D. Sarooshi, *supra* note 33, esp. pp. 159–60. This kind of control may be defined as 'political control': see M. MacDougall, *'United Nations Operations: Who Should be in Charge?', and* 33 *RDMDG* (1994) 21, p. 27. On the contrary, N. D. White, Ö. Ülgen, 'The Security Council and the Decentralised Military Option: Constitutionality and Function', 44 *NILR* (1997) 378, p. 387 maintain that a clearly defined mandate and an adequate reporting mechanism are sufficient to designate a particular military action as a *United Nations* operation.

[137] The military operations related to Albania and East Timor, led respectively by Italy and Australia and those carried out by ECOWAS represent exceptions.

[138] See *supra* pp. 16–17.

In this regard, the authorisation practice implies a significant degradation of the collective security system created to guarantee the common interests protected in Art. 1(1). Under the Charter, Member States have bestowed the Security Council with the extensive powers related to military enforcement measures knowing that the resort to enforcement measures, directly by the Security Council as envisaged in the Charter presupposes the agreement among the Great Powers not only for their commencement, but also for their continuation since otherwise the Military Staff Committee could not take any decision. In the authorisation practice, on the contrary, such guarantees are limited to the initial moment, namely the concession of the authorisation.

The problem of the *reverse veto* could be overcome, it has been proposed, by including in the resolution a temporal limit to the authorisation, or a provision allowing a particularly high number of members of the Security Council, without distinction between permanent and non-permanent, to suspend the authorisation partly or completely.[139] Neither of the options is completely satisfactory. The first would not affect the virtually absolute unaccountability of Member States until the expiring of the deadline, while the second implies a significant reduction of the veto power unlikely to be accepted by permanent members.

Alternatively, the resolution providing for the authorisation could allow the Security Council members, and perhaps the General Assembly, to request during the operations the verification of the continuing existence within the Security Council of a qualified majority to adopt a resolution under Chapter VII of the Charter. The majority could be different from that which originally voted in favour of the authorisation. Although not exempt from criticism, this appears a viable option to render more effective the control exercised by the Security Council and ensure that the use of force is based on the common will of the Organisation.[140]

The legal regime governing the authorisation granted to Member States to use force is far from satisfactory. The States willing to intervene militarily upon a Security Council authorisation have resisted all attempts made by several other Member States, especially those belonging to the non-aligned group, to create an effective control of the United Nations over military enforcement actions authorised by the Security Council. These attempts included the efforts to have the Military Staff Committee or the Secretary General involved in the decision-making and the conduct of the operations.[141]

[139] See D. D. Caron, *supra* note I-47, pp. 577 *et seq*.

[140] See *supra* note I-90.

[141] The rather ambiguous request included in para. 1 of Res. 665, to consult the Secretary General and to co-ordinate their action 'using, as appropriate, mechanisms of the Military Staff Committee', in turn, had no practical consequences. The role of Military Staff Committee, which met five times, was limited to exchange of information: see 62 *BYIL* (1991) 707. Paragraph 12 of Res. 794, in turn, requested both the Secretary General and the concerned States to make the necessary arrangements for the unified command and control of the forces involved. Less ambitiously, para. 13 provided for the attachment of a small United Nations Operation liaison staff at the headquarters of the unified command.

Only in Bosnia-Herzegovina, thanks to the dual-key procedure, could the Secretary General exercise, on behalf of the Security Council, his political judgement on the opportunity of a military response each time the use of force was prospected. Unlike the military enforcement measures carried out by UNOSOM II, in Bosnia-Herzegovina the Secretary General did not have the strategic and operational control over the troops. He could merely request or authorise military enforcement measures, the implementation of which depended on NATO forces. These arrangements, effectively in place until August 1995, minimised the risks of *reverse veto*. They permitted the United Nations to exercise effective control over the operations, and ultimately suspend or terminate them by refusing to authorise any further military coercive activities.[142]

The emergence of a rule allowing Member States to carry out military enforcement measures

When the United Nations retains effective political control over military enforcement measures – so far the exception rather than the rule – the first possible legal ground for the operations might be Art. 39. The debate on the competence of the Security Council to recommend military enforcement measures dates back to the war in Korea, when a permissive effect was attributed to Security Council Resolution 84.[143] Since then the Security Council has abandoned the practice of 'recommending' in favour of that of 'calling upon'[144] or, more recently, 'authorising'. Authors who invoke Art. 39 as the legal basis for such a practice consider the effects produced by a resolution ''recommending', 'authorising' or 'calling upon'

Actually, the United Task Force (UNITAF) operated entirely under the US chain of command and rules of engagement (see F. M. Lorenz, *supra* note 49, pp. 66–7). As admitted by the Secretary General, the United States President 'directed the execution of Operation Restore Hope on 4 December 1992. The United States command (USCENTCOM) was given the mission of conducting joint and combined military operations in Somalia, under United Nations auspices': see the letter dated 17 December 1992 (S/24976, Annex); and the Secretary General's report dated 19 December 1992.

[142] R. Falk, *'Questioning the UN mandate in the Gulf'*, IFDA Dossier (1991/2), pp. 81 *et seq*., p. 82, points out that the United Nations have 'an obligation to control the definition of war goals, the means chosen to achieve them and to use its authority to impose a cease-fire'. D. Sarooshi, *supra* note 33, p. 35 observes that 'the Security Council must at all times retain overall authority and control over the exercise of its delegated Chapter VII powers . . . and the competence to change the way that the delegated powers are being exercised'.

[143] D.W. Bowett, *supra* note 33, p. 32. This was also the position defended by the UK before the Security Council (S/PV. 477, 7 July 1950, p. 1).

[144] In Res. 221, 9 April 1966, the Security Council 'called upon' the UK to take the necessary measures to prevent arrival of vessels at Beira.

Member States to take military enforcement measures as substantially identical.[145] Apart from terminological questions, however, the admissibility under Art. 39 of recommended, authorised or called upon military measures is still controversial.[146] The argument that the Security Council's power to recommend or authorise military enforcement measures is logically and legally acceptable as a *minus* of the power to impose such measures – in analogy with economic enforcement measures[147] – is built on the false assumption that the Security Council could compel Member States to take such measures.[148]

The crux of the matter remains the degree of control exercised over the operations by the Security Council. Art. 39 may provide the legal basis of military enforcement measures only to the case in which – as for the NATO coercive military operations carried out in Bosnia-Herzegovina until August 1995 – the Security Council retains effective control over the operations. Otherwise, the action is far too different from that envisaged in the Charter. It is therefore unsound to read Art. 39 as permitting the Security Council to recommend or authorise military enforcement actions carried out entirely under the political, strategic and operational control of Member States.[149]

Art. 42 might constitute an alternative legal basis. Once it is accepted that the failure to implement Art. 43 has not deprived Art. 42 of any significance,[150] the reasoning may be further stretched through two extensive interpretations of the latter article. Article 42 being silent on the issue, it may be argued that the Security Council could take all necessary action to maintain international peace and security without necessarily assuming control and command over the forces provided by Member States.[151] Alternatively, Art. 42 *in fine* could be interpreted as

[145] See U. Villani, *Lezioni sull'ONU e la crisi del Golfo*, 2nd ed. (Bari: Cacucci, 1995); Y. Dinstein, *supra* note 43, p. 245 footnote 112. *Contra*, J. Verhoeven, 'Etats alliés ou Nations Unies? L'O.N.U. face au conflit entre l'Iraq et le Koweït', 36 *AFDI* (1990) 145, pp. 177 *et seq*.

[146] Among the authors admitting such practice, see: A. Malintoppi, *Le raccomandazioni internazionali* (Milano, Giuffrè, 1958), pp. 119 *et seq*.; G. Morelli, *supra* note I-38, p. 295; M. L. Picchio Forlati, *supra* note I-6, pp. 223 *et seq*.; N. D. White, *The United Nations and the Maintenance of International Peace and Security* (Manchester: Manchester University Press, 1990), p. 147; U. Villani, *supra* note 145, p. 102; B. Simma, *supra* note 121, pp. 138 *et seq*. *Contra*, see: H. Kelsen, *supra* note I-4, p. 934; J. Stone, *Legal Controls of International Conflict* (London: Stevens, 1959), p. 230; J. W. Halderman, *supra* note 33, p. 986; J. Quigley, 'The United States and the United Nations in the Persian Gulf War: New Order or Disorder?', 25 *CILJ* (1992) 1, pp. 33 *et seq*.; B. H. Weston, *supra* note 32, p. 521; B. Conforti, *supra* note I-15, p. 180. The latter author, who for decades has treated the US-led action in Korea as unlawful, has recently changed his mind and considers such an action as the first manifestation of the so-called authorisation practice (pp. 202–3).

[147] See *supra* note I-44.

[148] In the criticised sense, see O. Schachter, *supra* note 33, p. 462.

[149] See G. Gaja, *supra* note 128, p. 422.

[150] *Supra* pp. 35–7.

[151] On this point, see N. D. White, *supra* note I-9, pp. 117 *et seq*.; T. M. Franck, F. Patel and *supra* note 120, p. 66; O. Schachter, *supra* note 33, p. 462.

permitting Member States to contribute to the military enforcement operations through 'air, sea and land forces' which are neither necessarily put at the disposal of the Security Council nor operating under the command of the Military Staff Committee.[152] It is submitted that the contribution by Member States, which, according to the wording of Art. 42 *in fine* would have a complementary nature, could assume an exclusive character.

The suggested extensive interpretations of Article 42, however, cannot be stretched beyond the point at which the Security Council leaves to the States the operational control and even the strategic direction, while still maintaining effective political control over the operations. With the exception of the coercive military operations carried out in Bosnia-Herzegovina under the so-called dual key procedure, in all the instances of authorised use of force the Security Council could not exercise any effective control on the military actions. The actions were in fact unilaterally decided, carried out and terminated by Member States in accordance with their interests, objectives and strategies. In this sense, the authorisation is downgraded to a procedural guarantee and resembles a blank cheque.[153] As the authority of the Security Council is purely formal, Art. 42 ceases to be applicable. In these circumstances, the legal foundation of the military enforcement action has to be found elsewhere.

It is submitted that the so-called authorisation practice is legally based on a customary norm that emerged in the 1990s and informally modified the Charter. The emergence of the norm and the simultaneous modification of the Charter can be considered as two dimensions of the same process.[154]

As to the first dimension, the creation of customary law is the result of the extensive and uniform practice (*usus* or objective element) coupled with the conviction that the conduct is prescribed by a legal obligation or legally protects an interest (*opinio juris sive necessitatis* or subjective element). This theory is firmly established in the case law of the International Court of Justice[155] and is also

[152] According to H. Kelsen, *supra* note I-4, p. 756, 'The wording of Articles 39 and 42 does not even exclude the possibility of the establishment of an armed force of the Organisation different from and independent of the armed forces placed at the disposal of the Security Council by the Members'. See also J. Stone, *supra* note 146, p. 197.

[153] See J. Verhoeven, *supra* note 145, p. 181; B. H. Weston, *supra* note 32, p. 526; J. Quigley, *supra* note 118.

[154] On the interaction between international customary law and the Charter, see *infra* pp. 117 *et seq*.

[155] See, in particular: *North Sea Continental Shelf Cases*, Judgment, *ICJ Reports 1969*, p. 3, pp. 43 *et seq*.; *Continental Shelf (Lybian Arab Jamahiriya/Malta)*, Judgment, *ICJ Reports 1985*, p. 13, pp. 29–30; *Nicaragua case*, Merits, *infra* note IV-2, pp. 97 *et seq*. and 107–8; *Nuclear Weapons*, *infra* note V-127, pp. 253 *et seq*. For a critical analysis, see P. Haggenmacher, 'La doctrine des deux éléments du droit coutumier dans la pratique de la Cour internationale', 90 *RGDIP* (1986) 5.

generally accepted in doctrine,[156] although the relevance of the two elements may greatly differ.[157]

Defining such a legal consciousness and establishing whether and when it has emerged has proved rather problematic.[158] It has rightly been pointed out that

> elements other than law – social, economic, political and military necessities, may go into the formation of custom and provide the motive for its development. ... Nevertheless, the appreciation must ultimately be based upon some legal criterion and Article 38 [of the ICJ Statute] is quite explicit that the text is whether or not there is a general practice *accepted as law*.[159]

[156] As maintained by H. Waldock, 'General Course on Public International Law', 106 *RdC* (1962–II) 1, p. 49, 'The essential problem in each case . . . is to assess the consistency, duration and generality . . . But the ultimate test must always be: is this practice accepted as law? This is especially true in the international community, where those who participate in the formation of a custom are sovereign states who are the decision-makers within the community'. Among the most representative recent works entirely or partly dedicated to customary rules, see: G. Arangio-Ruiz, 'Consuetudine internazionale', in *Enciclopedia del Diritto* (Milano: Giuffrè, 1988), vol. VIII, p. 1; L. Condorelli, *'Consuetudine internazionale'*, in *Digesto* 4th ed. (Torino: UTET, 1989), vol. III, 1989, p. 490; M. E. Villiger, *Customary International Law and Treaties*, 2nd ed. (The Hague: Kluwer, 1997); K. Wolfke, *Custom in Present International Law*, 2nd ed. (Dordrecht: Nijhoff, 1993); V. D. Degan, *Sources of International Law* (Dordrecht: Nijhoff, 1997); G. M. Danilenko, *Law-Making in the International Community* (Dordrecht: Nijhoff, 1993).

[157] In addition to the authors cited *supra* note 156, compare, in particular: H. Kelsen, 'Théorie du droit international coutumier', 13 *RIDT* (1939) 253; M. Giuliano, *La comunità internazionale e il diritto internazionale* (Padova: CEDAM, 1950); R. Ago, *Scienza giuridica e diritto internazionale* (Milano, Giuffrè, 1950). For G. Fitzmaurice, 'Some Problems Regarding the Formal Sources of International Law', in *Symbolae Verzijl* (The Hague: Nijhoff, 1958), pp. 153 *et seq.*, footnote 2 at pp. 162–3, 'the theory which denies the existence of any factor of consent, assent, acquiescence or recognition, and attributes the emergence of the rule simply to the usage itself and the settled practice . . . irrespective of any subjective element . . . does not really bear examination'.

[158] For a discussion on the main theories on *opinio juris*, see M. Byers, *Custom, Power and the Power of Rules* (Cambridge: Cambridge University Press, 1999), esp. Chaps. 8 and 9. H. Thirlway, *International Customary Law and Codification* (Leiden: Sijthoff, 1972), pp. 53–4, 'the requirement of *opinio juris* is equivalent merely to the need for the practice in question to have been accompanied by either a sense of conforming with the law, or the view that the practice was potentially law'. According to M. H. Mendelson, 'The Formation of Customary International Law', 272 *RdC* (1998) 155, however, there is 'no particular reason to insist on proof of the presence of *opinio juris*' (p. 292) as customary international law materialises through the emergence of 'legitimate expectations' in the normative sense (pp. 179 *et seq.*).

[159] H. Waldock, *supra* note 156, p. 47, italic as in the original. M.H. Mendelson, *supra* note 158, p. 271, similarly observes that '*opinio necessitatis* . . . can play a part in the law-creating process, even though extra-legal necessity and reasonableness are not themselves sufficient to make law'.

Customary international law is then created through an incremental process[160] ignited by the proposal for a new legal regulation (*progetto di disciplina giuridica*)[161] put forward by some States. These States develop and manifest an *opinio necessitatis* to the effect that a norm ought to be created.[162] When the generality of the States composing the international community express their acceptance of, or at least acquiesce in, such a proposal, conscious of it potentially binding effect, a new norm has come into being.[163]

The existence of such a norm is to be established by resorting to the inductive method[164] 'through a flexible, global evaluation, aimed at assessing in synthetic fashion the whole set of behaviours, actions and reactions of the social actors, and not at counting their acts of consent analytically and adding them up'.[165] The process of creation of a customary international norm normally takes place over a significant period of time, because of the resistance of a segment of the international community, which is eventually overcome through the matching of States' claims and counter-claims.[166] Until that moment, a certain degree of legal uncertainty is physiological.[167]

[160] In the *Continental Shelf cases*, *supra* note 155, pp. 38–9, the Court referred to the 'definition, consolidation and crystalization of customary international law'. On the elusiveness of the notion of crystalization, see M. H. Mendelson, *supra* note 158, pp. 304 *et seq.*

[161] A. Miele, *La comunità internazionale*, 3rd ed. (Torino: Giappichelli, 2000), p. 11. According to M. Lachs, diss. op., *Continental Shelf cases*, *supra* note 155, p. 231, the process starts from 'voluntary unilateral acts relying on the confident expectation that they will find acquiescence or be emulated'.

[162] According to M. H. Mendelson, *supra* note 158, p. 281, these States believe that it would be *desirable* to have such a norm created, changed or extinguished. R. Walden, 'Customary International Law: A Jurisprudential Analysis', 13 *Isr. LR* (1978) 86, p. 97, speaks of 'a claim that it [the practice] ought to be legally binding'.

[163] K. Zemanek, *'Majority Rule and Consensus Technique in Law-Making* Diplomacy', in R. St Macdonald and D. M. Johnston (eds.), *The Structure and Process of International Law: Essays in Legal Philosophy Doctrine and Theory* (The Hague: Nijhoff, 1983), pp. 857 *et seq.*, p. 879, reminds that 'for the purpose of law-making, majority rule does not reflect the social conditions of a society which has no *volonté générale* but only a sum of values and interests which are in many respect conflicting'. Even a fervent positivist like P. Weil, 'Towards Relative Normativity in International Law?', 77 *AJIL* (1983) 413, p. 437, concedes that 'Explixit acceptance of a customary rule has never been required'.

[164] *Case Concerning Delimitation of the Maritime Boundary in the Gulf of Maine Area*, Judgment, *ICJ Reports 1984*, p. 246, at p. 299.

[165] L. Condorelli, 'Discussion', in A. Cassese J. H. H. Weiler (eds.), *Change and Stability in International Law-Making* (Berlin: W. De Gruyter, 1988), pp. 117 *et seq.*, p. 119. In general, see L. Ferrari Bravo, 'Méthodes de recherche de la coutume internationale dans la pratique des états', 192 *RdC* (1985–III) 237.

[166] A. A. D'Amato, *The Concept of Custom in International Law* (Ithaca: Cornell University Press, 1970), views the formation and change of a custom as a process by which the better of two conflicting claims articulated by national decision-makers and their legal counsels prevails, without necessarily fulfilling the requirement for a given absolutistic theory, because of its relative superiority of persuasiveness (pp. 18 *et seq.*, 73 *et seq.* and 270 *et seq.*). For a discussion and references on the so-called stages theory, see G. J. H. van Hoof, *Rethinking the Sources of International Law* (Deventer: Kluwer, 1983), pp. 91 *et seq.*

[167] For example, in 1984, the British government declared that humanitarian intervention could not be said to be 'unambiguously illegal', see document, *infra* note IV-315.

Coming back to the authorisation practice, it is maintained that the overwhelming majority of States, but also the United Nations as the subject of international law, have concurred in the emergence of a norm allowing Member States to resort to military force if so authorised by the Security Council. This organ has been entrusted with the determination of the conditions that may trigger the resort to non-defensive force – which are those indicated in Art. 39 of the Charter – and with the assessment of the soundness of the military intervention. In this perspective, the obligation to obtain the Security Council's authorisation thus derives from the newly emerged customary norm. Even adopting the strictest standard, the practice of Member States – including that of the specially affected States,[168] which in this context are presumably the permanent members of the Security Council – and the United Nations has been sufficiently uniform and general to generate such a norm, even taking into account the magnitude of the change it has introduced in the collective security system.[169]

As to the *opinio juris*, the belief that obtaining the Security Council authorisation was a legal condition to be satisfied before resorting to force clearly emerges from State practice. Suffice it to mention the insistence on the prior granting of the authorisation which characterised the offers advanced by some to the United States and France to intervene in Somalia and Rwanda;[170] as well as systematic invocation by NATO Member States of the Security Council as the legal basis of the coercive military operations carried out in Bosnia-Herzegovina,[171] and the equally systematic renunciation of taking such measures unless authorised or requested by the United Nations.[172] Until the Kosovo crisis, virtually all States

[168] See, for instance, *North Sea Continental Shelf*, *supra* note 155, p. 42.

[169] As observed by H. Lauterpacht, 'Sovereignty over Submarine Areas', 27 *BYIL* (1950) 376, p. 393, 'any tendency to exact a prolonged period for the crystallization of custom must be proportionate to the degree and the intensity of the change it purports, or is asserted, to effect'.

[170] France declared: 'In the spirit of Resolution 794 of 3 December 1992, our Government would like, as legal framework for their intervention, a resolution under Chapter VII', Letter to the Secretary General dated 21 June 1994 (S/1994/734, p. 1). During the parliamentary debate on the prospected military operation in Rwanda, the French Government declared: 'La France n'agira qu'avec un mandat du Conseil de Securité' (*Journal Officiel*, Débats parlementaires, 23 juin 1994, p. 3339).

[171] On 10 and 11 April 1994, in particular, NATO forces, responding to a request by the UN, executed two close air support missions against Bosnian Serb targets located around Goradze. The action was justified under Resolutions 836 and 844 as necessary to protect UNPROFOR forces from tank and artillery fire (Report of the United States President to the Congress, excerpts in 88 *AJIL* (1994) 525). Throughout the crisis, the Security Council Resolution had been indicated by NATO, although not always without ambiguity, as the exclusive legal basis for the use of force. See, in particular, NAC, *Decisions taken at the meeting of the NAC in Permanent Session*, Brussels, 9 February 1994; NAC, *Decisions on the Protection of Safe Areas*, Brussels, 22 April 1994; *Press Statement on Goradze following the NAC Meeting on 25 July 1995*. But see *Operation Deliberate Force*, *infra* pp. 69 *et seq*.

[172] For instance, on 28 February 1994, NATO aircraft shot down four unidentified Galeb violating the no-fly zone near Banja Luka (*supra* note 45). As Res. 816 was limited to the

regarded the Security Council authorisation as the only legal ground for the use force in addition to those expressly foreseen in the Charter. Up to then, intervening States relied – although on certain occasions not entirely convincingly – upon existing Security Council resolutions. Controversies have arisen with regard to the existence, the limits or the continuing validity of the resolution; never the necessity of obtaining the authorisation by the Security Council before resorting to non-defensive force.

The second dimension regards the informal modification of the Charter. Such a possibility is widely accepted[173] as consequential to the fact that contracting parties remain 'the transaction's exclusive and absolute *domini*'.[174] Uniform, prolonged and unchallenged non-application, or application in contrast with the Charter's provisions, could bring about a modification of the rights and obligations of Member States,[175] or at least their temporary adjustment.[176] For such a result to be achieved, unanimity among Member States,[177] or at least a constant and unchallenged State practice, is indispensable. According to the French Government, 'Depuis le début du fonctionnement des Nations Unies, il n'a pu se créer de règles coutumières ou de pratiques contraires à la Charte que si ces règles coutumières ou ces pratiques ont été constantes et non controversées'.[178]

For the purpose of informal modification of treaties, only the practice of Member States – including the conduct taken within the organs of international

Bosnian airspace, NATO aircraft did not enter Croatian airspace to engage the remaining two Galeb. Incidentally, virtually all NAC decisions on enforcement operations in the Yugoslav conflict were based upon and confined within the limits of Chapter VII resolutions.

[173] See S. Engel, 'Procedures for the de facto Revision of the Charter', *ASIL Proceedings*, 1965, p. 108; R. Zacklin, *The Amendments of the Constitutive Instruments of the United Nations and Specialized Agencies*, (Leyden: Sijthoff, 1968), pp. 171 *et seq*. For a critical analysis, however, see P. Spender, sep. op. in *Certain Expenses case*, *supra* note I-13, p. 191; Y. Z. Blum, *Eroding the United Nations Charter* (Dordrecht: Nijhoff, 1993), pp. 239 *et seq*.

[174] G. Arangio-Ruiz, *supra* note I-25, pp. 284–5, esp. note 183.

[175] S. Engel, 'The Changing Charter of the United Nations', 7 *YBWA* (1953) 71, p. 89. On the *de facto* modification of the Charter concerning Art. 27(2), see Y. L. Liang, 'Abstention or Absence of a Permanent Member', 44 *AJIL* (1950) 694; C. A. Stavropoulos, 'The Practice of Voluntary Abstention by Permanent Members of the Security Council under Article 27, Paragraph 3, of the Charter of the United Nations', 61 *AJIL* (1967) 737.

[176] R. Zacklin, *supra* note 173, p. 195.

[177] P. Spender, sep. op. in *Certain Expenses case*, *supra* note I-13, p. 197. See also W. Karl, *Vertrag und spätere Praxis in Völkerrecht* (Berlin: Springer, 1983), p. 351.

[178] *Certain Expenses case*, *supra* note I-13, *Pleadings*, p. 133. According to B. Winiarski, diss. op. in *Certain Expenses case*, *supra* note I-13, pp. 230–1, 'if a practice is introduced without opposition in the relations between the contracting parties, this may bring about, at the end of a certain period, a modification of a treaty rule, but in that event the very process of the formation of the new rule provides the guarantee of the consent of the parties'. In contrast, M. Akehurst, 'The Hierarchy of the Sources of International Law', 47 *BYIL* (1974–5) 273, p. 278, prefers to apply, by way of analogy, the qualified majority required for formal modifications of the Charter.

organisations – has to be taken directly into account. The organisation not being a party to the Charter, its organs 'are in law and in fact incapable, so to speak, of a subsequent practice'.[179] Whereas the organs are obviously entitled to interpret and apply the Charter in the performance of their functions, their conduct cannot as such bring about any informal modification of the Charter, no matter how uniform and widespread it is. The practice of the organisation could, however, concur to the development of customary international law and it cannot be excluded that this may eventually have an impact upon the Charter.

The two dimensions are strictly interrelated and reflect the constant interaction between the Charter and customary international law.[180] On the one hand, the Organisation serves as the most important forum where States put their claims and counter-claims, thereby contributing to the formation and development of customary international law.[181] The content of customary international law, especially in the field of use of force, cannot be ascertained without considering the attitude adopted, the will manifested and the action taken by States within the framework of the United Nations, as well as by the United Nations itself as subjects of international law.[182] On the other hand, the Charter remains a treaty to be applied and

[179] G. Arangio-Ruiz, *supra* note I-25, p. 287. *Contra*, R. Zacklin, *supra* note 173, p. 172, observes: 'The organic nature of constitutive instruments subjects them to twin forces of change, for both the individual members of an organisation and its organs may act as a catalyst. . . . But with the retreat of the unanimity procedure . . . it is possible to assert that an organ of an organisation is capable of acting as a force of change, independently of the individual members who make up the organ'. For P. Spender, sep. op. in the *Certain Expenses case*, *supra* note I-13, p. 192, 'Not only as such an organ is not a party to the Charter, but the inescapable reality is that both the General Assembly and the Security Council are but mechanisms through which the members of the United Nations express their views and act'. The second part of the statement proves too much insofar as it reduces in all cases the political organs of the United Nations to common organs of States.

[180] See *infra* pp. 117 *et seq*.

[181] For judge K. Tanaka, diss. op., *South West Africa case*, Second Phase, Judgement, *ICJ Rep. 1966*, p. 6, p. 291, 'A State . . . has the opportunity, through the medium of the Organisation, to declare its position to all members of the Organisation and to know immediately their reaction on the same matter': this greatly facilitate and accelerate the formation of customary rules. He then concludes that 'what is required for customary international law is the repetition of the same practice. Accordingly . . . resolutions, declarations, etc., on the same matter in the same, or diverse, Organizations must take place repeatedly'. While accepting that the existence and activities of the Organisation permit to multiply geometrically the elements to be taken into account in determining the exact content of customary rules, G. Arangio-Ruiz, *supra* note I-25, pp. 54 *et seq*., prefers to limit the role of the Organisation to providing the material facility. According to R. Higgins, *supra* note 62, p. 2, 'With the development of international organizations, the votes and views of States have come to have legal significance as evidence of customary law'. See also A. Pellet, 'La formation du droit international dans le cadre des Nations Unies', 6 *EJIL* (1995) 401.

[182] As noted by G. Arangio-Ruiz, *supra* note I-25, 'Recommendations, together with the many other components of UN practice, are part of that practice of States which brings about the formation of customary rules' to the extent that they are demonstrations of *opinio iuris* (p. 48) or may lead to the desuetude of a rule (p. 41).

interpreted taking into account customary international law which has come into existence or developed after the establishment of the United Nations or independently of its functioning. Those rules may fill the gaps and offer indications as to the content of the Charter, even in evolutionary terms.[183]

The final result of these developments is the emergence of a third form of collective use of force in addition to the enforcement actions carried out either directly by the Security Council under Chapter VII or by regional organisations under Chapter VIII. The authorisation is 'a reflection of the corporate will of the Security Council, not the aggregation of the wills of the members of that body',[184] and as such it should be representative of the whole membership willingness to suspend the prohibition of the use of force with regard to a given State. Reminiscent of Article 2 of the 1924 Geneva Protocol,[185] the authorisation produces a permissive effect by rendering lawful a conduct which otherwise would have been unlawful.[186] At the same time, it guarantees a preventive control, limited to the starting phase, over the military enforcement carried out by States.

It is therefore more accurate to describe the role of the Security Council as authorisation rather than delegation of powers. The latter qualification presents two problems. On the one hand, the Security Council is normally prevented from modifying, suspending or terminating the delegation. Thus, a fundamental element of the delegation of powers is missing. On the other hand, under the so-called non-delegation doctrine, the Security Council cannot delegate 'back' powers that has been conferred on it by Member States through Chapter VII of the Charter.

[183] See, with regard to Art. 22 of the Covenant, *Namibia case*, *supra* note I-28, pp. 31–2. In general, see Art. 68 of the 1964 ILC *Draft Article on the Law of Treaties*, 16 *YBILC* (1964–II), p. 198. See also F. Capotorti, 'L'extinction et la suspension des traités', 134 *RdC* (1971–III) 417, pp. 517 *et seq*.

[184] N. D. White, 'The Will and Authority of the Security Council after Iraq', 17 *LJIL* (2004) 1, p. 4.

[185] *Supra* note I-67.

[186] See, in particular, M. Iovane, *La tutela dei valori fondamentali nel diritto internazionale* (Napoli: Ed. Scientifica, 2000), esp. pp. 476 *et seq*. This position stands in contrast with that maintained by P. Picone, *Interventi delle Nazioni Unite*, *supra* note 133, pp. 517 *et seq*. According to this view, in the event of paralysis or inaction of the United Nations, intervening States act *uti universi* on behalf of the international community and on the basis of general international law. Far from being a condition of lawfulness, the Security Council authorisation would amount to nothing more than a second and further level of control of legitimacy. Apart from the difficulties in admitting actions *uti universi* in the horizontally structured international community (on this point see G. Arangio-Ruiz, *supra* note I-89, and the previous works by the same author referred to in footnotes 7 and 13), such a theory is scarcely supported by State practice. At least until the Kosovo crisis, in fact, the Security Council authorisation was universally considered by member States as a *conditio sine qua non* for the lawfulness of the intervention. In this regard, the circumstance that member States would have *probably* intervened even without authorisation has little importance for the alleged right to intervene under general international law. More importantly, the theory is clearly useless when, as in the Kosovo crisis, there is such a sharp division within the international community on how to tackle the situation.

The authorisation practice has hardly any resemblance to the collective security system envisaged in the Charter.[187] However distant it might be from the original scheme envisaged by the Charter, the authorisation practice, *faut de mieux*, ensures that the use of force is at least subject to the initial approval of the Security Council. Since both attempts by the United Nations to carry out directly military enforcement actions or to exercise over such measures at least an effective political control had failed; the next best option was to authorise Member States to intervene militarily, thus reducing the Security Council's role in ascertaining the conditions for the use of force and to ensure that the need for a military reaction is widely shared by the members of the Organisation. It cannot be denied that this represents a remarkable retreat from the ambitious project elaborated in the Charter. Furthermore, as observed by the Secretary General, the authorisation practice provides the Organisation with an enforcement capability it would not otherwise have, but also implies the risk that 'the States concerned may claim international legitimacy and approval for forceful actions that were not in fact envisaged by the Security Council when it gave its authorisation to them'.[188]

The end of the Cold War eventually put an end to decades of paralysis of the Security Council. On only one occasion, during the Somali crisis, could the Security Council effectively take military coercive measures. The operations were conducted by the armed forces provided by some States on the basis of *ad hoc* agreements and put under the strategic control of the UN Secretary General. They did conform to the spirit and the letter of the Charter. In all the other crises in which it was involved, the Security Council limited itself to authorising Member States to use military force. With the possible exception of NATO coercive military operations conducted in Bosnia-Herzegovina until August 1995, the operations were carried out by Member States without any effective control by the Security Council. The legal basis of these operations is to be found in a customary rule that emerged throughout the 1990s as a result of a uniform practice supported by an adequate opinio juris. Simultaneous to the emergence of this rule is the informal modification of the Charter. The authorisation has a permissive effect in that it makes the resort of force lawful in spite of the general prohibition to use force existing under Art. 2(4) of the Charter and in customary international law. It has enabled the collective security system to function, albeit in a rather selective manner and with a limited centralised control over the use of force.

[187] See, in particular, J. Verhoeven, *supra* note 145, p. 181; E. Rostow, 'Until What? Enforcement Action or Collective Self-Defence?', 85 *AJIL* (1993) 506, p. 508.

[188] Report dated 25 January 1995 (S/1995/1, p. 19).

III

The attempted dismantling of the collective security system

Although at variance with the collective security system envisaged in the Charter, the so-called authorisation practice guarantees a minimum of international control over the use of force. Its functioning, however, depends on the lasting agreement among the permanent members of the Security Council. As soon as such an agreement fades away, States may be tempted to resort to force unilaterally. This chapter deals with the numerous recent cases of use of force without, or with controversial, Security Council authorisation and assesses their impact on the collective security system.

Main deviations from the so-called authorisation practice

Military operations in and against Iraq in the aftermath of the Gulf Crisis

In the years following the Iraq–Kuwait crisis, some States resorted to force, essentially to protect the Kurdish and Shiite populations and to ensure compliance with the disarmament obligations imposed on Iraq.[1] The main cases include the following. On 17 April 1991, a coalition force intervened in northern Iraq where it established safe havens over a significant part of Iraqi territory.[2] The United States invoked Resolution 688 as the legal ground for the intervention[3] whereas the United Kingdom preferred to rely on the doctrine of humanitarian intervention.[4] Iraq protested against what it perceived as a unilateral action carried out with no

[1] The 2003 military invasion will be discussed separately *infra* pp. 78 *et seq*. On the border incidents which occurred along the Iraq–Kuwait border, see C. Gray, 'After the Ceasefire: Iraq, the Security Council and the Use of Force', 65 *BYIL* (1994) 135, pp. 146 *et seq*. On the air strikes carried out in June 1993 in relation to the former US President's alleged assassination attempt, see *infra* p. 204 *in fine*.

[2] See P. Malanczuk, 'The Kurdish Crisis and allied Intervention in the Aftermath of the Second Gulf War', 2 *EJIL* (1991) 114

[3] *Public Papers of the Presidents of the United States*, Washington, 1995, vol. I, p. 379.

[4] See *infra* p. 176, text corresponding to note IV-338.

Security Council authorisation.[5] Apart from some exceptions,[6] however, the lawfulness of the intervention was not openly challenged by Member States.[7]

The intervention cannot be legally justified on the basis of Resolution 688. The text and the drafting history clearly exclude that this resolution, which was not adopted under Chapter VII of the Charter and contained an express reference to the domestic jurisdiction clause enshrined in Art. 2(7) of the Charter, authorised Member States to intervene militarily in or against Iraq.[8] It is worthwhile noting that the United Kingdom, which preferred to justify its action as permissible on humanitarian grounds, admitted that the intervention was not specifically mandated by the United Nations as 'Res. 688 did not actually authorise it'.[9]

Subsequently, no-fly zones over the Iraqi airspace north of the 36-degree and south of the 32-degree parallels were declared and enforced by the United States, the United Kingdom and France.[10] France relied on Resolution 678,[11] whereas the United States invoked Resolution 688, read in conjunction with Resolution 678. The United Kingdom, in turn, declared that the imposition of no-fly zones was dictated by 'overwhelming humanitarian need'[12] and that aircraft engaged in monitoring compliance with Resolution 688 had 'the inherent right to self-defence against Iraqi threat to their safety'.[13] The operations were generally tolerated by other States,[14] and those States apparently critical, in particular China, the Russian Federation and the members of the Arab League, did not voice any formal protest before the Security Council.

[5] See the letters S/22513, S/22531 and S/22599, dated respectively 22, 25 April and 14 May 1991.

[6] See, for instance, the protest of Sudan (S/22656, 30 May 1991).

[7] J. Delbrück, 'A Fresh Look at Humanitarian Intervention Under the Authority of the United Nations', 67 *ILJ* (1992) 887, p. 985/986, argues that the Security Council 'clearly acquiesced in the temporary presence of Americans, British and French military forces in Northern Iraq'. More prudently, N. Rodley, 'Collective intervention to Protect Human Rights and Civilian Populations: The Legal Framework', N. Rodley (ed.), *To Loose the Bands of Wickedness* (London: Brassey's, 1992), p. 33, limits himself to record no objections among Security Council members.

[8] Among many, see P. Malanczuk, *supra* note 2; A. Daems, 'L'absence de la base juridique de l'Opération Provide Comfort', 25 *RBDI* (1992) 261; G. Gaja, *supra* note I-6, p. 314; C. Gray, *supra* note 1, p. 162; D. Sarooshi, *supra* note II-33, pp. 229 *et seq*.; S. Chesterman, *supra* note I-65, pp. 196 *et seq*.

[9] *Declaration by the FCO Legal Counsellor,* 63 *BYIL* (1992) 827–8.

[10] On the establishment of the no-fly zone in the north, see Keesing's, 1991, pp. 38307, 38357 and 38540. The no-fly zone in the south was declared on 26 August 1992: see *Statement issued by the Members of the Coalition*, in M. Weller (ed.), *Iraq and Kuwait. The Hostilities and Their Aftermath* (Cambridge: Grotius, 1993), p. 725.

[11] See the statement dated 14 January 1993, in M. Weller (ed.), *supra* note 10, p. 744.

[12] See the statement dated 20 August 1992, in M. Weller (ed.), *supra* note 10, p. 724.

[13] See the statement dated 25 January 1993, partly reproduced in 64 *BYIL* (1993) 737–8.

[14] At the London Summit, the G7 noted that the humanitarian crisis required 'exceptional action by the international community, following Res. 688', but urged 'the United Nations and its affiliated agencies to be ready to consider similar action in the future if the circumstances requires it' (16 July 1991).

Military coercive measures against Iraq had been finally resorted to within the context of the controversial programme of destruction of that country's chemical, biological and nuclear weapons, and the related inspections.[15] In January 1993, the use of force against Iraq was justified by the United States, the United Kingdom and France[16] as being necessary to guarantee the respect of Security Council Resolution 687,[17] whose violations by the Iraqi Government[18] rendered applicable the authorisation to use military force included in Resolution 678. The intervention was eventually tolerated by the Security Council, which met in private session.[19]

Throughout 1998, the United States and the United Kingdom attempted to obtain a resolution authorising Member States to use force to ensure the observance of Security Council resolutions. Several other Member States, however, were opposed to such an authorisation and insisted that in the event of violations of existing resolutions, a further express resolution by the Security Council was necessary in order to resort to force.[20] On 5 November, the Security Council condemned the decision by Iraq to cease co-operation with the Special Commission as a flagrant violation of Resolution 687 and other relevant resolutions.[21] Maintaining that Resolution 1205 implicitly revived the authorisation to use force given in Resolution 678,[22] the United States and the United Kingdom launched a series of new air strikes. This time, a large part of the international community

[15] See *infra* especially, p. 223 and pp. 226 *et seq*.

[16] See, respectively, US State Department, *Press Briefing*, 19 January 1993, at the State Department site (www.state.gov); the documents collected in 64 *BYIL* (1993) 736; *Press Statement Issued by the Ministry of Foreign Affairs of France*, 14 January 1993, in M. Weller, *supra* note 10, p. 744. This position was endorsed by the UN Secretary General see the *Press Release*, 14 January 1993, in M. Weller, *supra* note 10, pp. 741–2.

[17] Adopted on 3 April 1991 (12–1–2).

[18] See the Statements issued by the President of the Security Council on 8 and 11 January 1993 (S/25081 and S/25091) respectively.

[19] Even the Russian Federation acquiesced to the military operations: see the *Statement of the Foreign Minister*, in M. Weller, *supra* note 10, pp. 744–5.

[20] Russia, in particular, declared that any 'hint of automaticity with regard to the application of force has been excluded' (S/PV.3858, p. 4); whereas France stressed: 'It is the Security Council that must evaluate the behaviour of a country, if necessary to determine any possible violations, and to take the appropriate decisions' (*ibid*., p. 18). See also the declarations by Costa Rica, Brazil, Kenya, Sweden and China (*ibid*., pp. 7 *et seq*.).

[21] Res. 1205, adopted unanimously. In para. 7, it decided, in accordance with its primary responsibility under the Charter for the maintenance of international peace and security, to remain actively seised of the matter. See also Res. 1154, adopted unanimously on 2 March 1998.

[22] See, respectively, the letters sent to the Security Council, S/1998/1181 and S/1998/1182, as well as the interventions before that organ (S/PV 3955, 16 December 1998, pp. 5 and 9). Within the Security Council, only Japan expressly approved the action (*ibid*. p. 11). France limited itself to deplore the serious human consequences for Iraqi civilian population (*ibid*. pp. 12–13).

strongly protested against what it perceived as a unilateral unlawful resort to force.[23]

The theory of the reviviscence of Resolution 678, even if taken jointly with Resolution 688, does not provide a sound basis for the military operations. Certainly, the original cease fire on the ground, subsequently formalised by Resolution 687, was a decision of the coalition.[24] It is equally clear, however, that with that resolution the Security Council intended to terminate the authorisation to use force granted with Resolution 678 and to assume direct responsibility over the effective respect of the obligations incumbent on Iraq.[25] Contrary to Resolution 686, which suspended the existing authorisation of force, Resolution 687 definitively extinguished it upon the acceptance by Iraq of the cease-fire conditions. Additionally, Resolution 678 was addressed to all Member States acting in co-operation with the Government of Kuwait and could hardly be invoked by a coalition in which this government was extraneous and in a crisis completely different from that in which the authorisation was originally granted.[26] This would not have excluded a new authorisation in favour of Member States using force, but in that case a new resolution under Chapter VII of the Charter would have been indispensable.[27]

Under the so-called authorisation practice, the determination of the existence of a threat to international peace and the finding by the Security Council of material breaches of Resolution 687 are not sufficient for the purpose of military enforcement measures. Military force could have been resorted to only following a positive assessment by the Security Council of the effectiveness, from a cost–benefit perspective, of the intervention.[28] In this regard, Resolution 1205

[23] According to the Russian Federation, in particular, the Security Council 'alone has the right to determine what steps should be taken in order to maintain or restore international peace and security. . . . The resolutions of the Security Council proved no grounds whatsoever for such actions' (*ibid.* p. 4). China stated that the action 'violated the United Nations Charter and norms governing international law' (*ibid.* p. 5). See also the protests of Iraq (*ibid.* p. 2), Sweden (*ibid.* p. 10), Brazil (*ibid.* p. 11) and Kenya (*ibid.* p. 12)

[24] R. Wedgwood, 'The Enforcement of Security Council Resolution 687: The Threat of Force Against Iraq's Weapons of Mass Destruction', 92 *AJIL* (1998) 724, p. 726.

[25] This was clearly stated by those members who addressed the question, and in particular by India, the Soviet Union and the UK: see S/PV.2981, 3 April 1991, respectively at pp. 78, 101 and 103. In literature, see in particular, P. Picone, 'La guerra contro l'Iraq e le degenerazioni dell'unilateralismo', 86 *RDI* (2003) 329, p. 365; D. Fleck, 'Developments of the Law of Arms Control as a Result of the Iraq–Kuwait Conflict', 13 *EJIL* (2002) 105, p. 111.

[26] *Contra*, Y. Dinstein, *Remarks*, 97 *ASIL* (2003) 147, p. 148.

[27] See, in particular, C. Gray, *supra* note 1; P. Palchetti, 'L'uso della forza contro l'Iraq: la ris. 678 (1990) legittima ancora l'azione militare degli Stati?', 81 *RDI* (1998) 471; U. Villani, 'La nuova crisi del Golfo e l'uso della forza contro l'Iraq', 82 *RDI* (1999) 451; N.D. White, R. Cryer, 'Unilateral Enforcement of Resolution 678: A Threat too Far?', 29 *Cal. Western Int. LJ* (1999) 243.

[28] As noted by G. Gaja, *supra* note I-6, p. 314, with regard to Res. 688 (1991), 'il ne saurait être question de contremesures collectives lorsque le Conseil se borne à constater la violation d'une obligation et une menace à la paix, mais la résolution est invoquée par la suite par certains Etats pour justifier, du moins sur le plan politique, une action militaire'.

cannot be interpreted as rendering permissible the resort to force. Such an automaticity has been clearly and consistently denied by many Member States.[29] Quite to the contrary, with Resolution 1205 the Security Council envisaged severe consequences in the event of non-observance by Iraq of its obligations and remained seised of the matter in order to ensure the implementation of the resolution.

Liberia

In August 1990 ECOWAS became involved in the Liberian crisis and established a Cease-Fire Monitoring Group (ECOMOG).[30] ECOMOG was expressly qualified as a peace-keeping force,[31] although its alleged consensual basis was shaky because of the opposition by the main belligerent faction (NPFL). Additionally, its mandate ambiguously referred to the power to conduct military operations to restore law and to create the conditions for free and fair elections.[32]

On the ground, ECOMOG progressively became embroiled in the conflict and actively took part in the hostilities. Some of the States involved, namely Nigeria and Benin, justified the operations as the exercise of self-defence, but this position was not formally endorsed by ECOWAS.[33] Moreover, some members contested the legitimacy of the decisions since they were not taken by the plenary organ and protested against what they deemed to be a joint action of certain States, led by Nigeria, rather than of the Organisation itself.[34] With regard to the military operations carried out in October 1992, it is worth noting that the UN Secretary General referred to the Security Council the fact that ECOMOG came under NPL attack and therefore was obliged to adopt a peace enforcement model in order to defend itself and to protect the capital.[35]

On 19 November 1992, the Security Council determined that the deterioration of the situation in Liberia constituted a threat to international peace and commended ECOWAS for its role in the *peaceful* resolution of the crisis.[36] Most of the

[29] The Russian Federation, in particular, declared that the resolution sought a political solution to the crisis and 'contains no language that could arbitrarily interpreted as some kind of permission to use force' (S/PV.3939, 5 November 1998, p. 4). See also the statements of Brazil and China, respectively pp. 6 and 9–10.

[30] *ECOWAS Regulations for the Cease-Fire Monitoring Group in Liberia*, adopted in Banjul, 13 August 1990, in M. Weller (ed.), *Regional Peace-keeping and International Enforcement: The Liberian Crisis* (Cambridge: Grotius, 1994), p. 77.

[31] ECOWAS Standing Mediation Committee, *Final Communiqué*, point 12, in M. Weller (ed.), *supra* note 30, p. 72.

[32] ECOWAS Standing Mediation Committee, *Decision A/DEC.1/8/90*, adopted in Banjul, 7 August 1990, Art. 2(2), in M. Weller (ed.), *supra* note 30, p. 67.

[33] A. Mindua, 'Intervention armée de la CEDEAO au Liberia: illégalité ou avancée juridique?', 7 AJICL (1995) 257, p. 269.

[34] As a result of their protest, the political control over the operations returned to the Assembly, defined by Art. 7 of ECOWAS Treaty, as the 'supreme institution of the Community'.

[35] S/26422, 9 September 1993.

[36] Res. 788, adopted unanimously.

States that took part in to the debate equally referred to ECOWAS forces as a traditional peace-keeping operation and avoided any suggestion of the coercive measures that the force had already taken or was about to take.[37] In July 1993 ECOMOG was charged with the principal responsibility for supervising the implementation of the peace agreement concluded by the main belligerent parties in Cotonou.[38] Under the heading 'peace enforcement powers', in the event of violations of the cease-fire, ECOMOG could take the 'corrective measures' required by the Violation Committee, should the parties fail to take such measures upon an invitation from the Committee itself.[39] The Security Council welcomed the agreement, supported the role prospected for ECOMOG which was described as a peace-keeping operation[40] and decided to establish the United Nations Observer Mission in Liberia (UNOMIL). Indirectly, nonetheless, it admitted that ECOMOG could undertake enforcement measures. It did so, firstly, by excluding that UNOMIL could participate in enforcement operations,[41] then by referring to the last Secretary General's report on the crisis, dealing *inter alia* with UNOMIL temporary withdrawal from the area where ECOMOG should 'enter into planned peace enforcement involving combat operations'.[42]

Bosnia-Herzegovina

On 25 July 1995, the NAC decided to launch extensive air strikes under the authority of existing Security Council resolutions, in the event of a Bosnian Serb attack against Goradze.[43] On 10 August, CINCSOUTH and UNPROFOR commanders concluded a memorandum of understanding on the execution of air strikes by NATO forces. The memorandum became operative on 30 August 1995, when the second Sarajevo market massacre triggered massive NATO airstrikes, supported on the ground by artillery attacks carried out by the Rapid Reaction Force. The decision to initiate the *Operation Deliberate Force* was jointly taken by NATO and UNPROFOR commanders.

[37] China, the US, France and the UK, in particular, declared that ECOWAS was seeking a peaceful solution of the crisis (S/PV. 3138, 19 November 1992, respectively pp. 71–2, p. 73, 78 and 80.

[38] Concluded on 25 July 1993, in S/26272, 9 August 1993, Annex. Also in M. Weller (ed.), *supra* note 30, p. 343.

[39] Art. 8. The Committee was composed of one person for each of the parties and ECOMOG and the United Nations Observer Mission.

[40] Res. 866, adopted on 22 September 1993 (unanimously), Preamble.

[41] Para. 3 (h).

[42] S/26422, 9 September 1993, p. 4.

[43] NATO Secretary General, *Press Statement on Goradze following the NAC meeting*, 25 July 1995, in *NATO Review*, September 1995, at 7. The warning was later extended to the remaining safe areas: see NATO Secretary General, *Press Statement on other Safe Areas following the NAC meeting*, 1 August 1995, *ibid*. On that occasion it was also stated that, if requested by the UN, NATO would use air power to provide close air support to any UN personnel throughout Bosnia and in the UN Protected Areas in Croatia.

On 8 September 1995, the Russian Federation requested the immediate cessation of the operations and strongly contested their lawfulness on several grounds. Because of their punitive, disproportionate and extensive nature, the operations were considered as being contrary to existing Security Council resolutions, which were based on the principle of proportionality and limited to the defence of UNPROFOR and the safe areas. It was further argued that the new arrangements substantially revised the 'dual-key procedure', thus depriving the United Nations of the power to suspend or terminate the operations.[44] Within the Security Council, only China[45] and the FRY[46] supported the Russian position. All other States rejected the Russian objections and admitted – though in a rather summary fashion[47] – the conformity of *Operation Deliberate Force* with existing Security Council resolutions, and in particular with Resolution 836[48].

The operation ended when the Bosnian Serbs eventually accepted compliance with the conditions established by UNPROFOR and NATO commanders. This led to the conclusion of the conflict in Bosnia-Herzegovina which was formalised with the peace accords concluded in Dayton and signed in Paris.[49] Then the Security Council authorised the Member States, acting through or in co-operation with NATO, to establish a multinational implementation force responsible for discharging the duties specified in Annex 1–A and Annex 2 of the Peace Agreement.[50]

The lawfulness of *Operation Deliberate Force* is extremely precarious. In the first place, the radical transformation of the military operations, which assumed a clearly hostile nature,[51] could have been decided exclusively by the Security

[44] Although the document has not been made available even to the Security Council's members, it was apparently agreed that the operations would have continued until *both* commanders had determined that they had achieved their aims, See the letter by the US President to the Congress, dated 1 September 1995, in *Public Papers of the Presidents of the United States*, Washington, 1995, vol. II, pp. 1279–80.

[45] *Ibid.*, p. 8.

[46] *Ibid.*, at pp. 12–13. See also the Statements dated 30 August, 7 and 8 September 1995, respectively S/1995/759, S/1995/777, S/1995/778.

[47] See M. Weller, *supra* note II-123, p. 161.

[48] Germany, for instance declared: 'What is being enforced is international law, in the form of decisions by the competent United Nations organ, that is the Security Council' (S/PV.3575, 8 September 1995, at p. 6). Similarly see the declarations by France, the US and Italy (*ibid.*, respectively, pp. 4, 5 and 9).

[49] S/1995/999. See Sorel, 'L'accord de paix sur la Bosnie-Herzegovine du 14 Septembre 1995: un traité sous bénéfice d'inventaire', 41 *AFDI* (1995) 65; Szasz, 'The Dayton Accord: The Balkan Peace Agreement', 30 *CILJ* (1997) 759.

[50] Res. 1031, adopted on 15 December 1995 (unanimously), para. 14.

[51] In the report dated 23 November 1995 (S/1995/987 at 3), the UN Secretary General observed that there had been a change in the roles of UNPROFOR and NATO, both of which became militarily engaged against the Bosnian Serbs. In a document issued on 8 June 1995, the International Committee of the Red Cross maintained that the 1949 Geneva Convention Relative to the Treatment of Prisoners of War (75 *UNTS* 135) was applicable in the relationship between the United Nations and the Bosnian Serbs (on file with author).

Council.[52] Additionally, the operations definitively lost their impartiality because of the substantial toleration, despite the strong formal condemnation[53] and NATO warnings,[54] of the military offensive by the Croatian forces. The changes in the procedural arrangements, and in particular the abandonment of the so-called dual-key procedure, finally deprived the United Nations of any form of effective control and meant that the operations could not have been revised, suspended or terminated without the NAC consent.

Sierra Leone

In May 1997, the overthrown democratically elected government requested that ECOWAS restore the constitutional order.[55] Allegedly on that basis, Nigeria and Guinea intervened militarily through what appears to have been a joint unilateral operation. The request can hardly be said to constitute a valid legal basis for the use of force by the two States since it emanated from an entirely ineffective government and at any rate was addressed to the organisation and not to its Member States. Nor can self-defence be invoked to justify the resort to force as sustained by Sierra Leone, since there were no allegations on substantial military involvement from outside.[56]

ECOWAS met at the end of June and resolved to reinstate the 'legitimate' government, if necessary through the use of military force.[57] The document is silent on the requirement to obtain an authorisation from the Security Council in order to resort to military force as envisaged. The UN Security Council's reaction was confined to a private discussion and to a Presidential statement endorsing ECOWAS efforts to solve the crisis *peacefully*. The statement reveals no intention on behalf of the Security Council to condemns or authorise either the military measures already jointly taken by some members of ECOWAS, or those contemplated by ECOWAS itself.[58]

[52] See the reports by the UN Secretary General dated 1 December 1994 and 30 May 1995, respectively S/1994/1389 and S/1995/444. He maintained this position even after *Operation Deliberate Force*, when he envisaged the creation of a multinational force acting upon a Security Council mandate: see the letter dated 18 September 1995 (S/1995/804).

[53] Res. 1009 adopted on 10 August 1995 (unanimously). See also the Presidential Statement issued on 16 June 1995 (S/1995/30) and the reports by the UN Secretary General dated 10 February 1993 (S/25264), 9 June 1995 (S/1995/470) and 7 August 1995 (S/1995/666).

[54] NATO Secretary General, *Press Statement on other Safe Areas following the NAC meeting*, 1 August 1995.

[55] UN Press Release, *Press Conference by the Permanent Representative of Sierra Leone*, 27 May 1997, p. 4.

[56] UN Press Release, *Press Conference by the Permanent Representative of Sierra Leone*, 9 June 1997.

[57] *Foreign Ministers Final Communiqué*, 26 June 1997, para. 9 (iii), available at www.ecowas.int and in S/1997/499, 27 June 1997, Annex.

[58] S/PRST/1997/36, 11 July 1997.

On 29 August, ECOWAS authorised ECOMOG to use all necessary means to ensure the respect of the complete embargo imposed against Sierra Leone, to monitor the cease fire and 'to restore peace'.[59] Subsequently, the Security Council, acting under Chapter VIII of the Charter, authorised ECOWAS, co-operating with the democratically elected Government of Sierra Leone, to prevent violations of the sanctions, if necessary by halting inward maritime shipping in order to inspect and verify their cargos and destinations.[60] The authorisation to use force was addressed *exclusively* to the regional organisation, thus excluding any individual or joint unilateral initiative of Member States. During the debate leading to the adoption of the resolution, the Russian Federation insisted that regional organisations could not undertake enforcement action, such as naval interdiction operations, without an authorisation by the Security Council.[61]

In February 1998, after the failed implementation of the Conakry agreement,[62] a military offensive by armed forces composed essentially of Nigerian troops eventually brought about the return of the democratically elected Government. The question of the lawfulness of the intervention was not discussed by the Security Council. The Security Council merely welcomed the outcome of the crisis[63] and commended ECOWAS and ECOMOG for the role they were playing in support of the efforts undertaken by the newly re-established government.[64]

Kosovo

On 23 September 1998, the Security Council declared the situation in Kosovo a threat to peace and issued several injunctions to the Belgrade Government.[65] The brief debate within the Security Council reveals the significantly divergent interpretations given to the resolution. The Russian Federation emphasised that despite the reference to Chapter VII, no use of force was contemplated,[66] whereas the United States announced that NATO was planning military operations to guarantee, if necessary, compliance with the resolution.[67]

A couple of weeks later, the NATO Secretary General declared that, although the adoption by the Security Council of a further resolution clearly authorising an

[59] *Final Communiqué*, available at www.ecowas.int and in S/1997/695, 8 September 1997, Annex I. See also *Decision on Sanctions Against the Junta in Sierra Leone*, Art. 7, *ibid*., Annex II.

[60] Res. 1132, 8 October 1997 (unanimously). Despite some formal differences, the authorisation is in substance identical to that granted in Res. 787 (1992); see *supra* II-72.

[61] S/PV.3822, 8 October 1997, p. 9.

[62] Text in S/1997/824, 28 October 1997, Annexes I and II.

[63] Res. 1156, adopted unanimously on 16 March 1998.

[64] Res. 1162, adopted unanimously on 17 April 1998.

[65] Res. 1199 adopted on 23 September 1998 (14–0–1), para. 9.

[66] S/PV.3930, 23 September 1998, p. 3. During a press conference held the same day, the French Government declared that the Security Council 'est le seul organisme qui a le droit de décider du recours à la force' (44 *AFDI* (1998) 737).

[67] *Ibid*., at 5.

enforcement action was unlikely, the Alliance could legitimately resort to force to put an end to the humanitarian catastrophe and ensure compliance with the relevant Security Council resolutions.[68] On 13 October, the NAC issued an activation order for limited air strikes and a phased air campaign in the FRY.[69]

The military threat pushed the Belgrade Government to sign two agreements establishing, respectively, the OSCE Kosovo Verification Mission (KVM) which was charged with monitoring compliance with Security Council Resolution 1199,[70] and the NATO air surveillance mission over Kosovo.[71] The Security Council rapidly endorsed both agreements and confirmed that, in the event of an emergency situation, action may be needed to ensure the safety of the OSCE personnel involved in the monitoring mission.[72] Other references to the use of force included in the draft resolution were deleted in order to avoid Chinese veto. Concern over NATO military threat was expressed by the Russian Federation, which urged NATO to abstain from taking any unilateral action and to withdraw the activation order.[73] China declared the NATO initiative as being contrary to the Charter and general international law.[74] The United Kingdom and the United States, in turn, underlined the need to take concrete action to ensure the effective compliance of Security Council resolutions, and ultimately to prevent a humanitarian catastrophe.[75] Adopting a more prudent approach, France affirmed the centrality of the Security Council in the field of use of force and considered Resolution 1203 as necessary to legitimate the accords signed by the FRY.[76] At the time, the view that the express authorisation of the Security Council was indispensable for the lawful resort to military force was shared by many European

[68] See the letter dated 9 October 1998, partly quoted in B. Simma, 'NATO, the UN and the Use of Force: Legal Aspects', 10 *EJIL* (1999) 1, text corresponding to note 13.

[69] *Statement by the Secretary General Following Decision on the Accord*, Brussels, 13 October 1998.

[70] *Agreement on the OSCE Kosovo Verification Mission*, Belgrade, 16 October 1998, in S/1998/978. See also *OSCE Permanent Council Decision No. 263*, 15 October 1998, in S/1998/994, Annex; UN Secretary General's report dated 12 November 1998, in S/1998/1068, para. 43; OSCE report for September–October 1998, in S/1998/1068, Annex I, para. 30; *OSCE Oslo Ministerial Draft Statement on Kosovo*, in S/1998/1221, Annex II, para. 10.

[71] *KVM Agreement between NATO and the FRY*, Belgrade 15 October 1999, in S/1998/991, Annex.

[72] Res. 1203, adopted on 24 October 1998 (13–0–2), para. 9. This had already been foreseen in Art. 7 of the agreement with the OSCE.

[73] S/PV.3937, 24 October 1998, at 12.

[74] *Ibid*, at 14. See also the criticism expressed by Costa Rica, *ibid.*, p. 6, and Brazil, *ibid.*, p. 10.

[75] *Ibid.*, respectively pp. 13 and 15.

[76] *Ibid.*, pp. 15–16.

States[77] and the Russian Federation.[78] On 23 March, following the failure of the Rambouillet negotiations, NATO forces initiated a broad range of air operations against the FRY.

Intervening States failed to elaborate a unique and coherent legal argument to support the lawfulness of their action. They relied primarily on humanitarian grounds.[79] The clearest position in that sense was taken by the United Kingdom, which maintained that 'in the exceptional circumstances of Kosovo it was considered that the use of force would be justified on the ground of overwhelming humanitarian necessity, without Security Council authorisation'.[80]

The humanitarian argument, however, was normally integrated by other justifying elements, and in particular by the determination operated by the Security Council of both the existence of a threat to international peace and security and the violation by the Belgrade Government of its international obligations. The United States, in particular, argued before the International Court of Justice that 'the resolutions of the Security Council . . . have determined that the actions of the Federal Republic of Yugoslavia constitute a threat to peace and security in the region and, pursuant to Chapter VII of the Charter, demanded a halt to such actions'.[81] France considered the action 'a response to the violations by Belgrade of its international obligations, which stem in particular from the Security Council resolutions adopted under Chapter VII of the Charter'.[82] The United Kingdom,

[77] France, in particular, declared that NATO actions not based on Art. 5 of the 1949 Treaty 'doivent être placés sous l'autorité du Conseil de sécurité' (*Discours du Ministre des Affaires étrangères*, Bruxelles, 8 décembre 1998, in *DAI*, 15 janvier 1999, p. 60). Similarly, see the declaration of the Foreign Minister before the Foreign Affairs Commission, 22 December 1998, which reads in part: 'les Etats-Unis ont envisagé que l'OTAN agisse sans mandat du Conseil de sécurité au nom de l'urgence humanitaire. Ceci était contraire à la Charte de l'ONU et au Traité de Washington, et la France a fait prévaloir sa position' (44 *AFDI* (1998) 738). But see *infra* note 86.

[78] See Declaration of the Russian Government, 4 October 1998, *DAI*, No 23, 1 December 1998, p. 888.

[79] See, for instance, the *Chairman's summary of the Deliberations on Kosovo of the Informal Meeting of EU Heads of States*, 14 April 1999, S/1999/429, Annex; and the reference made by the US and Canada to the humanitarian emergency (S/PV.3988, 23 March 1999, p. 5).

[80] *Declaration by the Parliamentary Under Secretary of State*, 69 *BYIL* (1998) 593. See also the position expressed before the Security Council (S/PV.3988, 23 March 1999, at 12).

[81] *Legality of the Use of Force* (Yugoslavia v. United States), Verbatim Record, 11 May 1999, CR 99/24, para 1.7. On the same occasion, but also before the Security Council, see S/PV.3989, 26 March 1999, at 4–5; they also claimed that the action was permitted in order to prevent a further deterioration of the security of neighbouring countries.

[82] S/PV.3988, 23 March 1999, p. 9. This position is hardy compatible with that previously held by France; see *supra* note 77. The *revirement* is quite striking in the following declaration made on 15 April 1999 by the Prime Minister before the Senate: 'Le légitimité de notre action actuelle en République fédérale de Yougoslavie aux côtés de nos alliés est fondé sur les résolutions et les exigences du Counseil de sécurité des Nations Unies. Le gouvernement français, en accord avec le président de la République, est convaincu que c'est au même Conseil de sécurité qu'il reviendra de définir le cadre d'une solution politique au Kosovo et les mécanismes de sa mise en œuvre' (45 *AFDI* (1999) 885).

in turn, declared itself to have been compelled by the circumstances to take 'exceptional measures in support of the purposes laid down by the Security Council'.[83] Belgium distinguished itself from the other allies by expressly invoking the state of necessity as one of the legal base of the intervention.[84]

NATO action was criticised by a significant number of States as being contrary to Articles 2(4) and 53 of the Charter as well as contrary to the customary norm prohibiting the use of force in international relations. It was made abundantly clear that no coercive action could be undertaken by States or regional organisations without a Security Council authorisation.[85] On 26 March 1999, the members of the Security Council opposed to the intervention unsuccessfully submitted a draft resolution calling for the immediate cessation of the air strikes.[86]

The air campaign ended on 9 June after the FRY and Serbian Governments signed an agreement with NATO. Based on the general principles previously adopted by the G-8, the agreement established the procedures for the full withdrawal of the Yugoslav Security Forces from Kosovo and the deployment by the Security Council, acting under Chapter VII of the Charter, of a multinational force operating with unified NATO chain of command and under the political control of the NAC, in consultation with non-NATO force contributors.[87] The force was charged with taking any measure, including the use of force, necessary to main-

[83] See the Secretary of State for Defence's statement made to the House of Commons on 25 March 1999. The Government subsequently explained that the adoption of forcible measures would depend 'on an objective assessment of the factual circumstances at the time and on the terms of relevant decisions of the Security Council' (*Response to the 4th Report from the Foreign Affairs Committee*, Session 1999–2000, para. 20).

[84] *Legality of the Use of Force* (*Yugoslavia* v. *Belgium*), Verbatim Record, 10 May 1999, CR 99/15, pp. 17–18.

[85] See, in particular, the intervention of the Russian Federation, China, RFY, India, Cuba, S/PV.3988 and S/PV.3989, respectively 24 and 26 March 1999. See also: *Communiqué of the Rio Group of Latin American States*, 25 March 1999, S/1999/347, Annex; *Declaration of the Inter-Parliamentary Assembly of the Commonwealth of Independent States*, 3 April 1999, S/1999/461, Annex II; *Statement of the Movement of Non-Aligned Countries*, 9 April 1999, S/1999/451, Annex; *Ministerial Declaration of the Meeting of Foreign Ministers of the Group of 77*, 24 September 1999, available at the site of the Organisation: www.g77.org. The Organisation of Islamic Conference, in turn, limited itself to express regret that the Security Council had been unable to discharge its responsibilities under the Charter (*Declaration of the Ministerial Meeting*, 7 April 1999, S/1999/394).

[86] S/1999/328. It gathered only the votes of the Russian Federation, China and Namibia.

[87] *Statement by the Chairman*, 6 May 1999, in S/1999/516. The conditions were substantially identical to those listed by the NAC on 12 April 1999: stop to all military action; withdrawal of the military, police and paramilitary forces from Kosovo; stationing in Kosovo of an international military presence; unconditional and safe return of all refugees and displaced persons; unhindered access to international humanitarian assistance; credible assurance of the FRY willingness to work on the basis of the Rambouillet Accords in the establishment of a political framework agreement: see M-NAC, *Press Release* 1 (99) 51.

tain a secure environment in the province and facilitate the return of displaced peoples and refugees.[88]

The Security Council immediately endorsed the agreement and authorised the establishment of a multinational force whose responsibilities included deterring the renewal of the hostilities, maintaining and, where necessary, enforcing the cease fire.[89] During the debate, however, the Russian Federation declared that NATO forces acting 'in violation of the United Nations Charter and in circumvention of the Security Council, has severely destabilised the entire system of international relations based on the primacy of international law'. China further affirmed that 'NATO seriously violated the United Nations Charter and norms of international law, and undermined the authority of the Security Council'.[90]

Afghanistan

The Security Council declared the dramatic terrorist attacks that occurred on 11 September 2001 as a threat to international peace and security and recognised the right of individual and collective self-defence under Art. 51 of the Charter.[91] Two weeks later, acting under Chapter VII of the Charter, it reaffirmed the right of individual and collective self-defence and stressed the need to combat, still in accordance with the Charter, the terrorist threat by all means.[92]

Meanwhile, the United States Congress granted the President the power to use force against those nations, organisations or persons he determined were responsible for the terrorist attacks.[93] After having unsuccessfully attempted to obtain co-operation from the Kabul Government,[94] on 7 October the United States started a massive military campaign against Afghanistan. The action was justified by the United States[95] and the United Kingdom,[96] as the exercise of the right to self-defence.[97]

[88] *Military Technical Agreement between the KFOR and the Governments of the RFY and the Republic of Serbia*, Belgrade, 9 June 1999.

[89] Res. 1244, adopted on 10 June 1999 (14–0–1), paras 7 and 9.

[90] S/PV.4011, 10 June 1999, pp. 7 and 8 respectively.

[91] Res. 1368, adopted on 12 September 2001 (unanimously).

[92] Res. 1373, adopted on 28 September 2001 (unanimously).

[93] *Authorisation for Use of Military Force*, Pub. L. No. 107–40, 115 Stat. 224 (2001).

[94] The US requested the Taliban Government: (a) to deliver all Al Quaida leaders in their hands; (b) to release all foreign nationals unjustly imprisoned by Taliban authorities; (c) to protect foreign journalists, diplomats and aid workers operating in Afghanistan; (d) to close immediately and permanently every terrorist training camp in Afghanistan and to hand over every terrorist and every person supporting them; (e) to give the United States full access to terrorist training camps, see *President's Address Before a Joint Session of the Congress on the United States Response to the Terrorist Attacks of September 11*, 20 September 2001, 37 *Weekly Comp. Pres. Doc.*, pp. 1347 *et seq.*, p. 1348.

[95] See *Letter dated 7 October 2001 to the President of the Security Council*, S/2001/946.

[96] See *Letter dated 7 October 2001 to the President of the Security Council*, S/2001/947.

[97] On 12 September, the NAC declared that Art. 5 of the Washington Treaty was applicable if it was determined that the terrorist attack were directed from abroad against

The reaction to the preparation and the conduct of the military operations was overwhelmingly favourable. The permanent members of the Security Council expressed their support for what they saw as military action 'taken in self-defence and directed at terrorists and those who harboured them'.[98] Virtually all the members of the international community offered their participation in the operations or access to their airspace or expressed their support. Particular mention is deserved by the positive appreciation expressed by China and the Russian Federation, as well as the statements issued by the North Atlantic Treaty Organisation, the Organisation of American States, the Gulf Cooperation Council, the League of Arab States, and the Organisation for Islamic Conference.[99] Very few States criticised the military campaign.[100] The European Union confirmed 'its staunchest support for the military operations . . . which [were] legitimate under the terms of the Charter and of Resolution 1368'.[101]

The use of force in Afghanistan must be singled out because of the invocation by the intervening States of the right to self-defence. Leaving aside for the moment the self-defence claim, from the perspective of the collective security system, it is worthwhile noting that neither the United States nor any other State sought to obtain from the Security Council the authorisation to resort to force.[102] Consequently, the Security Council did not intend to authorise any military enforcement measures. It would therefore be unacceptable to read para. 2(b) of the resolution as allowing *any* States to take *any* measures, including those involving military force, against *any* other State or non-State entities.[103] The Security

---

the United States and on that basis for the first time it invoked the application of Art. 5 of the Washington Treaty *Statement by the NAC, Press Release (2001) 124. On 21 September, the OAS decided that 'all State parties to the Rio Treaty shall provide effective reciprocal assistance to address such attack and the threat of any similar attacks against any American State', Res. 1, para. 1, Doc.OAE/Ser.F/II.24/RC24/RES.1/01, also in 40* ILM (2001) 1273. Similarly, on 14 September, Australia, New Zealand and the US decided that the terrorist attacks were to be considered as armed attack for the purpose of the mutual defence pact concluded in San Francisco on 1 September 1951 (ANZUS Treaty, 131 *UNTS* 83).

[98] Press Statement on Terrorist Threats by Security Council President, 8 October 2001, SC/7167.

[99] An interesting survey may be found in S.D. Murphy, 'Terrorist Attacks on World Trade Centre and Pentagon', 96 *AJIL* (2002) 237, pp. 244 *et seq*. See also the US Department of State, Fact Sheet, *Operation Enduring Freedom Overview*, at www.state.gov.

[100] See, in particular, the positions expressed by Iraq, Iran, North Korea, Cuba and Malaysia before the General Assembly during the debate held on 10 November 2001; see L. Condorelli, *supra* I-50, p. 840, footnote 7.

[101] Declaration of the Heads of States or Governments of the European Union, Ghent, 19 October 2001.

[102] On this point, see O. Corten and F. Dubuisson, 'Opération "Liberté immuable": une extension abusive du concept de légitime défense', 106 *RGDIP* (2002) 51, p. 53.

[103] The view that Res. 1373 did not authorise the use of force was maintained, among others, by J. I. Charney, 'The Use of Force Against Terrorism and International Law', 95 *AJIL* (2001) 835; J. Delbrück, 'The Fight Against Global Terrorism: Self-Defense or Collective Security as International Police Action?', 44 *GYIL* (2001) 9, p. 13; C. Greenwood,

Council practice may be ambiguous in many regards, but each and every time the use of force was authorised, the target – either States, non-State entities, or belligerent groups or factions – was clearly identified. Incidentally, para. 2(b) was inserted into the section dealing with the measures *not* involving the use of force that Member States were compelled to take within their respective jurisdictions.[104]

The rapid military success of the United States-led forces paved the way to the creation of a transitional multi-ethnic Government. In accordance with the agreement concluded by the Afghan parties in Bonn on 5 December 2001,[105] the Security Council authorised the deployment of the International Security Assistance Force (ISAF) to assist it in the maintenance of security in Kabul and its surrounding areas.[106]

Iraq (2003)

On 8 November 2002, the Security Council decided that Iraq was in material breach of its disarmament obligations imposed, *inter alia*, by Resolution 687, and issued an injunction to comply with these obligations strictly in accordance with the established schedule.[107] One month earlier, the United States President had obtained from Congress the authorisation to use force against Iraq in order (1) to defend the national security of the United States; and (2) to enforce all relevant Security Council resolutions.[108]

At the United Nations, the United States faced insurmountable opposition to the military option by several members of the Security Council, including the Russian Federation, France and China. In vain it attempted to obtain from the Security Council a resolution authorising the resort to military coercion to compel Iraq to comply with its obligations, or at least formal certification that Iraq had failed to take the final opportunity provided by Resolution 1441. The support it was able to gather within the Security Council was so limited that it desisted from seeking even a simple majority vote, which would have expressed at least some moral or political legitimacy of the military action.[109] Supported by a minority of

'International Law and the "War against Terrorism"', 78 *IA* (2002) 301, p. 309; E. P. J. Myjer and N. D. White, 'The Twin Towers Attack: An Unlimited Right to Self-Defence?', 7 *JCSL* (2002) 5.

[104] This is clear, in particular, from the report submitted on 19 December 2001 by the US to the Security Council Committee established pursuant to Res. 1373, S/2001/1220, Annex; and it is confirmed that the modal 'shall', which would be erroneous if referred to military measures. See also the position of the Japanese Government, which rightly based the resolution on Art. 41 of the Charter, 45 *JAIL* (2002) 104.

[105] Letter of the Secretary General to the President of the Security Council (S/2001/1154, 5 December 2001).

[106] Res 1386 (unanimously), 20 December 2001, para. 1.

[107] Res. 1441 (unanimously).

[108] *House Joint Resolution Authorizing Use of Force Against Iraq*, Pub. L. 107–243, 10 October 2002.

[109] See S. D. Murphy, 'Use of Force and Arms Control', 97 *AJIL* (2003) 419.

States[110] and with troops contribution from the United Kingdom, Australia and Poland, on 19 March 2003, the United States eventually started a massive military campaign against Iraq.

Both domestically[111] and at the United Nations,[112] the Washington Government justified the military operations on two grounds: (1) the authority of existing Security Council resolutions, and in particular Res. 678 and Res. 687 coupled with the finding of material breach contained in Resolution 1441; (2) the need to defend the United States and the international community from the threat posed by Iraq. As to the first argument, it is based on the idea – already advanced in 1998 – that the non-respect of the conditions for the cease-fire imposed in 1991 by Resolution 687 would have reactivated the authorisation granted in Resolution 678.[113] For the same reasons indicated above with regard to the military operations carried out in the aftermath of the Gulf crisis,[114] the argument that Resolution 678 revived as a result of the material breaches by Iraq of its disarmament obligations is entirely unconvincing.

In a declaration made jointly with the United States and Spain,[115] as well as during the debate before the Security Council on the eve of the intervention,[116] the United Kingdom maintained that any action had to be taken in accordance with international law and be based upon relevant Security Council resolutions. Its official letter to the Security Council following the outbreak of hostilities, however, does not expressly refer to the authorisation of the use of force, but rather stresses

[110] See in particular the letter published by the leaders of the UK, Spain, Italy, Portugal, Denmark, the Czech Republic, Hungary and Poland, *Wall Street Journal*, 30 January 2003, at A14.

[111] *Address to the Nation on Iraq*, 17 March 2003, 39 *WCPD*, Doc. 338–9; *Letter to Congressional Leaders Reporting on the Commencement of Military Operations Against Iraq*, 21 March 2002 (*ibid.*, Doc. 348). See also *Bush Has Legal Authority to Use Force in Iraq. Remarks by the State Department Legal Adviser*, http://usinfo.state.gov.

[112] *Letter dated 20 March 2003 to the President of the Security Council*, S/2003/351.

[113] This argument was fully supported by Spain (see S/PV.4721, 19 March 2003, pp. 15–16), according to whom Res. 687 left in abeyance Res. 678. For Italy, Resolutions 678, 687 and 1441, jointly taken, authorise the use of force since any violation by Iraq of its obligations concerning weapons of mass destruction would imply a breach of the cease-fire and the restoration of the authorisation granted in 1990; see the Prime Minister's statement before the Parliament, *Comunicazioni del Governo sugli sviluppi della crisi irachena*, Camera dei Deputati, meeting n. 283, 19 March 2003. Australia took a less clear position when stating that the action was undertaken 'consistent' with Resolutions 678, 687 and 1441, *Letter dated 20 March 2003 to the President of the Security Council*, S/2003/352. In a *Memorandum of Advice on the Use of Force Against Iraq*, the Attorney General's Department and the Department of Foreign Affairs and Trade maintained that the authorisation contained in Res. 678 was still into force as a result of the violations of the cease-fire (www.pm.gov.au).

[114] See *supra* notes 24 *et seq.*

[115] *Statement of the Atlantic Summit: A Vision for Iraq and the Iraqi People*, 39 *WCPD*, No. 336, 16 March 2003.

[116] S/PV.4721, 19 March, p. 19.

the need to put an end to Iraqi's failure to comply with its disarmament obligations, as certified by Resolution 1441. The military action, in this perspective, was considered as indispensable to secure compliance of these obligations, apparently without a specific Security Council authorisation being necessary.[117]

The intervention provoked the firm protests of the overwhelming majority of the international community, including, significantly, some NATO members and other Western States. The Russian Federation, in particular, insisted on the central role of the Security Council and on the admissibility of non-defensive use of force exclusively when duly authorised by that organ,[118] whereas Germany declared that there is no substitute for the Security Council for its functions as a guardian of peace[119].

Following the military defeat of the Saddam Hussein regime, the United States-led forces occupied the territory of Iraq[120] and created the Coalition Provisional Authority, 'vested with all executive, legislative and judicial authority necessary to achieve its objectives, to be exercised under relevant U.N. Security Council resolutions, including Resolution 1483 (2003) and the laws and usages of war'.[121] On 22 May 2003 the Security Council, in addition to lifting the economic prohibitions on trading with Iraq, with the exception of those related to arms and related materials, recognised 'the specific authorities, responsibilities, and obligations under applicable international law' of the occupying States.[122]

After lengthy negotiations, the Security Council eventually stepped into the management of the military aspects of the crisis by authorising the deployment of a multinational force under unified command which was charged with taking all necessary measures to contribute to the maintenance of security and stability in Iraq.[123] France and Germany insisted on the creation of a single unified command and obtained the amendment of the first draft resolution submitted by the United

[117] *Letter dated 20 March 2003 to the President of the Security Council*, S/2003/350. It must be noted, however, that according to the UK Attorney General: 'Authority to use force against Iraq exists from the combined effect of resolutions 678, 687 and 1441' (*Written Answer to a Parliamentary Question on the Legal Basis for the Use of Force in Iraq*, 17 March 2003, in 52 *ICLQ* (2003) 811). See also British and Commonwealth Office, *Iraq: Legal Basis for the Use of Force*, *ibid*., p. 812.

[118] S/PV.4721, 19 March 2003, p. 7.

[119] *Ibid*., p. 4. That there were no alternative to multilateralism was stressed, with different tunes, by France (*ibid*., p. 6), Syria (*ibid*., p. 9), Pakistan (*ibid*., p. 12), Mexico (*ibid*., p. 12), China (*ibid*., p. 18), and Bulgaria (*ibid*., p. 19).

[120] See the *Letter dated 8 May 2003 from the United Kingdom and the United States to the President of the Security Council*, S/2003/538.

[121] *Coalition Provisional Authority Regulation Number 1*, CPA/REG/16 May 2003/01 (the date indicated in the document is not correct as Res. 1483 was adopted on 22 May 2003).

[122] Res. 1483 (14–0–0, Syria did not participate in the vote).

[123] Res. 1511, 16 October 2003 (unanimously), para. 13.

States on 4 September which did not exclude the continuing presence of a force composed of the existing Coalition troops.[124]

The political process towards the restoration of a fully independent Iraqi Government passed through the establishment of a Governing Council[125] and later the formation of an Interim Government endorsed by the Security Council.[126] On 8 June 2004, the Security Council declared the end of the occupation, with effect at the end of the month, and defined the timetable for the political transition to a democratically elected Government.[127] Contextually, it reaffirmed the authorisation for a multinational force under unified command established in Resolution 1511 as requested by the incoming Interim Government.[128]

It then decided that the mandate of the multinational force would be reviewed at the request of the Iraqi Government or twelve months after the adoption of the resolution, and would expire upon the complete restoration of the Iraqi Government. It also declared that the mandate would be terminated earlier if requested by the Government of Iraq.

The Security Council demonstrated a good deal of pragmatism. Since there was no independent and effective Government capable of validly requesting the deployment of foreign troops, the resolution provided the legal basis for the presence of the multinational force. Nonetheless, the new political situation existing in Iraq imposed some changes with regard to the authorisation given in Resolution 1511. The new mandate in fact is based on the idea of a partnership between the multinational force and the Government of Iraq. The formation of a subject of international law being an incremental process, Resolution 1546 allows the transitional Government gradually to assume its responsibilities and exercise its prerogatives. The sovereignty rights of the Government, once fully established, are preserved by the automatic extinction of the mandate of the multinational force.

The provision on the earlier termination of the authorisation should not be read as implying that the consent of the Interim Government – not yet subject to international law – is the legal basis for the operations carried out by the multinational force. Rather, it is aimed at preserving the prerogatives of the Security Council and its members. The opposition to the operation expressed by the Iraqi Government would radically alter the conditions under which the authorisation was granted in Resolution 1546 and render the adoption of a new resolution necessary for the continuation of the presence of the multinational force.

[124] French and German Amendments to the US Draft Resolution on Iraq, 10 September 2003.

[125] The establishment of the broadly representative Governing Council was welcomed by the Security Council in Res. 1500, adopted on 14 August 2003 (14–0–1).

[126] Res. 1546, adopted on 8 June 2004 (unanimously), para. 1.

[127] *Ibid.*, para. 2 *et seq.*

[128] See the side letters of the Prime Minister of the Interim Government of Iraq and of the US Secretary of State annexed to the Resolution.

The impact of State practice upon collective security law

In all of the cases examined above, the use of force was not duly authorised by the Security Council or was authorised only with regard to the post-conflict phase. *Individually taken*, these cases amount to clear deviations from the rule conditioning the lawfulness of any use of force – apart from self-defence – to the Security Council authorisation. What remains to be assessed is the impact, in terms of modification or even desuetude, of these departures *globally considered* upon the rule on the use of force existing in customary law and in the Charter. It is then necessary to explore whether the rule has merely been disregarded in a number of cases, or has rather undergone a further process of modification as to the form, timing and content of the authorisation, or even the downgrading of the authorisation itself from legal requirement to a matter of political expediency.

The discussion will focus on the claims put forward by the States resorting to force and on the reaction of the rest of the international community. The analysis is complicated by the fact that the States taking part in the operations have rarely relied upon the same legal grounds and their attitudes have not always been consistent and unambiguous. Furthermore, they have occasionally advanced legal arguments at least partially unrelated to the Security Council's resolution, namely self-defence and humanitarian intervention. These arguments will be treated separately in the respective headings in the paragraphs dedicated to unilateral or joint use of force.

International law is 'a dynamic, continually operating process of rejection or refinement of old rules; and the confirmation of new ones in supplement or replacement of the old'.[129] From the standpoint of customary international law, in particular, depending on the attitude of the States putting forward new claims and the reaction of the other States, deviations from existing norms may 'create occasions for emphatic confirmation of the custom and thus in the end contribute to its strengthening',[130] or lead to the desuetude or the modification of the custom.[131] The process of desuetude or modification is substantially identical to that of creation of new customary international law.[132] A process of modification or desuetude can be ascertained only on the basis of a uniform and coherent State practice contrary to the existing customary rule coupled with the justification of the conduct by reference to a new right or a new exception to the norm.[133]

[129] E. McWhinney, *The World Court and the Contemporary International Law-Making Process* (Alphen aan den Rijn: Sijthof & Noordhoff, 1979), p. 1. Adopting what has been defined as the 'legal realist approach', emphasis is to be put on the facts rather on the *a priori* legal categories: *ibid.*, p. 3.

[130] K. Wolfke, *supra* note II-156, p. 65.

[131] According to A. A. D'Amato, *supra* note II-166, p. 97, a departure from the existing customary law 'contains the seeds of a new legality'.

[132] See E. Jiménez De Arechaga, 'International Law in the Past Third of a Century', 159 *RdC* (1978–I) 1, p. 21; K. Wolfke, *supra* note II-156, p. 65.

[133] *Nicaragua case*, Merits, *infra* note IV-2, esp. p. 109. G. J. H. van Hoof, *supra* note II-166, p. 101, further points out that 'what only *opinio juris* can do, only *opinio juris* can undo'.

Beginning with the so-called subjective element, several factors greatly reduce the significance of the above-mentioned cases as manifestations of *opinio juris* for the purpose of modification or desuetude of the rule under examination. In the first place, until the Kosovo crisis, States resorting to force relied, in alternative or in addition to the Security Council authorisation, on other legal grounds.

The argument that overwhelming humanitarian necessity could exceptionally amount to a circumstance permitting the use of unilateral force in spite of the general ban embodied in Art. 2(4) of the Charter, in particular, was advanced by the United Kingdom with regard to *Operation Provide Comfort*, the enforcement of the no-fly zones, and the military intervention in Kosovo. Only in the later instance was this argument shared by other States.

Self-defence, in turn, was invoked by ECOWAS Member States, with the endorsement of the UN Secretary General, in the context of the Liberian crisis, as well as by the US-led coalition to justify the intervention in Afghanistan. A rather awkward claim to self-defence was also advanced with regard to the coercive operations carried out to enforce the no-fly zones in Iraq. The plea could be accepted only if the forces were lawfully operating in Iraqi airspace, a condition that is far from being satisfied precisely because of the fact that the enforcement action had not been authorised by the Security Council.

Additionally, in some cases the military action was described by the Security Council as having a peaceful character and being based upon the request or with the consent of the territorial government or the belligerent parties. This occurred in respect of the crises in Liberia and Sierra Leone, albeit that the existence, validity and genuineness of the request or consent of the parties was on some occasions doubtful.

In the second place, and more importantly, at least until the Kosovo crisis, the State resorting to force invoked the Security Council authorisation as the legal ground of their coercive military action. Although such a claim was often improper, the systematic reliance on the Security Council authorisation demonstrates the legal consciousness of Member States that non-defensive action could be lawfully be undertaken solely when so authorised. This deprives these cases of any value for the purpose of downgrading the Security Council authorisation from a legal requirement to a matter of political convenience. The controversies over the use of force in this period, in fact, did not concern the necessity of obtaining Security Council authorisation before using military force. Rather, they concerned the alleged existence of such an authorisation, the observance of its limits, or its continuing validity.

The question of the lawfulness of *Operation Provide Comfort* depended on the authorisation of the use of force allegedly granted by the Security Council in Resolution 688. In the case of *Operation Deliberate Force*, the invocation of Resolution 836 raised problems not with regard to the existence of the authorisation – which was undisputed – but rather to the observance of its substantial and procedural limits. The divergences on the lawfulness of the military operations carried out in and against Iraq, in turn, regarded principally whether Resolution 678 was still in force.

However improper the reliance on Security Council authorisation was, the attitude of concerned States reveals no intention to challenge the exclusive authority of the Security Council – except in the hypotheses of self-defence and arguably intervention on humanitarian grounds – temporally to suspend the observance of Art. 2(4) of the Charter. Quite to the contrary, they could be referred to as demonstrations that during the period under examination States continued to consider that obtaining a valid Security Council authorisation was *conditio sine qua non* for the lawful use military force for non-defensive purposes.[134]

A change in the *opinio juris* could eventually be detected in the positions maintained by certain States with regard to the recent interventions in Kosovo and Iraq. Until then, the States that had resorted to military force had relied – often on the basis of spurious arguments – upon Security Council resolutions allegedly authorising the use of force. In the Kosovo crisis, no consistent attempt was made by NATO Member States to base their action upon Security Council resolutions authorising the use of force. Alongside the humanitarian argument, for the first time they claimed the right to use force to enforce the Security Council resolutions in order to tackle a situation declared by that organ to represent a threat to international peace and security, even in the absence of a Security Council authorisation. The attitude of France, and in particular its *revirement* on the legal necessity to obtain the authorisation from the Security Council before resorting to force, is paradigmatic.[135]

During the 2003 crisis in Iraq, the challenge was essentially confined to the United States and the United Kingdom. The former claimed the right to use force whenever this was deemed necessary to protect its national security. Such a right was considered as independent from the other principal argument invoked to support the lawfulness of the military action, namely the continuing authorisation of the use of force provided by Resolution 678. This can be deduced from the admission that it was impossible to obtain a new resolution from the Security Council – which in a sense contradicts the view that the use of force was already permitted under the authority of the Security Council – coupled with the commitment to act unilaterally as long as the Security Council does not live up to its responsibilities.[136] In spite of certain differences, the United Kingdom put forward a substantially similar claim. It stressed with insistence that the action was permitted insofar as it was directed at enforcing previous Security Council resolutions, although that organ had stopped short of authorising the resort to force.

The two States remained rather isolated in openly challenging the rule that hinged the lawfulness of the use of force on the Security Council authorisation. The few States that supported that military action against Iraq, and especially

[134] According to the International Court of Justice, this attitude would strengthen rather than weaken the general prohibition to use force: see *Nicaragua case*, Merits, infra note IV-2, p. 98.

[135] See *supra* notes 77 and 82.

[136] *Address to the Nation*, *supra* note 111.

Australia, Spain and Italy, attempted to save the Security Council authority through the – rather unconvincing – theory of reviviscence of Resolution 678.[137]

In the third place, in some cases States have stressed the exceptionality of the circumstances in which the military actions took place and expressly excluded that they constituted a precedent that could contribute to the evolution of the rules governing the use of force in international law. However difficult it is to interpret the attitude of States, a distinction has to be made between intentional but occasional violations of a rule, and deliberate challenges to it aimed at its modification or abandonment. In the first case, the States acting in contrast with the norm continue to consider themselves bound by the norm, and are aware that their conduct amounts to an international wrongful act. As to the consequences, they hope that their conduct will be tolerated on the basis of extra-legal considerations, although they are probably prepared to face the possible reaction by other States under the law of State responsibility. At the normative level, however, they do not intend to affect in any way the value of the norm. In the second case, in contrast, the acting States show their disaffection for the existing law and test the reaction of the other States to its violation as well as their readiness to concur in, or at least acquiesce in, a process of change or desuetude.[138]

The Kosovo crisis falls into the first category. NATO Member States made any effort to get as close as possible to legality[139] and reaffirmed their commitment to the existing rules on the use of force. They also underlined that the intervention was to be considered as exceptional and did not bear any normative value nor raise any normative expectations.[140]

These considerations lead to the conclusion that no sufficient *opinio juris* has yet surfaced as to the modification of the rule requiring Security Council authorisation for the lawful resort to force apart from the case of self-defence. Indeed, just a very few States – and only in the last few years – have ceased to share such a legal conviction. As a result, the subjective element is far from being satisfied.

This alone, however, is not enough to affirm that the authorisation is still to be treated as a legal requirement – rather than a matter of political expediency – with regard to the use of force by Member States. Without arriving at denying any relevance to the subjective element, thus reducing the processes of change or desuetude to a matter of frequency and relevance of the contrary practice,[141] it can

[137] For the positions of Spain, Italy and Australia, see *supra* note 113.

[138] On the testing function of violations of international law, see M. W. Reisman, 'International Lawmaking: A Process of Communication', 75 *ASIL Proc.* (1983) 101, p. 111.

[139] See B. Simma, *supra* note 68.

[140] See, in particular, the positions of the German Foreign Minister before the Parliament, *Deutscher Bundestag*, Plenarprotokol 13/248, 16 October 1998, 23129, quoted in B. Simma, *supra* note 68, p. 13; and that of the Italian Under Secretary in Declaration before the Parliamentary Foreign Affairs Commission, 204[a] meeting, 12 May 1999, at http://notes3.senato.it/ODG_NSF/38b2113f.

[141] In this sense M. Weisburd, 'Customary International Law: The Problem of Treaties', 21 *VJTL* (1988) 1, p. 33.

safely be admitted that what States actually do is certainly more important than what they declare. It is normal that when breaching international law States attempt to prove that their behaviour is consistent with existing international law.[142] When no coherent and plausible legal rationale is provided by acting States, the material element has to be privileged and the *opinio juris* looked for in their concrete acts rather than in their formal documents or declarations.[143] Besides, when the norm to be changed has a restrictive character, such as the norm conditioning the use of force to the Security Council's authorisation, 'an express claim that States are entitled to act in a particular way is not necessary: it can be inferred from the fact that they do act in that way'.[144]

It is therefore appropriate to consider the relevant State practice also from the perspective of the objective element, bearing in mind that the modification or the desuetude of a norm requires a widespread State practice incompatible with the existing rule.[145] In the cases examined above, very few States have been actively involved in the military operations conducted without a valid Security Council authorisation. The Kosovo intervention witnessed the widest participation with all NATO Member States concurring in the decision to use force and most of them directly contributing to the military effort. In other important cases, namely in the aftermath of the Iraq–Kuwait crisis, the force was used by the United States, the United Kingdom and, occasionally, France. The recent intervention in Iraq, finally, was essentially an Anglo-American initiative.

For the purpose of modifying an existing norm, however, the material conduct contrary to it does not need to be widespread. Such a result could be achieved even if only a limited number of States actually behave in a way incompatible with the existing norm, provided that the generality of the other States support this behaviour or at least acquiesce in it.

This certainly has not occurred with regard to the norm under examination. In the recent major crises, resort to force not duly authorised by the Security Council met the firm and explicit condemnation of the overwhelming majority of States. Suffice it to recall the magnitude of the protest to the air strikes conducted against Iraq in 1998, the intervention in Kosovo and the recent invasion of Iraq. It must also be stressed that in the last case, the opposition was remarkably not only in quantitative terms but from a geo-political point of view as it included several NATO Member States as well as many other Western States.

[142] J. Brierly, *The Law of Nations*, 6th ed. (Oxford: Clarendon Press, 1963), pp. 69–70.

[143] A. D'Amato, 'Reply to Letter of Michael Akehurst', 80 *AJIL* (1986) 148, p. 149, warns against focusing too much on *opinio juris* since States 'may assert that even the most blatantly illegal acts are consistent with a rule of international law'. See also A. M. Weisburd, *Use of Force. The Practice of States Since World War II* (Pennsylvania: Pennsylvania State University, 1999), p. 23.

[144] M. Akehurst, 'Custom as a Source of International Law', 47 *BYIL* (1974–5) 1, p. 38.

[145] E. Jiménez De Arechaga, *supra* note 132, p. 21, observes that 'nothing prevents an established rule of custom from becoming extinct if an increasingly extended state practice contradicts it'.

These cases seems to clearly outweigh those in which the use of force has been substantially tolerated, namely the use of force related to the no-fly zone established in Iraq, the air strikes conducted against Iraq in 1993, and the military actions undertaken by ECOWAS forces without a valid Security Council resolution or beyond their limits.[146] *Operation Deliberate Force*, finally, must be singled out. In that case, the majority of States accepted the lawfulness of the operations, although certain others, and particularly the Russian Federation and China, protested in the strongest terms. The general attitude was influenced by contingent considerations, including the facts that the military operations were directed against a non-State entity, permitted to avoid the already planned withdrawal of UNPROFOR, and put an end to an intractable conflict.

Therefore, it can safely be excluded that a change of existing law has occurred in the sense of rendering the Security Council authorisation not indispensable. At best, it could be said that a process of modification has been ignited. The picture would not be different even assuming that no longer general, uniform and constant State practice may be sufficient to bring about the modification or extinction of the norm.[147] This view is debatable insofar as it does not adequately take into account the legally protected interests of the States respectful of the rule – which could still represent a significant part of the international community and even be the majority. This would undermine the *consuetude servanda est* rule which, since the inception of the international legal system, has served as basic rule alongside with *pacta sunt servanda*.[148] In any case, even applying this lower standard, it is impossible to affirm the change or desuetude of the norm under consideration because of the fact that the practice of the overwhelming majority of the States is still consistent with the norm.

The Kosovo and Iraqi crises witnessed the emergence, within a significant segment of the international community, of the *opinio necessitatis* that existing law conditioning the use of force to the Security Council authorisation ought to evolve with regard to certain situations strictly defined. Such an *opinio necessitatis* may play a pivotal role for the development of customary international law and the Charter regarding collective security.[149] In this initial phase of this process, the

[146] In particular, the coercive operations carried out on the territory of Sierra Leone – being unrelated to Res. 1132 – had never been authorised in any form by the Security Council. See K. Nowrot and E. W. Schabacker, 'The Use of Force to Restore Democracy: International Legal Implications of the ECOWAS Intervention in Sierra Leone', 14 *AUILR* (1998) 373, p. 365; V. Grado, 'Il ristabilimento della democrazia in Sierra Leone', 83 *RDI* (2000) 360, pp. 388 *et seq*.

[147] In this sense, see M. E. Villiger, *supra* note II-156, p. 55.

[148] A. Miele, *supra* note II-161, p. 88, considers these rules as necessarily pre-existing the system, and notes that neither any demonstration of their validity nor any explicit acceptance had ever been indispensable.

[149] See, in particular, A. Cassese, 'A Follow-Up: Forcible Humanitarian Countermeasures and *Opinio Necessitatis*', 9 *EJIL* (1999) 791.

behaviour contrary to the existing norm unavoidably amounts to illegal acts.[150] When such behaviour is gradually shared or tolerated by the generality of States and considered as compulsory under, or compatible with, international law, it becomes the new rule.

Being a matter of degree rather than kind, a period during which the law is a state of flux cannot be ruled out. Until the proposal for change put forward by these States gathers the consent or acquiescence of the generality of the members of the international community, the norms in this area may suffer from a degree of legal uncertainty. Deducing from such a legal uncertainty the non-existence of any rule prohibiting the use of force is not entirely convincing.[151] What needs to be demonstrated is precisely to what extent the challenge to the existing norm has been successful. The analysis must therefore focus primarily on the process of claims and counter-claims of the subjects of international law – to which considerations of power and even economic bargain are certainly not extraneous.[152] It is the progressive erosion of the resistance opposed by the States reluctant to change that may lead to the development of existent customary norms.[153] This critical phase and the tension between the two stands may persist for some time and may pass through an intermediate phase, when the conduct envisaged in the new claim is tolerated,[154] possibly on the basis of considerations of legitimacy.

The argument that such a normative change has not yet taken place is even more compelling if the general ban on the use of force – except the cases of

[150] E. Giraud, 'Le droit positif, ses rapports avec la philosophie et la politique', in *Hommage d'une génération de juristes au Président Basdevant* (Paris: Pédone, 1960), pp. 210 *et seq*., p. 233, observes that 'le fait qu'une règle de droit a subi des violations graves et répétées ne suffit à l'abolir. Toutes règles de droit sont destinées à être violées. Mais tant que la règle de droit a conservé sa valeur, ces violations suscitent des réactions telles que mesures de répression à l'égard des violateurs, représailles, protestations qui attestent le caractère anormal et illicite de la violation. Au contraire quand la règle paraît perdue de vue ou quand une pratique contraire à la règle se généralise, la règle en question a cessé de faire partie du droit positif'.

[151] M. J. Glennon, *Limits of Law, Prerogatives of Power. Interventionism After Kosovo* (New York: Palgrave, 2001), pp. 45 and 63.

[152] The importance of the contribution of Great Power to the development of customary international law has rightly been stressed by C. De Visscher, *Theory and Reality of Public International Law*, 2nd ed. (Princeton: Princeton University Press, 1956), p. 154, who underlines that 'every international custom is the work of power'. In the context of the law of the sea, see H. Lauterpacht, *supra* note II-169, p. 394.

[153] The development of the norms governing fishery zones provides an interesting example. See, in particular, the attitude of the UK that, after vigorously opposing the Icelandic claims to a 200-mile exclusive fishery zone, advanced a similar claim; D. J. Harris, *Cases and Materials on International Law*, 5th ed. (London: Sweet & Maxwell, 1998), pp. 446–7.

[154] Introducing a *tertium genus* between *lex lata* and *lex ferenda*, as suggested by M. E. Villiger, *supra* note II-156, p. 54, would not eliminate or reduce the uncertainty which would continue to characterise the passages between *lex ferenda* to *tertium genus* to *lex lata*.

self-defence and Security Council authorisation – is considered as a peremptory norm. The notion of peremptory norm is still struggling to find its place in the international legal order.[155] However, there is no doubt that a change in a peremptory norm cannot be brought about by less than an overwhelming acceptance by the subjects of international law.[156] Such a threshold has clearly not even approached with regard to the norm prohibiting the use of force.

The inadmissibility of *ex post facto* authorisations

Leaving aside for the moment the right of self-defence and without prejudice to the possible emergence of other exceptions to Art. 2(4),[157] it is submitted that the use of force is permitted only if authorised beforehand and expressly by the Security Council.

State practice hardly supports the admissibility of *ex post facto* authorisations. The only possible cases of *ex post facto* authorisation concern the military coercive operations undertaken in the context of the crises in Liberia and Sierra Leone.[158] Even these precedents, however, are of limited importance. In Liberia, the significance of the authorisation of the use of force is reduced by the fact that the ECOWAS operations action were allegedly undertaken with the consent of the concerned parties and, more importantly, were qualified by the Security Council and most of its members as peace-keeping operations. With regard to Sierra Leone, the naval coercive measures decided on and undertaken by ECOWAS had been authorised by the Security Council when they were underway, not afterwards.[159] Resolution 1132, additionally, is not exempt from ambiguity, considering that ECOWAS forces were supposed to co-operate with the democratically elected – although ineffective – Government. Finally, in both cases the authorisation was addressed to a regional organisation.

Apart from these possible exceptions, Security Council practice offers no cases of *ex post facto* authorisation.[160] Resolutions 1031, 1203, 1244 and 1511 do not

[155] On Art. 29(2) of the 1996 Draft Articles on State Responsibility, the British Government observed that 'The uncertainty which continues to surround the content of the category of *jus cogens*, and the lack of any practical mechanism for resolving that uncertainty, make the provision impractical'. 69 BYIL (1998) 555.

[156] N. D. White, *supra* note II-184, p. 19 observes that 'When practice is apparently violative of a peremptory norm, it is not enough to have acquiescence in the face of the violation in order to establish a new or extended right. It is argued that there needs to be more positive acceptance of the claim, positive proof in other words of *opinio juris*'.

[157] On the unilateral and joint use of force, see *infra* Chapters 4 and 5.

[158] See Res. 788, *supra* note 36 and Res. 1132, *supra* note 60.

[159] A. L. Sicilianos, 'L'autorisation par le Conseil de sécurité de recourir à la force: une tentative d'évaluation', 106 *RGDIP* (2002) 5, p. 41, is rightly reluctant to admit that the resolution had effect *ex tunc*.

[160] In literature, the admissibility of such an authorisation has been maintained, in particular, by C. Walter, 'Security Council Control over Regional Action', 1 *MPYUNL* (1997)

contain any *ex post facto* authorisation with regard to *Operation Deliberate Force*, NATO threat to use force and actual intervention in Kosovo or the intervention in Iraq. The reason is quite simple: on all these occasions the Security Council was prevented from taking any position as to the necessity and lawfulness of the military initiatives, either in the sense of authorising – or rather approving – them, or of condemning them. Because of the insurmountable contrasts existing among its permanent members, it could merely acknowledge the *fait accompli*, support the outcome of these initiatives, and attempt to restore – to the extent that it was possible – its authority in the post-conflict or post-confrontation environment.

This is particularly manifest in relation to the interventions in Kosovo and Iraq. In the first case, Resolution 1244 cannot be seen as a retrospective endorsement of NATO bombings.[161] The Russian Federation's and China's firm opposition persisted throughout the crisis, as demonstrated by their vehement protest against NATO expressed during the debate leading to the adoption of Resolution 1244. This categorically precludes that the Security Council has ever authorised the use of force by NATO forces. The resolution merely recognised the *fait accompli* [162] and amounted to little more than a damage limitation exercise.

Similar considerations can be made with regard to the recent Iraqi crisis. The overwhelming majority of States, including three permanent members of the Security Council, repeatedly and unambiguously expressed their opposition to the use of force. Without modifying their position as to the illegality of the intervention, they eventually opted for a diplomatic and constructive approach. Aware of the devastating effect that the unilateral military action had on the collective security system, they preferred not to exacerbate the political and legal confrontation in order to restore a consensus within the Security Council unity and permit it to assume and fulfil its responsibility in the management of the post-conflict Iraq and the maintenance of international peace in the region.[163] Certainly this cannot be treated as the slightest form of approval or acquiescence.

129, p. 177; B. Simma, *supra* note 68, p. 4. U. Villani, 'The Security Council's Authorization of Enforcement Action by Regional Organizations', 6 *MPYUNL* (2002) 535, pp. 556–7 suggests the reversal of the burden of proof. If in case of prior authorisation the lawfulness of the action is to be presumed, in case of *ex-post facto* authorisation, it is for the State resorting to force to demonstrate it.

[161] See N. Ronzitti, '*Raids* aerei contro la Repubblica federale di Iugoslavia e Carta delle Nazioni Unite', 82 *RDI.* (1999) 476, pp. 481 *et seq.*; P. Picone, 'La "guerra del Kosovo" e il diritto internazionale generale', 83 *RDI* (2000) 309, pp. 350 *et seq.*; N. White, 'The Legality of Bombing in the Name of Humanity', 5 *JCSL* (2000) 27, p. 32; H. Neuhold, 'Collective Security After "Operation Allied Force"', 4 *MPYUNL* (2000) 73, p. 100. *Contra*, see L. Henkin, 'Kosovo and the Law of "Humanitarian Intervention"', 93 *AJIL* (1999) 824, p. 826, according to whom the resolution 'effectively ratified the NATO action and gave it the Council's support'; R. Redgwood, 'NATO's Campaign in Yugoslavia', 93 *AJIL* (1999) 828, p. 830.

[162] F. Francioni, 'Of War, Humanity and Justice: International Law After Kosovo', 4 *MPYUNL* (2000) 107, p. 116.

[163] See, in particular, the views expressed during the debate by the Russian Federation, Germany, France and China, S/PV. 4844, 16 October 2003, respectively pp. 2, 3, 4 and 5.

The recognition made in Resolution 1483 of the obligations of the occupying States, in turn, does not imply any judgement on the lawfulness of the intervention. Occupation law applies, regardless of the action that led to the occupation, whenever a territory is actually placed under the authority of a hostile army.[164]

In addition to the absence of significant precedents and the evident risk of abuses,[165] the following theoretical considerations preclude the admissibility of the *ex post facto* authorisation. To start with, this kind of authorisation would contradict the rationale of the collective security system as the Security Council was meant to tackle ongoing situations threatening international peace and security.[166] The authorisation practice reserved to the Security Council at least the assessment of the necessity of the military action and the definition of the objectives and limits of the operations. Such an assessment cannot but have a preventive character.

Accepting that the Security Council authorisation could have a permissive effect with regard to measures already unilaterally undertaken by Member States or regional organisations would mean that the Security Council could modify *retroactively* the legal situation existing between the concerned parties.[167] In particular, the eventual exercise of individual or collective self-defence to resist these measures would be lawful until the adoption of the resolution approving them, but would become unlawful afterwards.

The authorisation *ex post facto*, therefore, would be in contrast with the principle of intertemporal law and the rules governing State responsibility. On the one hand, the lawfulness of an act has to be established by applying the law existing at the time of its commission, which in this case means without considering the authorisation granted *ex post facto*.[168] On the other hand, the authorisation can be invoked as a circumstance precluding the international wrongful act only if it existed at the time of the allegedly permitted use of force.

Serious problems could arise if either the legality of the initial use of force to be authorised or the claim of self-defence in response to it is submitted to

[164] Art. 42 of the 1907 Hague Regulations Respecting the Laws and Customs of War on Land (2 *AJIL* Suppl. (1908) 90) and Article 2 common to the 1949 Geneva Conventions (75 *UNTS* 31).

[165] These risks were already indicated, with regard to Art. 53 of the Charter, by M. Akehurst, 'Enforcement Action by Regional Agencies, with Special Reference to the Organisation of American States', 42 *BYIL* (1967) 175, pp. 214 *et seq*.

[166] In this sense, see M. Kohen, 'The Use of Force by the United States after the End of the Cold War and its Impact on International Law', in M. Byers and G. Nolte, *United States Hegemony and the Foundations of International Law* (Cambridge: Cambridge University Press, 2003), pp. 197 *et seq*., p. 217.

[167] O. Corten and F. Dubuisson, 'L'hypothèse d'une règle émergente fondant une intervention militaire sur un "autorisation implicite" du Conseil de sécurité', 104 *RGDIP* (2000) 873, p. 906.

[168] On the notion of intertemporal law, see *Island of Palmas*, Award of 4 April 1928, 2 RIAA (1949) 829.

adjudication, especially if this occurs before the concession of the authorisation.[169] The Security Council would find it extremely difficult to grant its authorisation if meanwhile an international tribunal has ordered, presumably as provisional measures, the cessation of the hostilities, or has considered as unlawful the use of force under consideration before the Security Council. Should such an order or decision be issued by the International Court of Justice, an institutional crisis within the United Nations would be unavoidable.[170]

Apart from the hypothesis of judicial proceedings, the Security Council would face quite an embarrassing situation should it receive from a State information about the exercise of right to self-defence, as required under Art. 51, while is considering whether to authorise the use of force that had triggered such an exercise.

The inadmissibility of implied authorisations

A question germane to the authorisation *ex post facto* concerns the admissibility of implied authorisations. It has been argued that the Security Council authorisation can be deduced from the conduct of that organ, without the adoption of a resolution containing a formal permission to take coercive military measures being necessary.

The argument is spurious. The authorisation needs not only to be granted beforehand but also be expressed in sufficiently clear terms. Normally when the Security Council intends to authorise the use of force it does so in quite a straightforward way. Hence, the resolution is adopted under Chapter VII of the Charter and contains one or more operative paragraphs in which the Security Council invites, authorises or calls upon Member States to take coercive measures proportionate to the objectives they aim to achieve.

Jargon expressions are often used to overcome the disinclination of some members to more explicit references to the use of military force. Yet, they not undermine the clarity of the resolution provided that it is possible, on the basis of the declarations made during the debate before the Security Council and of any other relevant conclusive acts, to establish a generally accepted interpretation of the expression. The expression 'all necessary means', which was several times unanimously referred to as including military measures, is an useful example.

[169] Furthermore, R. Y. Jennings, 'International Force and the International Court of Justice', in A. Cassese (ed.), *supra* note I-5, pp. 323 *et seq*., p. 330 observes that 'force, even lawful and justifiable force, should not be undertaken in respect of a matter which is *sub judice*'.

[170] In the *Nicaragua case*, Jurisdiction, *infra* note IV-1, p. 433, the ICJ held 'the view that the fact that a matter is before the Security Council should not prevent it being dealt with by the Court and that both proceedings could be pursued *pari passu*'. See also the *Genocide case*, *supra* note I-7; and *Case Concerning Armed Activities on the Territory of Congo* (Democratic Republic of the Congo *v*. Uganda), Provisional Measures, Order of 1 July 2000, para. 36.

Ambiguous resolutions are to be treated with the utmost prudence. Unless the debate or any other conclusive acts support the view that the Security Council intended to authorise the use of force, no permissive effect with regard to Art. 2(4) can be attributed to the resolution. This is clearly excluded when there is evidence – both in the debates before the Security Council and in declarations made inside and outside the United Nations – of the contrasts among the permanent members, as it was the case of the crises in Kosovo and Iraq.

It is also impossible to deduce the intention of the Security Council to authorise the use of force from the lack of its condemnation, and in particular, from the non-adoption of a resolution requiring the cessation of the hostilities, or the mere acknowledgement of the *fait accompli*. Both hypotheses occurred during the Kosovo crisis. The failed adoption of the draft resolution submitted on 26 March, in particular, cannot be treated as an implied authorisation.[171] The argument that, under certain circumstances, Member States, instead of seeking the authorisation from the Security Council, could unilaterally resort to force and subsequently neutralise the attempts of other States to obtain from that organ the order to terminate the action cannot be accepted.[172] It would foul the *ratio* behind Art. 27(3) of the Charter and rebuff the collective nature of the Security Council decisions. What is described as a 'shift of the burden of the veto', is in reality an unacceptable 'double reverse veto' in the sense that a single permanent member could not only prevent the Security Council from withdrawing an authorisation to use force (reverse veto), but also be allowed the use of force that was never authorised – nor condemned – by the Security Council.

In the context of the recent Iraqi crisis, it has also been argued that Resolution 1441 did not contemplate any 'automaticity' in the sense of immediately allowing the use of force, but affirmed that a new finding on material breach would have triggered the reviviscence of Resolution 678, without any further decision by the Security Council being necessary.[173] This line of reasoning relies upon literal arguments, and in particular on the fact that the Security Council would have *considered* the matter rather than *decided* what was needed to restore international peace.[174] It ends up with providing an interpretation which does not reflect the real positions existing within the Security Council.

[171] In the *Namibia case*, *supra* note I-28, p. 36, the Court made it clear that the failure to adopt a proposal does not necessarily imply a collective pronouncement in a sense opposite to that proposed.

[172] In the criticised sense, see L. Henkin, *supra* note 161, p. 827 On the value of this argument from the standpoint of legitimacy, see *infra* text corresponding to notes 191 *et seq*.

[173] The further observation made by the US that the resolution 'did not constrain any member to use force' is at best a truism considering that such an obligation does not exist, not even in respect to military operations decided upon and undertaken by the Security Council: see *supra* text corresponding to note II-36.

[174] See the position of the UK Attorney General, *supra* note 117.

Resolution 1441 warned Iraq that that any further failure to comply with disarmament obligations would be reported to the Security Council – which accordingly remained seised of the matter (para. 14) – for an *assessment* (para. 4) which could have led to the serious consequences, presumably the use of force upon authorised by the Security Council in a new resolution (para. 13). The intention to make the use of force dependent on a further collective decision based on a collective assessment of the attitude of the Iraqi Government is clear.[175]

The 'legislative history' of the resolution amply confirms this conclusion. The draft prepared on 2 October by the United States and the United Kingdom, which in case of material breach would have expressly authorised 'Member States to use all necessary means to restore international peace and security in the region'[176] was not even submitted to a formal vote because of the insurmountable opposition of several members.[177]

As is often the case, the resolution is the result of compromises which imposed mutual concessions at the expenses of the clarity and linearity of the text. It is nonetheless evident from the debates before the Security Council and the documents adopted at the national and international levels that several members of the Security Council – including three permanent members and probably representing the majority of the membership – were at all relevant times openly opposed to the use of force. Under the circumstances, attributing to the Security Council the will to allow the use of force without a further decision simply does not correspond to reality.[178]

The question of implicit authorisation, therefore, is nothing more than a question of interpretation of the relevant resolutions. What the interpreter is supposed

[175] The Legal Department of the Ministry of Foreign Affairs of the Russian Federation, *Legal Assessment of the Use of Force Against Iraq*, 52 *ICLQ* (2003) 1059, has observed that 'the whole mechanism of control and assessment with its obligations under the Security Council resolution is concentrated in accordance with resolution 1441 at the disposal of the Security Council'. In literature see, in particular, V. Lowe, 'The Iraq Crisis: What Now?', 52 *ICLQ* (2003) 859, pp. 856–7; R. Wolfrum, 'The Attack of September 11 2001, the Wars against the Taliban and Iraq: Is There a Need to Reconsider International Law on the Recourse of Force and the Rules on Armed Conflict?', 7 *MPYUNL* (2003) 1, pp. 14 *et seq*.

[176] Text posted at www.casi.org.uk/info/usukdraftscr021002.htlm.

[177] As noted by Fitzmaurice, dis. op., *Legal Consequences for States of the Continued Presence of South Africa in Namibia (South West Africa)*, Advisory Opinion, *ICJ Rep. 1971*, p. 56, at p. 275, 'Where a particular proposal has been considered and rejected, for whatever reason, it is not possible to interpret the instrument or juridical situation to which the proposal related as if the latter has in fact been adopted'. In general, see M. C. Wood, 'The Interpretation of Security Council Resolutions', 2 *MPYUNL* (1998) 73.

[178] In order to dissipate any possible doubt, on the very same day of the adoption of Res. 1441, France, the Russian Federation and China issued *Joint Declaration* pointing out that no use of force would have been lawful without a further Security Council authorisation (available at www.iraqwatch.org). In the same sense, see the Statements on Iraq made by France, Russia and Germany on 5 and 15 March 2003, available at http://special.diplomatie.fr.

to do is to ascertain whether the elements at its disposal – principally the text of the resolution and subsidiarily the debate leading to it and any other relevant documents – demonstrate beyond any reasonable doubt the will of the Security Council to authorise, in accordance with its own voting procedure, the resort to force.

Challenging the rule

The real challenge to the norm conditioning the lawfulness of the use of force on the authorisation by the Security Council comes neither from *ex post facto* nor from implicit authorisation. It is rather posed by the claim advanced by certain States militarily to enforce, under certain circumstance, Security Council resolutions without being formally authorised to do so. It would be sufficient, for the purpose of lawful resort to force, that the Security Council had determined the non-compliance with certain mandatory resolutions it had adopted with regard to a situation which continued to threaten international peace and security. Accordingly, Member States would be allowed to use all necessary means – including coercive measures – to put an end to the material breaches of the resolutions established by the Security Council itself.

From a practical point of view, it must be noted that this theory does not imply a better functioning of the authorisation technique. If the determination of a material breach could have a permissive effect, the State contrary to the military option will presumably oppose such a determination as otherwise they would have opposed the authorisation to use force. Seeing the problem from another perspective, one can safely assume that if there is no significant opposition the Security Council will take the next logical step and authorise in good and due form the military action. Member States are normally eager to obtain a mandate from the United Nations not only to dispel any doubt about the lawfulness of their action and disqualify any possible international claim, but also to facilitate the parliamentary approval of their action and appease public opinion.

As to the determination that a State is not acting in compliance with mandatory resolutions, the performance by the Security Council of judicial or quasi-judicial functions is undoubtedly problematic. Although it is perfectly admissible and indeed desirable that a political organ makes a judicial determination when necessary to the performance of its own functions,[179] it must not be forgotten that the Security Council is unfit to act as a court in terms of independence and impartiality, and was never intended to act as such.[180]

[179] See the *Namibia case*, *supra* note I-28, p. 49.

[180] During the discussion within the ILC, G. Arangio-Ruiz stressed that 'although the Security Council had the right to take measures to put an end to the fighting, it was not empowered to settle disputes or to impose a solution to a dispute' (44 *YBILC* (1992–I) p. 91). See also R. Higgins, 'The Place of International Law in the Settlement of Disputes by the Security Council', 64 *AJIL* (1970) 1; K. Harper, 'Does the United Nations Security

But this is neither the only nor the main problem. The International Court of Justice or international tribunal could subsequently find that the concerned State was in fact complying with the relevant Security Council resolutions, or that circumstances not depending on its will had prevented it from fully doing so.

Even assuming that the Security Council determination is not challenged before or is upheld by a judicial body, the fundamental problem is that the theory under examination is deliberately directed at neutralising the Security Council voting procedure, as was clear in the recent Iraq crisis. Although virtually all States condemned the material breaches of Iraqi disarmament obligations, diametrically opposed views emerged within the Security Council as to the consequences of such breaches. According to some States, the Security Council was effectively discharging its responsibilities and resort to military force – although not excluded – was for the time being considered as premature. For other States, unilateral action was needed and permitted because of the failure of the Security Council to enforce its own injunctions.

As a result, attributing a permissive effect to the determination of the commission of material breaches would overlook the fact that the overwhelming majority of States expressly ruled out the immediate use of force and reserved to the Security Council the exclusive competence to authorise it. In this regard, only a positive assessment by the Security Council of the ineluctability of the military option would have rendered lawful the use of force against Iraq.

The argument that, under Art. 60(2)(a) of the Vienna Convention on the Law of Treaties, Member States could invoke the Security Council determination of the material breaches committed by Iraq to suspend the application of Art. 2(4) of the Charter in their relations with Iraq is not convincing.[181] The indivisible character of the obligation stemming from Art. 2(4) makes it impossible for Member States to resort to force under the law of the treaties.[182] States can certainly take the measures they deem appropriate to react to what they and the Security Council perceive as serious violations of Iraqi disarmament obligations. They do so at their own risk, in the sense that it is not possible to equate the Security Council determination with a judicial finding. These measures, in any event, cannot amount to non-respect of *erga omnes* obligations, such as those deriving from Art. 2(4).

Council have the Competence to Act as a Court and Legislature?', 27 *NYUJILP* (1994–5) 103, pp. 105–6; F. L Kirgis, 'The Security Council's First Fifty Years', 89 *AJIL* (1995) 506, pp. 527 *et seq*.; U. Villani, 'Sul ruolo quasi giudiziario del Consiglio di sicurezza', 51 *CI* (1996) 25; K. Zemanek, 'Is the Security Council the Judge of its own Legality?', in E. Yapko and T. Boumedra (eds.), *Liber Amicorum M. Bedjaoui* (The Hague: Kluwer, 1999) 629, p. 630.

[181] See also F. Kirgis, 'Security Council Resolution 1441 on Iraq's Final Opportunity to Comply with Disarmament Obligations', *ASIL Insight*, November 2002. A reference to Art. 60(3) was made by Ireland before the Security Council (S/PV.4644, 8 November 2002, p. 8).

[182] See *supra*, pp. 20–2.

In this sense, Art. 60(2)(a) applies only if all United Nations members exercise their right to suspend the operation of such a norm in the relations between themselves and the allegedly defaulting State. In this case, it is the decision of all Member States to deprive the concerned State of the legal protection afforded by Art. 2(4) – and not the determination on the material breach – that produces the permissive effect.[183]

The attempted dismantling of the collective security system

The common feature of the cases examined above is the negative impact they had, in different ways and degrees, upon the collective security system and the limited centralised control over the use of force ensured by the authorisation practice. In the Bosnian conflict, in particular, NATO Member States resorted to the *escamotage* of the memorandum of understanding with UNPROFOR military commander in order to bypass the Security Council. In the aftermath of the Gulf crisis, the theory of reviviscence of Resolution 678 hid the attempt to further erode the Security Council authority. In the Kosovo and the recent Iraq crises, the repudiation of the Security Council authority was more evident. The case of Afghanistan, finally, must be singled out.

The last three cases deserve a closer scrutiny. In the Kosovo crisis, in particular, we assisted to the attempt to shift from a paradigm on the use of force based exclusively on legal arguments to one open to considerations of legitimacy.[184] In this perspective, States could exceptionally disregard the norm prohibiting the use of non-defensive military force without a Security Council authorisation, provided that its application would lead to an absurd result, namely unacceptable humanitarian suffering. It has been argued that legitimacy could be assessed objectively without reliance on moral or philosophical values,[185] through 'a process able to weight considerations of legality against the common public sense of legitimacy'.[186] Even assuming that the test of legitimacy can be so applied, the

[183] Such a decision would have been alternative to the Security Council resolution. In any case, a unilateral action is excluded. In general, according to H. Waldock, *2nd Report on the Law of Treaties*, 15 *YBILC* (1963–II) 36, p. 77, any question of terminating or suspending the operation of a provision of a constituent treaty of an international Organisation 'must be one for the competent organ of the Organisation and not for the individual parties to the treaty'.

[184] See, in particular, the Independent International Commission on Kosovo, *The Kosovo Report* (Oxford: Oxford University Press, 2000), p. 164. In the same sense, see T. Franck, *Recourse to Force. State Action Against Threat and Armed Attacks* (Cambridge: Cambridge University Press, 2002), pp. 163 *et seq.* and pp. 181–2.

[185] T. Franck, *The Power of Legitimacy Among Nations* (New York: Oxford University Press, 1990) pp. 208 *et seq.* For some interesting critical remarks on the distinction between legitimacy and justice, see J. Alvarez, 'The Quest for Legitimacy: An Examination of The Power of Legitimacy by T.M. Franck', 24 *NYUJILP* (1991) 199, pp. 245 *et seq.*

[186] T. Franck, *supra* note 184, p. 187.

crucial problem is not setting the criteria for legitimacy but rather to identify who is entitled to verify their compliance, and in particular to decide on the imperative necessity of the military action and, perhaps more importantly, on the impossibility of resolving the crisis through peaceful means.

Since the prospected action is directed at protecting common interests, considerations of legitimacy can be relevant only to the extent that they are shared by the majority of States, regardless of the possible opposition of one or more of the permanent members of the Security Council.[187] The collective dimension of legitimacy has been described as the multilateral endorsement of the position put forward by some States by 'as large and impressive a body of other States as may be possible'.[188]

At best, therefore, considerations of legitimacy can play a role when some States, supported by the majority of the international community, are willing to intervene militarily to tackle a situation that threatens international peace and security, but are unable to obtain an authorisation from the Security Council because of the opposition of one or more permanent members. Under the circumstances, the intervention remains unlawful but might be considered as legitimate.[189] In terms of legitimacy and certainly not of legality must we read the position expressed during the Kosovo crisis by the Italian Government, according to which no better-defined 'operational flexibility' would allow NATO States to intervene when the Security Council is blocked by the exercise for political purposes 'of the so-called veto right'.[190]

Again, in terms of legitimacy could be appreciated the argument, rejected above from the standpoint of legality,[191] concerning the non-condemnation by the Security Council of non-authorised use of force. The fact that the Security

[187] The generality requirement is also present in Franck's definitions (see *supra* note 185, p. 24); and 'The Relation of Justice to Legitimacy in the International System', in *Humanité et droit international. Mélanges R-J Dupuy* (Paris: Pédone, 1991), pp. 159 *et seq*., p. 160. Writing almost 100 years ago, A. Rougier, 'La théorie de l'intervention d'humanité', 17 *RGDIP* (1910) 468 at p. 501 observe that 'les interest collectives doivent faire l'objet de délibérations collectives. Le droit d'agir contre un gouvernement inhumain appartient proprement à la Société des Nations . . . Un Etat isolé, fût-il le plus civilisé du monde, ne saurait parler avec autorité en son nom ni celui de l'humanité'.

[188] I. Claude, 'Collective Legitimization as a Political Function of the United Nations', 20 *IO* (1966) 370.

[189] This does not exclude, from a normative point of view, that considerations of legitimacy – which in good substance are closely related to *opinio necessitates* defined by G. Scelle, 'Règles générales du droit de la paix', 46 *RdC* (1933–IV) 327, p. 434, as 'sentiments, tout au moins l'instinct d'obéir à une nécessité sociale' – could contribute to the development of international law, see D. Georgiev, 'Letter to the Editor', 83 *AJIL* (1989) 554.

[190] See the Report by the Government on the NATO Washington Summit, posted at http://notes3.senato.it/ODG_NSF/38b2113f. Leaving aside the fact that every vote, including the negative one cast by permanent members, is politically motivated, it remains to be seen by whom and upon which criteria would such a vote be assessed.

[191] See *supra* note 172.

Council does not adopt a resolution censuring the military action, nonetheless, might provide some legitimacy only if the majority of the organ members – and not merely a permanent member – have expressed a negative vote.

In the Kosovo crisis, a claim of legitimacy could have been plausible because of the fact that the Security Council was paralysed by the exercise of the veto power by China and Russian Federation, whereas a majority of members were not opposed to the military intervention, as demonstrated by the non-adoption of the draft resolution ordering the cessation of NATO military activities.[192] The fact that the decision to intervene had been taken unanimously within NATO, albeit obviously incapable of producing a permissive effect,[193] could at least reinforce its legitimacy.[194] What is problematical is that the majority existing within the Security Council did not reflect that of the Organisation membership, which was overwhelmingly contrary to the military intervention. This is also the reason why NATO members did not considered resorting to the General Assembly under the *Uniting for Peace* resolution.

It is against this background that the United States intervention in Afghanistan has to be appreciated from the standpoint of collective security law.[195] In contrast with other major crises, the Security Council was not prevented from fully discharging its responsibilities because of the opposition of certain permanent members. It had instead been deliberately excluded from the decision-making process with regard to the military operations. The fact that the action was justified by intervening States as exercise of the right to self-defence does not entirely explain this decision. Behind the decision may lie the interest of certain States – seconded or simply not noticed by others – to establish a significant precedent for the use of force without any control by the United Nations, nor even limited to the initial authorisation or approval. In this perspective, the episode could in future facilitate claims of unilateral or joint use of force, especially if the opposition of one or more permanent members could frustrate the attempt to obtain from the Security Council the authorisation to use force.

In spite of the absence of an authorisation by the Security Council, it may be argued that the consent, support or at least acquiescence expressed by almost all States belonging to all geo-political groups made it possible to deprive Afghanistan of the protection against the threat or use of force. The prohibition to threat or use military force safeguards an interest common to all States and the obligations stemming therefrom possess an *erga omnes* character.[196] The common

[192] See *supra* note 86.

[193] Paraphrasing A. Gros, diss. op. in *Interpretation of the Agreement of 25 March 1951 between the WHO and Egypt*, Order of 6 June 1981, *ICJ Reports 1981*, p. 104, conduct contrary to international law does not become lawful merely because it has been the object of a decision taken collectively, in this case within the framework of a regional organisation.

[194] On this point, see A. Cassese, *supra* note 149, p. 794.

[195] For a discussion of the intervention from the perspective of self-defence, see *infra* pp. 190 *et seq*.

[196] See *supra* pp. 20–2.

nature of the protected interest, however, does not prevent all States – except the State against which the measure is taken and possibly a marginal number of other States[197] – from suspending the effects of the norm with regard to a State that threatens international peace and security. If fifteen States sitting in the Security Council could authorise the use of military force, it is logically consequential to admit that the action of the whole international community could produce the same effects. Additionally, this instance of international governance, alternative to the collective security system established by the Charter, would satisfy – much better than any authorisation of the Security Council – any standard of legitimacy.

The difficulties lie in ascertaining whether and how all States could express their support or acquiescence to the suspension of the norm concerning the prohibition of the threat or use of force with regard to a given State. There is no need to comply with any formal requirement: support or acquiescence may be inferred from any conclusive acts. In the case of the Afghanistan intervention, the task has been facilitated by the numerous offers of material contribution as well as the wealth of declarations of support made by an impressive number of States, individually, jointly or within the framework of regional organisations. The fact that none of the Security Council submitted a draft resolution on the cessation of the military action – as happened during the Kosovo crisis – further demonstrates the extent of the consent existing within the international community.

The same result could be achieved through a resolution adopted by the General Assembly, provided that: (a) none of the permanent members of the Security Council oppose it; (b) at least nine members of the Security Council concur in its adoption; (c) the overwhelming majority of other members of the Organisation express their consent or acquiesce.[198] If these conditions are satisfied, no compelling reason would prevent the resolution from having a permissive effect.

Such a decision is reminiscent of the *United for Peace* resolution adopted by the General Assembly in 1950, although in that resolution the role of the General Assembly was confined to acts of aggression and breaches of peace.[199] It must be stressed, nonetheless, that what made the procedure established by that resolution rather indigestible – and indeed its essence – was the deliberate attempt to

[197] Dealing with international crimes of States, the ILC refused to equate the expression 'the international community as a whole' to unanimity among its members since this would have given each State an inconceivable right of veto (28 *YBILC* (1976–II) p. 73). Nonetheless, in the field of international peace and security such a right to veto would be conceivable indeed with regard to permanent members of the Security Council.

[198] In the *Certain Expenses case*, *supra* I-13, p. 162, the Court was somehow ambiguous on whether the General Assembly could recommend – not order – enforcement measures. N. D. White, *supra* note I-9, pp. 151–2 . . ., concludes that 'there appears to be no cogent objection to allowing the Assembly to recommend military measures to combat a threat to peace'.

[199] General Assembly Res. 377 (V), 3 November 1950. In literature see, in particular: J. Andrassy, 'Uniting for Peace', 50 *AJIL* (1956) 563; H. Reicher, 'The Uniting for Peace Resolution on the Thirtieth Anniversary of its Passage', 20 *CJTL* (1981) 1.

circumvent the Security Council's voting mechanism in order to overcome the opposition of the Soviet Union. A decision that respects the above-mentioned requirements would not disrupt the foundations of the collective security system established by the Charter and the Great Powers basic agreement underpinning it.[200]

To a large extent, however, the question is rather theoretical. If there is largely consent on the need to military action, it seems logical and likely that full use of the Security Council is made, probably in line with the authorisation practice. Member States resorting to force will benefit from the permissive effect of the resolution. The resolution would also strengthen the Security Council's authority and advance the main objective of the Organisation.

What needs to be underlined here is the awkward division of labour between the Security Council and the Member States. The efforts to deprive terrorists of any form of financial support and to ensure the most efficient co-operation on investigation and judicial matters have been pursued collectively, primarily through the conclusion of a network of conventions and the direct involvement of the Security Council. Military measures, on the contrary, have been the prerogative of States that have increasingly claimed, and tolerated, the right unilaterally or jointly to resort to force to curb terrorist activities.

Moving to the Iraq crisis, a legitimacy claim would be entirely misplaced. Here, the Security Council cannot be said to have been prevented from acting merely because some of its permanent members were opposed to the *immediate* recourse to force. The intervention not only enjoyed a limited support within the Security Council, as showed by the unsuccessful attempt to gather at least a simple three-fifths majority;[201] it was opposed by the overwhelming majority of the membership. Equally important for assessing the legitimacy claim is the unprecedented opposition to use of force by public opinion worldwide, including in the States directly involved in the military operations.

The introduction of considerations of legitimacy in order to make permissible the use of force without Security Council authorisation would undermine the already minimalist centralised control over the use of force and mark a dangerous step backwards to the discredited *bellum justum* doctrine. During the period which saw the emergence of the so-called authorisation practice, governments and scholars focused their attention on questions of the legitimacy of the Security Council,[202] on the dangers of marginalizing it,[203] on the selectivity of such types of

[200] In the *Certain Expenses* opinion, *supra* note I-13, p. 168, the Court showed a certain flexibility as to the internal competences of the different organs of the United Nations.

[201] See S. D. Murphy, *supra* note 109, p. 423.

[202] T. M. Franck, *supra* note 185; and *Fairness in International Law and Institutions* (Oxford: Clarendon Press, 1995); B. H. Weston, *supra* note II-32; D. D. Caron, *supra* note I-47; S. D. Murphy, 'The Security Council, Legitimacy, and the Concept of Collective Security After the Cold War', 32 *CJTL* (1994) 201, esp. pp. 246 *et seq.*

[203] *Supra* note II-118.

enforcement mechanism,[204] and of the lack of any effective control over its activities, and in particular the controversial power of judicial review by the International Court of Justice.[205] Unfortunately they overlooked the fact that the authorisation practice presupposes the lasting agreement between the permanent members not only on the qualification of a given situation as a threat to international peace, but also, and more crucially, on the need to intervene militarily.

Leaving aside for the moment the controversial question of humanitarian intervention,[206] it must be recalled that the collective security system established by the Charter is built on the absolute renunciation of non-defensive unilateral or joint use of force. The authorisation practice has not altered this. Albeit that it undeniably reduced the international control over the use of force to the initial approval of the military action, it preserved the authority of the Security Council and ultimately the notion of *bellum legale*. The lawfulness of the action continues to depend not on its intrinsic justice but on the observance of the Charter – and of the norm conditioning the use of force to the Security Council authorisation in particular – even at the price of sacrificing the individual interests of Member States.

Inherent in any form of international control over the use of force is the risk of not obtaining the authorisation to take coercive military measures. No reform of the composition or voting procedure of the Security Council, including the improbable abolition of the right to veto, would eliminate this risk. As long as the Security Council deliberates by qualified or unqualified majority – and it cannot be differently – the authorisation cannot be obtained if the States willing to resort to force do not manage to gather the necessary support.[207]

The United States' recent attitude reveals the intention to dismantle the institutionalised hegemonic collective system established by the Charter,[208] whose functioning was to a limited extent possible through the authorisation practice.

[204] *Supra* note II-119.

[205] See, in general, V. Gowlland-Debbas, 'The Relationship between the International Court of Justice and the Security Council in the Light of the Lockerbie Case', 88 *AJIL* (1994) 663; L. Caflish, 'Is the International Court Entitled to Review Security Council Decisions adopted under Chapter VII of the United Nations Charter?', in N. Al-Nauimi *et al.* (eds.), *International Legal Issues Arising under the United Nations Decade of International Law* (The Hague: Nijhoff, 1995); J. E. Alvarez, 'Judging the Security Council', 90 *AJIL* (1996) 1; M. N. Shaw, 'The Security Council and the International Court of Justice', in A.S. Muller *et al.* (eds.), *The International Court of Justice. Its Future Role after Fifty Years* (The Hague: Nijhoff, 1997), p. 219; D. Akande, 'The International Court of Justice and the Security Council: Is there Room for Judicial Control of Decisions of Political Organs of the United Nations?', 46 *ICLQ* (1997) 331; B. Martenczuk, *supra* note I-94.

[206] See *infra* pp. 174 *et seq*.

[207] This is without prejudice to the obvious consideration that the actual composition and voting procedure reflect the situation as it existed in 1945 and are today clearly obsolete.

[208] On this point, see generally D. Nincic, *The Problem of Sovereignty in the Charter and in the Practice of the United Nations* (The Hague: Nijhoff, 1970), pp. 125 *et seq*.

This is without prejudice to the role that the Security Council could play in regard to the adoption of non-military measures or its extensive normative powers.[209] The real objective of the United States strategy is to disconnect the lawfulness of the use of non-defensive force from the agreement among the permanent members of the Security Council. In this perspective, the non-concession by the Security Council of the authorisation to use force is equated to the failure of the collective security system. Not differently from the situation existing at the time of the League of the Nations, States would be able to use unilaterally or jointly resort to force in case of disagreement among the Great Powers.

This is not the first time that multilateralism has come under attack. In the Suez crisis, for instance, the United Kingdom, France and Israel defied the United Nations by conducted a military action that – as the British legal advisers made consistently and abundantly clear[210] – could in no way be defended under the Charter or general international law.[211] On that occasion, the United States became the advocate of multilateralism. Before the General Assembly it declared:

> If we were to agree that the existence in the world of injustices which this Organisation has so far been unable to cure means that the principle of the renunciation of force should no longer be respected that whenever a nation feels that it has been subject to injustice it should have the right to resort to force in an attempt to correct that injustice, then I fear that we should be tearing this Charter into shreds, that the world would be a world of anarchy, that the great hopes placed in this Organisation and in our Charter would vanish.[212]

For decades the United States saw, alongside with the other great powers, the Organisation as the vehicle for collaborative endeavour to keep order in international relations.[213] Now, it finds itself in a hegemonic position unprecedented in the history of international law[214] and its perception of the role of the United Nations is quite different. Hegemony is a factual phenomenon which has to be explained

[209] The normative powers of the Security Council in this field, indeed, have never been exercised so extensively as on the occasion of the adoption of Resolutions 1373 and 1540, *supra* text corresponding to note I-50.

[210] G. Marston, 'Armed Intervention in the 1956 Suez Canal Crisis: The Legal Advice Tendered to the British Government', 37 *ICLQ* (1988) 773.

[211] During the debate before the Security Council, the United Kingdom and France attempted to justify their action as necessary for the protection of their vital interests: see S/PV.751, 31 October 1956, pp. 8 and 10.

[212] A/PV. 561, 1 November 1956, p. 10 (First Emergency Special Session). S. Chesterman, *supra* note I-65, p. 236, rightly points out that 'unilateral enforcement is not a substitute for but the opposite of collective action'.

[213] I. L. Claude, 'The Security Council', in E. Luard (ed.), *The Evolution of International Organizations* (New York: Thames and Hodson, 1966), pp. 68 *et seq*., p. 77. S. D. Murphy, *supra* note 202, p. 256, concludes that the United Nations founded itself on a concept of relating responsibility for the maintenance of peace and security to the self-interest of the major powers.

[214] See H. Kissinger, 'America at the Apex: Empire of Leader', *Nat. Int.* (2001) 9.

in political terms. It escapes any legal definition, and leaves unaffected the structure of the international legal order.[215]

The radically changed political and military environment makes unlikely any major military action which does not enjoy the support of the United States and does not satisfy its national interest. At the same time, the decision-making process related to military action would be concentrated in Washington and assume a marked unilateral connotation, although it may be accompanied by a certain degree of consultation with other States[216] and by some form of participation – as *enthusiastic junior partners*[217] – in the operations.

In this perspective, the Security Council, or more precisely the right to veto and the majority requirement, are seen by the United States as potential obstacles to the pursuit of its national interest. This unilateral vision could reduce the Organisation to a 'forum precieux'[218] to tackle threats to international peace and security, a euphemistic expression reminiscent of the 'debating society' which labelled the League of the Nations.

What is at stake is nothing less than the centralised control over the use of force. The abandonment of the limited form of control exercised by the Security Council through the concession of the authorisation is resisted by the overwhelming majority of States. Paradoxically, the question is not any more one of protecting the rights of the minority against the corporate will of the Organisation, but rather the opposite. The time seems far away when the United States proclaimed that within the United Nations 'decisions are made by political processes involving checks and balances and giving assurance that the outcome will reflect considered judgment and broad consensus'.[219]

Apart from the 'quantitative' strength of the opposition to the dismantle of the collective security system, the United States' vision of the role of the United Nations, as it emerged during the Iraqi crisis, suffers from two main shortcomings. First, the non-adoption of a draft resolution that would have authorised the use of force does not necessarily mean that the system is paralysed. Quite to the contrary, the Security Council could be said to function perfectly well also when it does not grant its authorisation. It may in fact consider that the use of force is premature, because of the concrete possibilities of achieving a peaceful solution of the crisis, and reserve to itself the right to opt for military action at a later stage. Or, it could

[215] G. Arangio-Ruiz, *supra* I-87, p. 20–1. See also H. Triepel, *L'egemonia* (transl. G. Battino) (Firenze: Leonardo, 1949), esp. Chaps 10 and 11; D.F. Vagts, 'Hegemonic International Law', 95 *AJIL* (2001) 843.

[216] As noted by G. Schwarzenberger, *Power Politics*, 3rd ed. (London: Stevens, 1964), p. 181, compared with an imperialist domination, 'the hegemonial Power exercises more self-restrain. It pays more attention to the display of good manners. Discussion, rather than orders, is the normal form of communication. The emphasis lies on sparing the self-respect of the weaker Power'.

[217] The expression has been borrowed from B. H. Weston, *supra* note II-32, p. 527.

[218] L. A. Sicilianos, *supra* note 159, p. 48.

[219] A. Chayes, 'Law and the Quarantine of Cuba', 41 *FA* (1963) 550, p. 554.

reach the conclusion that the use of force is ineffective, disproportionate or unnecessary from a cost–benefit perspective.

Secondly, even assuming that the Security Council is ill-functioning as a result of the abusive resort to the veto power, the general prohibition on the use of force – which is at any rate independent from the effective functioning of that system[220] – would still prevent the unilateral or joint use of force, unless it may be justified as self-defence or under other possible exceptions. The argument that the non-authorised unilateral or joint use of force would be admissible merely because it is directed at protecting the vital interests of the acting States would amount to a denial of the prohibition on the use of force and ultimately would dismantle not only the collective security system but also the whole current legal regulation of the use of force.[221]

The practice of regional organisations and its impact on Chapter VIII of the Charter

The norms on the use of force by regional organisations[222] embodied in Chapter VIII of the Charter were the result of lengthy negotiations which had led to a substantial revision of the Dumbarton Oaks proposals.[223] Without prejudice to the right to individual and collective self-defence,[224] the purpose of these norms was to reconcile the principles of universalism and regionalism on the assumption that regional organisations could play a significant role in maintaining international

[220] See *infra* pp. 124 *et seq.*

[221] See the bald statement by J. Bolton, 'Is there Really "Law" in International Affairs?', 10 *TLCP* (2000) 1, p. 48, who does not hesitate to proclaim: 'We should be unashamed, unapologetic, uncompromising American constitutionalist hegemonists. International law is *not* superior to, and does not trump, the Constitution. The rest of the world may not like that approach, but abandoning it is the first step to abandoning the United States of America. International law is not law; it is a series of political and moral arrangements that stand or fall on their own merits, and anything else is simply theology and superstition masquerading as law.'

[222] For the purpose of this study, the expression 'regional organisations' is considered as equivalent to 'regional arrangements or agencies' used in Chapter VIII.

[223] On the innovative aspects of the Charter with regard to the Covenant, see Y. L. Liang, *Regional Arrangements and International Security*, 31 *Grotius Soc. Transactions* (1946) 221.

[224] It is well known that a specific article on self-defence was inserted during the San Francisco Conference. Art. 51 was developed within the Chapter devoted to regional organisations but never intended to be 'restricted to regional arrangements', see Subcommittee III(4) A, 12 *UNCIO*, p. 858. The Coordinating Committee, upon a recommendation of the Advisory Committee of Jurists, inserted Art. 51 in Chapter VII since otherwise it might have had the effect 'of limiting the right of self-defence only to regional arrangements, thus depriving a State with was not party to such arrangements of that right. Such a conclusion was clearly not to be permitted' (17 *UNCIO*, p. 287).

peace and security, provided that their coercive military activities are at least authorised by the Security Council.[225]

The Charter does not contain either a definition of 'regional organisation' or any indication with regard to its degree of institutionalisation and the geographical proximity or political affinities of its members.[226] Even a simple union of States, functioning as the co-ordination centre for national activities carried out through common organs, may qualify as a regional organisation,[227] provided that it has 'as its purpose the settlement at a regional level of matters relating to the maintenance of international peace and security'.[228] The occasional grouping of States, such as Groups of Contact, on the contrary, not being even an institutional or simple union of States, cannot be considered a regional organisation for the purpose of Chapter VIII.[229] As a result, the range of organisations potentially able to perform Chapter VIII activities is remarkably broad. In the *Agenda for Peace*, in particular, the UN Secretary General included among them 'regional organisations for the mutual security and defence, organisations for general regional development or for co-operation on a particular economic topic or function, and groups created to deal with a specific political, economic or social issue of current concern'.[230]

[225] It has been observed that 'In thus recognizing the paramount authority of the World Organisation in enforcement action as well as the inherent right of self-defence against armed attack pending the time the Security Council undertakes such action, this article [53] makes possible a useful and effective integration of regional systems of co-operation with the world system of international security' (in *Report to the President*, *supra* note I-10, p. 107).

[226] At the San Francisco Conference, the notion of regional organisation had been deliberately left vague. A restrictive definition proposed by the Egyptian delegation was rejected: see 12 *UNCIO*, p. 850.

[227] This view is supported by the *travaux préparatoires*: see, in particular, the discussion within the Advisory Committee of Jurists, 17 *UNCIO*, p. 396. In literature, see A. Gioia, *The United Nations and Regional Organizations in the Maintenance of Peace and Security*, in M. Bothe, N. Ronzitti and A. Rosas (eds.), *The OSCE in the Maintenance of Peace and Security* (The Hague: Kluwer, 1997), pp. 191 *et seq.*, p. 198.

[228] *Land and Maritime Boundary between Cameroon and Nigeria*, Preliminary Objections, Judgment, *ICJ Rep. 1998*, pp. 275 *et seq.*, p. 307. The UN Secretary General included among others 'regional organisations for the mutual security and defence, organisations for general regional development or for co-operation on a particular economic topic or function, and groups created to deal with a specific political, economic or social issue of current concern' (UN Doc. S/24111, 17 June 1992).

[229] J. M. Yepes, *Les accords régionaux et le droit international*, 71 *RdC* (1947–II) 235, p. 250. In the *Nicaragua case*, Jurisdiction, *infra* note IV-1, p. 440, the ICJ excluded that the Cantadora process could be considered as a regional organisation for the purpose of Chapter VIII.

[230] Report dated 17 June 1992 (S/24111). On the occasion of the 1991 London Conference on Yugoslavia sponsored by the EC, he did not hesitate to consider the EC as a regional organisation. See also the General Assembly Res. 49/57, adopted on 9 December 1994. It must be noted, however, that the military mission carried out in 2003 by the European Union on the basis of Art. 17(2) of the TEU (see Council Joint Action 2003/423/CFSP, 5 June 2003, in OJ L145, 11 June 2003, p. 50 and Council Decision 2003/432/CFSP, 12 June 2003, in OJ L147, 14 June 2003, p. 42) was authorised by the Security Council Res. 1484, adopted under Chapter VII of the Charter.

According to Art. 53(1), the Security Council can utilise regional organisations for enforcement action under its authority or authorise them to take such an action. In the first case, the Security Council exercises an effective political control over the operations.[231] The control necessarily includes the power to revise the objectives of the enforcement action, to assess when they are achieved, and ultimately to suspend or terminate the operations. Operational command and control, and possibly strategic direction, are left to the regional organisation. As the UN members have no obligation to take part in enforcement action in the absence of an agreement under Article 43, *a fortiori* such an obligation does not exist with regard to regional organisations, which are entitled to negotiate the conditions of their possible involvement or simply decline the Security Council invitation.

Under the second option, the Security Council merely authorises the resort to armed force following a determination of the existence of a threat to international peace and security.[232] The authorisation produces a permissive effect by depriving the concerned State of the legal protection it enjoys under Art. 2(4) and making lawful the otherwise prohibited conduct of the regional organisation. The normative phase initiated by the Security Council is then completed by a decision adopted by the regional organisation. The enforcement action effectively takes place only if, and to the extent to which the members of the latter organisation provide, on a case-by-case basis, the forces asked for. On the basis of the same arguments advanced with regard to the authorisation granted to Member States,[233] the authorisation under Art. 53(1) must be obtained beforehand.[234]

Since it is undisputed that the Security Council is entitled to authorise Member States individually to resort to armed force, the qualification of an organisation as regional organisation for the purpose of the enforcement action under Art. 53(1) has lost most of its practical interest. Furthermore, such a development has also

[231] Bearing in mind the consideration made above on the control exercised by the Security Council (see *supra* pp. 52 *et seq.*), the military coercive activities carried out by NATO to protect UNPROFOR until August 1995 are a case in point.

[232] NATO naval interdiction operations on the Adriatic Sea and aerial enforcement operations of the no-fly zone over Bosnian airspace may be indicated as instances of the authorised military enforcement action. M. Akehurst, *supra* note 167, pp. 185 *et seq.*, has convincingly demonstrated that, for the purpose of Art. 53(1), enforcement action is to be confined to measures involving military force. This conclusion is confirmed by the recent imposition of economic sanctions by ECOWAS and the OAS, without Security Council authorisation, respectively against Liberia and Haiti: see C. Gray, *International Law and the Use of Force* 2nd edn (Oxford: Oxford University Press, 2004), p. 306.

[233] See *supra* pp. 89 *et seq.*

[234] See M. Akehurst, *supra* note 167, p. 214; R. Pernice, *Die Sicherung des Weltfrieden durch regionale Organisationene und die Kapitel VIII der UN Charta* (Hamburg: Hansischer Gildenverlag, 1972), pp. 135 *et seq.*; L. Beyerlin, 'Regional Arrangements', in R. Wolfrum (ed.), *United Nations: Law, Policies and Practice* (München: C. H. Beck, 1995), vol. II, p. 1042; C. Schreuer, 'Regionalism v. Universalism', 6 *EJIL* (1995) 477, p. 492; G. Ress, 'Article 53', in B. Simma (ed.), *supra* note I-1, pp. 733 *et seq. Contra* C. Walter, *supra* note 162, pp. 177 *et seq.*

made immaterial the question whether a regional organisation may be authorised to carry out enforcement action against a non-Member State.[235] It would indeed be illogical to preclude a group of States from carrying out within the framework of a regional organisation activities that each of them could already lawfully carry out individually. The distinction between enforcement action against members or non-members, nonetheless, may be relevant assuming a norm allowing regional organisations – but not individual States – to resort to force without Security Council authorisation.

In general, the practice of regional organisations is too scarce in term of both *usus* and *opinio juris* to affirm the emergence of a norm allowing regional organisation to resort to force without Security Council authorisation as required by Art. 53(1). Not surprisingly, considering what is happening with regard to the authorisation granted by the Security Council to Member States, it must be admitted that certain States have expressed their disaffection to Art. 53(1). The division existing within NATO on the legal requirement to obtain such an authorisation before undertake military enforcement measures and the position expressed by those States that have pronounced on the question[236] demonstrate that the modification of Art. 53(1) is opposed by a large part of the international community representative of all geo-political areas. This latter position, which reflects that of the United Nations Special Committee on Peacekeeping Operations,[237] indirectly reinforces the conclusion reached above on the inadmissibility of unilateral or joint use of force without Security Council authorisation. The conditions upon which a regional organisation could resort to force, in effect, cannot be stricter than those existing for individual States.[238]

The recent activities carried out by NATO and ECOWAS as well as the establishment of the African Union present several elements of interest and will be briefly discussed in the later parts of this section.

[235] On the question, see in particular: H. Kelsen, *supra* note I-4, pp. 327 and 923; P. Vellas, *Le régionalisme international et l'Organisation des Nations Unies* (Paris: Pédone, 1948), p. 206; G. Gaja, *supra* note II-35, p. 41.

[236] See *infra* notes 252 and 253. In Revised Working Paper Submitted to the Special Committee on the Charter of the United Nations and on the Strengthening of the Role of the Organisation, 2 April 2001, A/AC.182/L.104/Rev.2, Belarus and the Russian Federation affirmed the 'immutability' of Art. 53(1) to the effect that no enforcement action shall be taken under regional organisations without the authorisation of the Security Council. See also *infra* notes 253 and 262.

[237] The Committee emphasised that 'in accordance with Article 53 of the Charter, no enforcement action shall be taken under regional arrangements or by regional agencies without the authorisation of the Security Council': see *Comprehensive Review of the Whole Question of Peacekeeping Operations in all their Aspects*, 11 March 2002, A/56/863, p. 13.

[238] Unless if it is so provided by the constituent instrument or other relevant treaties.

The North Atlantic Treaty Organisation

NATO was established first and foremost as a defensive military alliance. Article 5, the key provision of the Washington Treaty,[239] was accordingly modelled after Article 51 of the Charter. In the last decade, nonetheless, the Alliance has extended its range of activity to tackling international terrorism, sabotage, organised crime and disruption of the flow of vital resources,[240] and assumed new responsibilities in maintaining peace and security on the regional plane[241] and in coping with humanitarian emergencies.[242] Hence, most of the military activities carried out by its forces were at once undertaken out of area[243] and extraneous to Art. 5 of the Washington Treaty.

As to the practice of the Alliance on the ground, the military coercive and consensual activities conducted in the Yugoslav conflicts offer some *indicia* of the effective capability of the Alliance to function as a regional organisation. The forces involved were fully integrated in the Alliance military structure, and operated under NATO rules of engagement and NATO chain of command. The NAC exercised political control and strategic direction over the operations, while the troops were under exclusive NATO command and control. The only real obstacle to qualifying NATO as a regional organisation is the fact that so far the Alliance has accurately avoided defining itself as such, presumably in order not to assume the obligations related to the Security Council control on its military activities, including the submission of periodical reports as required under Art. 54 of the Charter. Under the circumstances, it seems appropriate to adopt a pragmatic

[239] Concluded on 4 April 1949, 34 *UNTS* 243. During the negotiations, however, opposing views were put forward as to the possibility that the Alliance could also operate as a regional organisation: see N. Henderson, *The Birth of Nato* (London: Weidenfeld & Nicolson, 1982), pp. 101 *et seq*. It was agreed not to include in the preamble the qualification of NATO as a regional organisation as proposed by France. It is, however, noteworthy that on 14 April 1949, France declared before the UN General Assembly that the Treaty 'represented an incontestably correct application of Articles 51 to 53' of the UN Charter (UN Doc. A/PV.194, p. 98).

[240] *Alliance Strategic Concept*, approved by the Heads of State and Government participating in the meeting of the NAC, Washington, 23–24 April 1999, para. 24. This stands in sharp contrast with *Alliance's New Strategic Concept*, agreed by the Heads of State and Government participating in the meeting of the NAC, Rome, 7–8 November 1991, para. 35, which partly reads: 'The Alliance is purely defensive in purpose: none of its weapons will ever be used except in self-defence . . . The role of the Alliance's military forces is to assure the territorial integrity and political independence of its member states'.

[241] See, in particular, para. 6 of the 1999 Strategic Concept.

[242] See the speech delivered by NATO Secretary General on 20 May 1999 before the Assembly of the Senior Civil Emergency Planning Committee.

[243] Lord Robertson, *Transforming NATO, NATO Review*, Spring 2003. The Strategic doctrine adopted in 1999 expressly foresees that the Alliance forces could be employed beyond the Allies' territory, either for collective defence purposes or for crisis response operations (paras 52 and 53).

approach and to focus on whether NATO may effectively function as a regional organisation rather than whether it qualifies itself as such.[244]

From an internal perspective, the strategic concepts are not legal instruments imposing or bestowing on Member States new obligations or duties.[245] Nonetheless, nothing prevents NATO Member States from performing, through the common organs of the Alliance, activities entirely outside those included in the constituent treaty, but not prohibited thereby, provided that the activities are based on a NAC decision taken unanimously or at least without opposition.[246] Through the decision – which may constitute international agreements concluded in simplified form[247] – Member States agree, on a case-by-case basis, upon the use of the Alliance's structure, chain of command, facilities and equipment, still reserving their individual position as to whether, how and how long participate to the military operations.[248] The forces voluntarily provided for by Member States are put under the command of the civilian and military authorities of the Alliance, acting as common organs of these States. It has been rightly pointed out that 'the fact that NATO might conduct operations outside the scope of its founding treaty means

[244] See D. W. Bowett, *infra* note IV-17, p. 222; M. Akehurst, *supra* note 167, p. 180. According to Akehurst, 'the question is not whether an organisation *is* a regional agency, but whether it is *functioning* as one *in a given situation*' (emphasis original).

[245] Suffice it to note that the US President issued a declaration that reads in part: 'I feel compelled to make clear that the document is a political, not a legal document. As such, the Strategic concept does not create any new commitment or obligation' (quoted in E. Cannizzaro, 'La nuova dottrina strategica della NATO e l'evoluzione della desciplina internazionale sull'uso della forza', in N. Ronzitti (ed.), *NATO, conflitto in Kosovo e Costituzione italiana* (Milano: Giuffrè, 2000), pp. 43 *et seq.*, p. 46, footnote 26). See also, for Canada, *Seventh Report on the Standing Senate Committee on Foreign Affairs*, April 2000, in E. Sciso (ed.), *L'intervento in Kossovo. Aspetti internazionalistici e interni* (Milano: Giuffrè, 2001), pp. 216 *et seq.*

[246] The position of the Greek Government in not concurring in the NAC decisions concerning the *ultimata* issued against the Bosnian Serbs strangling Sarajevo (*Decisions taken at the meeting of the NAC in Permanent Session*, Brussels, 9 February 1994) and Goradze (*Decisions taken at the Meeting of the NAC in Permanent Session*, Brussels, 22 April 1994; *Decisions on the Protection of Safe Areas*, Brussels, 22 April 1994), but not opposing them either, could be considered as an example of abstention. For want of any provisions in the 1949 Treaty, the admissibility of decisions taken without the participation of all members has emerged in the Alliance practice alongside the general application of the unanimity rule: see E. Cannizzaro, 'N.A.T.O.', *Digesto Discipline Pubblicistiche*, 4th ed. (Torino: UTET, 1995), vol. X, pp. 52, *et seq.*, 61–2.

[247] E. Stein and D. Carreau, 'Law and Peaceful Change in a Subsystem: "Withdrawal" of France from the North Atlantic Treaty', 62 *AJIL* (1968) 577, p. 613; E. Cannizzaro, *N.A.T.O.*, *Digesto Discipline Pubblicistiche*, IV ed., vol. X (Torino: Utet, 1995), pp. 52 *et seq.*, p. 65; A. Carlevaris, 'Accordi in forma semplificata e impegni derivanti dal Trattato NATO', in N. Ronzitti (ed.), *supra* note 246, pp. 67 *et seq.*, p. 87.

[248] With regard to the Kosovo crisis, for instance, the Italian Government excluded the use of its aircraft above the 44° parallel or in so-called 'non-defensive operations'.

not that such operations are illegal but that a Member State has no legal obligation to participate in them'.[249]

From the standpoint of the collective security system, until the Kosovo crisis NATO to a large extent respected the authority of the Security Council. The Alliance systematically based the coercive military operations carried out by its force on the relevant Security Council authorisations, although in some cases the substantial and procedural limits set up by that organ were disregarded.[250] It was during the Kosovo crisis that the Alliance, baldly challenging the Security Council monopoly on the use of force, unilaterally resorted to force. If, as observed above, no coherent legal argument was offered by the intervening States, the position of the Alliance on the legal necessity of obtaining the Security Council authorisation before resorting to force was even less clear.

Although adopted during the military campaign, the 1999 Strategic concept does not indicate any legal basis either for Kosovo intervention or for non-Art. 5 coercive operations the Alliance could carry out in future. In para. 31, in particular, while confirming that the Alliance could, on a case-by-case basis, undertake coercive operations under the authority of the Security Council, it was affirmed that 'NATO will seek, in co-operation with other organisations, to prevent conflict, or, should a crisis arise, to contribute to its effective management, consistent with international law, including through the possibility of conducting non-Article 5 crisis response operations'.

The ambiguous text of para. 31 reflects the diverging view held by Member States. For the United States, the strategic concept 'states the obvious point that NATO crisis response activity must be consistent with international law, but significantly, does not suggest that NATO must have permission from the United Nations or any other outside body before it can act'.[251] This stands in sharp contrast with the position of certain European States, and in particular France, which at the end of the Washington Summit declared that 'l'OTAN ne pourra et ne devra pas agir sans avoir l'assentiment de l'Organisation internationale'.[252]

[249] See Canada, *Seventh Report on the Standing Senate Committee on Foreign Affairs*, April 2000, in E. Sciso (ed.), *supra* note 245, pp. 216 *et seq*., p. 219. This position is reminiscent of the considerations made by G. Fitzmaurice, diss. op. in the *Certain Expenses case*, *supra* note I-13, p. 205, with regard to contribution to merely permissive operations of the United Nations. See *supra* notes II-108 and II-112.

[250] On the enforcement measures taken by NATO to curb international terrorism, see *infra* p. 189.

[251] See the declaration of the US Under Secretary of Defence dated 28 October 1999, quoted in E. Cannizzaro, *supra* note 246, pp. 64–5. The change of attitude was somehow anticipated by the North Atlantic Assembly that in November 1998 urged member States 'to seek to ensure the wildest international legitimacy for non-Article 5 missions and also to stand ready to act should the UN Security Council be prevented from discharging its purpose of maintaining international peace and security' (AR 295 SA). This view is shared by the British Minister of Defence: see the reply to the Third Special Report on the Future of NATO, 19 May 1999, available at www.parliament.the-stationery-office.co.uk.

[252] Available at www.elysee.fr.

The Economic Community of Western African States

ECOWAS's qualification as regional organisation is generally accepted both by the United Nations[253] organs and in literature.[254] ECOWAS was established in 1975 as a subregional organisation dealing with social and economic integration.[255] Through a series of subsequent legal instruments, including the 1978 Protocol on Non Aggression[256] and the 1981 Protocol on Mutual Assistance and Defence,[257] Member States extended the organisation's activities to collective self-defence and military co-operation and assistance. Under Art. 4(b) of the latter treaty, in particular, the organisation could establish an armed force to be used in 'in case of internal conflict within any Member State engineered or supported actively from outside likely to endanger the security and peace in the entire Community'.

ECOWAS practice is particularly ambiguous and incoherent, because of the attitude of the regional organisation itself, its Member States, and the Security Council. In the crises in Liberia and Sierra Leone, in particular, it was not always clear whether the operations were carried out by the regional organisation or by some of its members acting unilaterally. The practice was also contaminated by the overlapping of the different legal grounds invoked – ranging from self-defence to humanitarian intervention, from request from the Government or the belligerent parties to enforcement of peace agreements.[258]

In both crises the organisation's involvement in regional crisis went beyond peace-keeping operations. The new conception of the organisation clearly surfaces from the 1999 Protocol relating to the mechanism for conflict prevention, management, resolution, peace-keeping and security.[259] Maintenance and consolidation of peace, security and stability within the Community appear among the objectives of the mechanism as defined in Art. 3.

It remains that on some occasions ECOWAS forces carried out military enforcement action before the Security Council had granted its authorisation or beyond the limits of such an authorisation. It is nonetheless significant and encouraging that ECOWAS sought the Security Council's authorisation before resorting to coercive measures in the recent crisis in Côte d'Ivoire, although it

[253] See, in particular, Security Council Res. 1132. The Secretary General, in turn, declared that 'Liberia continues to represent an example of systematic and effective co-operation between the United Nations and regional organisations, as envisaged in Chapter VIII of the Charter': see SG S/26200, 2 August 1993.

[254] W. Hummer, M. Schweitzer, 'Article 52', in B. Simma, *supra* note I-1, pp. 807 *et seq.*; A. Gioia, *supra* note 228, p. 200; C. Gray, *supra* note p. 23, pp. 182 *et seq*.

[255] *Treaty of Ecowas*, signed in Lagos, 28 May 1975, 1010 *UNTS* 17.

[256] Signed in Lagos, 22 April 1978, in M. Weller (ed.), *Regional Peace-keeping and International Enforcement: The Liberian Crisis* (Cambridge: Cambridge University Press, 1994), p. 18.

[257] Signed in Freetown, 29 May 1981 (*ibid.*, p. 19).

[258] See *supra* p. 68 and p. 71.

[259] Signed in Lomé, 10 December 1999 (available at www.ecowas.int).

could have invoked the consent of the belligerent parties to justify its military presence and activities.[260]

Little attention has been paid to the relationships between regional organisations and the Security Council under Art. 53(1). On the one hand, ECOWAS and its Member States neglected to elaborate a consistent legal argument supporting their enforcement action. At any rate, they never articulated a claim to resort to force independently from the Security Council authorisation. On the other hand, the Security Council, its members and the members of the United Nations in general justified ECOWAS initiatives as having a consensual character or, when this was not possible, turned a blind eye on them. The few States that went beyond vague statements on the importance of the co-operation as envisaged in Chapter VIII, however, reaffirmed that in accordance with Art. 53(1) no enforcement action could be undertaken by regional organisations without the Security Council authorisation.[261]

African Union

The Constitutive Act of the African Union, which in July 2002 replaced the Organisation of African Unity, contains a provision that deserves a special mention. According to Art. 4(h), the African Union has the right 'to intervene in a Member State pursuant to a decision of the Assembly in respect of grave circumstances, namely: war crimes, genocide and crimes against humanity'.[262]

Considering that unilateral humanitarian intervention has not yet (re)emerged as an exception to the general ban on the use of force,[263] Art. 4 (h) is scarcely com-

[260] See *supra* note II-77.

[261] During the debate before the Security Council on the situation in Africa, which saw the participation of a remarkably high number of States, only Canada elaborated on this point: 'We cannot subcontract responsibility for the maintenance of international peace and security, even by default. Regional and subregional bodies should respond, not to vacuums created as a result of inaction on the part of the Security Council, but to collaborative programmes developed in close consultation with the Council. Such collaboration should be based on Articles 53 and 54 of the United Nations Charter and ought fully to reflect the Security Council's exclusive mandate for authorizing the use of force' (S/PV.3875 Resumption, 24 April 1998, p. 19). On 24 October 1998, Brazil declared before the Security Council that Art. 53 imposes on regional organisations 'the obligation of seeking Security council authorisation beforehand and abiding with the Council's decision' (S/PV.3937, pp. 10–11).

[262] Constitutive Act of the African Union, 11 July 2000, entered into force on 26 May 2001. The decision is taken by consensus or by a two third majority. According to the Protocol Relating to the Establishment of the Peace and Security Council of the African Union, 9 October 2002, entered into force on 26 December 2003, the Security Council of the African Union can recommend to the Assembly intervention to tackle one of the situations foreseen in Art. 4 (h) of the Constitutive Act, 'as defined in relevant international conventions and instruments'. Both documents are posted at www.africa-union.org.

[263] See infra pp. 174 et seq.

patible with the United Nations Charter.[264] The decision of the Assembly of the African Union, even if taken unanimously, would not remove the prohibition, incumbent upon all States, to refrain from threatening or using military force. The power to remove such a prohibition belongs exclusively to the United Nations Security Council. Coherently with the *erga omnes* character of the prohibition to use force, Member State of the African Union are not allowed to confer to the Assembly of the Organisation normative powers whose exercise would imply non-compliance with their obligations under the United Nations Charter. It is also maintained that the practice of the member States of the African Union can hardly generate a regional custom allowing humanitarian intervention in the continent. This would affect the legally protected right of all members of the United Nations with regard to Art. 2(4) of the Charter.

What cannot be ruled out, on the contrary, is that such a practice may contribute to the emergence in due course of a customary norm allowing the use of force on humanitarian grounds in or against a member of a regional Organisation provided that the competent organ of the Organisation has authorised it in accordance with its own constitutive instrument. In this perspective, the decision would have a permissive effect comparable to that of the Security Council, albeit limited to humanitarian emergencies. Such a development would ensure the collective character of the decision to intervene and permit to overcome one of the main objection to the right to humanitarian intervention.

The final phase of the Bosnian conflict, the military coercive activities carried out in the aftermath of the Gulf crisis (1991–99) and the Kosovo intervention marked a period of unilateralism that culminated with the recent massive intervention in Iraq. The United States, supported by its NATO allies or at least some of them, openly challenged the authority of the Security Council and attempted to downgrade its authorisation from a legal requirement to a matter of political convenience.

Individually taken, these instances of use of force are contrary to both the Charter and customary international law. Globally considered, however, they might have led to a further change of the rules on the use of force, provided that they were expressions of a new normative claim accepted by the generality of States. This can hardly be maintained since the attempt by a minority of States, however powerful, to relax the rules on the use of force for non-defensive purposes is steadily resisted by the overwhelming majority of States, representing all geo-political groups. For the time being, neither State practice nor *opinio juris* supports a change of existing law in the sense required by the United States.

At any rate, States must be aware that such a move would not imply a further involution of the collective security system but its definitive repudiation.

[264] The Protocol on Amendments to the Constitutive Act of the African Union, July 2003, not yet in force, is intended to add to the situations envisaged in Art. 4 (h) 'serious threat to legitimate order to restore peace and stability to the Member State of the Union'. Its incompatibility with the United Nations Charter is quite evident.

Part 2

The individual or joint use of force

IV

Self-defence and other forms of unilateral use of force

The collective security system and the unilateral or joint use of force are not sealed compartments. Their interaction is manifest in Art. 51 of the Charter, which temporally limits the right to self-defence until the Security Council discharges its responsibilities. Perhaps less evident, but nonetheless equally important, is the function of control exercised by the Security Council over the use of force in self-defence and on other legal grounds.

This chapter deals preliminarily with two general questions, namely the relationship between the rules on the use of force embodied in the Charter and those existing under customary law, and the alleged dependence of the ban on the use of force on the effective functioning of the collective security system. In spite of the shortcomings and failures of the collective security system, the continuing existence of the ban on the use of force is not questioned by States and has been systematically reaffirmed by the International Court of Justice. The content of such a ban is defined through the analysis of its exceptions (apart from those related to terrorism and weapons of mass destruction that will be dealt with in Chapter 5).

A prominent place has been accorded to the only exception expressly provided for in the Charter, namely self-defence . The rest of the chapter is dedicated to three exceptions to the general ban on the use of force that have been the object of controversy: armed reprisals, rescue operations of national abroad, and intervention on humanitarian grounds.

The relationship between the norms on the use of force under the Charter and under customary international law

Before discussing the legal regulation of individual or joint use of force, it is necessary to deal with the relationship between the rules on this field existing under the Charter and under customary international law. The question was crucial in the *Nicaragua case*. The United States' multilateral treaty reservation to the declaration under Art. 36(2) of the Statute of the International Court of Justice[1] precluded adjudication insofar as the Charter was concerned, but not with regard to customary law on the use of force. Already at the jurisdictional stage, the Court observed that the fact that the principles of customary law upon which Nicaragua had based its claims had been 'codified or embodied in multilateral conventions does not mean that they have ceased to exist and to apply as principles of customary law, even as regards countries that are parties to such conventions'.[2] The Court further affirmed that the customary norms on the use of force retain their separate existence and autonomous applicability,[3] regardless of their incorporation in the Charter[4] and even if their content is identical to those enshrined in the Charter itself.[5] In so doing, the Court dismissed the argument advanced by the United States that the Charter provisions on the use of force had subsumed and supervened the corresponding norms of customary international law.[6] The Court position is sound, even assuming that the Charter provisions codified the customary international law existing in 1945.[7]

In its attempt to overcome the United States' reservation, however, the Court focused more on the independent existence of the Charter and customary international law than on their interaction. Only cursorily did the Court note that the Charter and other relevant multilateral treaties must be taken into account in ascertaining the content of customary international law, and that in the last four decades customary international law had developed under the influence of the

[1] See relevant part of the reservation in *Case Concerning Military and Paramilitary Activities in and against Nicaragua*, Jurisdiction and Admissibility, *ICJ Reports 1984*, pp. 392 *et seq*., pp. 421–2. The reservation has been described by H. W. Briggs, '*Nicaragua* v. *United States*. Jurisdiction and Admissibility', 79 *AJIL* (1985) 373, p. 378 as 'nonsensical'.

[2] *Nicaragua case*, Jurisdiction, *supra* note 1, p. 424. This position was confirmed in *Nicaragua case*, Merits, *ICJ Reports 1986*, pp. 14 *et seq*., pp. 96–7.

[3] *Nicaragua case*, Merits, *supra* note 2, p. 95. While affirming that if the US reservation was to be interpreted in accordance with the effectiveness principle, the Court had no competence at all, S. Schwebel, diss. op. (*ibid*., p. 304), did not deny the separate existence of the rules on the use of force embodied in the Charter and those under international customary law. *Contra* R. Y. Jennings, diss. op. *ibid*., p. 530, according to whom 'there is no room and no need for the very artificial postulate of a customary law paralleling these Charter provisions'.

[4] *Nicaragua case*, Merits, *supra* note 2, p. 95. In another passage, the Court stated that the Charter 'gave expression' to principles already present in customary international law (p. 96).

[5] *Nicaragua case*, Jurisdiction, pp. 424–5; *Nicaragua case*, Merits, *supra* note 2, pp. 96–7.

[6] *Counter-Memorial*, *Pleadings*, vol. II, p. 91.

[7] In general, the codifying treaty 'does not replace existing customary law but is necessarily superimposed upon it' (R. Y. Jennings, 'The Progressive Development of International Law and its Codification', 24 *BYIL* (1947) 301, p. 306). See also E. Sciso, *Gli accordi confliggenti nel diritto internazionale* (Bari: Cacucci, 1986), pp. 326 *et seq*. Additionally, as maintained by J. Kunz, 'La crise et les transformations du droit des gens', 88 *RdC* (1955–II) 9, pp. 60–1, 'le droit international particulier d'une organisation internationale à vocation universelle peut disparaître mais le droit des gens continue'.

Charter.[8] The emphasis was placed instead on the different methods of interpretation and application of the two set of norms, as well as on the possibly different remedies available to ensure compliance therewith.[9]

The Court further noted that not *all* relevant customary international rules were identical to those embodied in the Charter.[10] None of the differences singled out by the Court, however, appears entirely convincing or of any appreciable significance.[11] To start with, proportionality and necessity, although not expressly referred to in Art. 51, constitute the basic criteria against which the lawfulness of self-defence is to be assessed, not only from the perspective of customary international law but also from that of the Charter. These criteria are well established in customary international law and as such are relevant in interpreting the Charter, if not even the principles underpinning it.[12] It is particularly significant that in the *Nuclear Weapons case*, the Court maintained that the requirements of necessity and proportionality apply equally to Art. 51 of the Charter, whatever the means of force employed.[13] Furthermore, the definition of 'armed attack', which according to the Court could be found only in customary law, is undoubtedly a question of treaty interpretation.[14] Deliberately left vague at the San Francisco conference, what amounts to an armed attack for the purpose of Art. 51 of the Charter is to be construed on the basis of the Organisation's and Member States' practice.[15] The only difference of some importance indicated by the Court was the report on the measures taken on self-defence Member States submit to the Security Council under Art. 51 of the Charter.[16] It is, however, disputed whether Art. 51 imposes an veritable obligation in that sense.[17]

Customary and conventional norms can not only co-exist: they also develop autonomously and possibly in divergent ways, even assuming their initially identical content. The application of the rules governing the interpretation of treaties, in particular, 'may and probably will change the content of the substantive rules

[8] *Nicaragua case*, Merits, *supra* note 2, pp. 96–7.

[9] *Nicaragua case*, Merits, *supra* note 2, p. 95. As to the remedies, M. H. Mendelson, *supra* note I-40, p. 85 *et seq.*, pp. 89, rightly stresses that 'the principle of reciprocity is a principle of customary law as much as of treaty law'.

[10] *Ibid.*, p. 93.

[11] *Nicaragua case*, Merits, *supra* note 2, pp. 93–4 and 105.

[12] M. H. Mendelson, *supra* note I-40, p. 89, observes that 'the *inherent* customary right of self-defence as it existed before 1945 included the notion of proportionality, and so part of the conceptual *baggage* taken over by the Charter included this principle' (emphasis as in original). See also L. Condorelli, 'La Corte internazionale di giustizia e gli organi politici delle Nazioni Unite', 77 *RDI* (1994) 897, p. 913; J. G. Gardam, 'Proportionality and Force in International Law', 87 *AJIL* (1993) 391.

[13] *Infra* note V-127, p. 245.

[14] See M. H. Mendelson, *supra* note I-40, p. 88.

[15] See *infra* pp. 133 *et seq.*

[16] *Nicaragua case*, Merits, *supra* note 2, p. 105.

[17] Compare, for instance, D. W. Bowett, *Self Defense in International Law* (Manchester: Manchester University Press, 1957), p. 197, and D. W. Greig, 'Self-Defence and the Security Council: What does Article 51 Require?', 40 *ICLQ* (1991) 366, p. 387.

which have been codified'.[18] Besides, subsequent practice of contracting parties may not only be relevant for the purpose of interpreting and applying the conventional rule;[19] it may also substantially modify its content,[20] not necessarily in line with the evolution of the codified customary rule.

These considerations, nonetheless, must be weighed against the mutual exposure and interaction between treaties and custom. In the case of codification, in particular, the treaty 'photographs'[21] the customary rule, but neither gives the conventional rule its final and perpetual shape nor freezes the development of the corresponding customary rule. On the one hand, conventional rules are to be interpreted taking into consideration any relevant rules of international law – irrespective of their conventional or customary nature[22] – applicable to the relations between the parties.[23] Customary norms may fill the gaps and offer indications on the content of a treaty, even in evolutionary terms.[24] It is therefore possible and indeed desirable that the interpreter brings the content of the conventional norms into line with the evolution of the corresponding customary norms. Treaties may even be partly or entirely modified by, or altogether terminated through, the subsequent formation of incompatible customary rules.[25] On the other hand, subsequent practice of States parties to the treaty may contribute to the development of the relevant customary rules on a larger scale. The same applies to a non-declaratory treaty, which may concur in the formation of new

[18] See R. Y. Jennings, *supra* note 7, p. 305.

[19] Art. 31(3)(*b*) of the *Convention on the Law of the Treaties*, 1155 *UNTS* 331 (hereinafter 'Vienna Convention').

[20] See *Air Transport Services Agreement Arbitration*, U.S. *v*. France, 22 December 1963, in 38 *ILR* (1969) 182, p. 249; *Case Concerning the Temple of Preah Vihear, ICJ Reports 1962*, p. 6. See also the position of the ILC, *Report to the General Assembly*, 17 *YBILC* (1966–II), p. 236. In literature, see: J. P. Cot, 'La conduite subséquante des parties à un traité', 70 *RGDIP* (1966) 632; F. Capotorti, 'Sul valore della prassi applicativa dei trattati secondo la Convenzione di Vienna', in *International Law at the Time of its Codification, Essays Ago* (Milano: Giuffrè, 1987), p. 197; I. Sinclair, *The Vienna Convention on the Law of Treaties* (Manchester: Manchester University Press, 1973), p. 137; H. Thirlway, 'The Law and Procedure of the International Court of Justice, 1960–1989, Part Three', 62 *BYIL* (1991) 1, pp. 48 *et seq*.

[21] R. R. Baxter, 'Multilateral Treaties as Evidence of Customary International Law', 41 *BYIL* (1965–6) 275, p. 299.

[22] See M. K. Yasseen, 'L'interprétation des traités d'après la Convention de Vienne sur le droit des traités', 151 *RdC* (1976–III) 1, p. 63.

[23] See Art. 31(3)(*c*) of the Vienna Convention.

[24] See, with regard to Art. 22 of the Covenant, the *Namibia case*, *supra* note I-28, pp. 31–2

[25] See Art. 68(*c*) of the Draft Articles prepared in 1964 by the ILC, *Report to the General Assembly*, 15 *YBILC* (1964–II), p. 198. The provision was not adopted at the Vienna Conference, because the relationships between treaty law and customary law were considered as extraneous to the object of the Convention. See F. Capotorti, 'L'extinction et la suspension des traités', 134 *RdC* (1971–III) 417, pp. 517 *et seq*. In general, see N. Kontou, *The Termination and Revision of Treaties in the Light of New Customary International Law* (Oxford: Clarendon Press, 1994).

customary rules, thereby binding also upon non-parties, provided that these rules possess a fundamentally norm-creating character.[26] The interaction between the two rules assures a certain degree of uniformity and coherence in their respective development, especially when the treaty has obtained widespread acceptance.

Such a process concerns also the constituent treaty of international organisations whose law, at once, is based upon, presupposes, and stands under the impact of customary international law; and exercises a continuous influence on customary international law.[27] The effects of the process are amplified when such a treaty has been ratified by virtually the whole international community, as in the case of the Charter, which can today be considered as part of general international law.[28] This has deprived of interest the question whether the participation of the majority of States, including the leading powers,[29] or a tendency of the Organisation to become almost universal,[30] would be sufficient to qualify the Charter as general international law or, on the contrary, whether the Charter remains particular law until the 'absolute universality' has been attained.[31]

Considering the interaction between the Charter and customary international law, and the fact that the addressees of the Charter and those of customary international law almost perfectly coincide because of the virtual universality of the Organisation, it is submitted that the norms on the use of force are substantially identically under the two sources. It has authoritatively pointed out that 'it would

[26] *Continental shelf cases, supra* note II-155, pp. 41–2. On the fundamentally norm-creating character, see R. Y. Jennings, 'What is International Law and How Do We Tell When We See it?', 37 *ASDI* (1981) 59, p. 64. The importance of treaties as evidence of the formation and development of customary law has been emphasised by A. A. D'Amato, *supra* note II-166, especially Chap. 5.

[27] J. Kunz, 'General International Law and the Law of International Organizations', 47 *AJIL* (1953) 456, p. 459.

[28] G. Tunkin, 'Is General International Law Customary Only?', 4 *EJIL* (1993) 534; and *Theory of International Law* (London: Allen & Unwin, 1974), pp. 137 *et seq.* On general multilateral treaties, see also R. Ago, 'Droit des traités à la lumière de la Convention de Vienne', 134 *RdC* (1971–III) 297, esp. pp. 314 *et seq.* As a matter of fact, general international law does not equate any more with customary international law. The contrary position expressed by H. Kelsen, *Principles of International Law* (New York: Rinehart & Company, 1952), p. 52, at the time irrefutable, must therefore be revised. In the 2nd edition, edited by R. W. Tucker and published in 1966, an attempt is made to consider at least some of the provisions of the Charter as general international law by admitting their applicability to non-Member States (pp. 486–7).

[29] See H. Lauterpacht, *Oppenheims's International Law*, 8th ed. (London: Longman, 1955), p. 28.

[30] See A. Verdross, *Völkerrecht* (Wien: Springer, 1973) p. 21.

[31] See G. Schwarzenberger, *International Law as Applied and Interpreted by International Courts and Tribunals*, 3rd ed. (London: Stevens, 1957) vol. I, p. 427. According to J. Kunz, *supra* note 27, footnote 1, the 'quasi universal' character merely denotes a greater extension of validity and not a legal difference.

be hard to believe that there can be any difference whatsoever in content between the notion of self-defence in general international law and the notion of self-defence endorsed in the Charter'[32].

The conclusion reached with regard to self-defence can safely be extended to the norms on the use of force enshrined in the Charter.[33] The exclusion of 'the existence of any legal distinction either of United Nations practice as a whole or of Assembly recommendations from States' practice at large'[34] further supports this conclusion.

Indeed, the striking feature of the *Nicaragua case* is the extent of the agreement on the essential correspondence between the rules of the Charter concerning the use of force and non-intervention, and the parallel rules to be found in customary international law.[35] The Court maintained that the prohibition on the use of force as expressed in Art. 2(4) represented 'not only a principle of customary interna-

[32] R. Ago, *Addendum to the 8th Report on State Responsibility*, 32 *YBILC* (1980–II) Part 1, p. 63. He further stressed that 'it is right to dismiss at the outset so unconvincing an idea as that two really divergent notions of self-defence, based respectively on general international law and on the United Nations system, could co-exist'. A. Constatinou, *The Right of Self-Defence under Customary Law and Article 51 of the Charter* (Athens: A. N. Sakkoulas, 2000), p. 204, observes that 'Article 51 represents the only content of the right of self-defence permitted by both the Charter and customary international law'.

[33] In *The Legality of United States Participation in the Defense of Viet-Nam*, 4 March 1966, in R. Falk, *The Vietnam War and International Law* (Princeton: Princeton University Press, 1968), p. 585, footnote 3, the US affirmed that 'it should be recognized that much of the substantive law of the Charter has become part of the general law of nations through a very wide acceptance by nations the world over. This is particularly true of the Charter provisions on the use of force'. See also R. Barsotti, 'Armed Reprisals', in A. Cassese (ed.), *supra* note I-5, pp. 79 *et seq*., p. 84; E. Sciso, 'L'intervento in Kosovo. L'improbabile passaggio dal principio del divieto a quello dell'uso della forza armata', in E. Sciso (ed.), *Intervento in Kosovo. Aspetti internazionalistici e interni* (Milano: Giuffrè, 2001), pp. 47 *et seq*., 54–5. *Contra*, S. Marchisio, 'La teoria dei due cerchi', in E. Sciso (ed.), *supra*, pp. 21 *et seq*. Nowadays there is therefore no need for a 'second-order level of legal inquiry', as suggested some years ago by R. A. Falk, 'The Beirut Raid and the International Law of Retaliation', 63 *AJIL* (1969) 415, footnote 39, pp. 430–1.

[34] G. Arangio-Ruiz, *supra* note I-25, p. 44. He also adds that 'Recommendations, together with the many other components of UN practice, are part of that practice of States which brings about the formation of customary rules' to the extent they are demonstration of *opinio iuris* (p. 48) or may lead to the desuetude of a rule (p. 41).

[35] In *Legal Consequences of the Construction of a Wall in the Occupied Palestinian Territory*, Advisory Opinion, 9 July 2004, para. 87, the ICJ relied on the *Nicaragua case* to affirm that 'the principles as to the use of force incorporated in the Charter reflect customary international law' (posted at www.icj-cij.org).

[36] *Nicaragua case*, Merits, *supra* note 2, p. 100. The Court recalled that the ILC described this provision as having the character of *jus cogens* (see ILC, *Report to the General Assembly*, 18 *YBILC* (1966–II) p. 247) and that this view was shared by the Parties. As to the alleged differences existing under the two sources, the Court stressed that they were not significant enough to render inappropriate a judgment based upon customary international law (*ibid*. p. 97).

tional law but also a fundamental or cardinal principle of such law'.[36] This view was shared by some of the judges who wrote separate or dissenting opinions[37] and by both the parties.[38] The United States, in particular, maintained without hesitation that the Charter '*is* the "customary and general international law" with respect to the questions concerning the lawfulness of the use of armed force'.[39] The same view is solidly supported in literature.[40]

In the light of these considerations, a static vision of the Charter must be rejected in favour of a more flexible approach.[41] The 'historical and functional interaction'[42] between the Charter and customary international law may have changed and developed the general prohibition to use force, and eventually brought about new exceptions to it. These exceptions, not expressly foreseen in the Charter, could have emerged – or re-emerged in the event that they existed prior to the entry into force of the Charter – through a sufficiently uniform and general practice. The content of the norms on the use of force, therefore, must be ascertained through the analysis of the successive interpretations given by the actors involved, whenever the provision was applied, and not merely by verifying the conformity of these behaviours with a prior, superior norm.[43] What matters, in large measure, is State practice, including the attitude adopted, the will manifested, and the action taken by States within the framework of the United Nations, as well as by the United Nations itself as subjects of international law.

[37] In particular, judge R. Ago, sep. op., *ibid.*, p. 183, spoke of a 'close correspondence', whereas judge S. Schwebel, diss. op., *ICJ Rep. 1984*, p. 614 noted that 'contemporary international law governing the use of force in international relations is essentially composed of Article 2, paragraph 4, and article 51 of the United Nations Charter'.

[38] Nicaragua took the view that 'the principles contained in Article 2 (4) of the Charter form part of general international law' (*Memorial*, *Pleadings*, vol. IV, p. 118).

[39] United States *Counter-Memorial*, *supra* note 6, p. 91. At p. 94, it further observed that 'Article 2(4) of the Charter *is* customary and general international law' (italics as in the original).

[40] See the references made in the US in the *Counter-Memorial*, *supra* note 6, pp. 94–5.

[41] N. Ronzitti, *Rescuing Nationals Abroad Through Military Coercion and Intervention on Ground of Humanity* (Dordrecht: Nijhoff, 1985), p. 19. According to I. Brownlie, 'Kosovo Inquiry: Memorandum on the International Law Aspects', 49 *ICLQ* (2000) 878, p. 894, 'There can be no doubt that the United Nations Charter can be modified by the congruent practice of the Member States crystallizing as a new principle of customary law'.

[42] *Argument of Professor Brownlie*, *Nicaragua Case, Pleadings*, vol. V, p. 224. This document, however, focuses on the mutual reinforcement and confirmation of the two set of rules, and seems to neglect their interaction in evolutive terms. Also, the US statement that 'subsequent State practice has necessarily evolved only by reference to the Charter', *Counter-Memorial*, *supra* note 40, p. 96, overlooks the impact that customary international law might have had on the interpretation, evolution or even informal modification of the Charter.

[43] See J. Combacau, *supra* note I-5, p. 9; and *supra* note I-40, pp. 48–61.

This approach renders superfluous dealing with the question whether the Charter provisions on the use of force codified[44] or developed[45] the corresponding existing customary rules, possibly leaving unaffected certain rights to self-defence or self-help previously enjoyed by States.[46] Whether there was in 1945 identity between the rules embodied in the Charter or to what extent States' freedom to resort to force under existing customary law had survived the Charter is nowadays of little practical value. The crux of the matter is rather to assess how the rules governing the use of force under customary law and under the Charter have subsequently developed under their mutual influence and interaction. Assuming that such an identity existed in 1945, it cannot be excluded that the Charter has since been modified in the sense of establishing a less restrictive regime of the use of force, even to the point of provoking a return to the pre-Charter customary law. If, on the contrary, it is maintained that, in 1945, the right lawfully to resort to force under customary international law was broader than under the Charter, it is necessary to explore whether State practice points to the erosion of the Charter provisions or to the development of customary law towards the Charter paradigm.

The alleged dependence of Art. 2(4) on the effective functioning of the collective security system

There is a universal agreement among governments that the prohibition on the use of force established in Art. 2(4) continues to be binding, regardless of its admittedly too frequent violations.[47] The very fact that States invariably invoke exceptions to the prohibition on the use of force – and especially self-defence – to justify the recourse to military measures implicitly confirm their legal conviction

[44] See, in particular, I. Brownlie, *supra* I-59, p. 274; R. Ago, *supra* note 32, p. 67. According to G. Arangio-Ruiz, *3rd Report on State Responsibility*, 43 *YBILC* (1991–II) Part 1, p. 9, it is very likely that an identity exists between Art. 51 and the customary rule on self-defence.

[45] See in particular R. Y. Jennings, diss. op., *Nicaragua Case*, Merits, *supra* note 2, p. 530; S. Schwebel, diss. op., *ibid*., p. 615.

[46] For a discussion on this point, see J. Stone, *Aggression and World Order. A Critique of United Nations Theories of Aggression* (London: Stevens, 1958), p. 44; D. W. Bowett, *supra* note 17, pp. 184–185; I. Brownlie, *supra* note I-59, pp. 272 *et seq*.

[47] As observed by Y. Dinstein, *supra* note II-43, p. 89, 'The plea that Article 2 (4) is dead has never been put forward by any Government'. Similarly, see O. Schachter, 'In Defense of International Rules on the Use of Force', 53 *UCLR* (1986) 113, p. 131; A. Cassese, 'Return to Westphalia? Considerations on the Gradual Erosion of the Charter System', in A. Cassese, *supra* note I-5, pp. 505 *et seq*., p. 514.

on the existence of such a prohibition.[48] This view is reflected in the ICJ case law[49] and largely shared in literature, despite some rather isolated attacks.[50]

The real debate has regarded the absolute or relative character of such a prohibition and ultimately the limits of the prohibition rather than its existence. Primarily on the basis of the preparatory works, it has been maintained that the prohibition has an 'all inclusive' character.[51] This view has been countered by literal and teleological arguments. It was contented that Art. 2(4) can be read as not including uses of force that do not undermine the territorial integrity and political independence,[52] or that use of force might be admissible and indeed desirable if aimed at promoting the purposes and principles of the Charter, or at ensuring minimum order.[53]

The above considerations allow us to assume the existence of a prohibition on the use of force. Bearing in mind that absolute compliance is not a condition for the existence of a rule in international law,[54] the correctness of this assumption, and eventually the definition of the content of the prohibition on the use of force, will be verified through an inquiry on what, on the basis of the assumption, can provisionally be considered as the exceptions – either expressly foreseen in the

[48] See *infra* note 75. In State practice, see, in particular, the case of the recent intervention in Afghanistan, *supra* pp. 76 *et seq.*

[49] See, in particular: *Corfu Channel case*, Judgment, *ICJ Reports 1949*, pp. 4 *et seq.*; *Nicaragua case*, Merits, *supra* note 2; *Legality of the Threat and Use of Nuclear weapons*, *supra* note V-127, pp. 244 *et seq.*; *Case Concerning Oil Platforms*, Merits, 6 November 2003, posted at www.icj-cij.org. See also the advisory opinion *supra* note 35, para. 87.

[50] The most virulent attacks may have been conducted by T. Franck, 'Who Killed Art. 2(4)? or: The Changing Norms Governing the Use of Force by States', 64 *AJIL* (1970) 809; E. Rostow, 'The Legality of the International Use of Force by and from States', 10 *YJIL* (1985) 286; M. Glennon, *supra* note III-151, esp. pp. 84 *et seq.*; J. Bolton, *supra* note III-221.

[51] According to M. Lachs, 'General Course in Public International Law', 169 *RdC* (1980–IV) 9, p. 162, Art. 2(4) is a 'residual catch-all provision'. See also C. H. M. Waldock, 'The Regulation of the Use of Force by Individual States in International Law', 81 *RdC* (1951–I) 455, p. 493; I. Brownlie, *supra* note I-59, p. 273; G. Arangio-Ruiz, *supra* note I-25, p. 104; L. Henkin, 'General Course in Public International Law', 216 *RdC* (1989–IV) 10, p. 148; Y. Dinstein, *supra* note II-43, p. 82. See also the position of the US delegation at San Francisco, 6 *UNCIO* p. 335.

[52] See, in particular, J. Stone, *supra* note 46, p. 43. The argument was advanced by the UK in the *Corfu Channel case*, *supra* note 49, *Pleadings*, vol. III, p. 296. As maintained by D. W. Bowett, *supra* note 17, p. 151, the Court made no specific reference either to this argument or indeed to Art. 2(4). More recently, in *Legality of the Use of Force*, Provisional Measures, Belgium argued that armed humanitarian intervention is compatible with Art. 2(4) since this article covers only interventions against the territorial integrity or political independence of a State (10 May 1999, Verbatim Record, CR 99/15).

[53] See, in particular, M. S. McDougal and F. Feliciano, *Law and Minimum World Public Order* (New Haven: Yale University Press, 1961), pp. 240–1; W. M. Reisman, 'Coercion and Self-Determination: Construing Charter Article 2(4)', 78 *AJIL* (1984) 642.

[54] On this point, see, *Nicaragua case*, Merits, *supra* note 2, p. 98; G. Arangio-Ruiz, *supra* note I-25, p. 46.

Charter or allegedly (re-)emerged after the entry into force of the Charter – allowing the individual or joint use of force.

Preliminarily, however, attention must be paid to the alleged dependence of such a prohibition on the effective functioning of the collective security system. Indeed, the most powerful argument advanced to refute the absolute character of the prohibition established in Art. 2(4) is an 'organic dependence of any renunciation of individual force in the Charter, on the effective establishment of collective institutions and methods'.[55] On the same note, it has been contended that since the guarantee upon which the norm was construed and accepted by contracting States does not function effectively, the norm itself is no longer binding and States have regained the rights they enjoyed before the entry into force of the Charter.[56]

The opposite view is shared by the majority of authors[57] and finds some support in the ICJ case law. In the *Corfu Channel case*, the Court maintained that 'The right of intervention as the manifestation of a policy of force . . . cannot, whatever be the present defects in international organisation, find place in international law'.[58]

The conclusion reached by the Court in the *Nicaragua case*, that customary norms prohibiting the use of force – which are substantially identical to those contained in the Charter – retain a separate existence has an important corollary: they are not conditioned by provisions relating to the collective security system envisaged by the Charter or to the implementation of Art. 43.[59] As a result, States would be still bound to respect these norms irrespective of any legal challenge concerning the norms embodied in the Charter.

[55] J. Stone, *supra* note 46, pp. 96 *et seq*. On the relative character of the prohibition, see also: G. Schwarzenberger, 'The Fundamental Principles of International Law', 87 *RdC* (1955–I) 190, p. 338; T. M. Franck, *supra* note 50; M. S. McDougal, 'Authority to Use Force on the High Seas', 20 *NWCR* (1967) 19, p. 28; W. M. Reisman, *supra* note I-81, p. 850; M. Virally, 'Article 2 Paragraph 4', in J. P. Cot and A. Pellet (eds.), *supra* note I-6, pp. 115 *et seq*., p. 116.

[56] J. Combacau, *supra* note I-5, esp. pp. 9 and 30. In its diss. op. appended to the *Nicaragua case*, Merits, *supra* note 2, p. 543/4, R. Y. Jennings concluded that 'the original scheme of the United Nations Charter, whereby force would have be deployed by the United Nations itself, in accordance with the provisions of Chapter VII of the Charter, has never come into effect. Therefore an essential element of the Charter design is totally missing'. The judge, however, does not challenge the prohibition on the use of force but rather suggests a broader notion of collective self-defence.

[57] See, in particular, D. Nincic, *supra* note III-208, pp. 76 *et seq*.; O. Schachter, *supra* note 47, pp. 125 *et seq*.; L. Henkin, 'The Reports of the Death of Article 2(4) Are Greatly Exaggerated', 65 *AJIL* (1971) 547; A. L. Sicilianos, *Les réactions décentralisées à l'illicite. Des contre-mesures à la légitime défense* (Paris: LGDJ, 1990), p. 407; A. Gianelli, *Adempimenti preventivi all'adozione di contromisure internazionali* (Milano: Giuffrè, 1997), pp. 309 *et seq*.

[58] *Corfu Channel case*, *supra* note 49, p. 35.

[59] *Nicaragua case*, Merits, *supra* note 2, p. 100.

This argument deprives of any practical relevance the question of the applicability of the *rebus sic stantibus* theory to the Charter norms on the use of force.[60] Furthermore, since the paralysis of the Security Council was foreseeable and indeed was largely envisaged in 1945,[61] an essential element required by Art. 62 of the Vienna Convention on the Law of Treaties is clearly missing.

At any rate, it must be underlined that the question of the alleged dependence of the prohibition on the use of force on the functioning of the collective security system is confined to situations threatening international peace and security but not amounting to armed attacks. In concluding the Charter, contracting States deliberately renounced on the use of force in hypotheses different from armed attacks. They bestowed on the Security Council the exclusive power to take such action by air, sea or land force as necessary to encounter threats to international peace and security while retaining the right to defend themselves – in accordance with the procedural and substantial limits of the Charter – in case of breaches of peace and acts of aggression.

Certainly, the failure by the Security Council to meet its responsibility had a negative impact on the notion of self-defence. The use of force in self-defence, which under Art. 51 had a provisional character pending the collective action undertaken by the Security Council,[62] assumed an entirely unilateral dimension. This, however, falls short of abolishing the prohibition on the use of force.

At the basis of the historical move accomplished by Art. 2(4) was the determination to render unlawful the use of force unless it was founded on a collective decision pursuing a common interest. The *raison d'être* of the Charter was to guarantee that, with the exception of self-defence, military force would be employed exclusively on the basis of the collective will of the Organisation members, expressed through the collective acts of the Security Council.[63] Contracting States were aware that the Security Council was doomed to failure. Nonetheless, they accepted that only defensive unilateral use of force would be permitted, even in the event of paralysis of the Security Council.[64]

It must not be forgotten, finally, that, thanks essentially to the authorisation practice, in the recent years the collective security system has started to function, albeit in a selective manner and at the price of substantially downgrading the original scheme. Hence, the question no longer concerns the existence of an organic

[60] With regard to humanitarian intervention, see, in particular, F. Teson, *Humanitarian Intervention: An Inquiry into Law and Morality* (New York: Transnational Publishers, 1997), pp. 157 *et seq.*

[61] See 11 *UNCIO* pp. 741 *et seq.* and pp. 753 *et seq.*

[62] H. Kelsen defines such an exercise as an 'interlude': see *infra* text corresponding to note 218.

[63] The Committee III concluded that 'The use of force . . . remains legitimate only to back up decisions of the Organisation' (6 *UNCIO* p. 459).

[64] At the San Francisco Conference, the US declared: 'If a major Power became the aggressor the Council had no power to prevent war. In such case, the inherent right of self-defence applied and the Nations of the world must decide whether or not they would go to war' (11 *UNCIO* 514).

dependence of the prohibition on the use of force on the effectiveness of the collective security system. After decades of 'structural paralysis', the Security Council has eventually begun to live up its primary responsibility in maintaining international peace and security. What is now necessary is to verify whether the Security Council is functioning in a given crisis. This requires setting the criteria to establish when the Security Council is able to handle a given crisis,[65] but also to identify who is entitled to make such a determination.

Whether the Security Council was effectively functioning was the object of controversy in most of the recent crises, and especially those concerning Kosovo and Iraq. The fact that the Security Council was prevented from authorising the use of force because of different evaluations of the necessity and effectiveness of the intervention among its permanent members can hardly be equated with the paralysis of the organ. The Security Council was actively involved in both recent crises. It was imposing economic sanctions, promoting a negotiated solution and, in the case of Iraq, conducting a vast verification operation. Its members, however, assessed differently the attitudes of the Belgrade and Baghdad Governments, the prospects of success of the Security Council's action, and the opportunity to resort to the military option.

In both instances, unilateral use of force does not integrate or correct the collective security system but is an alternative to it. In the first crisis, the fact that the overwhelming majority of the Security Council's members were in favour of the military intervention permitted the invocation of considerations of legitimacy to justify the bypassing of the Security Council.[66] In the second crisis, on the contrary, the challenge to the authority of the Security Council was flagrant. A few States deliberately used force on the basis of their own unilateral judgement which was contrary to that of the majority of the Security Council, this time perfectly reflecting the position of the international community.

Maintaining the independence of the prohibition on the use of force from the functioning of the collective security system,[67] nonetheless, does not mean that Art. 2(4) cannot evolve, know of new exceptions or even become obsolete through consistent and contrary practice. Under a dynamic vision of the Charter the admissibility of non-defensive use of force not authorised by the Security Council, already discussed above from the standpoint of legitimacy, might be defended on the basis of the (re-)emergence of exceptions not foreseen in the Charter, namely armed reprisals, rescue operations of nationals abroad and intervention on humanitarian grounds. The (re-) emergence of such exceptions is to be demonstrated on

[65] The problem was underscored within the US delegation by Hackworth, *United States Foreign Relations*, 1945, vol. I, p. 679.

[66] The opposition to the use of force by the majority of the United Nations members, however, reveals that in that occasion the Security Council was scarcely representative of the whole membership.

[67] In general, see R. Barsotti, *supra* note 33, pp. 79 *et seq.*, p. 103. Y. Dinstein, *supra* note II-43, pp. 83 *et seq.*, considers unlawful any non-defensive use of force not authorised by the Security Council. See also S. Chesterman, *supra* note I-65, p. 236.

the basis of a uniform practice accepted as law.[68] Such a course of events permits the Charter to evolve and meet the ever-changing needs of the international community without destroying the collective enterprise undertaken in 1945. Such a development would imply a redefinition of the content of the ban on the use of force, not necessarily a challenge to the existence of such a ban.

The right of self-defence

Among the different forms of self-help involving the use of force, self-defence needs to be singled out not only because it is the only exception to the prohibition on the use of force expressly provided for in the Charter,[69] but also, and more importantly, for its function and timing. In contrast with other forms of self-help, and in particular armed reprisals, self-defence cannot find application *ex post facto*. The reaction has a 'defensive' character since it is directed at preventing the armed attack from proceeding, succeeding and achieving its purpose.[70]

Self-defence can be described as the permissible military reaction by a State to an armed attack carried out by another State. The analysis in this chapter is accordingly confined to the exercise of self-defence in the relations between sovereign States on the assumption that that the notion of armed attack 'denotes a use of force that possesses the characteristic of an international wrongful act and must therefore be attributable to a State'.[71] When a State is incapable of preventing

[68] L. Gros, 'The United Nations and the Role of Law', 19 *IO* (1965) 537, p. 541, observes that 'the growth of customary international law within the framework of the Charter is not excluded, but assertion that such a growth has occurred should be treated with caution unless there is reliable evidence that there is not merely consensus as to practice but that this practice has become a matter of law'.

[69] According to R. Ago, *supra* note 32, p. 56, self defence is the *only* form of armed self-help permissible in modern international law. The ILC more prudently described it as *a* form of admissible armed self-help (*Report to the General Assembly*, 32 *YBILC* (1980–II) Part 2, p. 54).

[70] R. Ago, *supra* note 32, p. 54, quoting with approval R. Quadri, *Diritto internazionale pubblico* 6th ed. (Napoli: Liguori, 1968), p. 271, according to whom the action taken in self-defence 'is designed to prevent the consummation of the wrong'. The ILC entirely shared this approach when describing self-defence as an action 'used to resist to an offensive use of armed force' (*supra* note 69, p. 53). According to G. Schwarzenberger, *supra* note 55, 'self defence must be compelling and instant' (p. 334) whereas its function is to preserve or restore the *status quo* (p. 343).

[71] P. Lamberti Zanardi, 'Indirect Military Aggression', in A. Cassese (ed.), *supra* note I-5, pp. 111 *et seq.*, p. 112 (footnote omitted). In the *Oil Platforms case*, *supra* note 49, para 51, the ICJ stated that 'in order to establish that it was legally justified in attacking Iranian platforms in exercise of the right of individual self-defence, the United States has to show that attacks had been upon it for which Iran was responsible'. In the opinion on the wall in Palestine, *supra* note 35, para. 139, the ICJ stated that 'Article 51 of the Charter thus recognizes the existence of an inherent right of self-defence in the case of armed attack by one State against another State'. See however *infra*, note V-22. According to N. Ronzitti,

individuals or groups of individuals from conducting military operations against another State, the possible reaction cannot be regarded as self-defence. Since no prior breach of any international obligation has been committed, the reaction might be taken under the state of necessity doctrine, or 'by virtue of a right of necessity'.[72] We shall revert to the question in the next chapter, when dealing with international terrorism.

It is sequential to the premises that the *Caroline case* and in particular the so-called Webster formula, can hardly serve as paradigm for self-defence. At the time States still enjoyed the freedom to resort to unlimited war – considered as a paramount attribute of sovereignty[73] – and the notion of self-defence had little legal value.[74] It has been observed that 'The absolutely indispensable premise for the admission of the idea of self-defence, with its intrinsic meaning, into a particular system of law is that the system must have contemplated, as a general rule, the prohibition of the indiscriminate use of force'.[75] Hence, as the documents related to the *Caroline case* confirm, the notions of self-preservation, self-defence, necessity and self-help were 'not yet clearly differentiated as legal categories'[76] and were to a large extent used as interchangeable.[77] Additionally, it is doubtful that the British Government attributed to the United States the acts that triggered the military reaction. Quite to the contrary, the frequent reference to the 'piratical

---

supra note 41, p. 12, 'in order to be able to react on self-defence the attack must originate from a subject of international law or be ascribable to it by virtue of the norms regulating State international responsibility'. See also D. W. Bowett, *supra* note 17, p. 9.

[72] D. W. Bowett, *supra* note 17, p. 56.

[73] Q. Wright, 'The Outlawry of War', 19 *AJIL* (1925) 76, relying on the conclusion reached by the First World War Peace Conference Commission that even 'a war or aggression may not be considered as an act directly contrary to positive law' (p. 78), admits that at the time 'an act of war or a declaration of war which initiate a state of war is not illegal, in the absence of express treaty' (p. 83). On the undisputed freedom to wage war before 1915, see the authorities listed in Q. Wright, 'Changes in the Conception of War', 18 *AJIL* (1924) 755, pp. 756–7. See also D. Anzilotti, *Corso di diritto internazionale* (Roma: Athenaeum, 1915), esp. pp. 182 *et seq*.

[74] As observed by D. W. Bowett, *supra* note 17, p. 122, prior to 1915, 'it was impossible, as yet, to characterize force or war as being a delict, or self defence, or a sanction'. For E. Jimenez de Arechaga, *supra* note III-132, p. 96, 'before 1945 self-defence was not a legal concept but merely a political excuse for the use of force'. The invasion of Florida by the US, for instance, was described as 'a necessary measure of self-defence': see the Secretary of State's letter of 28 November 1818, in J. B. Moore, *Digest of International Law* (Washington: Government Printing Office, 1906), vol. II, pp. 402 *et seq*., p. 406. On the freedom to resort to force at the time of the Caroline, see *infra* notes 275–279.

[75] See R. Ago, *supra* 32, p. 52. See also the authorities referred to at p. 62, footnote 254; *Adde* Morelli, *supra* note I-38, p. 353.

[76] J. Stone, 'Book Review of I. Brownlie, International Law and the Use of Force by States', 59 *AJIL* (1965) 396, p. 399.

[77] See I. Brownlie, *supra* note I-59, p. 43.

character'[78] of the *Caroline case* suggests the comparison of the British action with military activities that would currently be included under the rubric of state of necessity.[79]

More than being an *ante litteram* – and probably unconscious[80] – attempt to elucidate the limits of self-defence in a period in which States were free to resort to force,[81] the so-called Webster formula was intended to avoid the qualification of coercive measures taken in the territory of another State as acts of war and prevent the instauration of a state of war between the two States.[82]

If the existence of the right to self-defence has never been disputed,[83] its content and limits have been the object of a passionate debate evolving around Art. 51 of the Charter. In line with the considerations made above on the relationship between the provisions on the use of force embodied in the Charter and those existing under customary international law, the argument that the right to self-defence under Art. 51 is narrower than that under customary international law is nowadays unconvincing.[84] Even assuming that the two notions did not coincide in

[78] See in particular the British notes of 6 February 1838, in W. R. Manning, *Diplomatic Correspondence of the United States: Canadian Relations* (Washington: Carnegie Endowment, 1943), vol. III, p. 422; and of 12 March 1841, in 29 *BFSP* (1840–1) 1126 *et seq*., p. 1127. On the local authorities' incapability of preventing the disturbances, see R. Y. Jennings, 'The *Caroline* and *McLeod* Cases', 32 *AJIL* (1938) 82, p. 86, footnote 12.

[79] See, in particular, R. Ago, *supra* note 32, pp. 39–40; *ILC Report to the General Assembly*, 32 *YBILC* (1980–II) Part 2, p. 44, footnote 155. J. Crawford, *The International Law Commission's Articles on State Responsibility* (Cambridge: Cambridge University Press, 2002) p. 179, observes that the *Caroline case* 'involved the plea of necessity at a time when the law concerning the use of force had quite a different basis than it now has'. See also *Draft Articles on Responsibility of States for Internationally Wrongful Acts*, *ILC Report to the General Assembly*, 2001, A/56/10, p. 196.

[80] R. Y. Jennings, *supra* note 78, p. 92.

[81] According to I. Brownlie, '*Interational Law and the Use of Force by States* Revisited', 21 *AYIL* (1999) 21, p. 24, 'The reference to the period 1838 to 1842 as the critical date for the customary law said to lie behind the Charter, drafted in 1945, is anachronistic and indefensible'.

[82] W. M. Reisman, 'Article 2(4): The Use of Force in Contemporary International Law', 78 *ASIL* (1984) 74, p. 75, observes that 'Presumably one of the functions of this doctrine in the context in which it was installed was to permit States to avert the conclusion that another State's resort to coercion was an act of war'.

[83] On the notes submitted by the US and other States on the interpretation of the 1928 *General Treaty for Renunciation of War*, 94 *LNTS 57*, see I. Brownlie, *supra* note I-59, pp. 237 *et seq*.

[84] Such a co-existence could have been plausible at the time it had been asserted by J. Stone, *supra* note 46, p. 44; A. L. Goodhart, *The North Atlantic Treaty of 1949*, 79 *RdC* (1951–II) 183, p. 192; D. W. Bowett, *supra* note 17, pp. 185 *et seq*. On the question see also I Brownlie, *supra* note I-59, pp. 272 *et seq*. With regard to the mission directed at rescuing the American hostages in Iran, T. L. Stein, 'Contempt, Crisis, and the Court. The World Court and the Hostage Rescue Attempt', 76 *AJIL* (1982) 499, footnote 8, observes that the operation could have been lawful 'not because the right of self-defence under the Charter is coexistensive with the preexisting international law right of self defense, which extended beyond defense against armed attack . . . but because the right of self-defense against armed attack has arisen'.

1945, the survival to the entry into force of the Charter of the broader notion of self-defence under customary international law – which needs to be demonstrated by the attitude of States – would have progressively modified Art. 51. The opposite course of events, namely the progressive evolution of customary law because of the impact produced upon it by the Charter, must equally be supported by the practice of the Organisation and its Member States. In both cases, however, the end result would be the substantial correspondence between Art. 51 and customary international law.[85]

Any attempt to define the limits to self-defence, therefore, must be based on the analysis of the relevant practice. The preparatory work of the Charter and the text of Art. 51, on the contrary, scarcely provide any conclusive arguments. It must be borne in mind that Art. 51 was inserted during the San Francisco conference in order to harmonise existing regional organisations with the new Organisation. Moreover, it was discussed essentially in the context of attacks involving the trespass of regular armed forces.[86] Since then, developments such as the expansion of the so-called indirect intervention, the proliferation of weapons of mass destruction, and the growth of international terrorism have prompted a debate on the need to reconsider the notion of self-defence.

Article 51 had been deliberately drafted in rather general terms.[87] Its content depends primarily on the interpretation and application of a notion, that of 'armed attack', which leaves room for diverging views and has significantly evolved throughout the years.[88] Whether or not it coincides with the definition of aggression,[89] 'armed attack' remains the key concept for the purpose of interpreting and

[85] This view is indirectly endorsed by D. W. Greig, *supra* note 17, p. 380, who, with regard to the alleged duty to report to the Security Council the measures taken in self-defence, notes that 'it hardly seems possible to have a mandatory provision in the Charter, to which there is no counterpart in customary international law'.

[86] M. J. Glennon, *supra* III-151, p. 140, confirms that '[t]he *idée fixe* at which the Charter's core prohibitions are directed is invasion, the paradigm being the 1939 German invasion of Poland'.

[87] Concern over the vagueness of Art. 51 had been expressed within the US delegation, see *US Foreign Relations*, 1945, vol. I, pp. 665 and 670.

[88] M. N. Feder, 'Reading the UN Charter Connotatively: Toward a New Definition of Armed Attack', 19 *NYUJILP* (1986–7) 395, pp. 410–1, rightly underlines that 'the potentially high significant of the concept of armed attack has generally been ignored'.

[89] Among the authors supporting a substantial identity, see P. Rambaud, 'La définition d'agression par l'Organisation des Nations Unies', 80 *RGDIP* (1976) 835; B. Broms, 'The Definition of Aggression', 154 *RdC* (1977–I) 299, p. 370; H. McCoubrey and N. D. White, *International Law and Armed Conflict* (Aldershot: Dartmouth, 1992), pp. 39 *et seq*.; A. L. Sicilianos, *supra* note 57, p. 299. See also the declarations made by France and the UK before the UN General Assembly, respectively, A/AC.134/SR 46 and A/AC 134/SR 67. *Contra*, see C. T. Eustathiades, 'La définition de l'agression adoptée aux Nations Unies et la légitime défense', 28 *RHDI* (1975) 1; E. Sciso, 'L'aggressione indiretta nella definizione dell'Assemblea Generale delle Nazioni Unite', 66 *RDI* (1983) 253, pp. 272 *et seq*. It must in any case be emphasised that the definition is neither exhaustive nor legally binding: it was rather meant to provide the Security Council with some guidance in the discharging of its responsibilities under Chapter VII of the Charter.

applying Art. 51.[90] It must be construed in accordance with the claims put forward by States and the reactions they provoked,[91] bearing in mind that 'what constitutes proportional and necessary self-defence can only be gauged in the light of situational problems which are created by the factors of weapons capability, and evolving tactics'.[92]

Armed attack as a prerequisite for self-defence

The notion of armed attack has generally been associated with the threshold of military hostile activities below which resort to force in self-defence is not admitted.[93] State practice, however, scarcely supports this view. Governments do not tolerate any hostile military activities carried out by the land, naval or air forces of other States, and reserve their right to counter them *extrema ratio* by military measures. The so-called 'unit self-defence',[94] 'on-the-spot' reaction[95] or 'defensive action'[96] – describing immediate, necessary and proportionate military reaction to small-scale hostile activities – are not qualitatively different exercises of the right of self-defence on a larger scale.

This casts some doubts on the validity of the distinction between armed attack and frontier incidents.[97] Reactions to armed incursions by small contingents, or limited hostile military activities across the frontier, may satisfy the two elements of the proposed definition of self-defence: they amount to violations of Art. 2(4) and are attributable to a subject of international law. The victim State is accordingly allowed to resort to military force, both within its territory and in the

[90] See P. Lamberti Zanardi, *La legittima difesa nel diritto internazionale* (Milano: Giuffrè, 1972), p. 228. On the feasibility and desirability of the definition of aggression, see, in particular, G. Fitzmaurice, 'Definition of Aggression (Speech in United Nations General Assembly)', 1 *ICLQ* (1952) 137; J. Stone, *supra* note 46; S. M. Schwebel, 'Aggression, Intervention and Self-Defense', 136 *RdC* (1972–II) 411; B. Broms, *supra* note 89.

[91] *Contra* J. Combacau, *supra* note I-5, p. 23, according to whom the notion of armed attack 'remains as indeterminate legally as it was when the Charter was drawn up, and can be freely construed case by case by its authorised interpreters'.

[92] D. P. O'Connell, 'International Law and Contemporary Naval Operations', 44 *BYIL* (1970) 19, p. 82, who also describes as 'naïve' the expression armed attack (p. 25).

[93] See the *Nicaragua case*, Merits, *supra* note 2 , p. 101; the *Oil Platforms case*, *supra* note 49, esp. paras 51 and 63.

[94] See D. Stephens, 'Rules of Engagement and the Concept of Unit Self-defence', 45 *NLR* (1998) 126.

[95] See Y. Dinstein, *supra* note II-43, pp. 192 *et seq.*

[96] See B. Simma, sep. op. in the *Oil Platforms case*, *supra* note 49, paras 12 *et seq.* Nevertheless, in para. 14, the judge concedes that 'there is in international law on the use of force no "qualitative jump" from iterative activities remaining below the threshold of Article 51 of the Charter to the type of "armed attack" envisaged there'.

[97] For a discussion on this distinction, see C. Gray, *supra* note III-232, pp. 145 *et seq.*

territory of the offending State, to put an end to these acts, within the limits of immediacy, proportionality and necessity.[98]

Self-defence equally provides a legal ground for the use of force against unlawful aerial intrusion by military aircraft.[99] Military aircraft that violate a State's airspace, disregard the orders of territorial authorities and represent a potential threat to military or civilian targets can be considered as conducting a hostile mission and forced to land, be diverted or, ultimately, shot down.[100] Although national rules of engagement differ,[101] the right to use the military force to the extreme consequences in order to neutralise intruding State aircraft has never been challenged. In all controversies regarding the shooting of State or civilian aircraft, objections to the armed reaction have been raised on grounds concerning not the existence of such a right, but rather its lawful exercise in the concrete case.[102] In order to increase national security and prevent incidents, several States have unilaterally declared air defence identification zone (ADIZs)

[98] G. Venturini, *Necessità e proporzionalità nell'uso della forza militare in diritto internazionale* (Milano: Giuffrè, 1988), p. 46, observes that an excessive reaction to an incursion could amount to a violation of Art. 2(4) or a threat to international peace, even if it is limited to the territory of the reacting State.

[99] On the problematic definition of 'military aircraft', see in M. Bourbonniere, L. Haeck, 'Military Aircraft and International Law: Chicago Opus 3', 66 *JALC* (2001) 885.

[100] See: Q. Wright, 'Legal Aspects of the U-2 Incident', 54 *AJIL* (1960) 836; O.J. Lissitzy, 'Some Legal Implications of the U-2 and RB 47 Incidents', 56 *AJIL* (1962) 135; I. Brownlie, *supra* note I-59, p. 373; A. A. Majid, 'Treaty Amendment Inspired by the Korean Plane Tragedy: Custom Clarified or Confused?', 29 *GYIL* (1986) 190, p. 224; K. G. Park, *La protection de la souveraineté aérienne* (Paris: Pédone, 1991), esp. pp. 312 *et seq.*; M. Kido, 'The Korean Airlines Incident on September 1, 1983 and Some Measures Following It', 62 *JALC* (1997) 1049; E. Cannizzaro, *Il principio della proporzionalità nell'ordinamento internazionale* (Milano: Giuffrè, 2000), pp. 260 *et seq.*

[101] Compare, for example, Art. 36 of the Law on State Boundary of the former Soviet Union, disposing that the use of weapons and combat equipment shall be used 'in order to repel an armed attack or intrusion on the territory of the USSR . . . in response to the use of force by them' (22 *ILM* (1983) 1074); with 'the use of force of arms without prior warning applies to unidentified aircraft entering Swedish airspace under circumstances indicating hostile intention', quoted in J. Sundeberg, 'Legitimate Responses to Aerial Intruders: The View from a Neutral State', 10 *AASL* (1985) 251, pp. 266–7. See also the position of the Japanese Government: 28 *JAIL* (1985) p. 142 *et seq.* According to O.J. Lissitzy, *supra* note 100, p. 138, 'intruding aircraft could be shot down, in certain circumstances, even without previous warning or order to land', whereas for Q. Wright, *supra* note 100, p. 850, 'the only legal issue is the extent of warning which should be given before a plane is shot down'.

[102] Most common objections include the location of the involved aircraft over international airspace, the alleged hostile nature of the flight and the avoidable or disproportionate nature of the military reaction. See, in particular the position taken by Israel, the US and the UK, in the respective memorial on the *Aerial Incident of 27 July 1955*, *ICJ Pleadings*, esp. pp. 84, 239 and 358. See also A. Yokaris and G. Kyriakopoulos, 'La juridiction de l'Etat côtier sur l'espace aérien national et international. A propos de l'affaire de CESSNA abattus par la chasse cubaine', 101 *RGDIP* (1997) 493.

and warned that intruding aircraft could be considered as engaged in hostile military missions.[103]

The powers of territorial States are obviously different in the event of intrusion by civilian aircraft since in normal conditions these aircraft cannot have a hostile nature.[104] Articke 3 (*bis*) of the Chicago Convention prohibits the use of weapons against civilian aircraft, but allows the use of force necessary to intercept them, provided that the lives of persons on board and the safety of aircraft are not endangered.[105] It must be noted, nonetheless, that the exercise of self-defence against civil aircraft is by no means excluded in absolute terms.[106]

The use of military force is also permitted for defensive purposes against ships and submarines carrying out or threatening to carrying out hostile military activities in another State's territorial waters[107] or from a location outside them.[108] Although recent practice offers few precedents, the coastal State possesses an undisputed right to take the appropriate military measures in order to put an end to these activities or neutralise these threats, including *extrema ratio* the destruction of the ship and submarine.[109]

Self-defence has also often been invoked by States as the legal basis to prevent or to put an end by military means to hostile activities carried out against their

[103] See, for instance, for the US, *Security Control of Air Traffic*, 14 CFR § 99 (1987). In general, see E. Cuadra, 'Air Defence Identification Zones: Creeping Jurisdiction on the Airspace', 18 *VJIL* (1978) 485; K. G. Park, *supra* note 100, pp. 268 *et seq.*

[104] But see *infra*, pp. 182–3.

[105] Art. 3 was amended following the shooting of Korean civilian aircraft and on the basis of a proposal put forward by the Soviet Union: see. B. Cheng, 'The Destruction of KAL Flight KE 007 and Art 3 bis of the Chicago Convention', in J. W. E. Storm Van Gravesonde and A. Van der Veen Vonk (eds.), *Air Worthy* (Deventer: Kluwer, 1985), 49 *et seq.*, pp. 62–3. In the resolution adopted on 14 June 1993, ICAO *reaffirmed* the principle of non-use of weapons against civilian aircraft, in 187 *RFDAS* (1993) 376. See also *Report of the ICAO Fact-Finding Investigation*, in 23 *ILM* (1984) 864, and the resolution adopted on 6 March 1984 (*ibid.*, p. 937).

[106] Art. 3 *bis* (a) *in fine*. But see B. Cheng, *supra* note 105, pp. 67–70, who questions the relevance of self-defence in the contest of civilian aircraft.

[107] This holds true *a fortiori* for internal waters.

[108] On the functional nature of the notion of territorial sea, see L. Sico AND L. Leanza, *La sovranità territoriale. Il mare* (Torino: Giappichelli, 2001), Pp. 19 *et seq*. R. C. Haerr, 'The Gulf of Sidra', 24 *SDLR* (1987) 751, pp. 764 *et seq.*, argues that, at least in principle, Libya could have resorted to force in self-defence against US carriers located outside its (claimed) territorial waters.

[109] N. Ronzitti, 'Sommergibili non identificati, pretese baie storiche e contromisure dello Stato costiero', 66 *RDI* (1983) 5, esp. p. 9; G. Cataldi, *Il passaggio delle navi straniere nel mare territoriale* (Milano: Giuffrè, 1990), Pp. 277 *et seq.*; Y. Dinstein, *supra* note II-43, p. 178. According to I. Delupis, 'Foreign Warship and Immunits for Espionage', 78 *AJIL* (1984) 53, p. 75, the right to self-defence 'is not limited to cases of an actual armed attack but exists also in the case of espionage or other illicit intrusions'. For a discussion on Art. 15 of the Swedish Law, see R. Sadurska, 'Foreign Submarines in Swedish Waters: The Erosion of an International Norm', 10 *YJIL* (1984–5) 34. See also the position of the Italian Government on the occasion of an unauthorised intrusion by a Soviet submarine in

ships or aircraft located on or over spaces open to international navigation.[110] Challenges to these claims have focused on the factual circumstances of the incident, the location of the ship or aircraft, and the respect of the limits within which States are allowed to exercise their right to self-defence, but have never regarded this right in itself. That the right to self-defence could be triggered by the attack conducted against a single military vessel has been confirmed by the ICJ in the *Oil Platforms case*.[111]

The repeated military clashes between the United States and Libya over the Gulf of Sidra in 1981,[112] 1986[113] and 1989 provide some useful examples, in spite of the uncertainty surrounding the facts and the underlying controversial Libyan claims over the area. For the purpose of this discussion, suffice it to note that the United States insisted on the location of its carriers on international waters and, more importantly, on the 'routine peaceful' nature of manoeuvres in progress. The unprovoked use of force by Libya, according to its view, had been lawfully countered by military means on the basis of Art. 51 of the Charter.[114] These claims were supported by some Western States, and in particular the United Kingdom.[115] It must be underlined that none of the States that criticised or condemned the United States' reactions contested the right recognised to any State to protect its ships, if

the waters of the Taranto Gulf in N. Ronzitti, *supra*, pp. 45–6. See also the Danish Law of 16 April 1984, quoted in D. Fleck, 'Rules of Engagement for Military Force and the Limits of the Use of Force Under the UN Charter', 31 *GYIL* (1986) 165, p. 184 footnote 75.

110 I. Brownlie, *supra* note I-59, p. 305, states that undoubtedly 'the armed forces of the flag State may use reasonable force to defend vessels from attack whether by pirates or forces acting with or without the authority of any State' (footnote omitted). The Japanese Government recently declared that 'if a ship, private or public, is attacked on the high seas, the target State can exercise individual right of self-defence' (43 *JAIL* (2000) 158). By concluding the *Agreement on the Prevention of Incidents on and over the High Seas*, 25 May 1972, 11 *ILM* (1972) 778 and the *Agreement on the Prevention of Dangerous Military Activities*, 12 June 1989, 28 *ILM* (1989) 877, the US and the former USSR intended to ensure the safety of air and naval navigation during military manoeuvres.

111 *Supra* note 49. In para 72, in particular, the Court 'does not exclude the possibility that the mining of a single military vessel might be sufficient to bring into play the inherent right of self defence'.

112 See F. Francioni, 'The Gulf of Sirte Incident (United States and Libya) and International Law', 5 *IYIL* (1980–1) 85; S. R. Ratner , 'The Gulf of Sidra Incident of 1981', 10 YJIL (1984) 59.

113 Y. Z. Blum, 'The Gulf of Sidra Incident', 80 *AJIL* (1986) 668.

114 See the letters sent to the Security Council on 19 August 1981, S/14632; 25 March 1986, S/17938; and 4 January 1989, S/20366. The incident has become the paradigm of the so-called unit self-defence, see *Commander's Handbook on the Law of Naval Operations*, available at www.cpf.navy.mil, which affirms that unit self defence 'is the act of defending from attack or threat of imminent attack . . . this concept relates to localized, low-level situations that are not preliminary to prolonged engagement'.

115 S/PV.2669, 27 March 1986, pp. 32 *et seq*.

unavoidable by force; they rather disputed the exercise of such a right by the United States in this specific case.[116]

During the Iran–Iraq war, finally, some Western States, while admitting the right of belligerents to visit and search neutral ships,[117] reserved to themselves the right to use force in order to protect not only their warships but also their commercial vessels.[118] The most tragic incident occurred in 1988, and regarded the accidental shooting of an Iranian civilian aircraft believed to be 'a military aircraft with hostile intention'.[119] The United States' claim that the shooting was justified as self-defence was not rejected by the ICAO, which elaborated on the factors to be taken into account in the process of determination of the military and hostile nature of the aircraft.[120] Iran itself admitted that, in order lawfully to invoke self-defence for using force, 'it will be necessary to examine whether the United States was subject to an armed attack when it destroyed IR 665. The fact that the targeted aircraft was a civilian aircraft with absolutely no military capability presents the United States with an insurmountable hurdle in this respect'.[121]

It must finally be observed that the hostile military activities may take place within the territory of the offending State as it may occur when the target of these activities is the diplomatic and consular personnel or premises.[122] The question

[116] The former Soviet Union, in particular, stated that 'There was absolutely no reason for the United States to use armed force, for nobody had attacked the aircraft or the ships of the United States in the region' (S/PV.2670, 27 March 1986, p. 67).

[117] Curiously, the UK maintained that this right derived from Art. 51 of the Charter.

[118] C. Gray, 'The British Position in regard to the Gulf Conflict', 37 *ICLQ* (1988) 420 and 40 *ICLQ* (1992) 464; I. F. Dekker and H. H. G. Post (eds.), *The Gulf War of 1980–1988: The Iran–Iraq War in International Legal Perspective* (Dordrecht: Nijhoff, 1992); A. De Guttry and N. Ronzitti (eds.), *The Iran–Iraq War (1980–1988) and the Law of Naval Warfare* (Cambridge: Grotius, 1993). The *Secretary of Defence Report to the Congress*, 15 June 1987, in 26 *ILM* (1987) 1433, p. 1458, reads: 'In accordance with our inherent right to employ proportional military force as necessary in self-defense, the United States will act only in the face of attack, or hostile intent indicating imminent attack, against warships or commercial vessels of its flag'. See also the rules of engagement: *ibid.*, p. 1454. On the admissibility of self-defence claims with regard to civil ships, compare A. V. Lowe, 'Self-Defence at Sea', in W. E. Butler, *supra* note I-40, pp. 185 *et seq.*, pp. 197–198, with C. Greenwood, 'Comments', in I. F. Dekker and H. H. G. Post (eds.), *supra*, pp. 212 *et seq.*, p. 214.

[119] *Aerial Incident of 3 July 1988*, *United States Memorial*, *ICJ Pleadings*, vol. II, p. 42, available at the Court website. The case was discontinued in 1996; see Order of 22 February 1996, *ICJ Reports 1996*, p. 9. See also *Agora*, *The Downing of Iran Air Flight 665*, 83 *AJIL* (1989) 318.

[120] *Report of ICAO Fact-Finding Investigation*, November 1989, 28 *ILM* (1989) 900, esp. pp. 913 and 923. See also the resolution adopted on 17 March 1989 (*ibid.*, p. 898).

[121] *Aerial Incident of 3 July 1988*, *Iran Memorial*, *ICJ Pleadings*, vol. I, p. 215, available at the Court website.

[122] The US justified the 1980 rescue mission in Iran as 'an exercise of its inherent right of self-defence with the aim of extricating American nationals who have been and remain the victim of Iranian armed attack on our Embassy', quoted by the Court in *United States Diplomatic and Consular Staff in Tehran*, *ICJ Reports 1980*, p. 3, at p. 18. See also T. L. Stein, *supra* note 84. In general, see G. Arangio-Ruiz, *supra* note I-25, p. 105; and *supra* note I-73, p. 27.

whether self-defence can also constitute the legal basis for military intervention directed at protecting nationals abroad will be discussed later.[123]

It is submitted that State practice offers enough evidence to refute the existence of a threshold of hostile military activities below which self-defence cannot be invoked.[124] Setting such a threshold would deprive States of the right effectively to counter hostile uses of force amounting to violations of Art. 2(4), but not reaching the level of gravity required to be qualified as armed attacks. This would expose them to unacceptable risks with regard to both their national security and potential human and material losses.

The resulting situation of powerlessness in case of breaches of the prohibition on the use of force would represent an unrealistic loophole in the whole normative framework on the use of force, even assuming the effective functioning of the collective security mechanism. When the situation does not amount to a threat to international peace, in fact, the Security Council cannot resort to measures involving the use of force. Admitting that States are allowed to resort to force in order to defend themselves against any hostile military activities appears to be the most plausible interpretation of Art. 51 and certainly that which better reflects State practice. The limits of immediacy, proportionality and necessity would provide an adequate safeguard against abuses.[125]

It may be argued that this view is in large measure compatible with the *Nicaragua case*, at least as far as individual self-defence is concerned. The Court left unanswered the question whether force can be used by the State victim of hostile military activities that – although not amounting to an armed attack – could qualify as threat or use of force.[126] Arguably, the Court did not exclude a military reaction by the concerned State, although this would have been justified on a legal basis other than self-defence, most probably as armed reprisals.[127]

Apart from the difficulties in setting a threshold of military activities for the purpose of qualifying them as armed attack, there is no compelling reason for a legal distinction, based on the trespassing of such a threshold, between measures

[123] See *infra* pp. 171–2.

[124] In this sense, see, in particular, J. Kunz, 'Individual and Collective Self-Defense in Article 51 of the Charter of the United Nations', 41 *AJIL* (1947) 872, p. 878; G. Fitzmaurice, *supra* note 90, p. 139; J. L. Hargrove, 'The Nicaragua Judgment and the Future of the Law of Force and Self-Defense', 81 *AJIL* (1987) 135, p. 139; G. M. Badr, 'The Exculpatory Effect of Self-Defence in State Responsibility', 10 *GJIL* (1980) 1; Y. Dinstein, *supra* note II-43, p. 176.

[125] See, for instance, R. Higgins, *Problems and Process: International Law and how we use it* (Oxford: Clarendon Press, 1994), p. 251.

[126] *Nicaragua case*, Merits, *supra* note 2, pp. 103–4, pp. 126–7. The Court here limited itself to noting that supplying arms and no better specified 'other support' does not amount to an armed attack, although it may be qualified as a threat or use of force. See the criticism on this point expressed in their diss. opinions by S. Schwebel (*ibid.* p. 348 *et seq.*), and by R. Y. Jennings (*ibid.* pp. 542 *et seq.*).

[127] According to J. L. Hargrove, *supra* note 124, p. 138, the Court strongly suggested that the materially victim State – but not other States – could resort to armed reprisals.

taken in self-defence and armed reprisals.[128] State practice reveals that governments invariably consider use of force to counter *any* military hostile activities as an exercise of self-defence. They also affirm the inadmissibility of armed reprisals.[129] Incidentally, treating any forcible reaction to hostile military activities as self-defence permits the underlining of their defensive nature and classifying more accurately under the rubric of 'armed reprisals' other kinds of measures involving the use of force.

The so-called indirect aggression

It is traditionally held that in order to trigger the right to self-defence, the military hostile activities must be attributed to States or other subjects of international law.[130] It is immaterial whether these activities are conducted by the regular forces or by irregular forces.[131] The existence of a real link between the individuals or groups carrying out the operations and the State machinery prevails over the lack of a formal legal *nexus* between them.[132] The crux of the matter lies in the degree of effective control exercised by the concerned State over the irregular forces.

There is no reason not to apply the effectiveness test, that generally governs the international responsibility of States for conduct of individuals or groups acting as its *de facto* organs to violations of the prohibition on the use of force. Yet, because of its peculiar nature, the violation does not only entail the typical legal consequences from the perspective of the international responsibility of the State involved in the military activities; it also allows the victim State to invoke the right of self-defence and request the military assistance of other States.

The International Law Commission, the International Court of Justice and the International Criminal Tribunal for the former Yugoslavia have contributed to the

[128] But see C. H. M. Waldock, *supra* note 51, p. 496; S. Schwebel, diss. op., *Nicaragua case*, Merits, *supra* note 2, p. 348, who admits that, under certain circumstances States could invoke self-defence as the legal basis for using force even if no armed attack has occurred.

[129] See Art. 50, para. 1(a) of the 2001 ILC *Draft Articles*, *supra* note 79, pp. 333 *et seq*. See also the position of the US in 1973, in 71 *AJIL* (1979) 489. Preference to a broadening of the notion of self-defence, rather than the introduction of new exceptions, has been expressed by R. Y. Jennings, dis. op., *Nicaragua Case*, Merits, *supra* note 2, p. 544.

[130] See *supra* note 71. Referring to D. Anzilotti, R. Ago, *2nd Report on State Responsibility*, 22 *YBILC* (1970–II) Part 1, p. 189, explained that the notion of 'imputability' indicates the link between the wrongful act or omission and its author in the sense that 'the international legal order must be able to regard the action or omission concerned as an act of State, if it is to be allowed further to assume the creation of those new subjective legal situations which . . . are covered by the overall, synthetic expression "international responsibility of States"'.

[131] *Nicaragua case*, Merits, *supra* note 2, p. 103.

[132] See the ILC Commentary to Art. 8, *Report to the General Assembly*, 26 *YBILC* (1974–II) Part 1, p. 283. See also R. Ago, *3rd Report on State Responsibility*, 23 *YBILC* (1971–II) Part 1, pp. 262 *et seq*.

elaboration of the criteria to ascertain when individuals or groups of individuals not integrated in the official structure of the State may nevertheless act as its *de facto* organs.[133] The ILC initially defined *de facto* organs as persons or group of persons acting in fact on behalf of the State,[134] in the sense that the former have been appointed and instigated by the organs of the latter 'to discharge a particular function or to carry out a particular duty'.[135]

The notion was applied and developed by the ICJ in the *Nicaragua case*. Here, the Court maintained that the so-called indirect aggression[136] implies that the relationship between the State and its *de facto* organs is so much one of control of the one side and dependence on the other.[137] International responsibility arises when the State exercises such an effective control over the *de facto* organs to put it in a position to direct or enforce the perpetration of certain acts.[138] The involvement of a State over irregular forces for the purpose of their qualification as *de facto* organs implies, in addition to instruction and instigation, the effective control which consists in the exercise of certain authority.[139]

Applying this test with regard to the *Contras*, the Court denied that they acted as *de facto* organs of the United States, despite the participation of this State in the financing, organising, training, supplying and equipping of the *Contras*, in the selection of their targets, and in the planning of the whole of their operation.[140] The opposite conclusion was reached with regard to UCLAs since the Court established that agents of the United States participated in the planning, direction,

[133] In the most recent literature, see, in particular: C. Kress, 'L'organe *de facto* en droit international public. Réflexions sur l'imputation à l'Etat de l'acte d'un particulier à la lumière des développements récents', 105 *RGDIP* (2001) 93; A. J. J. De Hoogh, 'Articles 4 and 8 of the 2001 ILC Articles on State Responsibility, the *Tadic* Case and Attribution of Acts of Bosnian Serb Authorities to the Federal Republic of Yugoslavia', 72 *BYIL* (2001) 255; F. Dopagne, 'La responsabilité de l'Etat du fait des particuliers: les causes d'imputation revisitées par les articles sur la responsabilité de l'Etat pour fait internationalement illicite', 34 *RBDI* (2001) 492.

[134] See Art. 8(*a*) of the *Draft Articles on State Responsibility*, 26 *YBILC* (1974–II) Part 1, pp. 283 *et seq*., adopted in the first reading in 1996, 48 *YBILC* (1996–II) Part 2, p. 59.

[135] Commentary to Art. 8, *supra* note 130, p. 285. With regard to abductions, the ILC observed that the *de facto* organs have to act in concert with and at the instigation of the State (*ibid*. p. 284).

[136] On the inaccuracy of the adjective 'indirect', see P. Lamberti Zanardi, *supra* note 71, p. 112. See also R. Ago, sep. op., *Nicaragua case*, Merits, *supra* note 2, p. 189 footnote 1.

[137] *Nicaragua case*, Merits, *supra* note 2, p. 61.

[138] *Nicaragua case*, Merits, *supra* note 2, p. 64. L. Condorelli, 'L'imputation à l'Etat d'un fait internationalement illicite: solutions classiques et nouvelles tendances', 189 *RdC* (1984–VI) 19, p. 101, underlines the similarities with the *Hostages* case, *supra* 122, p. 29, where the ICJ affirmed that Iran was not responsible for the initial phase of the attack against the embassy since the militant had not been charged by some competent organ of the Iranian State to carry out specific operations.

[139] See, however, the remarks made by R. Ago, sep. op., *Nicaragua case*, Merits, *supra* note 2, p. 189 footnote 1.

[140] *Nicaragua case*, Merits, *supra* note 2, pp. 64–5.

support and execution of the activities carried out against Nicaragua.[141] What made qualitatively different the relationship of the United States with UCLAs from that with the *Contras* was the more effective degree of control maintained by the United States and expressed by the direction exercised over the execution of certain unlawful operations.

Being a matter of degree, the assessment of the control–dependence relationship is likely to be problematic. It must be pointed out, nonetheless, that it regards the level of involvement of the State in the unlawful activities, not the gravity of the activities themselves, as it was apparently held in the *Nicaragua case*.[142] The qualification of the military activities as armed attack – in the sense described in the previous paragraph – and the question of the effective control for the purpose of attribution of these activities to a State or another subject of international law, must be kept separate. No right of self-defence may be invoked until the *de facto* organs have concretely been engaged in hostile military activities or represent an imminent and concrete threat *and* the control over the *de facto* organs is effective enough to engage the international responsibility of the parent State responsibility. Under the proposed definition, if one of the two elements is missing, self-defence does not come into play, although the use of force on other legal grounds cannot, *a priori*, be ruled out.

The 'effective control' test established in the *Nicaragua case* was utilised on several occasions by the ICTY.[143] In *Prosecutor* v. *Tadic*, in particular, the Trial Chamber observed that the Serb Republic and the FRY, with their respective armies, were highly dependent allies, but remained distinct legal entities.[144] Setting a particularly high threshold for effective control, it further pointed out that 'Coordination is not the same as command and control'[145] and denied that the relationship between the FRY and the Serb Republic was characterised by a sufficient degree of control and dependence.[146]

[141] *Nicaragua case*, Merits, *supra* note 2, pp. 50–1.

[142] The Court stated that the right of self-defence may arise when the sending of armed bands, 'because of its scale and effects', would have been classified as an armed attack had it been carried out be regular forces (*Nicaragua case*, *supra* note 2, Merits, p. 61).

[143] The ICTY did not fail to underline the differences between the ICTY and the ICJ nature and functions: see, for instance, *Prosecutor* v. *Rajic*, Rule 61, Judgement of 13 September 1996, 108 *ILR* (1998) 142 *et seq*. For a critique on the reliance on the *Nicaragua case* for the purpose of qualifying the Yugoslav conflicts, see T. Meron, 'Classification of Armed Conflicts in the Former Yugoslavia: Nicaragua's Fallout', 92 *AJIL* (1998) 326.

[144] *Prosecutor* v. *Tadic*, Trial Chamber, Judgment of 7 May 1997, in 36 *ILM* (1997) 908, paras 584 *et seq*.

[145] *Ibid*., para 598.

[146] *Ibid*., para 605. The Court, however, conceded that the 'volunteers' sent by the FRY on temporary, if not indefinite, assignment to the Bosnian Serb army were to be considered as agents of the FRY (para. 601). See also *Prosecutor* v. *Nikolic* (Rule 61), Judgment of 20 October 1995, 108 *ILR* (1998) 21, para. 30. In *Prosecutor* v. *Karadzic and Mladic* (Rule 61), Judgment of 11 July 1996 (*ibid*. p. 86), the Chamber, on the one hand, found that the Belgrade Government exercised a 'major control' over the Bosnian Serb forces (para. 58)

In *Prosecutor* v. *Rajic*, the application of the same criteria led to the opposite conclusion with regard to the relationship between Croatia and the Bosnian Croat forces. Here, the Court accepted both the Prosecutor's arguments that Croatia intervened in Bosnia with its regular force[147] and, subordinately, that it exercised a degree of control over the political and military authorities of the Bosnian Croat forces sufficiently effective to permit to equate the latter to *de facto* organs of the former.[148]

In 1999, however, the Appeals Chamber made a *revirement* by dismissing as not entirely persuasive the test elaborated in the *Nicaragua case*. For the purpose of the qualification of *de facto* organs, it introduced a distinction between the control States have to exercise over individuals or groups of individuals, on the one side, and militarily organised groups, on the other side. In the first case, international responsibility arises only if the individuals or groups of individuals receive specific instructions from the State. In the second case, it is sufficient that the State exercises an overall control, which implies a role in organising, co-ordinating or planning the acts of the *de facto* organs, without the issuing of specific instructions concerning the commission of each act being necessary.[149]

Meanwhile, the ILC had revised Art. 8(a) and replaced the expression 'acting on behalf of a State' with the more precise 'acting on the instructions of, or under the direction or control' of a State.[150] It was stressed that these requirements are to be considered as alternative, and that, for the purpose of attribution, 'it is not sufficient that such *direction or control* be exercised at a general level; it must be linked to the specific conduct under consideration, as indicated by the addition of the words *in carrying out the conduct*'.[151]

Art. 8(a) seems flexible enough to allow a sound application of the effectiveness test. Thanks to the relatively broad alternative criteria provided for, the interpreter will assess, on a case-by-case basis, the degree of control exercised by the State, taking into account any relevant circumstances including its involvement in the planning, preparation and execution of the illicit acts, and the means at its disposal to compel the individual or groups of individual to carry out certain acts. Although Art. 8(a) does not explicitly endorse the distinction suggested by

---

and on the other hand, admitted that the two defendants, respectively, 'assumed functions typical of a head of State' (para. 69) and 'demonstrated absolute control' over the troops (para. 77). It nonetheless concluded that at the time the Bosnian Serb forces were under the control or acted together with the FRY (para. 88).

147 *Prosecutor* v. *Rajic*, *supra* 143, paras 13 *et seq*.

148 *Ibid*., paras 22 *et seq*.

149 *Prosecutor* v. *Tadic*, Appeal Chamber, Judgment of 15 July 1999, in 38 *ILM* (1999) 1518, paras 115 *et seq*.

150 See Art. 8(a), adopted in 2001 without changes with regard to the 1998 version, ILC *Draft Articles*, *supra* note 79, pp. 43 *et seq*.

151 See also *Statement by the Chairman of the Drafting Committee*, 13 August 1998, available at www.law.cam.ac.uk/RCIL/ILCSR/rft/Simma(98dcrep)rft. This conclusion was endorsed in 2001 by the ILC: see Commentary to Art. 8, *supra* note 79, p. 108.

the Appeal Chamber in the *Tadic* case, the level of organisation reached by the groups can certainly be an element to be taken into account.

Wherever is located the threshold of effective control required to qualify *de facto* organs, it remains to consider the legal regime of activities carried out by individual under less intense control by any State. The question will be discussed in Chapter V, in the context of activities carried out by terrorists. For the time being, suffice it to note that the question of the lawfulness of military action to counter activities carried out by individuals or groups of individuals acting independently enough not to be considered as *de facto* organs of a State has arisen, in substantially similar terms, in the context of activities of armed bands and of terrorists.[152]

Conditions for and limits to the resort to force in self-defence

Immediacy

By stating that self-defence can be exercised 'if an armed attack occurs', Art. 51 requires that the military reaction must take place when the armed attack is in progress. This temporal requirement presents two dimensions. This section discusses when the armed attack is to be considered as terminated, with the consequent cessation of the right to use force in self-defence. The beginning of the armed attack which occasions the exercise of self-defence and the controversial question of anticipatory self-defence will be treated in the next paragraph.

When the armed attack has an instantaneous character,[153] in the sense that it ceases to product its effects once the hostile military operations are terminated, the right to react militarily is justified only for the duration of the operations. This is the case, for instance, in an aerial incursion which cannot be countered by force once the aircraft is no longer in a position to conduct hostile missions.[154] From this moment, all the victim State could do is resort to the remedy not involving the use of force admitted in international law, and possibly appeal to the Security Council.

A certain degree of flexibility is nonetheless admitted when a State is victim of a number of hostile military activities apparently distinct but in reality carried out within a single aggressive plan. In this regard, mention should be made to the so-called 'accumulation of events' theory, elaborated by Israel since the 1950s.[155]

[152] Significantly, I. Brownlie, 'International Law and the Activities of Armed Bands', 7 *ICLQ* (1958) 734, treats the activities of armed bands alongside those of terrorists.

[153] On instantaneous and continuous international wrongful acts, see R. Ago, 'Le délit international', 68 *RdC* (1939–II) 419, pp. 518 *et seq*.

[154] In the Memorial submitted in *Aerial Incident of 27 July 1955*, *Pleadings*, p. 240, the US asserted that 'The rule must apply, as is well established in various context of international law, that a prior emergency situation justifying hostile action by one government against the national of another is no longer justified when the emergency is over'.

[155] See, in particular, See D. W. Bowett, 'Reprisals involving Armed Force', 66 *AJIL* (1972) 1, pp. 6–7; Y. Z. Blum, 'State Response to Acts of Terrorism', 19 *GYIL* (1976) 223, pp. 232 *et seq*.

This theory is normally used qualitatively to transform a series of acts which, taken individually, would be considered a violation of the rules on the use of force, into an armed attack.[156]

The operation is unnecessary if – as submitted above – it is accepted that the right of self-defence arises regardless of the scale of the hostile military activities and the crossing of any alleged threshold of gravity. The theory of accumulation of events rather serves to assess the requirement of the immediacy of the self-defensive action, which 'would have to be looked at in the light of those acts as a whole'.[157] This is of particular importance in the context of international terrorism.[158]

The question is more complex when the hostile military activities produce continuous effects, as in the case of the annexation or occupation of foreign territory. Compliance with the requirement of immediacy must be assessed on a case-by-case basis, taking into account several elements. In the first place, a reasonable delay in the reaction may in certain circumstances be justified. It is possible that the victim State needs some time to organise its resistance, especially when the theatre of the operations is geographically quite distant, as illustrated with the Falkland–Malvinas crisis.[159]

More importantly, the obligation to settle the dispute by peaceful means, which derives not only from positive rules such as Art. 2(3) of the Charter but also from the requirement of necessity, must not undermine and even less deprive of significance the right to self-defence. Should the search for a negotiated solution or non-forcible remedies prove ineffective, force could be resorted to in self-defence. Hence, a balance thus has to be struck between the views put forward in the Falkland–Malvinas crisis. According to Argentina, 'self-defence can be used only to repel imminent and grave danger' and therefore unavoidably ceases with the end of the military operations leading to the occupation.[160] For the United Kingdom, on the contrary, self-defence would be admissible as long as force is being used 'to occupy British territory and to subjugate the Falkland Islanders'.[161]

The requirement of immediacy must also take into account the possible involvement of the Security Council in the crisis. The 1990–91 Gulf crisis provides a useful example. Almost immediately after the Iraqi invasion of Kuwait, the Security Council affirmed the inherent right of individual or collective self-

[156] In the *Oil Platforms case*, *supra* note 49, para. 64, the Court observed that 'Even taken cumulatively . . ., these incidents do not seem to the Court to constitute an armed attack on the United States. This approach, clearly influenced by the *Nicaragua case*, *supra* text corresponding to note 93, induced the Court to neglect immediacy as a limit to self-defence alongside necessity and proportionality. See the critical remarks by W. H. Taft IV, 'Self-Defense and the *Oil Platforms* Decision', 29 *YJIL* (2004) 295, pp. 298 *et seq*.

[157] R. Ago, *supra* note 32, p. 70.

[158] See *infra* pp. 191 *et seq*.

[159] See, in particular: A. Cassese, 'Article 51', in J. P. Cot and A. Pellet (eds.), *supra* note I-6, pp. 771 *et seq*., p. 773; H. McCoubrey and N.D. White, *supra* note 89, p. 97.

[160] S/PV2360, 21 May 1982, pp. 21 *et seq*.

[161] *Ibid*., pp. 37 *et seq*.

defence in response to the armed attack.[162] Meanwhile, on the basis of Art. 51 and a request for assistance from the Kuwait Government,[163] the United States[164] and the United Kingdom[165] undertook naval interdiction operations in the Gulf and surrounding areas. Other States limited the role of their warships to monitoring the compliance with the embargo and excluded resort to coercive measures against foreign vessels.[166] The lawfulness of interdiction operations was challenged by several States,[167] but any doubt was dissipated with Resolution 665.[168]

Subsequently, Resolution 678 authorised Member States *co-operating* with Kuwait to use military force to obtain Iraqi withdrawal. With the benefit of several years of hindsight, the resolution can be treated as the first instance of authorisation to resort to force granted by the Security Council to States. The use of force, nevertheless, could alternatively have been lawful as an exercise of collective self-defence, without any prior authorisation being necessary. In this sense, the resolution might be interpreted as implying the admission, by the Security Council, of its own incapability to tackle the crisis effectively, therefore allowing Member States to intervene militarily.[169] Whether such an admission or the authorisation itself is considered as legally required or merely as politically opportune,[170] the requirement of immediacy appears to have been satisfied.[171] Assuming,

[162] Res. 661 (1990), adopted on 6 August 1990, preamble. In the aftermath of the Iraqi invasion of Kuwait, the US and UK insisted that the Security Council involvement in the crisis was without prejudice to the right to collective self-defence (S/PV. 2934, respectively pp. 7 and 48).

[163] See the letter to the Security Council dated 13 August 1990 (S/21498).

[164] See the letters sent to the Security Council on 10, 13 and 16 August, respectively S/21492, S/21498, and S/21537. Before the Security Council, the US declared that Res. 665 provided an additional legal basis for the naval coercive activities (S/PV.2938, 16 August 1990, p. 48). On 17 August 1990 and on the basis of Art. 51 of the Charter, the US ships were instructed to use the minimum level of force necessary to ensure compliance with Res. 665: see *Special Warning No. 80 issued by the United States Department of the Navy*, in E. Lauterpacht (ed.), *The Kuwait Crisis: Basic Documents* (Cambridge: Grotius, 1991), p. 248.

[165] See *Press Conference of the British Minister of State*, 13 August 1990, in E. Lauterpacht (ed.), *supra* note 162, p. 245. While concurring in the adoption of Res. 665, the UK stressed that a sufficient legal authority already existed under Art. 51 (S/PV.2938, 16 August 1990, p. 47).

[166] This was the position of the Italian warship *Libeccio*: see A. Miele, *La guerra Irachena* (Padova: CEDAM, 1991), pp. 28 *et seq*.

[167] Among them, see the letters sent to the Security Council by Iraq (S/21563, S/21564 and 21568, all dated 20 August), Libya (S/21650, 17 August), Jordan (S/21571, 20 August) and Sudan (S/21574, 21 August).

[168] See *supra* note II-70.

[169] G. Gaja, 'Il Consiglio di sicurezza di fronte all'occupazione del Kuwait: il significato di una autorizzazione', 74 *RDI* (1991) 696, p. 697.

[170] The British Government considered that Res. 678 provided 'an additional political basis' (H.C. Debates, vol. 182, col. 824, 11 December 1990). According to O. Schachter, *supra* note II-33, p. 460, 'The resolution served the political purpose of underlining the general support of the United Nations'.

[171] In this sense, see emphatically Y. Dinstein, *supra* note II-43, p. 213. *Contra*, see T. Yoxall, 'Iraq and Article 51: A Correct Use of Limited Authority', 25 *IL* (1991) 967, p. 985.

for the sake of the argument, that the Security Council had granted no authorisation, use of force would still have been admissible in self-defence.

The months that elapsed between the Iraqi invasion and the reaction by the military coalition are explained by the attempt conducted primarily by the Security Council to induce Iraqi withdrawal by peaceful means. Throughout the crisis the right to collective self-defence had simply been frozen: the United Nations expressly recognised it and some Member States systematically reserved to themselves the right to use force in self-defence. This is without prejudice to the international control over self-defence claims.[172]

It is noteworthy to observe that in the 1990–91 Gulf crisis, the sequence foreseen in the Charter has been reversed. Under Art. 51, the individual or joint initial reaction by Member States is considered as an exceptional decentralised response to the armed attack temporally limited to the period necessary to activate the collective security system. In the intention of the drafters of the Charter, this response had to be followed and replaced by the centralised action conducted by the Security Council. In the case under examination, instead, the Security Council almost immediately became involved in the management of the crisis, and Member States' exercise of self-defence was confined to the naval interdiction operations carried out before the adoption of Resolution 665. With Resolution 678, the Security Council abdicated its responsibilities and paved the way for the use of military force in self-defence.

Necessity

As maintained by the ICJ in the *Nuclear Weapons case*, the principles of proportionality and necessity, being 'inherent in the very concept of self-defence', limit the exercise of self-defence both under international customary law and under Art. 51.[173] The requirement of necessity must in the first place be assessed taking into account the collective security system. Unless urgent defence action is indispensable to prevent irreparable damages, a State shall seek the Security Council involvement in the crisis before using force in self-defence. It is only when the Security Council is unable or unwilling to take effective measures to protect the concerned State that the latter is entitled to resort to force.

The use of force in self-defence, at any rate, satisfies the necessity requirement in the first place when the armed attack cannot be effectively countered by measures not involving the use of force or by military operations on a lesser scale.[174]

The requirement of necessity must be respected not only at the moment of the initial decision to resort to military measures but also throughout the operations.

[172] See *infra* pp. 153 *et seq*.

[173] *Nuclear Weapons case*, *infra* note V-127, paras 40–1. See also the *Oil Platforms case*, *supra* note 49, esp. paras 76–7. The inherent character of the principles of necessity and proportionality have been stressed by P. Lamberti Zanardi, *supra* note 90, pp. 267–8.

[174] R. Ago, *supra* note 32, p. 69.

The right to react in self-defence terminates[175] or at least is suspended should the attacking State demonstrate its willingness to desist from its unlawful action and to accept the settlement of the dispute in the sense pursued by the action undertaken in self-defence. This would imply, in particular, the immediate withdrawal of the armed forces in case of occupation of part of the territory of the defending State.

In these circumstances, the prolongation of the defensive military action no longer satisfies the requirement of necessity as the rights of the concerned State can be safeguarded effectively by peaceful means. Hence, the general ban on the use of force – in respect of which self-defence represents an exception – recommences to be binding with regard to the State previously acting in self-defence. The temporary suspension of the application of the ban as between the parties concerned terminates and any other State has a subjective right in its respect of the ban which was meant to protect an interest common to all States.

The Iraq–Iran war (1980–88) provides an interesting example as during the conflict Iraq manifested the will to put an end to the conflict. Assuming that the Iraqi attitude was sincere, Iran could no longer invoke the right to self-defence. The argument that it was entitled to carry on with the war effort, even to the point of completing defeating the enemy,[176] is untenable for two reasons. First, whatever the motives on the basis of Iraqi offer, Iran had at its disposal an alternative to military force. From that moment, use of force did not satisfy the necessity requirement. Second, this view postulates that the use of force in self-defence is a question limited to the relationship between the parties concerned and neglects the legal right of all other States to the respect of the prohibition of the use of force and the conditions under which such prohibition could be unilaterally and temporally suspended to permit a State to defend itself.

Proportionality

Closely related to the principle of necessity is the principle of proportionality,[177] which can be considered as the essence of self-defence.[178] The proportionality requirement of the defensive action is to be satisfied not only at its inception: it must be constantly kept under review while the military operations persist. How the proportionate character of the military reaction has to be assessed has been rather controversial.

[175] In this sense, see K.H. Kaikobad, 'Self-defence, Enforcement Action and the Gulf Wars, 1980–88 and 1990–91', 63 *BYIL* (1992) 299, pp. 336 *et seq*.

[176] See S. H. Amin, 'The Iran–Iraq Conflict: Legal Implications', 31 *ICLQ* (1982) 167, p. 186; Y. Dinstein, *supra* note II-43, p. 211.

[177] According to R. Ago, *supra* note 32, p. 69, the two requirements are 'two sides of the same coin', whereas for G. Venturini, *supra* note 98, p. 34, they may be indistinguishable.

[178] I. Brownlie, *supra* note I-59, pp. 261 *et seq*.

According to one view, the proportionality test is based on the comparison drawn *a posteriori* between the quantum of force and counter-force used.[179] It has also been suggested that such criteria are valid with regard to defensive measures against minor hostile military activities, whereas when massive operations in self-defence take the form of a legitimate war the proportionality requirement would fade away, leaving the State free to obtain the total defeat of the enemy.[180] According to another view, the military reaction has to be weighed against the danger posed to the State invoking self-defence.[181]

A more convincing view underlines the functional nature of self-defence. The terms of comparison are the objective of the reaction – namely stopping the hostile military activities – and the force employed to achieve it. As a result, 'The action needed to halt and repulse the attack may well have to assume dimensions disproportionate to those of the attack suffered. What matters in this respect is the result to be achieved by the defensive action, and not the form, substance and strength of the action itself'.[182]

Self-defence must therefore not exceed the limits of *executio juris*, even if these limits are, because of the urgency of the action, at least initially defined unilaterally by the reacting State.[183] This approach has several advantages. It does not resort to such an indeterminate notion as that of danger, which is likely to pave the way for non-defensive military initiatives and to deprive of any significance the eventual centralised control over the claim. It also guarantees an effective protection to the State victim of the hostile military activities. A strictly symmetric reaction, in fact, is not always sufficient to put an end to these activities. It also avoids the artificial distinction between minor and major military defensive reaction.

Self-defence claims may be advanced only to the strictest extent that the reaction is directed at stopping the activities that have triggered it, regardless to their dimensions. If this limit is deliberately disregarded, and in particular if the reacting State pursues the total defeat of the enemy force,[184] the action becomes unavoidably unlawful.

[179] See, in particular, O. Schachter, 'The Right of State to Use Armed Force', 82 *MLR* (1984) 1620, p. 1637.

[180] Y. Dinstein, *supra* note II-43, pp. 208 *et seq*. According to K. H. Meyn, *Debellatio*, *EPIL* vol. I (1992), pp. 969 *et seq*., p. 971, 'it would not be a proportionate response to annihilate a State on the basis of her prior aggression'. For J. Zourek, *La notion de légitime défense* (Leiden: Sijthoff, 1974), p. 49, 'le droit de détruire l'armée de l'agresseur et si l'Organisation internationale n'intervient pas pour protéger la victime de l'agression d'une manière efficace, d'imposer à l'agresseur des mesures tendant à éviter une éventuelle répétition des agressions'.

[181] See, in particular, G. Schwarzenberger, *supra* note 55, p. 333.

[182] R. Ago, *supra* note 32, p. 69, quoted with approval by R. Higgins, diss. op., *Nuclear Weapons case*, *infra* note V-127, p. 583. See also G. Venturini, *supra* note 98, p. 34 and the authorities referred to in footnote 51.

[183] A. Miele, *supra* note II-161, p. 16.

[184] Such an action is considered as lawful by Y. Dinstein, *supra* note II-43, p. 211.

The functional approach, however, must be qualified. The fact that there is no upper limit to the use of force in self-defence does not necessarily imply that force can always be used, regardless of the consequences it may produce. Similar to enforcement measures decided by the Security Council,[185] also in the context of self-defence the so-called ethic of responsibility principle is to be respected, even if this means that no forcible remedy are available to the aggrieved State. Such a situation may occur, for instance, when the foreign forces that have occupied a small area of a neighbouring State cannot be driven out without a major conflict. Without prejudice to the possible involvement of the Security Council, use of force might be precluded as the reaction is manifestly unsound from a costs–benefits perspective.

Anticipatory self-defence

Article 51 expresses the fundamental tenet of the Charter that a State can resort to force, individually or within regional arrangement, exclusively to defend itself against hostile military activities. In the words of the French representative, it

> makes a clear distinction between the prevention and the repression of aggression . . . As far as prevention of aggression is concerned, it vests in the Security Council the task of making the necessary provision and taking whatever measures are necessary . . . But as far as repression of aggression is concerned, and that is a form of legitimate individual or collective defence, the text indicates the right of the signatories of regional understandings or treaties of mutual assistance to act immediately without awaiting the execution of the measures taken by the Security Council.[186]

From the outset, however, the distinction was undermined by the controversial question of anticipatory self-defence.[187] Advocates of anticipatory self-defence argue that the Nuremberg International Military Tribunal indirectly admitted the lawfulness of such an use of force by rejecting on the factual evidence – and not in principle – the claim that Germany had been forced to invade Norway in order to forestall an imminent Allied landing.[188]

Leaving aside for the moment the recent and less recent developments related to international terrorism and weapons of mass destruction, State practice does not offer many cases of claims of anticipatory self-defence. Although potentially a fine case of preventive action, the 1962 Cuban crisis hardly provides a

[185] *Supra* note I-11.

[186] 11 *UNCIO*, p. 58.

[187] Anticipatory and preemptive self-defence in the contest of the fight against international terrorism will be discussed in Chap. V.

[188] International Military Tribunal, *Judgements and Sentences*, 1 October 1946, 41 *AJIL* (1947) 172, pp. 205 *et seq*. On the position taken in 1946 by the UN Atomic Energy Commission, which is equally relied upon to support the admissibility of anticipatory self-defence, see *infra* p. 219.

precedent.[189] The United States preferred not to invoke Art. 51 of the Charter and relied instead upon other legal grounds, namely Art. 52 of the Charter and Art. 6 of the 1947 Rio Treaty, the latter dealing with threats to peace other than armed attack.[190] The choice was dictated precisely by the intention to preserve the notion of self-defence.[191] It has indeed been observed that:

> It is a very different matter to expand [Article 51] to include threatening deployments or demonstrations that do not have imminent attack as their purpose or probable outcome. To accept that reading is to make the occasion for forceful response essentially a question for unilateral national decision that would not only be formally unreviewable, but not subject to intelligent criticism either.[192]

Equally doubtful is the contribution of the Israel military offensive of June 1967 to the affirmation of the right to anticipatory self-defence. The Israeli claim in this sense[193] was not adequately elaborated before the Security Council and was even partially modified before the General Assembly. Israel rather preferred to justify its military action as an exercise of self-defence in response to the armed attack being conducted by the Arab States and including a typical institute of war such as blockade.[194] Although limited to a few States, the reaction was in any case consistently negative.[195]

Finally, in 1981, Israel justified the air strike against the Iraqi nuclear reactor, relying specifically upon the right of anticipatory self-defence.[196] The action was unanimously condemned in the Security Council.[197] The episode may be regarded

[189] See J. Combacau, *supra* note I-5, footnote 66, p. 36.

[190] See the US President's Address, *The Soviet Threat to the Americas*, 47 *DSB* (1962) 715; the resolution adopted on 23 October 1962 by the Council of the OAS (*ibid.* p. 722); and the US letter to the Security Council, dated 22 October 1962 (S/5181). In literature, see: L. C. Meeker, 'Defensive Quarantine and the Law', 55 *AJIL* (1963) 515, p. 523; Q. Wright, 'The Cuban Quarantine', *ibid.*, pp. 546 and 559 *et seq.*; M. S. McDougal, 'The Soviet–Cuban Quarantine and Self-Defence', 57 *AJIL* (1963) 597; A. Chayes, *supra* note III-219, p. 554; P. Lamberti Zanardi, *supra* note 90, pp. 244–5; S. A. Alexandrov, *Self-Defense Against the Use of Force in International Law* (The Hague: Kluwer, 1996), pp. 154 *et seq.*

[191] M. Akehurst, *supra* note III-165, p. 223.

[192] A. Chayes, *The Cuban Missile Crisis* (Oxford: Oxford University Press, 1974), pp. 65–6.

[193] See, in particular, S/PV.1348, pp. 14 *et seq.*

[194] See M. Weisburd, *supra* note III-143, pp. 135 *et seq.*; C. Gray, *supra* III-232, pp. 130–1.

[195] P. Lamberti Zanardi, *supra* note 90, pp. 238–9; J. Combacau, *supra* note I-5, p. 24; A Alexandrov, *supra* note 190, p. 154. R. Higgins, 'The Attitude of Western States Towards Legal Aspects of the Use of Force', in A. Cassese (ed.), *supra* note I-5, pp. 435 *et seq.*, p. 443, however, denotes 'a general feeling, certainly shared by the Western states, that taken in context this was a lawful use of anticipatory self-defence, and that for Israel to have waited any longer could well have been fatal to her survival'.

[196] S/PV.2280, 12 June 1981, pp. 52 *et seq.*

[197] Res. 487, 19 June 1981. On 12 June the IAEA Board of Governors condemned the Israeli operation and invited the General Conference to withdraw the assistance to Israel and suspend its privileges and rights. See also the firm condemnation of the air strike

as a firm denial of the existence of a right of anticipatory self-defence[198] or as a rejection on factual circumstances of such a claim – which, therefore, could be assumed to be admissible in principle.[199]

These instances can hardly have led to the emergence of a consensus on the right to anticipatory self-defence intended as forcible action in response to a threat considered as concrete in the immediate future.[200] On the one hand, the claims in this sense were not always put forward in a coherent and sufficiently well-defined way; on the other, the reaction of a remarkable number of States has been unfavourable, if not openly hostile.[201]

The so-called interceptive self-defence theory permits the striking of a balance between the national security concerns of States and the common interest to outlaw non-defensive use of force.[202] States are allowed to resort to force, within the limits of proportionality and necessity, when faced with 'a clear intention to attack accompanied by measures of implementation not involving crossing the boundary of the target State'.[203]

---

expressed by the EEC before the General Assembly (A/36/PV.53, p. 33). C. Greenwood, however, points out that the notion of anticipatory self-defence was rejected on the basis of the factual circumstances, not in principle (United Kingdom, p. 157).

[198] This position was forcefully expressed, among other States, by France (S/PV. 2282, 15 June 1981, pp. 4 *et seq.*); China (*ibid.*, pp. 8–9); Soviet Union (S/PV.2283, 15 June 1981, pp. 6 *et seq.*).

[199] In this sense, the condemnation expressed by several States, including the US (S/PV.2288, 19 June 1981, p. 14) and the UK (S/PV.2282, 15 June 1981, pp. 9 *et seq.*), was based on the violation of the requirements of proportionality, immediacy and necessity. The operations was a lawful exercise of self-defence according to T. L. H. McCormack, *Self-defense in International Law. The Israeli Raid on the Iraqi Nuclear Reactor* (New York: St Martin's Press, 1996), esp. pp. 295 *et seq*. While denying the action was a lawful exercise of self-defence, Y. Dinstein, *supra* note II-43, p. 169, justifies it since there was a state of war between the two countries.

[200] J. Combacau, *supra* note I-5, pp. 24–5, concludes that 'Certainly no legal régime of anticipatory self-defence can be inferred from such a limited and equivocal body of precedent'.

[201] Interestingly, the bald attempt by Iraq to justify its military operation against Iran in 1980 as 'preventive self-defence' (see S/14199, 26 September 1980) was immediately abandoned.

[202] See Y. Dinstein, *supra* note II-43, p. 172; C. C. Joyner and M. A. Grimaldi, 'The United States and Nicaragua: Reflections on the Lawfulness of Contemporary Intervention', 25 *VJIL* (1984) 621, pp. 659–60; I. Pogany, 'Book Review of Dinstein's War Aggression and Self-Defence, 1st ed.', 38 *ILCQ* (1989) 435. Similarly, in spite of the denomination, A. Cassese, *supra* note 47, p. 515 states that 'consensus is now emerging that under Art. 51 anticipatory self-defence is allowed, but on the strict conditions that (i) solid and consistent evidence exists that another country is about to engage on a large scale armed attack jeopardizing the very life of the target State and (ii) no peaceful means of preventing such attack are available'.

[203] United Kingdom, House of Commons, *Foreign Affairs Committee*, 2nd Report, Session 2002–3, para. 151. D. W. Bowett, *supra* note 17, pp. 188–9, recalls 'the right [to self-defence] has, under traditional international law, always been "anticipatory", that is to say its exercise was valid against imminent as well as actual attacks or dangers'.

The beginning of the hostile military activities that trigger the right to self-defence does not coincide with the moment the hostile military activities reach the sphere of sovereignty of the target State.[204] It would be unrealistic to read Art. 51 as imposing an obligation on Member States to refrain from resisting with military force the commission of a violation of Art. 2(4) once such a violation has become practically unavoidable, although it has not yet begun to produce its effects.[205]

The armed attack is to be considered as occurring when, beyond any reasonable doubt and despite any effort to defuse the crisis by peaceful means, the other State has clearly manifested, through conclusive behaviour, its intention to carry out hostile military activities, and is not only potentially in the position to hit but is concretely about to do so.[206] The hypothetical use of force by the United States against the Japanese fleet en route to Pearl Harbour is the perfect example.[207]

There is, however, no reason to confine interceptive self-defence to massive hostile military activities or to those that put the existence of the target State at

[204] In the criticised sense, see P. Lamberti Zanardi, *supra* note 90, p. 245. Equally unsatisfactory is the position of the beginning of the armed attack at the moment at which the missiles or the armed forces leave the attacking State, as maintained by N. Singh, *Nuclear Weapons and International Law* (London: Stevens, 1959), p. 126.

[205] H. McCoubrey and N. D. White, *supra* note 89, p. 91, observe that 'to interpret article 51 to mean that a state must wait for the missiles to cross its frontiers before it can respond would appears to be condemning the state, a victim of aggression, to destruction in whole or in part'. Paragraph 4.3.2.19. of the *United States Navy Commander's Handbook* reads: 'International law recognizes that it would be contrary to the purposes of the United Nations Charter if a threatened nation were required to absorb an aggressor's initial and potentially crippling first strike before taking those military measures to thwart an imminent attack' (available at www.cpf.navy.mil).

[206] According to C. H. M Waldock, *supra* note 51, p. 498, 'Where there is convincing evidence not merely of threats and potential danger but of an attack being actually mounted, then an armed attack may be said to have begun to occur'. Similarly, see M. S. McDougal and F. P. Feliciano, *supra* note 53, p. 240.

[207] See E. Jimenez de Arechaga, *supra* III-132, p. 97; Y. Dinstein, *supra* note II-43, pp. 171–2. Even such a firm opponent of anticipatory self-defence as I. Brownlie, *supra* note I-59, p. 368, concedes that 'a naval force of a state which has stated its intention to attack, approaching territorial waters, might be regarded as offensive and intercepted on the high seas'. It might be presumed that the intention does not need to be expressly stated; it is sufficient that it is 'unequivocal': see p. 367. In this sense, the 1962 Cuban and 1967 Middle East crises could hardly have justified resort to force in interceptive self-defence. On the first crisis, however, C. G. Fenwick, 'The Quarantine Against Cuba: Legal or Illegal?', 55 *AJIL* (1963) 588, p. 590, considers that 'a missile base armed with an atomic warhead in such a close striking distance that no defensive radar equipment could operate effectively could be and was properly interpreted as an armed attack if in the hands of one whose hostile declarations and whose past conduct indicated an evil intention'. In the second crisis, Israeli action was not considered as lawful by A. Shapira, 'The Six Days War and the Right of Self-Defence', 6 *Isr. LR* (1971) 65, p. 76. *Contra* Y. Dinstein, *supra* note II-43, p. 173. In both cases, there was certainly a potential risk of military hostile activities but the attack had not been mounted yet. The last author seems to be correct when affirming that the soundness of the claim has to be assessed on the basis of the information available at the time of the operations.

stake.[208] Force may indeed be used to intercept any hostile military activities, regardless of their scale, provided that the proportionality and necessity limits are strictly respected. With regard to the Gulf War, it has been noted that Israel could have lawfully shot down Iraqi missiles before they had crossed the State frontiers.[209] A military operation directed at neutralising the hostile military activities at the launching bases or over Iraqi airspace could have been justified, as interceptive self-defence, had the launching sequence been irrevocably started. Needless to say, the decision to resort to force in order to intercept hostile military activities is one of the gravest consequences. The notion itself is dangerously open to abuses and exacerbates the problem of the centralised control over claims of self-defence.

The international control over self-defence claims

The lawfulness of military action undertaken by States as exercise of self-defence must ultimately be subject to international investigation and adjudication if international law is ever to be enforced.[210] The power of control over self-defence claims belongs in the first place to the Security Council.[211]

In the case of hostile military activities immediately exhausting their effects, such as unlawful aerial intrusions or isolated attacks against a single target, the forcible reaction normally remains entirely in the hands of the target State, without any involvement of or control by the Security Council during the operations. Once the emergency is over and hence the right of self-defence is no longer available to the concerned State, the Security Council has a role to play only insofar as the situation threatens international peace and security, or use is made of the

[208] For this argument, see A. Cassese, *supra* note 202. P. De Visscher, 'Cours général de droit international public', 136 *RdC* (1972–II) 1, p. 148 writes: 'autant il me paraît certain que la Charte a condamné l'exercice préventif de la légitime défense, autant il me paraît évident que tout Etat qui aurait conscience d'être directement, immédiatement et mortellement menacé, n'hésiterait jamais à faire usage de la légitime défense préventive s'il estimait que cet usage présente une chance de le sauver de la destruction totale'.

[209] H. McCoubrey and N. D. White, *supra* note 89, p. 91. Had such an action taken place over a third State airspace, the interception could have been more accurately be based on the state of necessity doctrine.

[210] International Military Tribunal (Nurenberg), *German Major War Criminals*, 1946, 1 *IMT*, pp. 171 *et seq.*, p. 208.

[211] In his diss. op. on the *Nicaragua case*, Merits, *supra* note 2, p. 285, S. M. Schwebel concludes that the Security Council is clearly 'entitled to adjudge the legality of a State's resort to self-defence and to decide whether such recourse is legitimate or, on the contrary, an act of aggression'. J. Stone, *supra* note II-146, p. 264, notes that the right to self-defence is 'subject at least to review by the Security Council, which may find that self-defence was not properly invoked, and act to enforce peace against the invoking State (subject to the veto power)'. In the same sense, see I. Brownlie, supra note I-59, p. 274; T. Franck, *supra* note II-12, p. 313; Independent International Commission on Kosovo, *supra* note III-184, p. 167.

mechanisms for peaceful settlement of international disputes provided for in Chapter VI. As to the international control over the self-defence claim, the possible approval or condemnation by the Security Council cannot be equated to a judicial finding affecting the rights and obligations of the parties.[212]

It is not before the Security Council, but before the judicial bodies, provided there exists a jurisdictional link, that States should seek the establishment of violations of Art. 2(4) and the determination of the lawfulness of the forcible reaction.[213] On the justiciability of self-defence claims, it has been conclusively observed that

> There is not the slightest relation between the content of the right of self-defence and the claim that it is above the law and not amenable to evaluation by law. . . . Like any other dispute involving important issues, so also the question of the right to recourse to war in self-defence is in itself capable of judicial decision, and it is only the determination of States not to have questions of this nature decided by a foreign tribunal which may make it non-justiciable.[214]

Conversely, when the allegedly defensive military activities have a continuous character, the sequence of individual and collective reactions foreseen in Art. 51 may take place. The target State is entitled to resort to force until the Security Council has taken the measures necessary to maintain international peace and security. It is for the State to determine 'in the first instance' and 'at its own risk'[215] whether and in which form a military reaction is permitted.[216] The obligation to

[212] See, for instance, Res. 487, 19 June 1981, condemning Israeli air strike against an Iraqi nuclear reactor (para. 1) and affirming that Iraq was entitled to appropriate redress (para. 6). As observed by G. Arangio-Ruiz, *supra* note I-21, p. 631, any finding of such a nature would be 'outside the scope of the Security Council's competence'. See also K. Harper, *supra* note III-180.

[213] See, for instance, *Aerial Incident of 3 July 1988*, *supra* note 117.

[214] H. Lauterpacht, *The Function of Law in the International Community* (Oxford: Clarendon Press, 1933), pp. 179–80. After examining the ICJ case law, C. Gray, 'The Use and Abuse of the International Court of Justice: Cases Concerning the Use of Force after *Nicaragua*', 14 *EJIL* (2003) 867, p. 904, concludes that 'there is no general, principled reluctance by States to submit cases on such controversial subject matter to the Court. Even those States which initially challenged the Court's jurisdiction to hear claims on the use of force, like the United States and Nigeria, subsequently revised their position in making counterclaims on the same subject matter'.

[215] See the identical position of the Nuremberg and Tokyo International Military Tribunals in the passages quoted in T. L. H. McCormack, *supra* note 199, respectively pp. 255–6 and 258. H. Kelsen, 'Collective Security under International Law', 49 *ILS* (1954) p. 27 observes that the exercise of self-defence, being permitted only as a reaction against an illegal use of force, 'involves a certain risk if a legal authority must eventually confirm its lawfulness'.

[216] The ILC has stressed that 'Only in specific situations where, by its very nature, the use of force by the agencies of the central authority cannot resort promptly and efficiently enough to protect a subject against an attack by another does the use of means of defence involving force by the subject in question remain legitimate' (*Report to the General Assembly*, 32 *YBILC* (1980–II) Part 2, p. 52).

immediately report to the Security Council on the measures taken seems to have an essentially procedural character; hence, non-compliance therewith does not necessarily vitiate the action taken in self-defence.[217] The main function of the reporting obligation is to facilitate the setting in motion of the centralised reaction to the violation of Art. 2(4). Within a system of collective security, the initial unilateral reaction has been appropriately described as 'an exceptional and provisional interlude between an act of illegal use of force, an act of aggression, and the collective enforcement action which the community, through its central organ, is to take as a sanction against the illegal use of force'.[218]

The sequence envisaged in Art. 51 has rarely found application in the Organisation practice. It presupposes not only that the Security Council is not prevented from functioning because of the absence of the required majority; it also implies that organ's willingness and capability to take the measures necessary to tackle the crisis. In fact, even when there exists a sufficient agreement among the members of the Security Council, there is no guarantee that measures will be taken to effectively restore international peace and security, nor that these measures will be successful.

Five options are available to the Security Council to deal with a crisis involving self-defence claims.

(1) The Security Council could limit itself to rejecting the claim of self-defence and to intimating the State advancing such a claim to immediately desist from any military operations, and, when applicable, to withdraw its forces. This occurred, for instance, with regard to the military operations carried out by South Africa – allegedly on the ground of self-defence – against certain countries in the region.[219]

While remaining a political decision taken by a political body, a binding resolution in this sense has certain legal consequences. It imposes upon the concerned State the obligation to adopt certain conduct regarding the current military situation (mandatory effect) and deprive it of the right to invoke self-defence as the justification for further armed activities (prohibiting effect).[220] The resolution, nevertheless, is not a judicial pronouncement.[221] Should the dispute be the object

[217] P. Lamberti Zanardi, *supra* note 90, p. 275; J. Combacau, *supra* note I-5, p. 17; H. McCoubrey and N. D. White, *supra* note 89, p. 101.

[218] H. Kelsen, *supra* note I-81, p. 785.

[219] With regard to the military activities conducted against Angola, in particular, see Res. 545, 20 December 1983 (14–0–1); Res. 546, 6 January 1984 (13–0–2); and Res. 574, 7 October 1985 (14–0–1).

[220] The resolution implies the risk of reverse veto. As observed by D. W. Bowett, 'Collective Security and Collective Self-Defence: The Errors and Risks in Identification', in M. Rama-Montaldo (ed.), *International Law in an Evolving World, Liber Amicorum E. Jiménez de Arechaga* (Montevideo: Fundación de cultura universitaria, 1994), pp. 425 *et seq.*, p. 426, during the Gulf crisis the coalition partners were unwilling 'to abandon self-defence as a basis upon which they might wish to act without the approval of the Council'.

[221] Nor is a judicial pronouncement the finding of the Secretary General: see the indication of Iraq as the responsible for the Gulf War (1980–1988), S/22115, 9 December 1991. Iraq immediately declared that it considered the document as devoid of any legal value and reflecting only the Secretary General's personal opinion (S/22156, 12 December 1991).

of international litigation, the concerned State could still defend before the tribunal the lawfulness of its conduct prior to the adoption of the resolution. Conversely, the military activities conducted after the adoption of the resolution are unavoidably unlawful, provided that the resolution has been validly adopted.[222]

(2) The political nature of the decision and the related law-making power of the Security Council are even more evident when that organ, after rejecting the self-defence claim put forward by one or more of the States, orders all the States involved in the crisis to abstain from carrying out any military activities. In Resolution 1304, in particular, the Security Council maintained that Uganda and Rwanda had violated the sovereignty and territorial integrity of the Democratic Republic of Congo (hereinafter DRC) and enjoined them to withdraw all their forces from the latter State's territory.[223] The Security Council disallowed all the legal grounds invoked by Uganda in order to justify the presence and activities of its armed forces in the DRC and most prominently self-defence.[224]

This notwithstanding, it called on *all* parties to cease hostilities throughout the territory of the DRC and to fulfil their obligations under the cease-fire agreement and the relevant provisions of the 8 April 2000 Kampala agreement plan.[225] That both the RDC and Uganda were obliged, under the binding Security Council resolution, to refrain from any further military action was confirmed a few days later by the ICJ.[226] The Court unanimously indicated some provisional measures, including the order addressed to both parties to abstain from carrying out any armed action that could prejudge the rights of the other, and to take all necessary measures to fully comply *inter alia* with Resolution 1304.[227]

[222] Y. Dinstein, *supra* note II-43, p. 188, affirms that the States deprived of the right to use force in self-defence have no remedy under the Charter. Perhaps the statement is too categorical: see *infra* text corresponding to notes 248 *et seq*.

[223] Res. 1304, adopted unanimously on 16 June 2000, para. 4(a).

[224] These arguments were further elaborated by Uganda in the context of the ICJ order referred to *infra* note 226. In addition to self-defence (para. 28), they included the alleged invitation from the territorial government and the state of necessity resulting from the alleged political vacuum existing in some parts of the territory of the DRC (para. 24).

[225] Para. 1.

[226] *Case Concerning Armed Activities on the Territory of the Congo* (Democratic Republic of Congo *v*. Uganda), Provisional Measures, Order of 1 July 2000, posted at the Court website. For a comment, see L. Savadogo, 72 *BYIL* (2001) 357. In *Armed Activities on the Territory of the Congo (New Application: 2002)* (Democratic Republic of Congo *v*. Rwanda), Provisional Measures, Order of 10 July 2002, the Court declined to indicate provisional measures after concluding that it had no *prima facie* jurisdiction. On the question of provisional measures in the context of contentious cases on the legality of the use of force, see C. Gray, *supra* note 214, pp. 888 *et seq*.

[227] It rejected the argument put forward by Uganda that following the adoption of Res. 1304 the request for provisional measures had become moot (para 36 of the decision). In *Case Concerning Armed Activities on the Territory of Congo (New Application: 2002)* (Democratic Republic of Congo *v*. Rwanda), Provisional Measures, 10 July 2002, para. 55, the Court affirmed its responsibilities in the maintenance of international peace and security under the Charter.

(3) Alternatively, the Security Council could intimate to the parties to put an end to the fighting without passing any judgement on the self-defence claims nor allocating to the parties any specific responsibilities for the crisis. With Resolution 598, in particular, the Security Council determined the existence of a breach of the peace as regard to the conflict between Iraq and Iran, and issued an injunction to both the belligerents to immediately cease their military activities and withdraw their forces to the internationally recognised boundaries.[228]

More recently, the Security Council condemned the use of force in the conflict between Ethiopia and Eritrea and urged both parties to refrain from taking any military action and to seek a negotiated solution of the border dispute.[229] The competing self-defence claims put forward by the parties[230] were not the object of any assessment by the Security Council. Furthermore, in Resolution 1298, the Security Council imposed an arms embargo on both States.[231]

In all these cases, the Security Council imposed its own assessment of the situation and its own will upon those of the concerned States.[232] The conclusion may certainly be considered as unsatisfactory, and even unfair by the State victim of hostile military activities and the States prepared to assist it, but is logical from the perspective of the collective security system. The political judgement on the effectiveness and necessity of the military reaction expressed by the whole mem-

[228] Adopted unanimously on 20 July 1987. In the Presidential statement issued on 16 March 1988 (S/19626), the Security Council expressed 'grave concern that resolution 598 (1987), which has a binding character, has not yet been implemented'. On the binding character of the resolution, which was adopted under Arts. 39 and 40, see K. H. Kaikobad, *supra* note 175, p. 344 and the authorities relied upon.

[229] Res. 1177, adopted unanimously on 26 June 1998. In Res. 1227, adopted unanimously on 10 February 1999, the Security Council condemned the recourse to force by both countries.

[230] See, in particular, the documents submitted by Ethiopia on 14 May 1998 (S/1998/396), 3 June (S/1998/459) and 9 June (S/1998/483); and by Eritrea on the same days (S/1998/399, S/1998/467 and S/1998/492). See also the letters sent by Ethiopia on 18 May 2000 (S/2000/448) and by Eritrea on 22 May 2000 (S/2000/464).

[231] Adopted unanimously on 17 May 2000. Both States complained that the resolution undermined their right to resort to force in self-defence. In the letter dated 19 May 2000 (S/2000/464), Eritrea observed that the resolution 'unjustly applies an arms embargo on Eritrea, the victim, along with Ethiopia, the aggressor. It punishes equally Eritrea, which complied with, and Ethiopia, which defied Security Council resolutions. It deprives Eritrea of its legitimate right to defend itself'. See also the letter sent by Ethiopia on 18 May 2000 (S/2000/448, Annex).

[232] The power of the Security Council to order a State not to use force, regardless to the soundness and genuineness of the claim of self-defence, is widely accepted: see, for instance: N. Quoc Dihn, 'La légitime défense d'après la Charte des Nations Unies', 52 *RGDIP* (1948) 223, p. 243; C. H. M Waldock, *supra* note 51, pp. 495–6; Y. Dinstein, *supra* note II-43, p. 188; O. Schachter, *supra* note II- note 33, p. 459; S. A. Alexandrov, *supra* note 190, pp. 146 and 266.

bership through the Security Council prevails over that of the individual Member State(s).[233]

The Security Council's order alone will hardly defuse the crisis. The chances of success depend primarily on the attitude of the parties, and on the measures of pressure and coercion the United Nations might take, alongside with other international organisations and individual States, to promote and eventually impose a peaceful settlement of the dispute. The difficulties faced in resolving the conflicts between Iran and Iraq,[234] and between Ethiopia and Eritrea,[235] clearly illustrate how problematic and complex this process can be.

The power to terminate the right to resort to force in self-defence implies as *a minus* the power to limit the exercise of such a right. Resolution 678 has been read as including a temporal limitation on the exercise of the right to collective self-defence, which had been suspended until 15 January 1991.[236] Resolution 713, concerning the maintenance of the arms embargo during the Bosnian crisis, provides another interesting example.[237] Here, the Security Council deprived Bosnia–Herzegovina not of the right to use force in self-defence, but rather of the right to receive military assistance from third States.[238] During the conflict, the Security Council did not exempt Bosnia–Herzegovina from the arms embargo in spite of the repeated requests in this sense coming from several international organisations and Member States.[239] A draft resolution submitted by 22 States in

[233] Y. Dinstein, *supra* note II-43, p. 188, concludes that the particular interest of a Member State is immolated to the general interest of international peace. This may be inaccurate insofar as the right of self-defence presupposes violations of *erga omnes* obligations and consequently all States have a common legal interest in the compliance of these obligations (which is the essence of collective self-defence). In this context, the so-called veto power could be welcomed as ensuring an adequate protection of the interests of the States invoking self-defence: *supra* note I-92.

[234] The conflict terminated only on 17 June 1988, when Iran eventually decided to comply with Res. 598.

[235] On 18 June 2000, the parties concluded an *Agreement on Cessation of Hostilities*, brokered by the OAU (S/2000/601). Successively, the Security Council established the UNMEE (United Nations Mission in Ethiopia and Eritrea): see Res. 1312, 31 July 2000. On these developments, see B. Simma and D. E. Khan, 'Peaceful Settlement of Boundary Disputes under the Auspices of the Organisation of African Unity and the United Nations: The Case of the Frontier Dispute Between Eritrea and Ethiopia', in N. Ando, E. McWhinney and R. Wolfrum (eds.), *Liber Amicorum Judge Oda* (The Hague: Kluwer, 2002), vol. 2, pp. 1179 *et seq*.

[236] C. Dominicé, 'La sécurité collective et la crise du Golfe', 2 *EJIL* (1991) 85, p. 104.

[237] See *supra* p. 8.

[238] Despite some oddities in the method followed by the Security Council to extend to the new subjects the embargo originally imposed on the FSRY, the intention to extent the arms embargo to Bosnia–Herzegovina is clear, as maintained by E. Lauterpacht, diss. op., *Genocide Convention*, Order of 13 September 1993, *supra* note I-7, p. 438.

[239] See, in particular, the letters of the Sarajevo Government dated 28 September 1992 (S/24601), 25 September (S/24588), 11 May 1993 (S/25755); the documents adopted by the Islamic Conference on 23 September 1992 (S/24604, Annex), 25–29 April 1993

order to lift it with regard to Bosnia–Herzegovina mustered only six votes including only one (that of the United States) from the permanent members.[240]

Throughout the conflict, the Security Council decision's was – at least formally – respected. The explicit appeals made by the Organisation of the Islamic Conference for 'a unilateral response by members of the international community'[241] were not followed by concrete action accompanied by declarations contesting the validity of the embargo. Quite to the contrary, States accused of supplying arms to Bosnia–Herzegovina preferred to deny any allegation rather than attempt to justify their conduct by contesting Resolution 713[242]. The United States, in turn, came rather close to openly breaching Resolution 713, but the President eventually managed to block a decision that would have 'severely undermined' the Security Council's authority.[243]

The question of the maintenance of the arms embargo against Bosnia–Herzegovina permits appreciation of whether there is any remedy available against a mandatory decision of the Security Council depriving a State of the right to self-defence or limiting its exercise. Uninhibited by Art. 12 of the Charter, the General Assembly first affirmed the right to self-defence of Bosnia–Herzegovina,[244] then invited all Member States 'to extend their co-operation to the Republic of Bosnia and Herzegovina in exercise of its inherent right of individual and collective self-defence in accordance with Art. 51'.[245] The General Assembly's stand amounted to an open challenge to the Security Council's primary responsibility in the field of maintenance of international peace and security, and risked provoking an institutional crisis at the United Nations.

The ICJ, in turn, has demonstrated its reluctance to pass judgement on a Security Council decision allegedly affecting the right to self-defence. In the *Genocide Convention case*, Bosnia–Herzegovina requested the Court to declare, alongside with other provisional measures, that Resolution 713 was not to be construed as preventing the exercise of its right of self-defence. The Court declined to make such a declaration, because in so doing it would have clarified the legal

(S/25714 Annex), 14 August 1994 (S/1994/949 Annex), 18 May 1995 (S/1995/45, Annex); the documents adopted by the non-aligned members of the Security Council dated 15 April 1993 (S/25605, Annex) and 14 May 1993 (S/25782, Annex).

[240] The embargo remains in force until 18 June 1996: see Res. 1021, adopted on 22 November 1995. Incidentally, it must be noted that the opposition of one permanent member would have been enough to prevent the Security Council from lifting the embargo.

[241] See the document adopted on 19 September 1994 (S/1994/1121, Annex). See also the document adopted on 4 August 1994 (S/1994/949, Annex).

[242] See, for instance, the reply of Iran dated 14 May 1993 (S/25783) to the censure of the Federal Republic of Yugoslavia (see the letter dated 22 February 1993, S/25318).

[243] See the passage of the State Department's document quoted in M. P. Sharf and J. L. Dorosin, 'Interpreting UN Sanctions: The Ruling of the Yugoslav Sanctions Committee', 19 *BJIL* (1993) 771, p. 777.

[244] Res. 46/242, 25 August 1992.

[245] Res. 48/88, 20 December 1993 and Res. 49/10, 3 November 1994.

situation for the entire international community.[246] Such a conclusion was not shared by judge *ad hoc* Lauterpacht who, however, noted that through such a finding the Court would have identified 'a source of doubt' regarding the validity of the resolution and requested the Security Council to reconsider the maintenance of the embargo *vis-à-vis* Bosnia–Herzegovina.[247]

Under the circumstances, the only effective remedy at the disposal of States remains the so-called right to last resort, on the basis of which Member States may refuse to comply with Security Council resolutions they perceive as unlawful,[248] and in particular as contrary to peremptory norms.[249] Such a conduct by Member States, which is already admitted in general terms, gains in terms of legitimacy when openly supported by the General Assembly.

(4) When the Security Council does not impose upon a State the obligation to stop all military activities, the right of self-defence can be exercised until the Security Council itself takes the measures necessary to maintain international peace. In this sense, a resolution inviting or ordering the State believed to be violating Art. 2(4) of the Charter to refrain from using armed force hardly precludes military reaction in self-defence. Nonetheless, if the concerned State decides to comply with the Security Council's resolution and shows its intention to find a negotiated solution of the dispute, which must necessarily include the commitment to restore the territorial status *quo ante bellum* when applicable,[250] the conditions for the exercise of self-defence cease to exist.

The right of self-defence is conditioned to neither a hortatory or binding resolution addressed by the Security Council to the State deemed to be carrying out hostile military activities, nor to the authorisation or approval granted by the same organ to the State invoking such a right. The very nature of the right of self-defence excludes that its exercise depends upon any kind of authorisation,[251] although the self-defence can be exercised in the context of Security Council's approval.[252]

[246] *Genocide Convention*, Order of 13 September 1993, *supra* note I-7, p. 345.

[247] *Ibid.*, p. 442.

[248] *Supra* pp. 28 *et seq*.

[249] According to W. P. Nagan, 'Rethinking Bosnia and Herzegovina's Right of Self-Defence: A Comment', 52 *RICJ* (1994) 34, p. 44, Member States could have unilaterally disregarded the resolution as (unintentionally) contrary to *jus cogens*.

[250] Otherwise, the offending State would be in a position to negotiate the withdrawal of its forces or the international status of the territory unlawfully occupied.

[251] As observed by R. Ago, *supra* note 32, p. 70, 'a State which considers itself the victim of an armed attack or, in more general terms, of conduct entitling it to react in self-defence against the author of that conduct, should not have to seek anybody's permission beforehand to do so; to maintain the opposite would be to contradict the very essence of the notion of self-defence'.

[252] In Res. 546, see *supra* note 219, para. 5, for instance, the Security Council reaffirmed 'the right of Angola to take all the measures necessary to defend and safeguard its sovereignty, territorial integrity and independence'. In general, see, E. Rostow, 'The International Use of Force after the Cold War', 32 *HILJ* (1991) 411, p. 420.

The Security Council may take a step further and adopt concrete measures against the State allegedly breaching Art. 2(4). This would be the case, in particular, of the imposition of economic enforcement measures, possibly accompanied by the authorisation to Member States to ensure their implementation by coercive means. Whether these measures can be considered as 'measures necessary to maintain international peace and security' for the purpose of pre-empting the right of self-defence can be established only on a case-by-case basis.

The text of Art. 51 is the result of lengthy negotiations during which, upon the insistence of the Soviet Union, the adjective 'necessary' was preferred to 'adequate', and the expression 'maintain international peace and security' to 'restore international peace an security'.[253] Apart from terminological choices, however, the content of Art. 51 is clear: self-defence can be exercised until the Security Council takes measures that will *effectively* tackle the crisis.[254] It is only when the Security Council action is unsuccessful that States regain the right to use force in self-defence.

The real problem lies in the determination of who is entitled to make such an assessment. The debate on whether such a determination has to be made by the Security Council[255] or by the concerned State[256] is characterised by a certain dogmatism. It is submitted that, as long as the Security Council is actively dealing with the crisis, the concerned State is allowed to question the effectiveness of the centralised action and to express its concern about the outcome. Before taking any individual military initiative, however, it has a duty to inform the Security Council. Such a duty derives generally from Art. 2(2) and Art. 2(5), compelling Member States, respectively, to fulfil in good faith the obligations assumed in accordance with the Charter, and to give the Organisation every assistance in any action it takes; and, more specifically, from the second part of Art. 51, according to which Member States must not affect in any way the authority and responsibility of the Security Council.[257]

[253] For a summary of the legislative history of Art. 51, see P. Lamberti Zanardi, *supra* note 90, pp. 261 *et seq*.; M. Halberstam, 'The Right to Self-defence once the Security Council Takes Action', 17 *MJIL* (1996) 229, pp. 240 *et seq*.

[254] See, in particular, O. Schachter, *supra* note II-33, p. 458. M. Halberstam, *supra* note 253, p. 248, observes that these measures must 'have succeeded in restoring international peace and security'.

[255] See, in particular, *A Commentary to the Charter of the United Nations*, Cmd 6666, London, 1945, p. 9. See also J. Stone, *supra* note II-46, p. 244; A. Chayes, 'The Use of Force in the Persian Gulf', in L. Fisler Damrosch and D. J. Scheffer (eds.), *Law and Force in the New International Order* (Boulder: Westview Press, 1993), pp. 3 *et seq*., p. 5; S. A. Alexandrov, *supra* note 190, p. 105; C. Gray, *supra* note III-232, p. 104.

[256] See, for instance, L. M. Goodrich and E. Hambro, *Charter of the United Nations*, 2nd ed. (Boston: Peace Foundation, 1949), p. 300; F. J. Krezdorn, *Les Nations Unies et les accords régionaux* (Speyer am Rhein: Jägershe Buchdr, 1954), p. 122; D. B. Rivkin, 'Commentary on Aggression and Self-Defense', in L. Fisher Damrosch and D. J. Scheffer (eds.), *supra* note 255, pp. 54 *et seq*., p. 57.

[257] Informing the Security Council is also a matter of convenience since the State probably wants to avoid the risk, underlined by D. W. Bowett, *supra* note 17, p. 196 and

At that point, the Security Council may share the concerned State's assessment of the situation and admit, through a resolution, a presidential statement or any other concluding behaviour, that the measures in place are not effective.[258] This would pave the way for the individual or joint use of defensive military force within the limits of immediacy, necessity and proportionality. If, on the contrary, the Security Council is still confident of the chances of success of the centralised reaction, it may confirm that the right of self-defence is suspended. This obviously presupposes that it is possible to reach the required majority within that organ.[259] In these conditions, and subject to the right of last resort, the State is prevented from invoking self-defence as the legal ground for initiating or resuming its military operations. The most problematic situation arises when the Security Council is not able to express any view because of the division between its permanent members. In this event, the concerned State would have a strong case to invoke self-defence to justify the unilateral or joint recourse to force, although it may consider submitting the question to the General Assembly whose support will greatly increase the legitimacy of its claim.

(5) Finally, the Security Council could be unable or unwilling to step in at all. Here, the failure of the centralised reaction as envisaged in the Charter is complete. The risk that, when a major power is directly involved or has strategic interests in a given crisis, the Security Council would have been powerless was well perceived at the San Francisco conference. The constant impossibility of realising the two-phase sequence as established in Art. 51 which characterised the Cold War came as no surprise. The Security Council's role was reduced to the occasional rejection of self-defence claims advanced by certain member States whose policies were generally censured.[260] It was normally before the General Assembly that abusive self-defence claims were condemned. The General Assembly resolutions, however, were doomed to be essentially symbolic acts.[261]

Nonetheless, to attribute to the Cold War confrontation and to the voting procedure established under Art. 27(3) of the Charter all the deficiencies of the centralised reaction under Art. 51 proves too much. The risk of paralysis is unavoidable in any organ functioning on a majority basis, regardless of the possible qualification of such a majority or the enjoyment by all or some of its members of the so-called veto power. The centralised reaction is effective only

---

Y. Dinstein, *supra* note II-43, p. 189, that its initiative is considered as a threat to international peace and instigates an adverse decision by the Security Council.

[258] This is a plausible interpretation of Res. 678: see *supra* text corresponding to note 169.

[259] Again, the so-called veto power protects the rights of the State that challenges the effectiveness of the measures adopted by the Security Council: *supra* I-92.

[260] See, for instance, the claims of self-defence of Israel and South Africa referred to by J. Combacau, *supra* note I-5, pp. 17–18.

[261] See, for instance, Res. ES-6/2, 14 January 1980, condemning the Soviet invasion of Afghanistan.

when voting rules are strict enough to ensure that such a reaction is backed by an adequate political and military support. No centralised reaction is feasible, and indeed desirable, when insurmountable contrasts among major powers prevent the Security Council from expressing the collective will upon which the collective security system is based.

There is more: the Security Council may deliberately refuse to deal with a crisis involving self-defence claims or ignore the complaint by Member States suffering from allegedly defensive armed activities. A remarkable example is the military operations carried out by Iran and Turkey on Iraqi territory since the end of the Gulf crisis. The two States justified their intervention, respectively, as self-defence and under the theory of state of necessity.[262] For years, the Security Council has paid no heed to the dozens of letters of protest by Iraq, denouncing violations of its territorial sovereignty and of the prohibition on the use of force.[263]

The paralysis of the Security Council or to its unwillingness to step in are likely to pave the way – today, as it was during the Cold War – for unilateral or joint defensive use of force by States. Self-defence will cease to have an exceptional and provisional character and ultimately mean the replacement of the right to self-defence by the opposite principle of self-help.[264] Each State returns to be *judex in re sua* and, on the basis of its own unilateral judgement, may decide to resort to force. Not too differently from the 'just war' doctrine,[265] all States involved in a military confrontation may claim to be acting in self-defence.[266]

Armed reprisals to enforce international rights

It has been submitted above that States are entitled to resort to force in self-defence to counter any hostile military activities, regardless of the scale of such activities, provided that the principles of proportionality, immediacy and necessity are respected. This conclusion permits considering separately, under the rubric of 'armed reprisals', non-purely defensive military operations. Armed reprisals may provisionally be defined as conduct involving the use of force that, although normally contrary to international law, could be permitted when taken in response to a prior international wrongful act by the State against which it is directed.

[262] See infra pp. 206–7.

[263] See, for instance, the letter dated 18 July 2002 (S/2002/803) denouncing Turkey's armed incursions and urging the Security Council to intervene with a view 'to halting and ensuring that there is no recurrence of these Turkish acts of aggression, which are in flagrant violation of the Charter of the United Nations, public international law and international humanitarian law'.

[264] H. Kelsen , 'Collective Security and Collective Self-Defense under the Charter of the United Nations', 42 *AJIL* (1948) 783, p. 785.

[265] J. Kunz, *supra* note I-64, p. 533.

[266] A. Miele, *supra* note II-161, pp. 14 *et seq*.

They must be kept distinct from military reaction in self-defence.[267] Although both amount to military operations and follow previous violations of international law – which in the case of self-defence necessarily concerns Art. 2(4) – they are different with regard to their function and limits as well as the subjects allowed to react. Whereas the action taken in self-defence is strictly confined to defensive purposes,[268] armed reprisals may be aimed at obtaining the cessation and reparation of the illicit conduct, securing compliance with international obligations, inflicting a punishment, obtaining guarantees of non-repetition, or preventing further violations.[269]

Having denied that the hostile military activities must reach a given threshold before States can invoke the right to self-defence makes redundant the artificial category of defensive armed reprisals under which some authors classify as a sub-species of self-defence military reactions to minor hostile military activities. Military reactions strictly limited to halt these activities, directly related to them, and not carried out after their cessation can be treated as exercises of self-defence and as such will most probably be justified by the reacting State.[270]

Significant differences exist with regard to the limits to the exercise of self-defence and the resort to reprisals. The adoption of reprisals must be preceded by a demand of compliance and accompanied by an offer of negotiations.[271] Such a requirement does not necessarily limit the exercise of self-defence, which on the contrary usually consists in immediate response. Besides, in the context of armed reprisals, the principle of proportionality must be assessed by comparing the gravity of the violation and that of the reaction.[272] This stands in sharp contrast

[267] During the debate of the IDI on 'Le Régime des représailles en temps de paix', C. de Visscher observed that 'Il est essentiel de distinguer nettement les deux notions. Les conditions de la légitime défense devraient être précisées dans de sens suivant: existence d'une agression contraire au droit qui, en raison du danger actuel ou imminent qu'elle implique, ne laisse à l'Etat qui en est menacé d'autre moyen de protection que le recours à la force', *Annuaire*, 1934, pp. 144 *et seq.*, p. 154.

[268] See R. Ago, *supra* note 32, p. 54; P. Lamberti Zanardi, *supra* note 90, pp. 131 *et seq.*

[269] Normally, countermeasures pursue several objectives: see *Responsabilité de l'Allemagne à raison des dommages causés dans les colonies portugaises du Sud d'Afrique* (*Naulilaa case*), 2 *UNRIAA* p. 1011, p. 1025. For a discussion on the function and purpose of reprisals, see G. Arangio-Ruiz, *3rd Report on State Responsibility*, 43 *YBILC* (1991–II), Part 1, pp. 15 *et seq.* The lawfulness of punitive countermeasures has been excluded by the ILC (*Report to the General Assembly*, 48 *YBILC* (1996–II), Part 2, p. 67).

[270] *Contra* Y. Dinstein, *supra* note II-43, pp. 194 *et seq.*, who admits the lawfulness of post-attack armed reprisals under the rubric of self-defence. He also consideres that striking a military target a thousand miles away from the place where the hostile military activities has been carried out could still qualify as self-defence.

[271] *Naulilla case*, *supra* note 269, p. 1027; *Air Services Case*, *supra* note 20, p. 444 *et seq.*; *Gabcíkovo-Nagymaros* (Hungary/Slovakia), *ICJ Reports 1997*, p. 7, at p. 56. See also Art. 52 of the ILC, *Draft Articles on State Responsibility, supra* note 79, pp. 345 *et seq.* In general, see A. Gianelli, *supra* note 57, esp. Ch. 6.

[272] In the *Corfu Channel case*, *supra* note 49, the UK argued that countermeasures must not be disproportionate to the suspected offence (*Pleadings*, Vol. IV, p. 579).

with the functional character of the principle of proportionality which governs self-defence. Finally, unlike self-defence, armed reprisals are confined to the relationships between the two concerned States without any room for collective action.[273]

Moving to the lawfulness of armed reprisals, before the emergence of the ban on the use of force, they were certainly admitted as a *minus*[274] within the right 'inherent in sovereignty'[275] to wage war 'in order to assert and vindicate their rights'.[276] The watershed between armed reprisals (or reprisals or measures short of war in general) and war was the *animus belligerendi* on behalf of at least one of parties.[277] Armed reprisals were in fact considered as permissible acts of taking the law into its own hand (*Selbsthilfehandlung*) by the concerned State. This conduct was not intended to initiate a state of war with the consequent 'unlimited *licentia laedendi*'[278] and the application of the rights and duties of belligerents and neutrality. A state of war, nonetheless, could arise should the State against which armed reprisals had been taken regard them as acts of war.[279]

The right to armed reprisals was limited by Art. 1 *in fine* of the 1907 Hague Convention (II) Respecting the Limitation of the Employment of Force for the Recovery of Contract Debts.[280] It was left substantially unaffected by the Covenant of the League of the Nations, as demonstrated by the judicial pronouncement in the *Naulilaa case*.[281] A distinguished feature of the Charter of the United Nations, as already mentioned, is the general ban on any kind and form of threat or use of

---

G. Arangio-Ruiz, *4th Report on State Responsibility*, 44 *YBILC* (1992–II), Part 1, p. 23 refers to the principle of 'reasonableness'. See also Art. 51 of the ILC, *Draft Articles*, *supra* note 79, pp. 341 *et seq*.

[273] In the *Naulilaa case*, *supra* note 269, p. 10 it has been stated that a countermeasure 'a pour effet de suspendre momentaneament, dans le rapport des deux Etats, l'observance de telle ou telle règle du droit de gens'.

[274] D. Anzilotti, *supra* note 73, p. 156.

[275] A. S. Hershey, *Essentials of International Public Law* (New York: Macmillan, 1912), p. 349.

[276] W. Phillimore, *Commentaries upon International Law* (London: Butterworths, 1885) vol. III, p. 77, describes war as 'the exercise of the international right of action, to which, from the nature of things and the absence of any common superior tribunal, nations are compelled to have recourse, in order to assert and vindicate their rights'.

[277] See A. D. McNair, 'The Legal Meaning of War, and the Relation of War with Reprisals', 9 *GS* (1926) 7; R. Quadri, *supra* note 70, pp. 266 *et seq*. See also the Report prepared by the League of the Nations' Secretary General, 17 May 1927, *Official Journal*, 1927, p. 834.

[278] T. E. Holland, *Letters to 'The Times' upon War and Neutrality* (London: Longmans, 1921), p. 19. See also the Italian declaration regarding the Corfu incident (*League of Nations Official Journal*, 1923, p. 1314) which reads in part: 'These reprisals are legitimate. No act of war and no violation of international law therefore took place'. See also A. Miele, *supra* note II-161, p. 116.

[279] See A. D. McNair, *supra* note 277, pp. 35 and 43 (with regard to the Corfu incident).

[280] 2 *AJIL* (1908) Suppl. p. 81.

[281] *Supra* note 269.

force, including armed reprisals.[282] Since then, the unlawfulness of armed reprisals has been systematically reiterated on every possible occasion. Suffice it to mention the 1975 Helsinki Final Act[283] and the United Nations General Assembly Resolutions 2625 (XXV).[284] This view is shared in literature by the overwhelming majority, although there are significant dissenting positions.[285]

An unavoidable consequence of the prohibition of armed reprisals was that, apart from the right of self-defence, 'The delinquent State which is in actual possession of the illegal advantage is protected by the Charter against any enforcement action other than that taken by the Security Council'.[286] The decision to renounce forcible self-help was freely and conscientiously taken by contracting parties as the price to pay to legally protect their common interest to prevent the unilateral or joint non-defensive use of force and ultimately to maintain international peace. Like any other right under customary international law, the right of forcible self-help may also be limited (as in the case of the 1907 Hague II Convention) or excluded altogether (as in the case of the Charter of the United Nations).[287]

Similar to the general prohibition on the use of force, the ban on armed reprisals is not dependent on the effectiveness of the collective security system.[288] This was one of arguments prospected by the British Government in the 1956 Suez crisis.[289] It is important to note that the United Kingdom's Law Officers admitted that 'It cannot . . . be said that Egypt has so far committed any act which would justify the use or threat of force by the United Kingdom in self-defence. The failure of the Security Council to take an effective decision will not in itself alter this'.[290]

The *Corfu Channel* case confirmed that in 1945 States had relinquished their right to forcible self-help to ensure compliance with what they perceived as their international rights. Despite a certain degree of ambiguity, the decision can

[282] See 6 *UNCIO* p. 459. C. H. M Waldock, *supra* note 51, p. 492; G. Arangio-Ruiz, *supra* note I-25, p. 104; I. Brownlie, *supra* note I-59, p. 281; P. Lamberti Zanardi, *supra* note 90, pp. 143 *et seq*.; L. Henkin, 'Use of Force: Law and United States Policy', in L. Henkin *et al*., *Right* vs. *Might: International Law and the Use of Force*, 2nd ed. (New York: Council on Foreign Relations Press, 1991), pp. 37 *et seq*., p. 40.

[283] 14 *ILM* (1975) 1292.

[284] *Declaration on Principles of International Law Concerning Friendly Relations and Cooperation among States*, adopted on 24 October 1970, para. 6.

[285] See a full discussion in R. Ago, *supra* note 32, pp. 42 *et seq*.; G. Arangio-Ruiz, *4th Report on State Responsibility*, 44 *YBILC* (1992–II), Part 1, pp. 23 *et seq*.

[286] H. Kelsen, *supra* note I-4, p. 269. See also G. Fitzmaurice, 'The Foundations of the Authority of International Law and the Problem of Enforcement', 19 *MLR* (1956) 1, p. 5; M. S. McDougal and F. P. Feliciano, *supra* note 53, p. 208.

[287] On this point, see G. Schwarzenberger, *A Manual of International Law*, 5th ed. (London: Stevens, 1967), p. 184.

[288] See *supra* pp. 124 *et seq*.

[289] See the Foreign Secretary's declaration of 30 October 1956 (6 *ICLQ* (1957) 326).

[290] Quoted in G. Marston, *supra* note III-210, p. 792. See also the US position in the crisis, *supra* note III-210.

scarcely be read as allowing States to affirm their right through measures involving the use of force.[291] Quite on the contrary, the Court admitted the legality of the British passage of 22 October on the basis of its innocent character. The Court declared that the reasonable precautionary measures taken by the United Kingdom to meet the event of hostile military operations did not make the passage offensive, not even considering that the operations was aimed at testing Albania's attitude and amounted to a demonstration of force.[292] The characterisation of the passage as inoffensive is certainly debatable.[293] Nonetheless, the decision is to be interpreted as permitting the use of force only in self-defence, which included the right to take precautionary measures and to react – within the limits admitted in international law – to any hostile military activities impeding the right to passage.[294]

That the Court was not ready to tolerate military self-help emerges clearly from the unanimous condemnation of *Operation Retail* and the unambiguous rejection of the claim advanced by the United Kingdom both with regard to the abating of a nuisance and to securing the evidence with a view to submission to the Security Council. The unfortunate reference made by the Court to the affirmation of unjustly denied rights does not affect this conclusion.[295] It may be inferred from the characterisation of the passage as inoffensive and the condemnation of *Operation Retail* that such an affirmation cannot amount to measures involving the use of force.

This reference, nevertheless, invites the following considerations of general character. The very fact that a State needs to affirm a right implies that the exercise of the alleged right is resisted by the other States and that therefore there is an international dispute. State A could attempt to ensure the enjoyment of what it perceives as its legally protected right through non-forcible measures. State B, in turn, may react through similar measures on the assumption that State A's action is in breach of international law. The lawfulness of the respective conduct depends primarily on the existence of the right State A intends to affirm and the alleged unlawfulness of the conduct of State B. Such a determination can be made exclusively by an international tribunal – provided that adjudication is possible.

Without a judicial settlement, the outcome of the dispute will be determined by non-legal factors and there is no guarantee that the better claim will

[291] C. H. M Waldock, *supra* note 51, p. 500.

[292] *Corfu Channel case*, *supra* 49, p. 31. See R. Y. Jennings, 'International Force and the International Court of Justice', in A. Cassese (ed.), *supra* note I-5, pp. 323 and 332.

[293] For a critical appraisal of the qualification as innocent of the British passage, see the diss. opinions of S. Krylov, pp. 68 *et seq.* and 75; P. Azevedo, pp. 78 *et seq.* and 109; B. Ečer, p. 115 *et seq.* and 130.

[294] G. Schwarzenberger, International Law Association, *Report of the 48th Conference*, 1958, p. 573, observes that 'If it is legal to take precautionary measures of the kind discussed, it must be compatible with the international quasi-order of the United Nations to take armed action in self-defence against any actual armed interference with the enjoyment of rights under international law'.

[295] I. Brownlie, *supra* note I-59, p. 286.

effectively prevail. Refraining from using force, States might have found themselves without any effective remedies. The situation is undoubtedly unsatisfactory, but at least its negative consequences are confined to the two concerned States. The enjoyment by one or even both of them of their subjective rights might ultimately be sacrificed to the interest common to all States not to resort to force in order to maintain international peace.

The scenario changes significantly if one of the two States opts for armed reprisals. Such an option involves the risk of an escalation of the military engagement without altering the fact that the dispute will still be resolved in favour of the most powerful State, which by no means must coincide with the State having the best legal case.[296] It was precisely to avoid this course of events that in contracting the Charter Member States resolved to outlaw armed reprisals, regardless of the soundness of the claim underlying them and even at the price of leaving the concerned State without any effective remedy, apart from action by the Security Council when feasible.

Since the common interest protected by Art. 2(4), namely the prevention of armed violence in the relations among States, prevails over the individual interests of Member States, armed reprisals remain inadmissible when directed at obtaining the execution of an international award.[297]

This conclusion is supported by the most convincing interpretation of Art. 2(4).[298] It is also reinforced by Art. 94(2) of the Charter, which expressly entitles Member States to recourse to the Security Council to give effect to the International Court of Justice. The *ratio* beyond Art. 94(2) is precisely to ensure a collective judgment on the necessity to resort to enforcement measures in order to compel recalcitrant States to comply with the international decision. This view is strengthened if it is admitted that this provision functions regardless of the fact that non-compliance with the decision creates a situation that threatens international peace.[299]

Incidentally, Art. 94(2) would have been rather superfluous had the power of the Security Council to take enforcement measures been dependent on the

[296] Compare, for instance, the outcome of the actions undertaken by India and Argentina to enforce their claims with regard to the islands of Goa and the Falklands–Malvinas respectively.

[297] See, in particular, O. Schachter, 'The Enforcement of International Judicial and Arbitral Decisions', 54 *AJIL* (1960) 1, pp. 14 *et seq.*; S. Rosenne, 'L'exécution et la mise en vigueur des décisions de la Cour Internationale de Justice?, 57 *RGDIP* (1953) 532, pp. 559 *et seq.*; A. L. Sicilianos, *supra* note 57, pp. 378 *et seq. Contra*, C. Vulcan, 'L'exécution des décisions de la Cour Internationale de Justice après la Charte des Nations Unies' 51 *RGDIP* (1947) 187, pp. 193 *et seq.*; W. M. Reisman, *supra* note I-81, pp. 846 *et seq.*

[298] *Supra* note 282.

[299] In this sense, see H. Kelsen, *supra* note I-4, p. 542; O. Schachter, *supra* note 297, pp. 21 *et seq.*; G. Arangio-Ruiz, *supra* note I-21, pp. 621 *et seq. Contra*, see E. Jimenez De Arechaga, *Derecho constitutional de la Naciones Unidas. Comentario teorico y pratico de la Carta* (Madrid: Escuela de funcionarios internationales, 1958), p. 560; T. M. Franck, *supra* note III-184, p. 111.

existence of such a threat. The alleged dependence of the forcible measures taken by the Security Council upon a prior determination under Art. 39, in any case, is to a large extent an academic question for which there are no precedents in that organ's practice.[300] Paradoxically, in recent years the real question has not been the role of the Security Council as enforcement agent, but rather whether and eventually on what conditions Member States could resort to force to obtain the observance of the Security Council's resolutions.

Moving to State practice, most of the cases allegedly supporting the admissibility of armed reprisals concern the fight against international terrorism and will be discussed separately in Chapter V. As to the remaining cases, the paucity of potential cases and the almost absolute absence of *opinio juris* confirm that no right to resort to force in order to enforce what States perceive as their rights has not survived the entry into force of the Charter or (re-)emerged afterward.[301] In the few potential precedents, the use of force has normally been defended as measures of self-defence and accompanied by a clear rejection of armed reprisals.[302] When not justified on this ground, the claim met a firm and widespread opposition within the Security Council and the international community.[303] The argument that the ban on armed reprisals has rapidly degenerated to the point of rendering its normative value doubtful,[304] therefore, can safely be dismissed, at least as far as reprisals not directed at fighting international terrorism are concerned.

[300] In general, see A. Tanzi, 'Problems of Enforcement of Decisions of the International Court of Justice and the Law of the United Nations' 6 *EJIL* (1995) 539. With regard to the request advanced by Bosnia–Herzegovina on 16 April 1993 (S/25616) concerning the enforcement of the provisional measures decided upon by the Court, it must be noted, on the one hand, that the Security Council was urged 'pursuant to Art. 94 (2)' to take immediate measures under Chapter VII of the Charter; on the other hand, that the situation had already been the object of several determinations under Art. 39.

[301] After an accurate analysis of State practice, including terrorist-related reprisals, R. Barsotti, *supra* note 33, observes, on the one hand, that 'actual practice, is not so serious to give grounds to the belief that there is a process of degeneration of the ban in question (p. 90); on the other hand that 'not only is there absolutely no sign of *opinio juris* in the conduct of the State in question, but there is even evidence of an awareness of the unlawfulness of reprisals' (p. 92).

[302] See, for instance, the case concerning the Fort Harib, which occurred in 1964, including the position of the UK (S/PV.1111, 9 April 1964, p. 6).

[303] In 1961, for instance, India justified the forcible recovery of Goa on the basis of the alleged evolution of international law in the sense of allowing use of force to end colonial ruling (S/PV.988, 18 December 1961). The action was supported by the Soviet bloc and Third World States, but vigorously condemned by Western States (see, in particular, the position of the US, S/PV.987, 18 December 1961).

[304] See R. Falk, *supra* note IV-33; D. W. Bowett, *supra* note 155. More recently, T. M. Franck, *supra* note III-184, p. 132, has considered these measures as admissible on the basis of extreme necessity justified by evident legitimacy.

Protection of nationals abroad

Before the entry into force of the Charter, States enjoyed an undisputed right to resort to military force in order to protect the lives and property of their nationals within the jurisdiction of another State.[305] During the Cold War, military operations allegedly directed at rescuing nationals abroad, conducted essentially by certain Western States, invariably stirred great controversy. This occurred especially when the situation of danger in which nationals had been caught was merely the pretext for hegemonic interventions directed at pursuing completely different objectives.[306] Most of these operations have been justified by the intervening State – sometimes alongside with other legal or political grounds – as permissible exercises of self-defence.[307] Occasionally, they have been based on considerations of necessity or on humanitarian grounds.[308] These claims systematically met significant opposition that in some cases reached remarkable proportions and occasionally permitted the adoption by the General Assembly of a resolution of condemnation.[309] It must be concluded that the claims advanced in this regard by some Western States failed to gather the general support necessary to transform them into law.[310]

Recent State practice offers a significant quantity of cases of military interventions aimed at rescuing foreigners abroad.[311] In contrast with the past, these inter-

[305] See M. Huber, *Rapport sur les responsabilités de l'Etat dans les sistuations visées par les réclamations britanniques*, 2 RIAA (1949) 639, esp. p. 641. In literature, see in particular, E. Borchard, *The Diplomatic Protection of Citizens Abroad* (New York: Banks Law Pub., 1915), pp. 346 *et seq.* and pp. 448 *et seq.*; D. W. Bowett, *supra* note 17, pp. 87 *et seq.* According to I. Brownlie, *supra* note I-59, pp. 289 *et seq.*, such a right had been relinquished with the acceptance of the General Treaty of 1928: see *supra* note 83.

[306] The claim to protect the nationals abroad has been described, with regard to the Suez crisis, as a 'palpably inadequate excuse': see R. Higgins, *supra* note II-62, pp. 220–1; and with regard to the Grenada and Panama cases as 'juridical figleaf': see R. Lillich, 'Forcible Protection of Nationals Abroad: The Liberian "Incident" of 1990', 35 *GYIL* (1992) 205, p. 222.

[307] This was in particular the interventions by the UK in Suez (see 6 ICLQ (1957) 325 *et seq.*); by the US in the Dominican Republic (see S/PV.1196, 3 May 1965, p. 14); in Cambodia (Mayaguez incident, S/11689,15 May 1975); in Iran (S/13908, 25 April 1980); in Grenada (S/PV.2491, 27 October 1983, p. 8; S/16076, 25 October 1983; and the documents collected in 78 *AJIL* (1984) 200 *et seq.*); in Panama (S/PV.2902, 23 December 1989, pp. 9–10; S/21035, 20 December 1989; and the documents collected in 84 *AJIL* (1990, pp. 545 *et seq.*)); by Israel in Uganda (*Entebbe incident*, S/PV.1939, 9 July 1976, p. 57); and by Egypt (*Larnaca Incident*, 82 *RGDIP* (1978) 1096–7).

[308] See, in particular, the interventions by Belgium in Congo in 1960 (S/PV.879, 21–22 July 1960, pp. 28–9); and by Belgium and the US in Congo in 1964 (respectively S/6063, 24 November 1964, and S/6062, 24 November 1964).

[309] See Res. 38/7, 2 November 1983 (108–9–27), and Res. 44/240, 29 December 1989 (75–20–40), condemning respectively the interventions in Grenada and Panama.

[310] See, in particular, N. Ronzitti, *supra* note 41, pp. 62 *et seq.*

[311] The recent State practice include the following instances of unchallenged rescue operations: the US in Liberia (1990); France in Gabon (1990) 94 *RGDIP* (1990) 1071;

ventions have gone entirely unchallenged, on either political or legal grounds. In none of these cases has the territorial State or other States officially protested against nor raised the matter before the Security Council.

The lawfulness of forcible protection of nationals abroad has generated an endless debate and continues to divide scholars.[312] Article 2(4) of the Charter, in particular, has been the object of radically different interpretations. Relying primarily on the *preparatory works* and subsequent documents adopted by the United Nations, the authors who contest the lawfulness of military operations to rescue nationals abroad read Art. 2(4) as encompassing any form of unilateral use of force, including military rescue operations.[313] For others, on the contrary, Art. 2(4) prohibits only the use of force against the territorial integrity and political independence, at the exclusion of military operations genuinely aimed at saving human lives.[314]

Bearing in mind the non-static character of the Charter's provisions, Art. 2(4) cannot be treated as postulating – on the basis of literal or teleological explanations – either an absolute and perpetual prohibition on the use of force, or the admissibility of military action directed at promoting the respect of human rights in a manner not harmful to the territorial integrity and political independence of the concerned State. The content of this provision rather depends on how it has been concretely interpreted and applied by Member States and the Organisation.

An alternative argument advanced in support of the lawfulness of these operations is based on the assumption that a threat or hostile activities against the nationals of a State can be equated to a threat or hostile activities to the State itself for the purposes of Art. 51 of the Charter.[315] Consequently, the parent State is

France and Belgium in Rwanda (1990, 1993, 1994) 95 *RGDIP* (1991) 746; 24 *RBDI* (1991) 208; France in Chad (1990); France and Belgium in Zaire (1991); the US and France in Central African Republic (1996); the US in Sierra Leone (1997); and the US in Liberia (1998). For a survey of the US operations, see R. F. Grimmett, *Instances of Use of United States Forces Abroad, 1798–2001*, updated February 2002, *CRS*, Order Code RL30172.

[312] See the discussion held within the ILC in the context of diplomatic protection, in *Report to the General Assembly*, 45th Session, 2000, A/55/10, pp. 149 *et seq*. and the following Summary records: A/CN.4/SR.2617 to A/CN.4/SR.2620, from 9 to 12 May 2000; A/CN.4/SR.2624 to A/CN.4/SR.2627, from 19 to 25 May 2000; and A/CN.4/SR.2635, 9 June 2000). For an accurate summary of the debate in literature, see A. C. Arend and R. J. Beck, *International Law and the Use of Force* (London: Routledge, 1993), Chapter 7.

[313] See, in particular, I. Brownlie, *supra* note I-59, pp. 298 *et seq*.; M. Akehurst, 'The Use of Force to Protect Nationals Abroad', 5 *IR* (1977) 3. More recently, see M. Bennouna, *Preliminary Report on Diplomatic Protection*, A/CN.4/484, 9 February 1998, p. 4.

[314] See, in particular, C. H. M Waldock, *supra* note 51, p. 503; J. Stone, *supra* note 46, p. 43; R. Lillich, 'Forcible Self Help to Protect Human Rights', 53 *Iowa LR* (1967) 325; J. Paust, 'Entebbe and Self Help: The Israeli Response to Terrorism', 2 *FF* (1978) 86, pp. 89 *et seq*.; D. W. Bowett, in Cassese (ed.), *supra* note I-5, p. 40.

[315] Israel, in particular, justified the Entebbe raid as self-defence: see S/PV.1939, 9 July 1976, pp. 51 *et seq*. It must be noted, however, that very few States openly supported the claim. The US, in particular, defended the Israeli operation and maintained that 'there is a well-established right to use limited force for the protection of one's own nationals . . .

entitled to resort to force in self-defence, provided that the principles of proportionality, immediacy and necessity are respected. This analogy is not implausible, although its applicability can be accepted only insofar as the territorial State is responsible for violating Art. 2(4) with regard to the nationals of the intervening State. It would be inapplicable when the situation of danger is determined by events outside its control of the territorial State or when there is no government at all. Additionally, this view is not entirely convincing when the rescue operation concerns also third States' nationals. Assuming that the operations are lawful, it would be illogical to exclude them from the military protection.[316] Characterising the operation as collective self-defence, however, would stretch Art. 51 beyond recognition.

It has also been argued that the failure of the collective security system has implied the return to Member States of the right to protect their nationals abroad as measures of self-help.[317] This view must be rejected since the ban on the use of force does not depends on the effective functioning of the collective security system. Additionally, such a view postulates that the situation in which rescue operations take place threatens international peace and security, which is not necessarily the case. The argument has further lost credibility considering that the Security Council is no longer permanently paralysed.

The state of necessity doctrine has also been indicated as the legal basis of military rescue operations.[318] The admissibility of such a claim depends on whether the subjective right of the concerned State to have its territorial sovereignty respected might be sacrificed for the sake of the interest of the intervening State to protect its nationals. Military protection of nationals abroad could satisfy the

flowing from the right of self-defense' (S/PV.1941, 12 July 1976, p. 31). In general, the claim found the rather firm opposition from a large part of the Organisation membership, including several Western States: see, for instance the position of France (S/PV.1939, 9 July 1976, p. 88), and of the UK (S/PV.1940, 12 July 1976, pp. 11 *et seq*.). In literature, see L. C. Green, 'Rescue at Entebbe. Legal Aspects', 6 *IYHR* (1976) 312; L. M. Salter, 'Commando Coup at Entebbe: Humanitarian Intervention or Barbaric Aggression?', 11 *IL* (1977) 331. According to a British Government released in 1986, Art. 51 of the Charter is the most plausible, although far from undisputed, legal basis of the right to intervene to protect nationals abroad: see *Foreign Policy No. 148*, in 57 *BYIL* (1986) 614, p. 617. Similarly, see S. A. Alexandrov, *supra* note 190, p. 190. See also D. W. Bowett, *supra* note 17, pp. 91 *et seq*.; G. Fitzmaurice, 'The General Principles of International Law', 92 *RdC* (1957–II) 1, pp. 172–3; J. R. Dugard, *1st Report on Diplomatic Protection*, A/CN.4/506, 7 March 2000, pp. 16 *et seq*. *Contra* J. E. S. Fawcett, 'Intervention in International Law. Study of Some Recent Cases', 103 *RdC* (1961–II) 343, p. 404; J. Zourek, *supra* note 179, pp. 54–5; A.F. Panzera, '*Raids* e protezione dei cittadini all'estero', 61 *RDI* (1978) 759.

316 See J. R. Dugard, *supra* note 315, p. 22. He further states that when the preponderance of threatened persons are not nationals of the intervening States, the operation should be classified as humanitarian intervention.

317 P. Jessup, *A Modern Law of Nations* (New York: Macmillan, 1948), pp. 169–70; M. W. Reisman, *supra* note I-81, pp. 848 *et seq*.

318 See J. Raby, 'The State of Necessity and the Use of Force to Protect Nationals', 26 *CYIL* (1988) 253.

requirements elaborated throughout the years by the ILC.[319] In any event, the doctrine cannot be applied when the territorial State has violated international law by creating, supporting, endorsing or tolerating the situation threatening the foreigners.[320]

Finally, there is the qualification of rescue operations as humanitarian intervention.[321] Undoubtedly, these operations possess at once a defensive and a humanitarian dimension.[322] They should nonetheless be kept separate from intervention on humanitarian grounds as they pursue different objectives through different means.[323] They are in fact directed at extracting foreign nationals in danger, regardless of any violation of international law by the territorial Government. Equally important, they do not attempt to influence the conduct of the territorial Government. In contrast, humanitarian interventions normally target that Government and are aimed at compelling it to change its attitude in the exercise of its sovereign powers upon essentially its own nationals. Additionally, rescue operations normally concern small groups of individuals and imply the engagement of strictly limited force, in terms both of means and time, whereas humanitarian intervention, being directed at putting an end to massive and widespread violations of human rights, might involve military operations of significant proportions and duration.

In reality, the use of force to protect nationals abroad defies attempts to fit it into predetermined categories. Under the circumstances, the most appropriate approach is to verify whether State practice confirms the re-emergence of the right forcibly to rescue nationals abroad as a new exception to Art. 2(4). It is submitted that a rule allowing – under certain conditions – the use of force to rescue foreign abroad had re-emerged or at least is crystallising because of the uniform practice accepted as law by the generality of States. The process has been initiated by the claim, put forward by certain Western States. After decades of opposition by the majority of the international community, the claim seems to have eventually overcome any resistance.[324]

[319] ILC, *Report to the General Assembly*, *supra* note 79, p. 202.

[320] The commission of international wrongful acts distinguishes state of necessity from other institutes and in particular self-defence or reprisals: see C. De Visscher, *supra* note 267. This position has been endorsed by the ILC: *supra* note 69, p. 34; and *supra* note 79, p. 195.

[321] L. Henkin, 'The Invasion of Panama under International Law: A Gross Violation', 29 *CJTL* (1991) 293, pp. 296–7, for instance, considers genuine protection of nationals abroad as a subspecies of humanitarian intervention.

[322] See N. K. Tsagourias, *supra* note I-65, Ch. 6.

[323] The need to keep the two notions separate has been affirmed by J .R. Dugard, *supra* note 315, p. 19.

[324] R. Lillich, *supra* note 306, p. 223, underlines that 'affirmation of U.S. and many other States's normative expectations concerning the international acceptance of such rescue operations'. See also T. C. Wingfield *et al.*, *Lillich on the Forcible Protection of Nationals Abroad*, (Newport: Naval War College, 2002); Y. Dinstein, *supra* note II-43, p. 205. More prudently, C. Gray, *supra* III-232, p. 129, speaks of acquiescence. In 1983, the Department of State's Legal Adviser maintained that the right of States to use force to

Needless to say, the right to use force must be defined in the strictest terms. Tentatively, the following conditions may be inferred from States' practice:[325]

(a) nationals of the intervening State – and incidentally nationals of third States – are exposed to a concrete and immediate threat of, or are the target of activities that could cause grave and irreparable injury;
(b) the territorial State is responsible for the situation threatening the foreigners, or is unable or unwilling to guarantee them an adequate protection;
(c) measures not involving the use of military force have proved useless or are not practicable because of either the attitude of the territorial State or the time constraint posed by the emergency;[326]
(d) when practicable, the consent of the territorial State to the operations has been requested in vain;[327]
(e) the operation is genuinely defensive;[328]
(f) force is used to the extent necessary, in terms of time, space and means, to rescue the nationals;[329]
(h) a report on the operations is immediately submitted to the Security Council.[330]

Humanitarian intervention

The lawfulness of individual or joint military interventions duly authorised by the Security Council in the context of humanitarian crisis threatening international

---

protect their nationals is among the 'well established legal principles providing a solid legal basis' for the US action in Grenada. On the abusive character of the claim in this specific case, see R. Lillich, *supra* note 306.

[325] The *Entebbe incident*, *supra* note 315, may be considered as a sort of model for genuine rescue operations: see, for instance, Y. Dinstein, *supra* note II-43, pp. 205–6; J. R. Dugard, *supra* note 315, p. 21.

[326] With regard to the *Mayaguez incident*, *supra* note 307, the US declared that it immediately sought to recover the vessel and to arrange the return of the crew through diplomatic channels.

[327] For an example of a rescue operation conducted with the consent of the territorial State, see the Mogadishu operation, in N. Ronzitti, *supra* note 41, pp. 79 *et seq*.

[328] The US State Department Legal Adviser observed that the right to protect nationals abroad 'does not encompass acts intended to punish or exact compensation' (73 *AJIL* (1979) 122, p. 123).

[329] According to the US Departments of the Navy, the Army, the Air Force and the Treasury, *Joint Doctrine for Military Operations Other than War*, Joint Pub 3–07, p. III-11, adopted on 16 June 1995, available at www.atic.mil.doctrine/jel/new_pubs/jp3–07.pdf, 'The operation involves swift insertion of a force, temporary occupation of objectives, and ends with a planned withdrawal. . . . Forces penetrating foreign territory to conduct a Noncombatant Evacuation Operation should be kept to the minimum consistent with the mission accomplishment and the security of the force and the extraction and protection of evacuees'.

[330] Regrettably, States conducting recent rescue operations have failed to keep the Security Council officially informed.

peace and security is today generally accepted.[331] On the contrary, since the entry into force of the Charter the unilateral use of force on humanitarian grounds is not permitted.[332] In accordance with the most convincing interpretation of Art. 2(4), the notion of humanitarian intervention is radically incompatible with the text of the Charter,[333] which expressly admits only strictly limited numbers of exceptions to the general ban on the use of force. Nonetheless, this does not preclude the possibility – through uniform and generally accepted contrary practice – of modifications of the Charter and the (re-)emergence of an exception allowing States to intervene militarily to tackle humanitarian emergencies.

The actual evidence, in terms both of practice and *opinio juris*, that such an exception has emerged or is emerging is clearly insufficient.[334] From a quantitative

[331] See, among others, R. Lillich, *supra* note I-93, pp. 563–4; S. D. Murphy, *Humanitarian Intervention. The United Nations in an Evolving World Order* (Philadelphia: University of Pennsylvania Press, 1996), pp. 282 *et seq.*; F. Teson, *supra* note 60, p. 225; M. E. O'Connell, 'The United Nations, NATO, and the International Law After Kosovo', 22 *HRQ* (2000) 57, pp. 67 *et seq.*

[332] Among the immense literature available, see, in particular: I. Brownlie, *supra* note I-59, pp. 432 *et seq.*; *Id.*, 'Thoughts on Kind-Hearted Gunman', in R. B. Lillich (ed.), *Humanitarian Intervention and the United Nations* (Charlottesville: University Press of Virginia, 1973), pp. 193 *et seq.*; L. Henkin, *How Nations Behave*, 2nd ed. (New York: Columbia University Press, 1979), pp. 135 *et seq.*; M. Akehurst, 'Humanitarian Intervention', in H. Bull (ed.), *Intervention in World Politics* (Oxford: Clarendon Press, 1984), pp. 95 *et seq.*, pp. 106 *et seq.*; N. Ronzitti, *supra* note 41, Ch. IV; A. C. Arend, R. J. Beck, *supra* note 312, Ch. 8.; P. Malanczuk, *Humanitarian Intervention and the Legitimacy of the Use of Force* (Amsterdam: Het Spihuis, 1993); S. D. Murphy, *supra* note 331, esp. pp. 355 *et seq.*; C. Antonopoulos, *The Unilateral Use of Force by States in International Law* (Athens: A. N. Sakkoulas, 1997), pp. 452 *et seq. Contra*: R. B. Lillich, 'Forcible Self-Help by States to Protect Human Rights', 53 *IoLR* (1967) 325; M. W. Reisman and M. S. McDougal, 'Humanitarian Intervention to Protect the Ibos?', in R. B. Lillich (ed.), *supra* note 332, pp. 167 *et seq.*; F. Teson, *supra* note 60. For an alternative discursive framework, see N. K. Tsagourias, *supra* note I-65. See also the rather awkward position of the NATO Parliamentary Assembly, which suggested an extended interpretation of the right to self-defence that would embrace 'defence of common interests and values, including when the latter are threatened by humanitarian catastrophes, crimes against humanity, and war crimes' (*Resolution 283 on Recasting Euro-Atlantic Security*, para. 15(e)). The lawfulness of humanitarian intervention before 1945 could be less clearly established than generally believed. See the interesting analysis by A. Rougier, *supra* note III-189. As noted by I. Brownlie, *supra* note I-59, pp. 339–40, the intervention in Syria carried out in 1860 by France might be the only true case of humanitarian intervention in the Ottoman Empire. And even the value of this precedent is doubtful: see I. Pogany, 'Intervention in Syria Re-examined', 35 *ICLQ* (1986) 182.

[333] N. Ronzitti, *supra* note 41, p. 108. *Contra*, relying on teleological and literal arguments or on the cumulative effect of Articles 1, 55 and 56, M. McDougal and M. W. Reisman, *supra* note 332, p. 172.

[334] See, in particular, A. Cassese, *supra* note III-149, p. 796; I. Brownlie, 'Kosovo Crisis Inquiry: Memorandum on the International Law Aspects', 49 *ICLQ* (2000) 876; C. Chinkin, 'The Legality of NATO Action in the Former Republic of Yugoslavia (FRY) under International Law', *ibid.*, 910, pp. 918–20; S. Chesterman, *supra* note I-65, pp. 226 *et seq.*; Y. Dinstein, *supra* note II-43, pp. 66 *et seq.*; M. E. O'Connell, *supra* note 331, p. 82.

standpoint, during the Cold War, very few cases could have potentially contributed to the normative process leading to the formation of a humanitarian exception. Even in these cases intervening States refrained from relying on the doctrine of humanitarian intervention – although they occasionally referred to humanitarian emergencies – and relied instead on self-defence. Equally importantly, the overwhelming majority of States unambiguously ruled out that humanitarian motives could justify military interventions.[335] Several General Assembly resolutions[336] and the *Nicaragua case*[337] corroborate this conclusion.

After the fall of the Berlin Wall, State practice on humanitarian intervention remained scarce and incoherent. The relevance of the military intervention in Iraq to protect the Kurd and Shiite populations in the aftermath of the Gulf crisis, in particular, is rather limited. Among intervening States, only the United Kingdom invoked the right to humanitarian intervention allegedly existing in customary law. Being based on a vague and entirely undocumented reference to State practice, the argument is far from convincing.[338] Significantly, this position was not shared by the United States and France.

The normative value of the intervention in Kosovo is equally doubtful. Both the poor legal articulation of the humanitarian claim[339] and, more importantly, the magnitude of the opposition to the claim, militate against the emergence of a rule allowing the use of force on humanitarian grounds.[340] At best, it could be said that

[335] For a useful analysis of the main relevant cases, and in particular the interventions carried out by India in East Pakistan in 1971, by Vietnam in Cambodia (Kampuchea) in 1978, and by Tanzania in Uganda in 1979, see N. Ronzitti, *supra* note 41, pp. 95 *et seq*.

[336] See in particular Res. 2131, adopted on 21 December 1965; Res. 2625, adopted on 24 October 1970; Res. 3314, adopted on 14 December 1974; and Res. 36/103, adopted on 9 December 1981.

[337] *Supra* note 2, pp. 134–5.

[338] During the debate before the House of Commons, the Government admitted that 'There is no general doctrine of humanitarian necessity in international law' although a limited use of force could be permitted depending on 'an objective assessment of the factual circumstances at the time and on the terms of relevant decisions of the Security Council' (16 November 1998, in 69 *BYIL* (2001) 693). This position is close to the so-called common-lawyer approach, which maintained that the use of force might be justified not solely on the basis of certain limited specific legal grounds but also upon the evaluation of all relevant circumstances globally assessed, even if each of them would be insufficient by itself see A. D. Sofaer, 'International Law and Kosovo', 36 *SJIL* (2000) 1.

[339] NATO Member States failed to elaborate a common position and some of them insisted that the intervention did not set a precedent: see the position expressed by Belgium on 25 September 1999 before the General Assembly (A/54/PV.14, p. 18) and by German Minister of Foreign Affairs, J. Fisher, 'Vortrag vor den Mitgliedern der DGAP', 55 *Int. Politik* (2000–2) 58.

[340] The Russian Federation, in particular, was categorical in stating that humanitarian intervention was based neither on the Charter nor on generally recognised rules of international law (S/PV.3988, 23 March 1999, p. 2). The Independent International Commission on Kosovo, *supra* note III-186, para. 132 *in fine*, could detect 'at the very least, a tenuous legal basis'. Similarly, see International Development Centre, 'International Commission on Intervention and State Sovereignty. The Responsibility to Protect', Canada, 2000, at www.iciss-ciise.go.ca/report_e.asp.

the Kosovo intervention constitutes a clear manifestation, on behalf of certain States belonging to NATO, of the *opinio necessitatis* to introduce an humanitarian exception to Art. 2(4).

The British Government has taken a leading role in promoting the doctrine of humanitarian intervention and elaborated a set of principles that should govern it. The following principles, which to a large extent reflect those suggested in literature,[341] can be extrapolated from the relevant documents:

(a) there must exist a serious humanitarian crisis;
(b) the territorial Government is unable or unwilling to take effective measures to tackle it;
(c) non-forcible remedies have proved ineffectual or are not available;
(d) the Security Council is not discharging its responsibilities;
(e) the intervention is effective from a costs–benefits perspective;
(f) the intervention is collective;
(g) the military means employed are proportionate.[342]

Three major objections are to be raised. First, criteria under (c), (d) and (e) can hardly be assessed objectively by Member States as claimed by the British Government. Second, the role of the Security Council and its relationships with the States willing to intervene does not receive adequate treatment.[343] Finally, it is not clear when an intervention can be considered as collective. The mere fact that many States, belonging or not to an international organisation, participate in the operations does not change the situation from a legal point of view, although it might provide some degree of legitimacy.

The international community is currently sharply divided on the issue of humanitarian intervention. As admitted by the British Government itself, many countries still 'have reservations about the concepts involved, fearing that their endorsement would undermine the principle of state sovereignty'.[344] As long as the

[341] See S. Chesterman, *supra* note I-65, pp. 227 *et seq*. Interestingly, the author concludes that none of the cases of State practice examined would satisfy these criteria.

[342] See the documents collected in 70 *BYIL* (1999), pp. 572 *et seq*.; 71 *BYIL* (2000), pp. 640 *et seq*.; 72 *BYIL* (2001), pp. 694 *et seq*.; and in particular the *Paper on Humanitarian Action in Response to Humanitarian Crises*, *ibid*., pp. 695 *et seq*. See also *Fourth Report from the Foreign Affairs Committee*, Session 1999–2000, Kosovo, esp. para. 20.

[343] According to V. Lowe, 'International Legal Issues Arising in the Kosovo Crisis', 49 *ICLQ* (2000) 934, p. 939, the principles should include both a prior determination by the Security Council of a grave crisis, threatening international peace and security, and the articulation still by the Security Council of specific policies for the resolution of the crisis.

[344] Intervention before the House of Commons, 2 May 2001, in 69 *BYIL* (2001) 695. See also A. Roberts, 'NATO's Humanitarian War', 41 *Survival* (1999) 102, p. 120. Additionally, according to J. Stromseth, 'Rethinking Humanitarian Intervention: the Case of Incremental Change', in J. L. Holzgrefe and R. O. Keohane (eds.), *Humanitarian Intervention. Ethical, Legal and Political Dilemmas* (Cambridge: Cambridge University Press, 2003), pp. 232 *et seq*., p. 264, the US is sceptical about the wisdom and utility of articulating criteria for humanitarian intervention and prefers an assessment in the light of the particular circumstances of the crisis in question.

majority of States are opposed in principle to the right to humanitarian intervention, setting criteria for the exercise of such a right may be a futile exercise from a strictly normative point of view. In perspective, it remains to be seen whether it could make it less difficult gathering the general acceptance of the claim.[345]

For the present, they may provide a framework for assessing when humanitarian intervention, although still inadmissible in international law, could be pardoned.[346] Unavoidably, the question is to be solved by resorting to extra-legal considerations[347] since 'the circumstances in which the law can be violated are not in themselves susceptible to legal regulation'.[348] Otherwise, we would have an exception of humanitarian nature to the rule. Such a result will be achieved, provided that this occurs, when the generality of States concur or at least acquiesce in the emergence of such an exception.

For the time being, the decision to intervene militarily to put an end to a humanitarian emergency belongs to the realm of policy. Intervening States wittingly decide to violate international law upon considerations of morality or legitimacy; they expect that the violation will be tolerated by the rest of the international community.[349]

The rules on the use of force enshrined in the Charter and those existing under customary international law are substantially identical because of the mutual exposure and interaction of the two sources.

There is no compelling argument in favour of the dependence of the general ban concerning the use of force on the effective functioning of the collective security system.

As to the main exception to such a ban, namely self-defence, it appears that any hostile military activities may trigger a forceful reaction, without the trespassing of a threshold of gravity being required. In spite of the contrary view held by the International Court of Justice, this conclusion is amply supported by State practice.

Self-defence has proved to be flexible enough to adapt itself to the modern forms of military attacks. States are justified in countering the so-called indirect

[345] In 1999, the Group of 77 declared: 'We reject the so-called "right to humanitarian intervention" which has no legal basis in the United Nations Charter or in the general principles of international law' (para. 171). See however *supra* pp. 113–14.

[346] O. Schachter, *International Law in Theory and Practice* (Dordrecht: Nijhoff, 1991), p. 126. S. D. Murphy, *supra* note 331, p. 384, however, warns that 'developing criteria might serve less to restrain unilateral humanitarian intervention and more to provide a pretext for abusive intervention'.

[347] A. Miele, *supra* note II-161, p. 34.

[348] S. Chesterman, *supra* note I-65, p. 230.

[349] Before the Security Council, the Member States of the European Union declared that they were 'under a moral obligation to ensure that indiscriminate behaviour and violence . . . are not repeated' (S/PV.3988, 23 March 1999, pp. 16–18). The UK Parliamentary Foreign Affairs Committee, Session 1999/2000, *Fourth Report*, para 138, maintains that 'NATO's military action, if of dubious legality in the current state of international law, was justified on moral grounds'.

aggressions as well in intercepting hostile military activities or in neutralising a concrete and imminent threat before such acts reach their target. Conversely, self-defence cannot be invoked to resort to force to tackle potential threats.

Given the unilateral character of the defensive action, the international control over self-defence claims is crucial. The Security Council may exercise its extensive normative powers and even enjoin a member not to use armed force in circumstances in which force could otherwise be lawfully resorted to. In so doing, it impose its will – which in principle represents that of all members of the United Nations – upon that of the concerned State.

As to the other possible exception to the ban on the use of individual or joint use of force, State practice seems to support the (re-)emergence of a rule allowing, under certain circumstance and within strict limits, military operations genuinely directed at rescuing nationals abroad. On the contrary, it is still premature to admit the admissibility of armed reprisals because of the lack of both practice and *opinio juris*. Finally, from a legal standpoint, intervention on humanitarian ground remains unlawful as the correspondent claim put forward by some States has failed to muster the critical mass necessary to transform it into law. Nonetheless, a few Governments and a substantial number of scholars have elaborated some criteria under which it may be tolerated upon consideration of justice, morality or legitimacy.

V

The international fight against terrorism and the proliferation of weapons of mass destruction

This chapter deals with the use of force in the related fields of international terrorism and weapons of mass destruction. It discusses in the first place to what extent the notion of self-defence, as it has emerged in the previous chapter, adequately protects States against international terrorism. On the basis of the rules on attribution developed in the context of State responsibility, it further explores the consequences, from the perspective of the use of force, of State involvement in terrorism. The most difficult questions probably concern the limits within which interceptive self-defence can be stretched and the admissibility of preventive military measures deliberately directed at eliminating potential but not yet immediate and concrete threats. The lawfulness of anti-terrorist military action on the ground of necessity is also considered.

The second part of the chapter deals with the use of force in relation to weapons of mass destruction. It discusses the lawfulness of the use of nuclear weapons in self-defence, which in 1996 was the subject of a controversial advisory opinion by the International Court of Justice. Still from the standpoint of self-defence, it then focuses on one of the most remarkable issues of the recent Iraqi crisis, namely the admissibility of pre-emptive military action against potential threats posed by the development of weapons of mass destruction. Finally, it considers collective and unilateral measures taken in order to ensure compliance with disarmament obligations, neutralise threats involving weapons of mass destruction and curb the proliferation and trafficking of these weapons.

Terrorist activities as armed attack

The first part of this chapter discusses to what extent existing legal categories provide an adequate legal framework to govern the use of force against international terrorism. The analysis cannot but start with self-defence, which is the legal ground almost systematically invoked by States to justify their military measures directed at curbing terrorist activities.

Terrorist activities may well amount to violations of Art. 2(4) of the Charter which prohibits any hostile activities involving threat or use of force, regardless of the means and the strategies utilised, including attacks on computer network.[1] What normally distinguishes terrorist activities from other hostile military activities is primarily their aim and the techniques employed.[2] Defining international terrorism, which in itself is a term without legal significance,[3] has proved a particularly difficult task.[4] For the purpose of this study, terrorist activities may be described as acts of violence intended to create a climate of terror within the population or to coerce governments or international organisations into given conduct. That the perpetrators of these acts are motivated by political, religious or ideological considerations is not necessary to qualify them as terrorist acts, at least according to the most recent international instruments,[5] nor can in any way justify them.[6]

As to the techniques employed, the use of civilian means of transportation by land is far from being a novelty. Terrorist attacks perpetrated by exploding vehicles placed in front of civilian or military targets dates back to 1983 at the latest.[7] In contrast, civilian vessels have been used for attacking warships for the first time in 2000, when the target of the attack was the *USS Cole* during a refuelling stop in the harbour of Aden.[8]

[1] In literature see, in particular, T. A. Morth, 'Considering Our Position: Viewing Information Warfare as a Use of Force Prohibited by Art. 2(4) of the UN Charter' 30 *CWRILJ* (1998) 567; M. N. Schmitt, 'Computer Network Attack and the Use of Force in International Law: Thoughts on a Normative Framework', 37 *CJTL* (1999) 885; Y. Dinstein, 'Computer Network Attacks and Self-Defence', in M. N. Schmitt and B. T. O'Donnell (eds.), *Computer Network Attacks and International Law* (Newport: Naval War College Press, 2002), pp. 163 *et seq.*

[2] It may be argued that military actions committed by belligerents might also be qualified as acts of terrorism, as could probably be the case of the bombing of Coventry or Dresden during World War II.

[3] R. Higgins, 'Introduction', in R. Higgins and M. Flory (eds.), *International Law and Terrorism* (London: Routledge, 1997), pp. 13 *et seq.*, p. 28.

[4] See, in particular, K. Skubiszewski, 'Definition of Terrorism', 19 *IYHR* (1989) 39; E. Hugues, 'La notion de terrorisme en droit international: en quête d'une définition juridique', 129 *JDI* (2002) 753; C. Walter, 'Defining Terrorism in National and International Law', in C. Walter *et al.* (eds.), *Terrorism as a Challenge for National and International Law: Security versus Liberty?* (Berlin: Springer, 2004), pp. 23 *et seq.*

[5] See the UN-sponsored *International Convention for the Suppression of the Financing of Terrorism*, General Assembly Res. 54/109, 9 December 1999; and the EU *Council Framework Decision of 13 June 2002 on Combating Terrorism* (2002/475/JHA), OJ L 164, 22 June 2002, p. 3. Art. 1(1) of the later document includes a catalogue of the acts deemed to constitute terrorist offences.

[6] See, in particular, Art. 5 of the Convention for the Suppression of the Financing of Terrorism, *supra* note 5; and para. 2 of the General Assembly Res. 57/27, 15 January 2003.

[7] See, for instance, the attack against UN Marine Corps barracks in Beirut in 1983. More recently, track bombs had been used in 1996 against US military residences in Saudi Arabia and in 1998 against the US embassies in Nairobi and Dar es Salam.

[8] See R. Perl and R. O'Rourke, 'Terrorist Attack on USS Cole. Background and Issues for Congress', 30 January 2001, CRS Report for Congress.

Terrorist activities have been more intense in the field of air navigation. Initially they comprised essentially the hijacking or the destruction of civilian aircraft.[9] In September 2001 the terrorists inaugurated a new phase by transforming civilian aircraft into devastating weapons. The radical change in the effective use of the aircraft implies the forfeiting of the protection normally ensured to civilian aircraft under the Chicago Convention and the assimilation of these aircraft to military ones. States reserve to themselves the right to neutralise – if necessary through destruction – civilian aircraft that represent a threat to military or civilian targets located within their territory or subjected to their jurisdiction. In the aftermath of the 11 September, in particular, the British Government closed its airspace and alerted the air defence aircraft whose role was 'to deter, to deflect and ultimately to destroy any threat from the sky'.[10] This attitude is less surprising than it might appear at first sight, considering that under the legislation of most States air defence forces are allowed to counter any threat to their national security, territorial integrity and population, with no exceptions.[11]

The use of civilian aircraft for terrorist attacks has imposed a revision of the air defence systems. In the United Kingdom, in particular, a procedure was established to take coercive measures – including shooting down – against civilian aircraft demonstrating an intention to imminently carried out a terrorist attack.[12] The legal basis for the use of force was indicated, with regard to municipal and international law, respectively, in s. 3 of the Criminal Law Act of 1967 and in Art. 51 of the Charter).[13]

From the standpoint of international law, the resort to force against civilian aircraft requires the strictest observance of the limits on self-defence, and in particular those of proportionality and necessity. No mention is made of the existence of the threshold of gravity terrorist attacks must reach in order to permit the defensive use of force by the concerned State. The British attitude, which reflects that

[9] On the phenomenon of hijacking, see, in particular, E. McWhinney, *Aerial Piracy and International Terrorism. Illegal Diversion of Aircraft and International Law* (Dordrecht: Nijhoff, 1987). Among the cases of explosion of civilian aircraft, see those which occurred in 1970 to Swissair aircraft bound to Beirut; in 1974 to TWA flying over Corfu; in 1988 to PAN AM aircraft flying over Lockerbie; and in 1989 to UTA aircraft flying over Chad.

[10] House of Commons *Hansard* Debates, 14 September 2001, col. 665.

[11] In France, for instance, Art. 1 of Ordonnance 59/147, 7 January 1959 states: 'La défense a pour objet d'assurer en tout temps, en toutes circonstances et contre toutes les formes d'agression, la sécurité et l'intégrité du territoire, ainsi que la vie de la population', quoted in L. Baby, 'Interception d'un aéronef civil par un moyen militaire': Conséquences en matière de responsabilité', 55 *RFDAS* (2001) 400, p. 407.

[12] The decision to shoot down civilian aircraft must be taken at the ministerial level. In the US, the decision is taken by the President or, when time does not permit, by a two-star military commander: House of Commons, Defence Committee, *Defence and Security in the UK*, 6th Report, Session 2002–3, posted at www.parliament.the-stationery-office.co.uk/pa/cm200203/cmselect/cmdfence/93/9302.htm, *Prevention and Protection*, para. 11.

[13] *Ibid.* para 8.

of the generality of States, confirms the position taken above).[14] States are allowed forcibly to counter *any* hostile military measures or terrorist activities threatening their national security or their population.

The debate on whether the terrorist attacks perpetrated on 11 September constituted an armed attack for the purpose of Art. 51 implies a foregone conclusion,[15] but largely misses the point. Clearly, there was an armed attack and the United States was allowed to take all necessary action, including by military means, to prevent the accomplishment of the terrorist plan. The crux of the matter was the lawfulness of military measures taken afterwards.

In the aftermath of the attacks, the Security Council recognised the Member States' right to individual and collective self-defence and expressed its readiness to take all necessary steps to counter the threat to international peace and security posed by terrorists.[16] There is no harm in recognising the right of self-defence in general terms and without proceeding to either a formal qualification of the terrorist attack for the purpose of Art. 51 or the identification of the responsible. In any case, a terrorist attacks may amount at once to an armed attack in the sense of Art. 51 and to a threat to international peace and security.[17] As such, it may trigger both the unilateral or joint defensive military measures by the Member States and the action by the Security Council under Chapter VII of the Charter. Yet, the question is to establish whether the Security Council is effectively discharging its responsibilities and consequently unilateral or joint military reaction ceases to be permitted.[18]

Resolution 1368 coordinates the exercise of the right to self-defence with the collective measures to be taken by the Security Council to counter the terrorist threat. The fact that the Security Council is actively dealing with the crisis does not necessarily preclude unilateral or joint defensive use of force. Member States continue to be allowed to defend themselves, in accordance with the limits of self-defence. In particular, they are allowed to take urgent military action against further attacks, provided that they immediately cease any military activities should the Security Council take effective measures.

From the standpoint of self-defence, characterising the 11 September terrorist acts as armed attacks is not sufficient. No military measures would be permitted exclusively in relation to the attacks carried out on 11 September since those attacks had manifestly ceased to produce their effects. The reaction, therefore, would not possess a defensive character. It would not be directed at resisting or putting an end to an armed attack, but would unavoidably have had a purely punitive or deterring function. This is not to say that States cannot take measures aimed at sanctioning attacks already ended or at deterring their renewal. International

[14] *Supra* pp. 133 *et seq.*

[15] See *supra* pp. 76–7.

[16] The resolution has been considered as ambiguous and contradictory by L. Condorelli, *supra* note I-50, p. 840; A. Cassese, *supra* Introduction-1, p. 996.

[17] See C. Greenwood, *supra* note III-103, p. 308.

[18] See *supra* pp. 160–2.

law certainly permits them to react, individually or jointly, provided that the measures decided upon do not imply military force.

Linking the armed attack already consumed with the possible military reaction, in contrast, would lead to the repudiation of the defensive character of self-defence. In this false perspective, the self-defence is not any longer directed to resist an armed attack, but rather to punish *ex post facto* those responsible for the armed attacks and to deter the commission of others. It is nonetheless possible to consider the 11 September 2001 attacks as acts forming part of a larger hostile plan. As a result, the armed attack against the United States assumes a continuous character and permits to invoke the right to self-defence as legal basis of the military reaction. In this regard, the armed attack has been put in the right perspective by the United States that invoked Art. 51 on the basis on the armed attack already suffered and the *ongoing* threat posed by the continuing terrorist activities of Al Qaeda. We shall revert to this point later.[19]

States' involvement in terrorism

Traditionally, the attribution of the armed attack to a subject of international law was considered as an indispensable element for the exercise of the right to self-defence.[20] In the recent opinion concerning the lawfulness of the construction of the wall in Palestine, the ICJ noted that under Art. 51 self-defence is allowed against armed attack carried out by States and that Israel did not invoke self-defence in relation to such an attack perpetrated by any State. In so doing, the Court carefully avoided taking a position on the admissibility of defensive armed action against non-State entities, provided that such an attack originates from outside the territory of the State acting in self-defence.[21] This attitude has been criticised by several judges who refused to read Art.51 as confining self-defence to reaction against armed attacks conducted by States.[22]

Since Resolutions 1386 and 1373 recognised the right to individual and collective self-defence without making any reference to armed attacks conducted by States, it is necessary to discuss the admissibility of the use of force in self-defence against hostile military activities carried out by a non-State entity. The question is crucial in the context of military action directed at curbing international terrorism.

[19] *Infra* pp. 191–3. It would have been more accurate to refer to the ongoing *armed attack*.

[20] See *supra* pp. 129–30. R. Ago, *supra* note IV-32, pp. 61–2, rightly stresses the need to limit the notion of self-defence to reaction to certain international wrongful acts committed by States, with the exclusion of acts of individuals or groups unrelated to the organisation of a State.

[21] *Supra* note IV-35, para. 139.

[22] This was maintained in the separate opinions of P. H. Kooijmans, paras 35–6, and R. Higgins, paras 33–4, as well as in the declaration made by T. Buergenthal, para. 6.

In the case of the recent Afghan crisis, the Taliban was the Government of a State in the sense of international law, regardless of the fact that it maintained official relations only with Pakistan and was regarded as 'illegitimate' by a large part of the international community.[23] The effective and independent exercise of governmental powers is indeed the necessary and sufficient condition to acquire international subjectivity. The lack of control over the entire territory comprised in the internationally recognised borders of Afghanistan, on the contrary, is immaterial.[24]

The problem is the legal status of Al Qaeda. It has been argued that the terrorists can be treated as *de facto* organs of the Taliban.[25] In this perspective, the effective control exercised by the Taliban – as a subject of international law – over the terrorists would have implied its international responsibility and exposed it to the defensive military reaction by other States in accordance with the traditional notion of self-defence and within the limits thereof. Other scholars prefer to consider Al Qaeda as a non-State actor, but are divided as to the qualification as self-defence of the resort to force against it.[26]

[23] According to D. Anzilotti, *Cours de droit international* (Paris: Sirey, 1929), vol. I, p. 169, 'il n'y a pas d'Etats légitimes et d'Etat illégitime; la légitimation de l'Etat réside dans son existence même'. Similarly, see: G. Arangio-Ruiz, *Sulla Dinamica della Base Sociale nel Diritto Internazionale* (Milano: Giuffrè, 1954), pp. 127 *et seq.*; R. Quadri, *supra* note IV-70, p. 458; I. Brownlie, *supra* note I-59, p. 323. See also: *Cuculla Claim,* U.S. v. Mexico (1876), in J. B. Moore, *International Arbitrations* (Washington: Government Printing Office, 1908), vol. III, p. 2873; *Affaire du Guano*, Tribunal Arbitral Franco–Chilien (1901), 15 *RIAA* p. 77; *Tinoco Case* (1923), 1 RIAA 369; *Wulfsohn* v. *Socialist Federated Soviet Republic* (1923), 2 *Annual Digest* (1923–24) p. 39; *Georges Pinson Claim*, Commission Franco–mexicaine des réclamations (1928), 5 *RIAA* p. 327, esp. p. 423; *Fubini Claim*, Italian–United States Conciliation Commission (1959), 14 *RIAA* p. 420, esp. 428/430.

[24] For the same reasons, it may be argued that the Northern Alliance also enjoyed international personality in spite of the fact that it was in control of a rather limited portion of territory. Significantly, the Security Council referred several times to the international obligations of the Taliban (awkwardly treated as a 'faction') with regard to the territory under their control; see, for instance, Res. 1267, 15 October 1999.

[25] C. Tomuschat, 'Der 11 September und seine rechtlichen Konsequenzen', 28 *EuGRZ* (2001) 535, p. 541; J. Delbruck, *supra* note III-103, p. 15.

[26] In general, R. Higgins, *supra* note II-62, pp. 200 *et seq.*, notes that Art. 51 covers all modes of attack as long as it is armed. M. N. Schmitt, 'Preemptive Strategies in International Law' 24 *MJIL* (2003) 513, p. 539, observes that 'It is incontrovertible that States now treat the law of self-defence as applicable to acts by non-State actors'. In the same vein, see: R. Wedgwood, 'Responding to Terrorism: The Strikes Against Bin Laden', 24 *YJIL* (1999) 559, p. 564; J. J. Paust, 'Use of Armed Force against Terrorists in Afghanistan, Iraq and Beyond', 35 *CILJ* (2002) 533, p. 534; T. Franck, 'Terrorism and the Right of Self-Defense', 95 *AJIL* (2001) 839, p. 840; S. D. Murphy, 'Terrorism and the Concept of "Armed Attack" in Article 51 of the U. N. Charter', 43 *HJIL* (2002) 41, pp. 45 *et seq.*; C. Stahn, 'International Law at a Crossroad?', 62 *ZaöRV* (2002) 183; C. Greenwood, *supra* note III-103, p. 307. *Contra*, A. Cassese, 'The International Community's "Legal" Response to Terrorism', 38 *ICLQ* (1989) 589, p. 596; L. Condorelli, *supra* note I-50, p. 838; M. E. O'Connell, 'The Myth of Preemptive Self-Defence', *ASIL*, August 2002, p. 7; O. Corten, F. Dubuisson, *supra* note III-106, pp. 65 *et seq.* G. Aldrich, 'The Taliban, Al Qaeda, and the Determination of Illegal Combatants?', 96 *AJIL* (2002) 891, p. 893, maintains that two separate armed conflicts have been waged against the Taliban and Al Qaeda.

The question must be addressed by discussing the relationship between the terrorists or terrorist groups and the State from which they operate. For this purpose, four categories may be conveniently indicated.

(1) The terrorists are *de jure* or *de facto* organs of the State. In both cases, the State is responsible for the activities carried out by the terrorists and exposes itself to the remedies admitted by international law including, when these activities amount to hostile military operations, the military reaction in self-defence.[27]

(2) The State actively supports the terrorists or terrorist groups. Such a support may take a virtually infinite varieties of forms, including typically the provision of financial means, logistic facilities, weapons and military training. In spite of the support, the State does not exercise over the terrorists control effective enough to qualify them as organ *de facto*, and therefore is not responsible for the acts committed by them. Its behaviour, however, implies the breach of the negative obligation to refrain from encouraging, promoting or support in any form terrorist activities against other States. Such an obligation derives from the well-established general rule, confirmed by the ICJ in the *Corfu Channel case*, that imposes upon States the obligation not to allow knowingly their territories for acts contrary to the rights of other States.[28] This negative obligation has been reiterated on several occasions by the General Assembly. In Resolution 2625 (XXV), in particular, the General Assembly proclaimed that States must abstain from organising, instigating, assisting, participating in terrorist activities against other States and from tolerating these activities being carried out within its territory.[29]

[27] Individual responsibility could arise alongside the responsibility of State. On the question, which goes beyond the purpose of this study, see A. Nollkaemper, 'Concurrence between Individual Responsibility and State Responsibility in International Law', 52 *ICLQ* (2003) 615.

[28] *Supra* note IV-49, p. 22. See also the *Hostages case*, supra IV-120, pp. 32–3. See also: *Affaire des biens britanniques en Maroc espagnol*, Award of 1 May 1925, II RIAA 615, pp. 640 *et seq*.; R. Ago, *4th Report on State Responsibility*, 24 *YBILC* (1972–II) p. 120. In Art. 1(1) of the Convention for the Prevention and Punishment of Terrorism, concluded in Geneva on 16 November 1937 but never ratified, the Contracting parties reaffirmed 'the principle of international law in virtue of which it is the duty of every State to refrain from any act designed to encourage terrorist activities directed against another State and to prevent the acts in which such activities take shape' (League of the Nations Doc. C.546 (I). M. 383 (I). 1937 V).

[29] General Assembly Res. 2625 (XXV), 24 October 1970, principle 1. The principle has been systematically reaffirmed since, lastly by Res. 57/27, 15 January 2003, para 5. The Security Council has repeatedly taken an identical position: see, for instance, Res. 1189, 13 August 1998, preamble, para. 5. The obligations imposed by para. 2(a) of Res. 1373 to 'refrain from providing any form of support, active or passive, to entities or persons involved in terrorists acts, including by suppressing recruitment of members of terrorist groups and eliminating the supply of weapons to terrorists', therefore, reflect obligations already binding under customary international law.

(3) The State is not actively involved in the terrorists' activities, but passively tolerates them. Here, it violates the positive obligation to take all reasonable measures to prevent and repress terrorists' activities conducted from its territory. The obligation does not have an absolute character and its compliance must be assessed in accordance with the due diligence principle.[30]

(4) The State is genuinely unable to tackle the terrorist activities effectively. No rules of international law will be therefore be breached, provided that the concerned States can prove its due diligence. It is submitted that under the due diligence principle, the State ought accept the assistance offered by the States targeted by the terrorists, or even give its consent to the adoption by these States of coercive measures within its territory.[31]

When the terrorist or terrorist groups cannot be considered as *de facto* organs of a given State, their international legal status appears controversial. Admitting the international personality of militarily organised terrorist groups that act independently from any government may be more than a provocation. The possession of a structure of power – which is the essence of international subjects[32] – and the independent exercise of authoritative powers over however a limited social basis composed of the militants could point to the international personality of the terrorist group. The control over a portion of territory, although not strictly indispensable, would clearly reinforce the claim. Without such a control, admitting the international personality of the terrorist groups may still be possible, albeit that it would entail the overlapping over a partly coincidental social basis of the 'jurisdictions' of the territorial State(s) and that of the terrorist groups.

[30] The legal opinion tendered in 1959 by the Legal Service of the Swiss Department of Political Affairs reads: 'L'Etat doit prévenir et punir les actes qui sont dirigés de son territoire contre l'intégrité extérieure et intérieure des Etats étrangers . . . Toutefois, ni l'obligation de prévenir ni celle de punition n'ont un caractère absolu. La première ne se réalise que dans le cadre d'un standard général, d'une responsabilité pour négligence . . . L'Etat doit faire preuve de due diligence; il n'est pas tenu d'empêcher n'importe quel incident d'une manière absolue, ce qui serait matériellement impossible', in 16 *ASDI* (1959) 225. Already in 1887, the US Supreme Court affirmed: 'The law of nations requires every government to use due diligence to prevent a wrong being done within its dominion to another nation with which it is at peace' (*United States* v. *Arjona*, 120 US 479 (1887), p. 484). In literature see, in particular: S. G. Kahn, 'Private Armed Groups and World Order', 1 *NYIL* (1970) 32, esp. pp. 49 *et seq*.; R. B. Lillich and J. M. Paxman, 'State Responsibility for Injuries to Aliens Occasioned by Terrorists Activities', 26 *AULR* (1977) 217, esp. pp. 26 *et seq*.; R. Pisillo-Mazzeschi, 'The "Due Diligence" Rule and the Nature of the International Responsibility of States', 35 *GYIL* (1992) 9; and *"Due Diligence" e responsabilità internazionale degli Stati* (Milano: Giuffrè, 1989), esp. Chap. 4.

[31] This would hardly be a novelty. At the beginning of the nineteenth century, the UK shelled Copenhagen and destroyed the Danish fleet. The justification was that 'when a State is unable of itself to prevent a hostile use being made of its territory or its resources, it ought to allow proper measures' by the threatened State, quoted in S. A. Alexandrov, *supra* note IV-190, p. 20.

[32] G. Arangio-Ruiz, *supra* note 23, pp. 99 *et seq*.

It may also be plausible – but still far from being undisputed[33] – to consider the individual terrorists as subjects of international law or simply the addressees of international rules. It has been suggested, in particular, that Art. 2(4) of the Charter should be read as imposing the prohibition on threat or use of force not only on States but also on individuals.[34] An inquiry on the controversial question of the legal position of individuals in international law goes beyond the purpose of this study. Suffice it here to mention that this theoretical and largely academic question could be overcome by considering the individuals as participants in the international legal system.[35]

What matters here is to explore when States can resort to military measures to counter hostile military activities carried out by terrorists or terrorists groups that cannot be treated as *de facto* organs of any State. Needless to say, within their respective jurisdictions and in spaces not subjected to the jurisdiction of any State, States can take all coercive measures necessary to curb terrorism, provided that the limits imposed by human rights law and, where applicable, humanitarian law are respected.

Problems arise, in the first place, when the terrorists are on board foreign vessels on the high sea. With all due precautions, an analogy could be drawn with the repression of piracy. It is undisputed that international law allows States to take coercive measures against any vessels engaged in piracy, regardless of its flag. This action, which would normally amount to an international wrongful act, is permitted by a customary norm – subsequently codified and developed in the conventions on the law of the sea.[36] Sharing a common interest in safe navigation, States have mutually accepted renouncing the exclusiveness of the flag State to exercise jurisdiction over the ship in favour of the concurrent jurisdiction of all States. A permissive customary norm thus emerged through uniform practice accepted as law. As a result, pirates became outlaw[37] and were exposed to the coercive action of any State. Significantly, in the *Le Luis* case, Lord Stowell maintained that 'With professed pirates there is no state of peace. They are the enemies

[33] According to Anzilotti, the so-called *delicta iuris gentium* – elaborated with regard to piracy and slave trade but applicable also to terrorists – are actions prohibited not by international law but rather by national law in order to comply with international obligations: see D. Anzilotti, 'L'azione individuale contraria al diritto internazionale', in D. Anzilotti, *Scritti di diritto internazionale* (Padova: CEDAM, 1956), vol. I, p. 209. See also G. Schwarzenberger, 'The Problem of an International Criminal Law', 13 *CLP* (1960) 263; G. Arangio-Ruiz, 'L'individuo e il diritto internazionale', 54 *RDI* (1971) 561.

[34] A-M. Slaughter and W. Burke-White, 'An International Constitutional Moment', 43 *HILJ* (2002) 1, p. 2.

[35] R. Higgins, *Problems and Process. International Law and How We Use It* (Oxford: Oxford University Press, 1994), p. 50.

[36] *Convention on the High Seas*, 29 April 1958, 450 UNTS 82, Art. 19; *Convention on the Law of the Sea*, 10 December 1982, A/CONF. 62/122 or 21 *ILM* (1982) 1261, Arts. 100 *et seq*.

[37] See J. B. Moore, diss. op., *The Case of the SS 'Lotus'*, PCIJ Series A, No. 9 (1927), p. 70.

of every country and at all times, and therefore are universally subject to the extreme rights of war'.[38] The same reasoning underpins, although in less dramatic terms, the claim recently advanced by NATO Member States to stop, visit and eventually take coercive measures against vessels suspected to be involved in terrorist activities, regardless of its flag.[39]

Much more complicated is the question of the lawfulness of military measures taken against terrorists located within the territory of another State. It has been argued that crucial State support of armed bands or terrorists, although not intense enough to qualify them as *de facto* organs, could nonetheless amount to an armed attack[40] or an act of aggression.[41] In this perspective, the acts committed by the terrorists still fall short of being imputable to the State: it is the gravity of the violation of the negative obligation not to support and encourage the terrorists that exposes the State to the consequences normally attached to armed attacks. The State would be responsible not for the acts perpetrated by the terrorists but rather for its own illegal conduct. The introduction of a further threshold in addition to – and as difficult to establish as – the one concerning the qualification of *de facto* organs is only partially satisfactory as it leaves unanswered the question of the remedies available when the State involvement is less significant.

The problem must be addressed by assessing the attitude of the State involved in terrorism towards the Security Council and other States, and especially those that, being the target of the terrorist activities, are specially affected. The refusal of the territorial State to stop supporting the terrorists or to take the action in its power to curb the terrorist activities conducted from its territory may amount to the adoption by that States of the activities carried out by the terrorists.[42] In this

[38] 2 Dodson, 210, p. 244 (1817).

[39] Following the attacks perpetrated on 11 September 2001, NATO member States decided to take, individually and jointly, eight measures to co-ordinate and enhance the Allied response to international terrorism: see *Statement to the Press by Nato Secretary General*, 4 October 2001. These measures included the deployment of a naval force on the Eastern Mediterranean Sea charged not only with surveillance and monitoring tasks, but also with enforcing duties in case of vessels suspected to be engaged in international terrorism, regardless of their flag. NATO forces are certainly allowed to undertake naval military operations aimed at protecting commercial vessels on the high sea and to react to any threat or hostile military activities against them. Under the current law of the sea, however, a Security Council authorisation is necessary to forcefully intercept and board third States's vessels suspected to be engaged in international terrorism, but not representing an immediate military threat to navigation.

[40] See R. Jennings, diss. op., in *Nicaragua case*, Merits, *supra* note IV-2, p. 543.

[41] See E. Sciso, 'Legittima difesa ed aggressione indiretta secondo la Corte internazionale di giustizia, 70 *RDI* (1987) 627, pp. 632–3.; R. Pisillo-Mazzeschi, *supra* note 30, p. 324–5. According to P. Lamberti Zanardi, *supra* note IV-71, p. 115, on the contrary, the term 'substantial' employed in Art. 3(g) of the definition 'can have legal significance only if it is understood to mean that the involvement must be so important as to transform the armed groups . . . into *de facto* organs of the State'.

[42] In international law, the faulty failure to prevent the commission of the illicit act may be equated to causing it: see R. Ago, *supra* note IV-153, pp. 502 *et seq*.; W. Wright, 'The

sense, Art. 11 of the Draft Articles on State Responsibility establishes that conduct may be attributable to a State to the extent that it 'acknowledges and adopts such a conduct as its own'.[43]

What generates the responsibility of a given State and exposes it to the remedies permitted by international law, including where applicable the exercise of self-defence, is the conduct that conclusively reveals its unwillingness to stop the terrorist activities from being carried out within its territory, and *a fortiori* its support to them. A formal endorsement of the acts of the terrorist is not necessary. This conduct must be kept distinct from the inability of the State to curb the terrorist activities within its jurisdiction. In this case, States cannot invoke self-defence to counter the hostile military activities; they have to rely on other legal grounds, presumably the state of necessity.[44]

The United States has implicitly made use of this reasoning. This occurred, in particular, in 1998 when air strikes were conducted against Afghanistan and Sudan following their refusal to comply with their international obligations not to support, instigate or tolerate terrorist activities.[45] In 2001, the United States denounced the 'central role' played by Al Qaeda, with the support of the Taliban Government, in the terrorist attacks and requested the former to surrender all the terrorists in Afghanistan and to close dawn their camps and operations.[46] It must be stressed that the request had been to a large extent endorsed by the Security Council that, acting under Chapter VII of the Charter, ordered the Taliban to take the measures necessary to put an end to the terrorist activities carried out in the

Prevention of Aggression', 50 *AJIL* (1956) 514, p. 527; G. Morelli, *supra* note I-38, p. 349; P. A. Pillitu, *Lo stato di necessità nel diritto internazionale* (Perugia: Libreria Editrice Universitaria, 1981), pp. 208–9.

[43] See the commentary in *Report to the General Assembly. 53rd Session* (2001), A/56/10, pp. 118 *et seq*. Here the ILC relied mainly on the *Hostages Case*, *supra* IV-122.

[44] See *infra* pp. 204 *et seq*.

[45] President Clinton, *Address to the Nation on Military Action Against Terrorist Sites in Afghanistan and Sudan*, 20 August 1998, in 93 *AJIL* (1999) 161 *et seq*., p. 162, declared: 'Afghanistan and Sudan have been warned for years to stop harboring and supporting these terrorist groups. But countries that persistently host terrorists have no right to be safe havens.'

[46] President Bush, *Radio Address*, 6 October 2001. In the document *supra* note III-100, the US declared: 'Despite every effort by the United States and the international community, the Taliban regime has refused to change its policy.' The British Secretary of State, in turn, declared: 'We gave the chance to surrender bin Laden and his associates for trial and to offer proof that thy no longer supported terrorism. They had more than two weeks to comply, but they continued to prevaricate and to lie. We warned the Taliban regime that they were running out of time. We warned them that they faced powerful military action', in 72 *BYIL* (2001) 684. Among the many precedents concerning Israel, mention can be made of the following statement made before the Security Council on 30 December 1968, S/PV. 1461, p. 10: 'The attention of the Lebanese government has been drawn on numerous occasions to the activities of the terror organisations within its borders. The Lebanese government, however, has not only continued to condone these activities, but has publicly identified itself with them.'

territory it controlled and to hand over Osama bin laden.[47] The refusal to meet these requests amounted to 'clear and unequivocal'[48] conduct for the purpose of attributing to the Taliban Government the acts committed by the terrorists. The United States concluded that the Taliban regime and Al Qaeda were 'virtually indistinguishable. Together they promote terror abroad and impose a reign of terror on Afghan people'.[49] Regardless of the possible qualification of Al Qaeda as a *de facto* organ of the Taliban Government, therefore, the use of force in self-defence could have been – at least in principle – permitted.

The fact that for decades the United Nations has rejected self-defence claims related to military measures against alleged terrorists[50] is not necessarily conclusive as to the inadmissibility of self-defence in this field. No compelling reasons prevent the qualification of terrorist activities as hostile military activities for the purpose of Art. 51 of the Charter, nor their attribution to a subject of international law. On the one hand, no State will hesitate to use force to protect civilian or military targets against terrorist attacks, regardless of the origin and proportions of the said attacks.[51] On the other hand, terrorist activities can be attributed to a State because of either its effective control over the terrorists or its conclusive behaviour in the sense of Art. 11 of the Draft Articles. As a result, States could justify their use of force as self-defence. The real challenge posed by terrorist activities regards the conditions and the limits within which the right to self-defence may be exercised rather than the applicability of the notion itself.

The limits of self-defence in the fight against international terrorism

Immediacy

It is undisputed that States are allowed to counter with military measures any terrorist attack during its execution. The capacity to do so, however, may be merely theoretical as terrorist attacks normally consist of largely unpredictable, sudden and instantaneous acts. An interpretation of Art. 51 of the Charter in the sense of

[47] See, in particular, Res. 1267, 15 October 1999, para. 2.

[48] The expression has been borrowed from the ILC, *Report to the General Assembly*, *supra* note 43, p. 122.

[49] President Bush's address before the UN General Assembly, 10 November 2001, A/56/PV.44, pp. 8–9. See also the *Address to a Joint Session of Congress and the American People*, 20 September 2001, at www.whitehouse.gov/news/releases/2001/09/20010920–8.html; *Presidential Address to the Nation*, 7 October 2001, at www.whitehouse.gov/news/releases/2001/10/20011007–8.html. This view was shared also by the British Government which described the relationship between Taliban and Al Qaeda in terms of symbiosis: see *Responsibility for the Terrorist Atrocities in the United States. 11 September 2001. An Updated Account*, esp. para. 19, at www.number10.hov.uk/output/page458.asp.

[50] On this point, see O. Corten, F. Dubuisson, *supra* note III-102, p. 59.

[51] *Contra*, A. Cassese, *supra* note 26, p. 596, according to whom self-defence can be invoked only in the event of a 'consistent pattern of violent terrorist action'.

confining the use of force in self-defence to the time during which the attack is in progress hardly accords with reality and would leave the target State powerless.

The doctrine of cumulative events does not serve to demonstrate that the terrorist activities have reached a given threshold of gravity and may trigger a response in self-defence. As maintained above, States militarily resist *any* hostile activities, regardless of their nature or proportions. The doctrine permits the global representation of the different attacks and their classification as a unique continuing action for the purpose of the immediacy requirement. Instead of expiring immediately after any single attack, the right to self-defence survives it and allows States to take the forcible action necessary to put an end to the chain of attacks.

State practice offers several instances in which States invoked self-defence to justify the use of force not against a specific episode of terrorism but in the context of repeated terrorist attacks.[52] This conduct has been almost systematically condemned by the Security Council, or at least a significant part of the Organisation membership, as being in violation of Art. 2(4). The defensive claims, however, were not rejected as legally unsound in principle: the negative attitude of other States was generally attributed to the unnecessary, disproportionate or punitive character of the military reaction.[53] What was considered unacceptable was not the claim in itself, but rather its invocation in the specific case.

The claim that force can be used in self-defence, even when a specific terrorist attack has been consumed, provided that it is part of a planned hostile strategy and there is reliable evidence that further attacks are imminent, seems to have gained a general acceptance. In 1998, in particular, the United States asserted that the air strikes against Afghanistan and Sudan were in conformity with Art. 51 of the Charter as they were directed at putting an end to the sequence of terrorist attacks, including those against the embassies in Kenya and Tanzania, and to prevent their recurrence.[54] A negligible number of States actually protested against

[52] In 1982, for instance, Israel justified its military action in Lebanon as 'exercise of its right of self-defence to arrest the never ending cycle of attacks against Israel's northern border' (S/PV.2374, 5 June 1982, p. 7). In 1986, the US invoked Art. 51 to respond militarily to 'an ongoing pattern of attacks by the Government of Libya' (Letter to the Security Council, 14 April 1986, S/17990). During the discussion before the Security Council, it further declared that it was compelled to resort to military force 'In the light of that reprehensible act of violence – only the latest in an ongoing pattern of attacks by Libya – and of clear evidence that Libya was planning a multitude of further attacks' (S/PV.2674, 15 April 1986, p. 17).

[53] In 1985, for instance, the US, while abstaining from voting Res. 573, which condemned Israel for the air strikes against PLO headquarters in Tunisia, recognised and strongly supported 'the principle that a State subjected to continuing terrorist attacks may respond with appropriate use of force to defend itself against further attacks' (S/PV.2615, 4 October 1985, p. 112).

[54] The US insisted that it was in possession of compelling evidence that further attacks were in preparation. On the basis of Art. 51 of the Charter, it invoked the right to prevent and deter the *continuation* of terrorist attacks (Letter to the Security Council, 20 August 1998, S/1998/780).

the action.[55] Although, from a factual standpoint, the claim concerning Sudan was abusive,[56] it was confirmed that the right to self-defence does not necessarily cease at the conclusion of each terrorist attack.

The massive use of force against Afghanistan in 2001 was defended as indispensable to counter the *ongoing* threat posed by the terrorist groups operating from that country with the support of the local Government.[57] The immediacy test is not to be applied simply taking into account the lapse of time dividing the armed attack and the military reaction.[58] It would have been more accurate for the United States to use the expression 'ongoing armed attack' rather than 'ongoing threat'. The rationale behind its position – accepted by the generality of other States – was that terrorist activities were being carried out from Afghan territory within the framework of a large hostile military plan. Because of the continuous character of the armed attack, coupled with the imminent and concrete risk of further attacks, States could resort to force in self-defence. Admittedly, the preventive and deterrent character of the reaction – which may be considered as inherent to most defensive measures – assumes here a stronger connotation and ultimately overlaps with the notion of interceptive self-defence. Once again, the collective assessment of the threat and control over the defensive claim is the only guarantee against the evident risk of abuses.

Necessity

As with any other defensive military action, those directed at curbing terrorism must also strictly respect the necessity requirement. When countering a terrorist attack which is still underway, States are allowed to take military measures only *extrema ratio* and at any rate they must opt for the smaller scale of use of force. This may imply dramatic choices, especially where civilian aircraft are concerned. The State acting in self-defence is provisionally the only judge of the necessity to use force, without any prior submission of proofs to the Security Council being required. Under Art. 51, however, the State must immediately report to the Security Council on the measures taken and provide it with the evidence that the action was necessary to repel the armed attack.

[55] Interestingly, the League of Arab States condemned the action against Sudan, but apparently condoned that against Afghanistan: see the *Letter to the Security Council*, 21 August 1998, S/1998/789. The different attitude could be explained by the lack of evidence on Sudan involvement in terrorism. A few days later, the Security Council, without passing any judgment on the US actions, ordered the Afghan factions to refrain from harbouring and training terrorists (Res. 1193, 28 August 1998).

[56] See *infra* note 67.

[57] See *Letter dated 7 October 2001 to the President of the Security Council*, S/2001/946. Similarly, the UK declared that the military action was indispensable to avert the continuing threat of attacks (*Letter dated 7 October 2001 to the President of the Security Council*, S/2001/947).

[58] In this sense, J. Delbrück, *supra* note III-103, p. 16, maintains that a lapse of little over three weeks does not appear unreasonably long.

The situation is quite different when the reaction takes place at a subsequent moment, as in the case of a response to what the concerned State perceives as a continuing attack. The factual circumstances in which the reaction is envisaged forces a reconsideration of Art. 51 from the standpoint of necessity. Without prejudice to the right of the concerned State to resort to force in order to intercept or counter any further attack, the military reaction does not present the character of absolute urgency that normally distinguishes the use of force in self-defence.[59] The harm has already been inflicted by the terrorist attacks. Consequently, the unilateral use of force must not only be defensive in nature;[60] it must also be preceded by unsuccessful resort to peaceful means.[61]

Bearing in mind that 'the right of self-defence is not a right which is left altogether outside the collective system for maintaining peace'[62] and that even the defensive use of force is subject to the international control,[63] it is submitted that the concerned State has a duty to report to the Security Council and to provide it with the evidence supporting the self-defence claim.[64] The evidence must concern the continuing involvement in terrorist activities of the State against which the use of force is considered, the exhaustion of peaceful means, and the need to take military action. Such a duty derives from Art. 2(2) of the Charter according to which Member States have accepted the fulfilment in good faith of the obligations related to the protection of common interests, and in the very first place the maintenance of international peace through the collective control of the use of force, including self-defence.[65]

The fact that, according to the text of Art. 51, States submit to the Security Council a report on the measures already taken must not necessarily be interpreted

[59] It may be worthwhile recalling that almost one month elapsed between the 11 September 2001 terrorist attacks and the beginning of the military operations against Afghanistan.

[60] Serious doubt may be cast on the defensive character of military actions such as the Israeli raid at Beirut airport in 1968, the US air strikes against Libya in 1986 and against Iraq in 1993. Their retributive and punitive nature may make them better qualified as armed reprisals. See R. A. Falk, *supra* note IV-33.

[61] State practice shows that reacting States feel legally obliged to resort to non-military measures before using force. In respect of the 1986 air strikes against Libya, the US observed before the Security Council that 'when quiet diplomacy, public condemnation, economic sanctions and demonstration of military force failed to dissuade Colonel Qaddafi, this self-defence action became necessary' (S/PV.2674, 15 April 1986, p. 16). The 1998 air strikes against Sudan and Afghanistan, in turn, were decided on by the US 'after repeated effort to convince the Government of Sudan and the Taliban regime in Afghanistan to shut terrorist activities down and to cease their co-operation with the Bin Laden organisation'.

[62] C. H. M Waldock, *supra* note IV- 51, p. 495.

[63] See *supra* note I-80.

[64] In this sense, see J. I. Charney, 'The Use of Force Against Terrorism and International Law', 95 *AJIL* (2001) 835, p. 836.

[65] See J. P. Müller and R. Kolb, 'Article 2 (2)', in B. Simma (ed.), *supra* note I-1, pp. 91 *et seq.*, p. 95.

as conclusive proof that the evidentiary requirement arises after – and not before – the right of self-defence has been exercised.[66] Article 51, in fact, clearly states that the measures taken in self-defence shall not in any way affect the authority and responsibility of the Security Council. The facts that, as a result of the substantial failure of the collective security system, the unilateral action in self-defence has lost its residual character and the temporal limitation foreseen in Art 51 has became obsolete do not mean that the Security Council cannot exercise a preventive control over self-defence claims.

If normally this is not feasible because of the urgency of the military reaction of the victim State, when the defensive use of force is deferred – as in the case of military operation against a continuous terrorist armed attack – the State concerned shall provide the Security Council with the evidence supporting its claim. The behaviour of the State accused of being involved in terrorism,[67] the practicability of diplomatic or economic means of pressure, and the necessity of military action cannot be left to the unilateral judgement of the State that intends to resort to force; it must be the object of collective assessment and control.[68] The move is not directed as obtaining from the Security Council the authorisation to resort to force, but at submitting the claim to a preventive and collective control.

The Security Council has basically four options at its disposal. First, it may evaluate the self-defence claim negatively either because it is not persuaded by the evidence produced or because it is not convinced of the necessity to use force from a costs–benefits perspective. Acting under Chapter VII of the Charter, it may consequently decide to deprive that State of the right to use force in self-defence. As a result, resort to self-defence would be excluded. Such a decision requires the participation, or at least the non-opposition, of all permanent members. This amounts to an effective guarantee against an abusive exercise by the Security Council of its powers.[69]

Second, it may express reservations, of either a political or a legal nature, on the self-defence claim, while limiting itself to recommending the concerned State to refrain from using force and to seek a peaceful settlement of the situation. The non-binding decision of the Security Council does not bar the use of force of self-defence, albeit that it may induce the concerned State to reconsider its position.

[66] *Contra*, T. Franck, *supra* note 26, p. 842.

[67] The need for a collective evaluation of the real intention of the State suspected of tolerating or supporting terrorism was evident with regard to the air strikes against Sudan in 1998. The US not only failed to produce reliable evidence; it also first rebuffed Sudanese co-operation in the investigation, and then prevented the dispatch of a fact-finding mission by the Security Council to investigate the circumstances surrounding the air strikes as requested by Sudan (Letter to the Security Council, 21 August 1998, S/1998/786). See also L. M. Campbell, 'Defending Against Terrorism: A Legal Analysis of the Decision to Strike Sudan and Afghanistan', 74 *Tulane LR* (2000) 1067, pp. 1090–1.

[68] See C. Greenwood, *supra* note IV-197, para. 156; C. Stahn, *supra* note 26, p. 238, argues that the Security Council exercises a 'preventive *droit de regard*'.

[69] See *supra* note I-92.

Third, it may pass no judgement on the claim, possibly because of the disagreement among permanent members either on the lawfulness of the action or on its political opportunity. Military action in self-defence would still be admissible. The State will act on its own unilateral judgement and at its own risk.

Fourth, the Security Council may express its satisfaction with the evidence produced and share the need for a military action. Nothing would prevent the Security Council from recognising beforehand the lawfulness of the resort to force, even in the form of approval or authorisation.[70] The authorisation would not have the permissive effect attributed to the resolutions authorising military enforcement measures in the sense described in Chapter II, albeit that it could constitute an additional legal ground for the military operations. Here, the concerned State is already allowed to use force in self-defence, independently from the Security Council authorisation. The resolution, nonetheless, could certify the Security Council's incapacity or unwillingness to take the measures necessary to tackle the threat to international peace probably posed by the situation in which self-defence is envisaged.[71]

Scepticism has been expressed as to the readiness of States to accept the assessment of the Security Council on the evidence upon which they base their 'defensive strategy of self-preservation'.[72] It is submitted that when time restraints do not make it impossible, States genuinely committed to pursuing the most important objective of the Organisation – namely the maintenance of international peace through effective collective measures in the common interest – shall seek the involvement of the Security Council, in the first place in the form of preventive assessment of the existence of the conditions to resort to force in self-defence. Renouncing the centralised control over self-defence claims would contribute to dismantling the collective security system and undermine the rules governing the use of force in international law.[73]

It must be underlined that before intervening in Afghanistan, the United States felt the need to submit the evidence in its possession to NATO allies.[74] The decision to exclude the Security Council involvement in the military aspects of the Afghan crisis, which has been discussed above from the perspective of collective security, is rather disappointing also with regard to self-defence, especially considering that the attitude of the Taliban Government had already been condemned by the Security Council.[75] Nonetheless, the virtually universal support for or

[70] See *supra* text corresponding to note IV-252.

[71] With regard to Res. 678, see G. Gaja, *supra* note IV-169.

[72] See T. M. Franck, *supra* note 26, p. 843.

[73] In this regard, it is illustrative that the last author quoted refers to 'self-preservation' rather than self-defence.

[74] In a Statement issued on 2 October 2001, NATO Secretary General described the evidence provided by the US as 'compelling' and 'conclusive'.

[75] See, for instance, Res. 1267 and Res. 1333, adopted on 15 October 1999 and 19 December 2000 respectively. That the US holds a permanent seat on the Security Council may be considered as a aggravating circumstance. See E. P. J. Myjer and N. D. White, 'The Twin Towers Attack: An Unlimited Right to Self-Defence?', 7 *JCSL* (2002) 5, pp. 9 *et seq.*

acquiescence in the intervention led by the United States could be assimilated to a decentralised form of collective control over the self-defence claim capable of replacing the Security Council decision. As a result, the necessity requirement would be satisfied.

Proportionality

In order to be permitted as self-defence, military measures taken to intercept or counter a terrorist attack during its execution must also satisfy the requirement of proportionality. It is not sufficient that the measures are necessary in the sense that the acting State has no alternative but to use force and no lesser use of force would be effective. The consequences of the military action – which most of the time are irreversible and irreparable – must be proportionate to the objective they pursue, namely preventing the accomplishment of the terrorist attack or at least minimising its effects.

This perspective is to be preferred to the comparison of the quantum of force and counter-force used, which may be acceptable when the defensive action targets the attacking armed forces, but may be inadequate with regard to terrorism. This second perspective, in fact, may be deformed by the techniques used by the terrorists, and in particular by suicide commandos on civil aircraft. Assuming that the action can be qualified as self-defence because of the role played by State A and that the aircraft belongs to State B, the defensive action of State C does not target State A forces, whereas it is State B which essentially suffers from the consequences of the action taken in self-defence. Consequently, when the aircraft is approaching its potential target and there is a concrete risk of causing a higher number of casualties, the reaction – presumably the shooting of the aircraft – has to be weighed against the consequences that the attack might provoke.

Applying the proportionality test to defensive action undertaken not to intercept or counter a single armed attack but to terminate a sequence of attacks is even more difficult. It is generally accepted that a State that has suffered and continues to suffer from a series of successive hostile military activities may resort to a single armed action on a much larger scale than the attacks – taken individually – it is intend to stop.[76]

As seen before, the theory of cumulative events introduces in the notion of self-defence the necessary flexibility with regard to the immediacy requirement, but is not adequate for the purpose of assessing the proportionality of the defensive action. Again, confining the exercise of self-defence to action proportionate – from a quantitative and qualitative standpoint – does not necessarily guarantee an effective defence of the State concerned. Such an action may fail to achieve its objective and leave the State exposed to further attacks. Yet, the action is lawful insofar as it is 'commensurate with the objectives that the plea of self-defence

[76] R. Ago, *supra* note IV-32, p. 69, observes that the lawfulness of self-defence 'cannot be measured except by its capacity for achieving the desired result'.

might reasonably entitle a State to achieve'.[77] The crux of the matter is precisely what must be intended for reasonable objectives.

The most important objective of the defensive action is to neutralise the terrorist groups or to reduce their capacity to conduct their activities. Air strikes directed at destroying terrorist training camps actively engaged in hostile military activities represent the typical defensive measure. Measures not expected to affect the terrorist network and activities, on the contrary, cannot be justified as self-defence as they do not directly contribute to the achievement of the objective. Rather, they may have deterring or punitive effects and have to be dealt with under the rubric of armed reprisals.[78]

It remains to be seen whether there is any limit to the defensive action. The question is of crucial importance when a State supports the terrorists or identifies itself with them. The main objectives of the intervention in Afghanistan declared by the United States included: (a) the destruction of the infrastructures and the facilities used by the Taliban and Al Qaeda; (b) the replacement of the Taliban Government; (c) the prevention of further terrorist attacks being launched from Afghanistan.[79] In order to achieve these objectives, the United States extended the military operations to the *debellatio* of the Taliban Government and the occupation of the Afghan territory.

Since 1945 at the latest, the right to self-defence has been intended as not allowing the annihilation of the State responsible for breaching Art. 2 (4) of the Charter, even in the event of aggression.[80] The picture may be different when the State supports the terrorist groups to the point of identifying itself with them and shows the firm intention to continue such conduct. In these circumstances, the acting State has a plausible argument to extend its defensive action to the destitution of the concerned Government, which may be followed by a period of occupation and the creation in due course of a new Government.[81]

Once again, the need for international control is compelling. The fact that in the Afghan crisis the Security Council sat back is to be regretted. It must, however, be recognised that the action led by the United States was not only supported or tolerated by virtually of the members of the United Nations; it was not criticised

[77] D. W. Greig, *International Law*, 2nd ed. (London: Butterworths, 1976) pp. 886–7.

[78] *Infra* pp. 203 *et seq*.

[79] See, in particular, the US President, *Address to a Joint Session of the Congress and the American People*, 20 October 2001: www.whitehouse.gov/news/release/2001/09/20010920–8.html. The British Government listed the following objectives: '(a) to bring Usama Bin Laden and other Al Qaida leaders to justice; (b) to prevent Usama Bin Laden and the Al Qaida network from posing a continuing terrorist treat; (c) to this end and to ensure that Afghanistan ceases to harbour and sustain international terrorism and enables us to verify that the camps where terrorists train have been destroyed; (d) and to achieve a sufficient change in the Afghan leadership to ensure that Aghanistan's links to international terrorism are broken' (73 *BYIL* (2002) 860).

[80] See K. H. Meyn, *Debellatio*, *EPIL* vol. I (1992), pp. 969 *et seq*., p. 971.

[81] J. Delbrück, *supra* note III-103, p. 18, concedes that 'the deposition of the Taliban regime could not be neatly separated from the fight against Al'Qaida network'.

from the standpoint of proportionality, either during the debates before the Security Council or in the plenary session of the General Assembly. Not even the few States that considered the intervention as lawful seriously addressed its disproportionate character.

The question of pre-emptive self-defence

Already with regard to conventional hostile military activities, the doctrine of interceptive self-defence has stretched the span of time during which States can use force in self-defence. In this sense, States are not obliged to wait until these activities concretely produce their effects: they are allowed to take the military measures strictly necessary to protect them against 'absolute imminent attacks'.[82]

Such an extensive interpretation of the concept of self-defence is essential in the fight against international terrorism. By their own nature, terrorists' attacks produce their effects unexpectedly, instantaneously and irreversibly, thus making it extremely difficult, if not impossible, to counter them during their execution. The chances of effectively tackling the phenomenon of terrorism largely depend on the ability to timeously detect and intercept the terrorists in the planning and preparation phases of their activities. To deny States the right forcibly to put an end to the preparation of terrorist activities would seriously undermine the effectiveness of the right of self-defence.

The argument was used in 1998 by the United States to justify the air strike against Afghanistan and Sudan as necessary and proportionate 'to prevent and deter additional attacks by a clearly identified imminent and concrete terrorist threat'[83]. Assuming, for the moment, the accuracy of the classification of the threat as immediate and concrete, it is submitted that the United States action could possess a defensive character, albeit that the execution phase of the terrorist plan had not yet been put in motion. The action consequently may be legally based on Art. 51 of the Charter, provided that the limits for the exercise of the right to self-defence are respected. The crux of the matter is to determine at which point the terrorist activities represent a concrete and immediate threat. The latitude of the resort to defensive force amplifies the risks of abuses and render more compelling than ever centralised control over self-defence claims.

Even this flexible approach has been considered as inadequate. The most remarkable claim has recently been elaborated by the United States in these terms:

[82] The expression has been borrowed from A. Roberts, *Letter to the Select Committee on Defence*, 31 March 2003 (on file with author).

[83] *Letter to Congressional Leaders Reporting on Military Action Against Terrorist Sites in Afghanistan and Sudan*, 21 August 1998, excerpts in 93 *AJIL* (1999) 163. In this perspective, interceptive self-defence may overlap with self-defence against continuous armed attacks.

> Legal scholars and international jurists often conditioned the legitimacy of pre-emption on the existence of an imminent threat – most often a visible mobilization of armies, navies, and air forces preparing to attack. We must adapt the concept of imminent threat to the capabilities and objectives of today's adversaries. . . . The United States has long maintained the option of pre-emptive actions to counter a sufficient threat to our national security. The greater the threat, the greater is the risk of inaction— and the more compelling the case for taking anticipatory action to defend ourselves, even if uncertainty remains as to the time and place of the enemy's attack. To forestall or prevent such hostile acts by our adversaries, the United States will, if necessary, act pre-emptively.[84]

The claim is by no means a novelty, although what is new is the magnitude of the terrorist threat and the military counter-terrorist reaction. It had already been put forward, both in words and in deeds, in the 1980s,[85] when the United States justified as self-defence the use of force against Libya in order to pre-empt and deter terrorists' attacks. With regard to the air strike against Libya carried out in 1986, the President affirmed: 'We believe that this pre-emptive action against the terrorist installations will not only diminish Colonel Qadhafi's capacity to export terror, it will provide him with incentives and reasons to alter his criminal behaviour'.[86]

The claim to use force pre-emptively, however, has not been adequately articulated or accompanied by sufficiently precise definitions and criteria.[87] Expressions such as 'sufficient threat to national security' pave the way for any sort of abuse. The fact that the United States has declared that it will 'not use force in all cases to pre-empt emerging threats, nor should nations use pre-emption as a

[84] *National Security Strategy of the United States*, at www.whitehouse.gov/nsc/nss.html. On deterrence against terrorism, the US President declared that 'the promise of massive retaliation against nations means nothing against shadowy terrorist networks with no nations or citizens to defend' (*Address at the Military Academy at West Point*, 1 June 2002, 38 *WCPD* 944, p. 946).

[85] On 25 October 1984, Secretary of State G. Shultz, while discussing self-defence against terrorism, declared: 'We must reach a consensus in this country that our response should go beyond passive defense to consider means of active prevention, preemption, and retaliation. . . . If we are going to respond or preempt effectively, our policies will have to have an element of unpredictability and surprise' (*Address before the Park Avenue Synagogue*, 84 *DSB*, December 1984, p. 12, at p. 16). A rather relaxed reading of the norms governing the use of force in international law was visible also in the National Security Strategy adopted in 1999, which partly reads: 'We will do what we must to defend [America's] interests, including when necessary and appropriate, using our military unilaterally and decisively', at www.dtic.mil/doctrine/jel/other_pubs/nssr99.pdf.

[86] *Address to the Nation on the Air Strikes against Libya*, 14 April 1986, Public Papers of the United States Presidents, 1986, Vol. I, pp. 468–9. See also *Testimony of the Legal Adviser of the Department of State*, 29 April 1986, in 80 *AJIL* (1986) 636, p. 641.

[87] The Defence Secretary, in particular, declared that 'Defending the United States requires prevention, self-defence and sometimes preemption' (quoted in A. Sofaer, 'On the Necessity of Pre-emption', 14 *EJIL* (2003) 209, footnote 3).

pretext for aggression' certainly does not represent a satisfactory guarantee.[88] Regrettably, the extension of the right of self-defence along the lines indicated by the United States doctrine 'has significant and potentially dangerous consequences in international law'.[89]

Aware of the difficulties, if not the impossibility of reaching a significant international agreement on this doctrine,[90] pre-emptive self-defence can be defined as military action against a potential adversary in advance of a suspected attack[91]. It differs from interceptive self-defence in the sense that it is deliberately future oriented. Although an element of deterrence may be considered as inherent in any form of self-defence, here the threat is merely potential and the military reaction deprived, strictly speaking, of defensive character.[92]

The line dividing interceptive self-defence and pre-emptive self-defence must be maintained.[93] Blurring it would undermine the whole legal regulation of the use of force. There is a point beyond which self-defence ceases to represent an exception to the general ban on the use of force and becomes the negation of the ban itself. Far from being an evolution or adaptation of existing legal categories, rendered impellent by the emergence of new forms of terrorism, it would represent a huge step backwards to the 'just war' doctrine and ultimately to unilateral and uncontrolled self-help.

The United States put forward a claim, however poorly articulated, that would ultimately put into question the general prohibition on the use of force[94]. It seems to have definitively abandoned the view previously maintained – at least verbally

[88] A. Roberts, *supra* note 82, regrets that the American doctrine was not accompanied by 'any statement of reassurance about the continuing importance of the non-intervention norm in international relations'.

[89] See the report *supra* note IV-203, para. 51.

[90] A. Roberts, *supra* note 82.

[91] United Kingdom, *Foreign Affairs Committee*, *supra* note 90, para 48. M. E. O'Hanlon, S. E. Rice and J. B. Steinberg, 'The New National Strategy and Preemption', at www.brook.edu/comm/policybriefs/pb113.htm, define pre-emption as the 'striking an enemy even in the absence of specific evidence of a coming attack'. For M. E. O'Connell, *supra* note 26, footnote 10, preemptive self-defence refers to the use of force 'to quell any possibility of future attack by another State, even where there is no reason to believe that an attack is planned and where no prior attack has occurred'.

[92] Pre-emptive self-defence goes much further than anticipatory self-defence. As observed by W. M. Reisman, 'Assessing the Claims to Revise the Laws of War', 97 *AJIL* (2003) 80, p. 87, the former implies a 'palpable and imminent threat of attack', whereas the latter is based on 'the conjectural and contingent threat of *possible* attack'. See also M. E. O'Connell, *supra* note 26, footnote 10.

[93] See L. Condorelli, *supra* note I-50, p. 843; R. N. Gardner, 'Neither Bush nor the "Jurisprude" ', 97 *AJIL* (2003) 585, p. 588.

[94] Equally disruptive is the projection of this claim in purely hegemonic terms. This approach amounts to the unacceptable rejection of the generality of the command of Art. 2(4) with the exemption of the US. See H. Kissinger, 'Beyond Baghdad', *New York Post*, 11 August 2002, at 24, who argued that 'America's special responsibility, as the most powerful nation in the world, is to work toward an international system that rests on more

– according to which, 'In contrast to an attack on a terrorist base in self-defence, the United States opposes peacetime attacks on a State's facilities on the mere possibility that they may someday be used against the attacking country'.[95]

Its new attitude, at once, reveals its disaffection with the limitation of the use of unilateral or joint use of force to the defence against imminent and concrete dangers, and challenges the exclusive authority to the Security Council to tackle situations susceptible to threaten international peace and security. The whole legal regulation of the use of force and the collective security system established by the Charter are based upon the Security Council authority. Its rejection would have marked the end of the collective control over the use of force and ultimately of multilateralism.[96]

Such a development is both unnecessary and unwarranted. The right to self-defence provides States with an adequate legal protection against State-supported terrorism and does not need to be substantially reconsidered.[97] On the one hand, the difficulties related to the qualification of these activities as armed attacks for the purpose of Art. 51 are more apparent than real, especially if it is admitted that there is no threshold below which a military reaction is not permitted. However, some degree of adjustment might be necessary. Because of the specific nature of the terrorist activities, the immediacy test cannot be applied as strictly limited to the phase of execution of each single attack. In order to be effective, the right to self-defence must permit a State to take the forcible action – in accordance with the principles of proportionality and necessity – expected to neutralise the terrorist groups engaged in hostile military action and posing a continuing, concrete and imminent threat to its national security and population. When the threat is merely potential, in contrast, States must refrain from unilaterally using force and rely instead on the collective security system.

---

than military power – indeed, that strives to translate power into co-operation. Any other attitude will gradually isolate and exhaust us . . . It is not in the American interest to establish preemption as a universal principle available to every nation'.

[95] A. Sofaer, 'Terrorism, the Law and the National Defense', 126 *Mil. LR* (1989) 89, p. 109.

[96] For J. Delbrück, *supra* note III-103, p. 19, States will have carte blanche for the unilateral use of force. See also the critical remarks made by O. Corten and F. Dubuisson, *supra* note III-102, p. 76; O'Connell, *supra* note 26; T. Farer, 'The Bush Doctrine and the United Nations Charter Frame', 37 *IS* (2002) 91, pp. 99–100. As observed by M. E. O'Connell, 'Evidence of Terror', 7 *JCSL* (2002) 19, apart from the case of self-defence, the assessment of the necessity of taking military action cannot be left to the unilateral judgment of States. The fact that States normally are not able to produce 'the kind of evidence that can stand up in an American court of law', as noted by G. Shultz, *supra* note 85, p. 16, does not necessarily affect this conclusion. Yet, the evidence must satisfy a political body that takes political decisions, not a tribunal.

[97] *Contra*, L. Sohn, 'The Missile Attack on Baghdad and its Justifications', *ASIL Newsletter*, June–August 1993, p. 4, believes that 'it remains necessary to continue to develop the law of permissible response to terrorist activities [which] is not part of the law of self-defence against armed attack contemplated by Article 51'.

On the other hand, the rules elaborated in the context of State responsibility allows to attribute the terrorist activities to the State that supports, encourages or merely tolerates them. Such an attribution would pave the way for the use of force in self-defence. Alternatively, when a State is genuinely unable to destroy terrorist networks operating from its territory, recourse to force could still be admissible under the state of necessity doctrine.

Armed reprisals against international terrorism

Armed reprisals in the context of the fight against State-supported international terrorism can be defined negatively as any military measures to the exclusion of those admissible under the rubric of self-defence (a) to intercept or counter any terrorist activities underway or amounting to an immediate and concrete threat against the military or civilian targets of the acting State; and (b) to neutralise terrorist groups involved in ongoing hostile military operations.[98]

In spite of some superficial similarities, including the deterrent effect, armed reprisals must be kept separate from pre-emptive self-defence. Pre-emptive self-defence implies the dissociation between the commission of the armed attack and the military action. Such an action is not directed at countering, intercepting, putting an end to or punishing military hostile activities, but rather at preventing a potential threat from concretising. The terms of the question are reversed in the case of armed reprisals. Here, the action is related to the armed attack that has already been committed. The real intention behind such an action is to punish the State believed to be involved in terrorism and to compel it to change its attitude.

The lawfulness of armed reprisals intended to curb international terrorism can be neither excluded nor upheld on the basis of theoretical or formal arguments. The reiteration of the unlawfulness of armed reprisals as corollary of the general prohibition on the use of force, or, in the opposite sense, the need of States to protect themselves effectively in an environment characterised by the ill-functioning of the collective security system, do not amount to conclusive proof. Whether armed reprisals are admissible or inadmissible is to be demonstrated by assessing the practice of States. In this sense, the (re-)emergence of a customary norm – which would have introduced a new exception to the general ban established by Art. 2(4) of the Charter – allowing the unilateral or joint use of force for non-defensive purposes cannot be ruled out in principle.

From the objective standpoint, State practice offers a significant amount of cases of unilateral or joint use of force in conditions that could hardly have triggered the exercise of the right to self-defence. The fact that these actions were carried out essentially by Israel and the United States does not necessarily deprive them of any value as potential precedents for the formation of a norm permitting

[98] For the admissibility of the use of force against terrorist groups not supported by the State from which they operate, see the next paragraph.

armed reprisals. The crucial element to consider is the reaction of the rest of the international community. Until recently, armed reprisals almost systematically met the opposition of the overwhelming majority of States, opposition that on some occasions was translated into a resolution of condemn adopted by the Security Council or the General Assembly.[99] The tide could have started to change in the 1990s. The air strikes conducted against Iraq in 1993 and against Sudan in 1998 were in fact generally tolerated.

Conversely, the subjective element remains clearly insufficient. States have never claimed the right to take armed reprisals. Quite to the contrary, they repeatedly denounced armed reprisals as incompatible with the current legal regulation of the use of force and preferred to justify their military action as exercise of the right to self-defence, even when these actions had exclusively or essentially a punitive or retributive character. The air strikes against Iraq conducted in 1993 is a case in point. Albeit that it should have been better classified under the rubric of 'reprisals',[100] the action was characterised by the United States and the few States that submitted a legal analysis as permissible under Art. 51 of the Charter. The claim was abusive since none of the requirements for the lawful exercise of the right of self defence – necessity, proportionality and immediacy – was respected. At any rate, this case, as well as that of Sudan, is scarcely relevant for the purpose of ascertaining the *opinio juris*. Considering the complete lack of *opinio juris*, coupled with the still not entirely coherent and uniform practice, admitting the lawfulness of armed reprisals is premature.

The doctrine of state of necessity in the context of international terrorism

After defining the limits within which unilateral or joint use of force can be resorted to in self-defence against a State involved in terrorism, it remains to consider the admissibility of military action taken to curb terrorist activities conducted without the active support or acquiescence of the territorial State. In this case, the latter State may be doing all in its power to prevent the use of its territory for the perpetration of terrorist acts, but is unable to achieve such a result. Its conduct, therefore, does not imply any violation of international law. Under the

[99] See, for instance, the air strikes carried out by Israel against Beirut airport in 1968 (Security Council Res. 262, 31 December 1968); and by the US against Libya in 1986 (General assembly Res. 41/38, 20 November 1986). R. Barsotti, *supra* note IV-33, has convincingly concluded that practice of States until 1986 permitted the upholding of the inadmissibility of armed reprisals.

[100] This is admitted, in spite of the diverging views on the lawfulness of the action, by M. Reisman, 'The Raid on Baghdad: Some Reflections on its Lawfulness and Implications', 5 *EJIL* (1994) 120; L. Condorelli, 'A propos de l'attaque américaine contre l'Irak du 26 juin 1993: Lettre d'un professeur désemparé aux lecteurs du JEDI' (*ibid*, p. 134); D. Kristiotis, 'The Legality of the 1993 US Missile Strike on Iraq and the Right of Self-defence in International Law', 45 *ICLQ* (1996) 162, p. 169.

circumstances, the State victim of the terrorist acts cannot resort to force in self-defence which, according to the definition proposed above, presupposes a violation of Art. 2(4) attributable to the State against which self-defence is invoked.

The unacceptable situation of powerlessness in which States can find themselves may be overcome through the invocation of the state of necessity as a ground precluding the wrongfulness of conduct otherwise contrary to international law. It is generally accepted that, in exceptional cases, States could be exempted from complying with their obligations in order to protect their essential interests threatened by a grave and imminent peril. This conduct, which is not related to a previous violation of international law by the subject which owns the right correspondent to the obligation breached on grounds of necessity,[101] is permissible insofar as the essential interests of the acting State cannot be protected by means compatible with international law.[102]

The state of necessity does not imply the conflict of two subjective rights. It opposes the essential interest of a State against the legally protected interest of another State or, more precisely, because of the *erga omnes* character of the obligation not to threat or use force, that of all States composing the international community.[103]

Whether the legally protected interest could be sacrificed on the altar of necessity is to be assessed, on a case-by-case basis, through the comparison of the two interests.[104] The definition of 'essential interest' is rather problematic. After rejecting the view that in order to qualify as essential an interest needs to concern the existence of the State,[105] the ILC has wisely declined to lay down pre-established categories and has limited itself to providing a few examples.

As to the use of force on ground of necessity, the ILC did not take a position on the lawfulness of:

> incursions into foreign territory to forestall harmful operations by an armed group which was preparing to attack the territory of the State, or in pursuit of an armed

[101] R. Ago, *supra* note IV-32, p. 53, observes that 'the State *vis-à vis* with another State adopts a form of conduct inconsistent with an international obligation without having any excuse other than necessity is a State which has committed no international wrong against the State taking the action'. See also D. W. Bowett, *supra* note IV-17, p. 10; G. Schwarzenberger, *supra* note IV-55, p. 343.

[102] According to D. Anzilotti, sep. op., *Oscar Chinn case*, PCIJ, 12 December 1934, Series A/B No. 63, pp. 107 *et seq*., p. 114, 'the plea of necessity . . . by definition, implies the impossibility of proceeding by any other method than the one contrary to law'. He further points out that the burden of proof is for the party invoking the state of necessity.

[103] The State of the territory in which force is used, nonetheless, would be the especially affected State.

[104] R. Ago, *supra* note IV-32, p. 19; *ILC Report to the General Assembly*, *supra* note IV-69, p. 48; J. Crawford, *supra* note IV-79, pp. 178 *et seq*.; *ILC Report to the General Assembly*, *supra* note IV-79, p. 195.

[105] *ILC Report to the General Assembly*, *supra* note IV-79, p. 49. See also P. A. Pillitu, *supra* note 42, p. 306 *et seq*.

> band or gang of criminals who had crossed the frontier and perhaps had their base in that foreign territory . . . or to eliminate or neutralize a source of trouble which threatened to occur or to spread across the frontier.[106]

According to the ILC, the question pertained to the interpretation of the Charter and was therefore reserved to the organs of the United Nations. It is nonetheless significant that it did not rule out in principle the admissibility of a plea of necessity involving military force, and this after treating Art. 2(4) of the Charter as *jus cogens*.

This is in line with the Special Rapporteur's view that the fact that the Charter expressly foresees only one exception to the prohibition of Art. 2(4), namely self-defence, does not logically or necessarily exclude in absolute terms the elimination of the lawfulness of conduct not in conformity with such a prohibition 'on the ground of the existence of other circumstances'.[107]

Coherently with the methodological approach adopted throughout this study, it may be further argued that there is no obstacle to the (re-)emergence of the state of necessity as legal justification for the use of force in derogation to Art. 2(4), provided that State practice adequately supports such a conclusion.

In this regard, recent State practice offers a useful example among others. In 1995 the Turkish army invaded part of Northern Iraq and has been permanently stationed there since. The Turkish Government declared:

> As Iraq has not been able to exercise its authority over the northern part of its country since 1991 for reasons well known, Turkey cannot ask the Government of Iraq to fulfil its obligation, under international law, to prevent the use of its territory for the staging of terrorist acts against Turkey. Under these circumstances, Turkey's resorting to legitimate measures which are imperative to its own security cannot be regarded as a violation of Iraq's sovereignty.[108]

The statement contains all the elements of a state of necessity plea. Iraq was not held responsible for any violation of international law. The coercive measures, which normally would have implied the infringement of Iraqi sovereignty, were considered by Turkey as admissible because they were indispensable to protect its essential interests.

Iraq protested against what it considered an aggression which it was entitled to resist in accordance with the right to self-defence, and repeatedly requested the

[106] *Ibid.*, p. 44.

[107] R. Ago, *supra* note IV-32, p. 41.

[108] See the letter dated 24 July 1995 (S/1996/605). In a letter dated 2 January 1997 (S/1997/7, Annex), the Turkish Prime Minister justified the armed activities as necessary to exercise its authority over the northern parts of its territory, to (a) restore peace and stability in the region; (b) enhance security in the region; (c) combat terrorism; (d) ensure the safety of the people of northern Iraq. She admitted that because of 'Iraq's inability to exercise its authority over the northern parts of its territory . . . Turkey is determined to take all appropriate measures with a view to safeguarding its legitimate security interests, defending its borders and protecting its people against terrorism'. See also the letter sent on 18 July 1997 by Turkey to the President of the Security Council (S/1997/552, Annex).

intervention of the Security Council.[109] Interestingly, it did not deny the right of Turkey to take coercive measures strictly limited to neutralise terrorist or terrorist groups operating from Iraq; it protested against the permanent invasion of part of its territory.[110] What is contested here is not the admissibility in principle of the use of force, on the ground of necessity, against terrorists located abroad, but rather the abusive character of the specific plea.

The view that military coercive measures could be taken, in exceptional circumstances,[111] in the territory of another State is to be shared, lest it leaves the concerned State no choice but to suffer and continue to suffer from the irreversible damaging effects of the terrorist activities.[112]

The use of force on the ground of necessity should be kept separate from that of self-defence for at least three reasons.[113] First, a State can lawfully resort to force on the ground of necessity only after having unsuccessfully requested the consent of the territorial State to carrying out coercive measures, or sought the Security Council's authorisation to use force. These obligations – that do not necessarily exist with regard to the use of force in self-defence – stem from the undisputed fact that state of necessity cannot be invoked unless it is impossible to protect the essential interests of the State without failing to comply with international law. Second, the criteria of proportionality are more stringent than in the case of self-defence in the sense that the action has to be not only proportionate with the objectives to achieve, but also weighed against the legally protected interest of the other State.[114] Third, the State lawfully resorting to force on grounds of

[109] See, for instance, the letters sent on 15 January and 7 February 2002 to the President of the Security Council, respectively S/2002/61 and S/2002/150.

[110] In the letter sent on 22 July 2002 to the President of the Security Council, in particular, it observed that 'The claim to be in pursuit of outlaw elements cannot justify the invasion of the territory of a neighbouring State' (S/2002/803).

[111] *Ibid.*, p. 50. The exceptional character of state of necessity claims has been confirmed by the ICJ in the *Gabcíkovo case*, *supra* note IV-271, pp. 40 *et seq*.

[112] *Contra* J. J. A. Salmon, 'Faut il codifier l'état de necessité en droit international?', in J. Makarczyk (ed.), *Essays in International Law in Honour of Judge Lachs* (The Hague: Nijhoff, 1984), pp. 235 *et seq*., p. 258, according to whom 'On a aurait pu espérer que la Commission aurait pris la position que l'article 2(4) de la Charte qui exclut tout recours à la force ne souffre pas d'exceptions au titre de l'état de necessité'.

[113] In favour of the distinction, see R. Ago, *supra* note IV-32, p. 15 and the authorities referred to in footnote 7; O. Schachter, 'The Lawful Use of Force by a State against Terrorists in Another Country', 19 *IYBHR* (1989) 209, pp. 228–9, J. J. A. Salmon, *supra* note 112, pp. 237–8. *Contra*, P. A. Pillitu, *supra* note 42, esp. pp. 211 *et seq*. The author notes that a situation of emergency similar to that foreseen in Art. 51 arises also when the military hostile operations are carried out by individuals or groups of individuals from the territory of a State that is unable to stop them. She suggests extending by analogy the notion of self-defence to a situation characterised by a state of necessity. Similarly, see Y. Dinstein, *supra* note II-43, pp. 213 *et seq*., who considers the distinction as artificial, and treats extra-territorial law enforcement actions as a form of self-defence.

[114] See P. A. Pillitu, *supra* note 42, esp. p. 217.

necessity, albeit not committing any violation of international law, has a duty to compensate the other State for the damages suffered.[115]

The first ground for distinguishing state of necessity from self-defence deserves closer scrutiny. As maintained above, the State unable to suppress the terrorist activities carried out from its territory against another State ought to accept, if not actually seek, the assistance of other States and in particular that of the States directly suffering from or exposed to the terrorist activities.[116] Seen from another perspective, the State that intends to resort to force to neutralise the terrorist groups operating from the territory of another State must request the permission of the local Government before entering the territory of the latter. This, at least when there is a Government capable of validly expressing its consent and the emergency of the situation, does not make it impracticable. If such a permission is granted, the use of force would be based on the consent. In the context of the Afghan crisis, the United States required the Taliban Government to allow 'full access to terrorist training camps, so that [the United States] can make sure they are no longer operating'.[117]

In practice, however, trying to obtain the permission may be a futile exercise. The refusal may be motivated in different ways, typically by denying that the terrorist activities are conducted from the territory of the concerned State or that the external assistance is not indispensable. Unless the refusal amounts to the adoption of the terrorist acts by the territorial State, thus paving the way for the use of force in self-defence,[118] the state of necessity may come into play.

The State considering the resort to force, however, can neither be the sole judge of the existence of the conditions for lawfully invoking the state of necessity, nor immediately proceed with the assessment of the interests at stake. It has to explore the other possible way to protect its essential interests through an action not implying non-compliance with its obligations, namely the Security Council authorisation of the use of force.

Provided that the situation could qualify as a threat to international peace, the Security Council authorisation would ensure a solid legal ground for the military action. Otherwise, the non-concession of the authorisation by the Security Council does not necessarily prevents the concerned State from invoking – upon its own unilateral judgement and at its own risk – the state of necessity as a ground for using force.

Yet, the Security Council could not only refuse to grant such an authorisation, but also order the State to refrain from resorting to force. Already admitted with regard to the exercise of self-defence,[119] the power of the Security Council to

[115] R. Ago, *supra* note IV-32, p. 21 and the authorities referred to in footnote 35. *Contra*, P. A. Pillitu, *supra* note 42, pp. 342 *et seq*.

[116] See *supra* text corresponding to note 31.

[117] US President, *Address Before the Joint Session of the Congress*, 20 September 2001, 37 WCPD 1347.

[118] See *supra* pp. 184 *et seq*.

[119] See *supra* pp. 153 *et seq*.

impose the obligation to abstain from carrying out any military action must be affirmed *a fortiori* in the context of state of necessity. Such an occurrence requires the agreement of the permanent members of the organ.[120]

The admissibility of a plea of state of necessity is therefore to be intended in residual terms. It is reduced to the cases in which (a) the urgency of the situation does not permit the acting State to require the consent of the territorial State or the Security Council authorisation; or (b) the territorial State refuses such permission and the Security Council does not take a binding decision preventing the use of force.

This argument presupposes that the State invoking the state of necessity must preliminarily resort to the Security Council and that that organ lives up its responsibilities. Unfortunately, the recent practice is not encouraging. The plea of state of necessity advanced by Turkey since 1995 with regard to its military operations in Iraq is hardly defendable. Given the impracticability of obtaining the territorial State consent, the Turkish should have resorted to the Security Council. Only after having unsuccessfully attempted to obtain that organ's authorisation to take coercive military measures, it could have considered unilateral action as the sole alternative at its disposal. Since the military operations lasted for several years, at any rate, no considerations of urgency or time restraint can justify the Turkish failure to make use of the collective security system. Incidentally, serious doubts must be cast on the absolute necessity of the permanent deployment by Turkey of massive forces in northern Iraq. The disproportionate character of the military action might reveal that the real intention of Turkey went beyond the repression of terrorist activities.

Although the European Parliament and the Parliamentary Assembly of the Council of Europe[121] condemned the Turkish invasion, the international community remained rather indifferent. The European Union limited itself to urge 'Turkey to exercise the utmost restrain, to respect human rights, not to endangered the lives of innocent civilians and to withdraw its military forces from Iraq territory as soon as possible',[122] whereas NATO reportedly took 'no formal position on the Turkish invasion of northern Iraq'.[123]

Regrettably, the Security Council took no action. However infamous the Iraqi regime was, there is no excuse for the Security Council's refusal to assume its

[120] The voting procedure, once again, affords an effective guarantee to the concerned State: see *supra* note I-92.

[121] Recommendation 1266, 26 April 1995, considered the Turkish military invasion 'as contrary to international law' (para. 4) and called for the immediate withdrawal of its forces from northern Iraq. See also C. Antonopoulos, 'The Turkish Military Operations in Northern Iraq of March–April 1995 and the International Law on the Use of Force', 1 *JACL* (1996) 33.

[122] See the letter of the Presidency of the EU to the Secretary General (A/52/157, 27 May 1997).

[123] House of Lords *Hansard*, Written Answers, 6 April 1995, Co. WA32. The UK itself took note of the Turkish assurances that 'their operations are temporary and aimed solely at destroying the PKK's capability to mount attacks against Turkey from northern Iraq'.

responsibilities in a situation that undoubtedly threatened regional peace and security and to decline to exercise the international control upon which the whole collective security system is based. Such a control is the only remedy against the vicious circle of the Turkish plea of state of necessity and the Iraqi claim of self-defence. It is also the last barrier – however imperfect – against the logic of self-help in international law.

Self-defence and weapons of mass destruction

Since the use of chemical and biological weapons is prohibited under any circumstances[124] and no State claims the right to possess, develop and use chemical and biological weapons for military operational use,[125] the question of the admissibility of the threat or use of weapons of mass destruction in self-defence[126] essentially concerns nuclear weapons. The question has proved rather intractable, as demonstrated by the advisory opinion rendered in 1996 by the ICJ, which has attracted a good deal of criticism.[127] Rather than embarking on another full analysis of the advisory opinion, it is appropriate to keep a certain distance from the views taken by the Court and by its judges – without nonetheless overlooking their valuable contribution – and to explore the current legal regulation of nuclear weapons by focusing on the recent practice of the United Nations and its Member States.

Four contentions seems undisputed. First, Art. 2(4) and customary international law prohibit any threat or use of use of force, and *a fortiori* those involving weapons that cause indiscriminate suffering and destruction. Second, as maintained by a substantial majority in the *Nuclear Weapons* advisory opinion, there

[124] According to W. Krutzsch and R. Trapp. *A Commentary on the Chemical Weapons Convention* (Dordrecht: Nijhoff, 1994), p. 13, in particular, the wording of Art. 1 of the Convention excludes any justification for the activities prohibited in the Convention itself 'whether for self-defence in case of armed attack with those weapons or in other exceptional circumstances'.

[125] See *Final Declaration of the Paris Conference of States Parties to the 1925 Geneva Protocol and Other Interested Parties*, 11 January 1989, CD/880, p. 49. Those States suspected of possessing chemical or biological military programmes have systematically denied their existence. Many States have publicly declared their commitment to renouncing to such programmes: see, for example, as far as NATO member States are concerned, para. 57 of the 1999 *Alliance's Strategic Concept*, *supra* note III-240; and *The Threat of Weapons of Mass Destruction*, para. 24, at www.nato.int.

[126] The expression 'weapons of mass destruction' is used here, as in *NATO Handbook* (Bruxelles, 2001), p. 160, footnote 3, as interchangeable with nuclear, chemical and biological weapons.

[127] *Legality of the Threat or Use of Nuclear Weapons*, Advisory Opinion, *ICJ Reports 1996*, p. 226. See, in particular, M.-P. Lanfranchi and T. Christakis, *La Licéité de l'emploi d'armes nucléaires devant la Cour internationale de justice* (Paris: Economica, 1997); L. Boisson de Chazournes and P. Sands (eds.), *International Law, the International Court of Justice and Nuclear Weapons* (Cambridge: Cambridge University Press, 1999).

exists neither a conventional norm of general scope nor a customary norm specifically proscribing the threat or use of force of nuclear weapons *per se*.[128] The Court dismissed the argument that the adoption by the General Assembly of a series of resolutions – beginning with Resolution 1653 (XV)[129] – proclaiming the illegality of nuclear weapons has brought about the emergence of a customary international norm in that sense. The significant number of abstentions and negative votes which characterised the adoption of these resolutions demonstrates, on the contrary, that no sufficient *opinio juris* has surfaced yet.[130] Third, the threat or use of nuclear weapons must at any rate conform to conventional and customary international law applicable to armed conflict, and most prominently international humanitarian law and the norms contained in legal instruments dealing with nuclear weapons.[131] Fourth, States must comply with the obligation to pursue in good faith and bring to a conclusion negotiations leading to nuclear disarmament'.[132] This is expressly provided for in Art. VI of the Non-Proliferation Treaty (NPT).[133] Whether such an obligation stems also from customary international law and as such is binding upon all States may be answered in the affirmative if account is taken of both the attitude of the handful of State that have not ratified

[128] *Nuclear Weapons case*, *supra* note 127, pp. 253 *et seq*. and para. 105(2) B (11 votes against 3). The General Assembly, in turn, regretted 'the absence of multilateral negotiated and legally binding security assurances against the threat or use of nuclear weapons against non-nuclear weapons' (Res. 51/45, 10 December 1996, preamble). The ICRC admits that 'Today there is no comprehensive and universal prohibition on the use of nuclear weapons in either customary or conventional international law' (www.icrc.org).

[129] Adopted on 24 November 1961 with 55 votes in favour, 20 against and 26 abstaining. It is worth noting that on that occasion Italy unsuccessfully put forward an amendment containing a reservation on the exercise of individual and collective self-defence (A/AC. 1/L.295).

[130] The Court noted that 'The emergence, as *lex lata*, of a customary rule specifically prohibiting the use of nuclear weapons is hampered by the continuing tension between the nascent *opinio juris* on the one hand, and the still strong adherence to the practice of deterrence on the other' (*Nuclear Weapons case*, *supra* note 127, p. 255). On the tension between the two opposite positions, see also M. Bedjaoui, sep. op., p. 273. Underlining the sharp division on the issue within the international community, N. Ronzitti, 'La Corte internazionale di giustizia e la questione della liceità della minaccia o dell'uso delle armi nucleari', 79 *RDI* (1996) 861, p. 873, prefers to refer to the *opinio juris* shared by a majority of States, albeit firmly opposed by the others, rather than an *opinio juris in statu nascendi* or *lex ferenda*.

[131] *Nuclear Weapons case*, *supra* note 127, pp. 259–60 and para. 105(2) D (unanimously). See also the *Final Document of the 2000 Review Conference of the Parties to the Non-Proliferation of Nuclear Weapons*, para. 15, posted at www.un.org/Depts/dda/WMD/nptrevhome.html#home.

[132] The existence of such an obligation was upheld unanimously by the Court in the *Nuclear Weapons case*, *supra* note 127, pp. 263–4, and para. 105(2) F.

[133] 729 *UNTS* 169, Art. VI. See also G. Cottereau, 'Obligation de négocier et de conclure?', in SFDI, *Le droit international des armes nucléaires* (Paris: Pedone, 1998) pp. 163 *et seq*.

the NPT yet[134] and the universal support for the General Assembly position on the irreversibility of the process of nuclear disarmament.[135] Although some concrete results have undoubtedly been achieved,[136] complete nuclear disarmament still remains rather distant.[137]

The thorny question concerns the threat or use of nuclear weapons in the exercise of the right to self-defence.[138] The choice is between two alternatives: either there is an absolute prohibition on the use of or the threat to use nuclear weapons under any circumstances; or such a prohibition is not absolute but admits of one exception, namely self-defence.

The ICJ declared itself unable to answer to this question.[139] In a rather cryptic way, it maintained that the threat or use of nuclear weapons would generally be contrary to international law applicable to armed conflict and in particular to international humanitarian law. Considering the current state of international law, nevertheless, the Court declared itself unable to decide on the lawfulness of such a threat or use in an extreme circumstance of self-defence in which the very survival of a State would be at stake.[140] The ambiguities of these findings and the dif-

[134] In this sense, see M. Bedjaoui, sep. op., p. 274. *Contra* S. Schwebel, diss. op., p. 329; N. Ronzitti, *supra* note 130, p. 879. For the position of India, for instance, see *Statement by the Minister of External Affairs*, 9 May 2000, available at www.indiaembassy.org/policy/npt/jsingh_npt_may_9–2000.htm.

[135] See, for instance Res. 56/24 R, adopted on 29 November 2001, para. 8.

[136] The main achievement has been summarised by the US representative on 15 February 2001 before the Conference on Disarmament, CD/PV.866, pp. 14 *et seq*.

[137] The recent decisions of the US not to ratify the CTBT (see 94 *AJIL* (2000) 137) and the Protocol to the BWC (see 95 *AJIL* (2001) 899) and to withdraw from the ABM Treaty (see R. Mullerson, 'The ABM Treaty: Changed Circumstances, Extraordinary Events, Superior Interests and International Law', 50 *ICLQ* (2001) 509) are far from encouraging. Ironically, in 1998 the US urged India and Pakistan to ratify the CTBT: see 93 *AJIL* (1999) 500.

[138] In the light of the conclusion reached *supra*, pp. 163 *et seq*., the Court finding that armed reprisals in time of peace are unlawful is to be shared (*Nuclear Weapons case*, *supra* note 127, p. 246). With regard to reprisals in time of war, an argument that goes beyond the purpose of this study, the Court limited itself to observe that the right of recourse to such reprisals would, like self-defence, be governed *inter alia* by the principle of proportionality. Here the Court seems to be excessively hesitant and prudent.

[139] R. Higgins, diss. op., p. 584, notes that the Court declined to answer a question that was in fact never put to it. The British Government excluded that the Court opinion 'imposed any new disarmament obligations on the United Kingdom or that it required either a change in our entirely defensive nuclear deterrence policy or in NATO doctrine of collective self-defence', in 71 *BYIL* (2001) 702.

[140] Paragraph 105(2)E (decided by the President' casting vote). In para. 43, the Court stressed that States must carefully assess the risk factor when considering the threat or use of nuclear weapons. The *non liquet* has been criticised by, among others, R. Higgins, diss. op., paras 37 *et seq*.; and N. Ronzitti, *supra* note 130, pp. 876 *et seq*. The *non liquet* contained in para. 105E2 notwithstanding, it may be argued that the Court came close to admitting, by implication, that the threat or use of nuclear weapons in self-defence may in exceptional cases be permitted. The findings that any such threat or use would be, on the

ficulties in reconciling them with each other have been underlined by several judges and commentators.[141]

The most powerful arguments advanced in support of the existence of an absolute prohibition to use or threat to use nuclear weapons concern humanitarian law and the law of neutrality.[142] It is maintained that the indiscriminate nature and effects of these weapons make them inherently incompatible with the rules of warfare. Under no circumstances, therefore, can they be resorted to. Besides, since these weapons are likely to produce their effects beyond the borders of the belligerent parties, there is an unacceptably high risk of seriously and indiscriminately affecting the rights of neutral States.

In spite of the importance of these arguments, the opposite view better reflects State practice. In the first place, most of the treaties directed at reducing the proliferation of nuclear weapons or establishing nuclear free zones have been regularly accompanied by reservations and declarations made by nuclear weapons States in order to preserve unaffected their right to resort to nuclear weapons in the exercise of individual or collective self-defence.[143]

In the context of the extension of the NPT, in particular, the Russian Federation, the United Kingdom, the United States and France accepted the obligation

---

one hand, unlawful if contrary to Art. 2(4) and not vindicated by Art. 51 (unanimously) and, on the other hand, generally – not in every circumstance (see G. Guillaume, sep. op., p. 290; C. A. Fleishhauer, sep. op., pp. 307 and 308; S. M. Schwebel, diss. op., pp. 321 *et seq*. *Contra* M. Bedjaoui, sep. op., p. 273) – incompatible with international law applicable to armed conflict (by a majority of 11 against 3) make plausible the argument that nuclear weapons could be resorted to in extreme circumstances of self-defence. Among the possible readings of para. 105(2)E, R. Higgins, diss. op., p. 589, does not exclude that the term generally, especially in the light of para. 96, suggests that 'if a use of nuclear weapons in extreme circumstances of self-defence were lawful, that might of itself exceptionally make such a use compatible with humanitarian law'.

141 G. Herczegh, declaration, pp. 275–6; R. Ranjeva, sep. op., pp. 301 *et seq*.; R. Higgins, diss. op., pp. 584 *et seq*. According to S. M. Schwebel, diss. op., p. 322, the Court should have declined to render the opinion. In literature, see, in particular, M. Kohen, 'The Notion of "State Survival" in International Law', in L. Boisson de Chazournes and P. Sands (eds.), *supra* note 127, pp. 293 *et seq*.

142 See, in particular, the written statement submitted by Malaysia, available at the Court website. See also Art. 7 of the resolution adopted on 9 September 1969 by the Institut de droit international, 53–II *Annuaire* (1969) 375.

143 Besides, when France ratified the Statute of the International Criminal Court (9 June 2000), it made the following interpretative declarations: '1. The provisions of the Statute of the International Criminal Court do not preclude France from exercising its inherent right of self-defence in conformity with Article 51 of the Charter. 2. The provisions of article 8 of the Statute, in particular paragraph 2 (b) thereof, relate solely to conventional weapons and can neither regulate nor prohibit the possible use of nuclear weapons nor impair the other rules of international law applicable to other weapons necessary to the exercise by France of its inherent right of self-defence, unless nuclear weapons or the other weapons referred to herein become subject in the future to a comprehensive ban and are specified in an annex to the Statute by means of an amendment adopted in accordance with the provisions of articles 121 and 123'.

not to use nuclear weapons against non-nuclear weapons States with the express exclusion of the exercise of self-defence in the event of an armed attack conducted by these States in association or alliance with nuclear weapons States.[144] This view was shared by the Security Council which in Resolution 984 reaffirmed 'the inherent right, recognised in Art. 51 of the Charter, of individual and collective self-defence if an armed attack occurs against a member of the United Nations, until the Security Council has taken measures necessary to maintain international peace and security'.[145] Similar declarations and reservations accompanied the treaties of Tlatelolco, Ratatonga, Bangkok and Pelindaba.[146]

Contracting parties to treaties on nuclear disarmament and nuclear-free zones proceeded from the assumptions that there was no absolute prohibition to the threat or use of nuclear weapons and that such a threat or use for defensive purposes was not ruled out. Since these reservations met no objections either from other contracting parties or from the Security Council or its members, it is submitted that nuclear weapons States have, at once, reaffirmed their right – accepted by the other States – to resort to nuclear weapons in self-defence and prevented the formation of an absolute prohibition on the use of these weapons.

This conclusion is further strengthened by the request, concession and acceptance of positive and negative security assurances. Here, a distinction has to be made between the threat or use of force among nuclear weapons States and among them and non-nuclear States.

Starting with the first kind of relationship, nuclear States have systematically and unambiguously claimed the right to use nuclear weapons to defend themselves against armed attacks.[147] The real debate, indeed, was over the acceptance not to use nuclear weapons *first*, which would have implied the renunciation to threat or use nuclear weapons to counter a conventional armed attack. The adoption of a non-first use largely depended and still depends on the capability to repel any armed attack not involving nuclear weapons. In 1982, for instance, the USSR, relying on its conventional weapons superiority, formally declared that it would not use nuclear weapons *first*.[148] In contrast, NATO refused – and continues to

[144] See the declarations contained in S/1995/261, S/1995/262, S/1995/263 and S/1995/264. Only China renounced the use of nuclear weapons against non-nuclear-weapons States 'at any time and under any circumstances', see S/1995/265.

[145] Adopted on 11 April 1995 (unanimously).

[146] For the text of the treaties and their protocols, and for the reservations and declarations made by nuclear States, see, *Status of Multilateral Arms Regulations and Disarmament Agreements* 3rd ed. (New York: United Nations, 1987), 4th ed. (1992) and 5th ed. (1996). When signing and ratifying the First Additional Protocol to the Tlatelolco Treaty, for instance, France declared: 'No provision of this Protocol of the articles of the Treaty to which it relates may detract from the full exercise of the right of self-defence confirmed in Article 51 of the Charter of the United Nations.'

[147] See, in particular, the declarations made by the USSR, the UK and the US in relation to Security Council Res. 255, adopted on 19 June 1968 (10–0–5), S/PV.1430, respectively pp. 3, 4 and 5. More recently, see the documents referred to *supra* note 144.

refuse, in spite of the changed strategic environment – to take a similar commitment. It rather opted for and never formally abandoned the so-called flexible response, which is based on the threat to use nuclear weapons against a massive conventional armed attack.[149] The question of non-first use is crucial also in the confrontation between India and Pakistan. Only the latter State has formally declared that it will not resort to nuclear weapons unless it has been the target of a nuclear attack.[150]

Moving to the second kind of relationship, non-nuclear States have claimed and obtained – at least as *interim measures* in the view of a complete nuclear disarmament[151] – security assurances from nuclear weapons States.[152] These assurances regard in the first place the pledge to defend non-nuclear weapons States against nuclear armed attack (positive security assurances). In the event of aggression or threat of aggression with nuclear weapons against a non-nuclear weapons State that has ratified the NPT, the permanent members of the Security Council undertook to seek Security Council action immediately. The limitation of the commitment to the States party to the NPT is questionable insofar as the permanent members should discharge their responsibilities – which means in the very first place activating the Security Council – whenever a situation threatening international peace materialises, regardless of the conventional engagements of the concerned States.

Aware of the shortcomings of the collective security system, the positive security assurances are integrated by the engagements concerning collective self-defence against armed attacks,[153] including self-defence in the context of a

[148] A/S-12/PV 12, p. 22. See H. Meyrowitz, 'Le débat sur le non-recours en premier aux armes nucléaires et la déclaration soviétique du 15 juin 1982', 28 *AFDI* (1982) 147. Unlike previous commitments (see, for example, the declaration made on 1 February 1966 before the Conference of the Eighteen Nation Committee on Disarmament, ENDC/167), this one was not conditioned by reciprocity.

[149] See A. Roberts, 'The Relevance of the Laws of War in the Nuclear Age', in J. Dewar (ed.), *Nuclear Weapons, the Peace Movement and the Law* (Basingstoke: Macmillan, 1986), pp. 25 *et seq*., p. 33; T. Graham and J. Mendelsohn, 'NATO's Nuclear Weapons and the No-First-Use Option', 34 *IS* (1999) 5; M. O. Wheeler, 'NATO Nuclear Strategy, 1949–90', in G. Schmidt (ed.), *A History of NATO . The First Fifty Years* (New York: Palgrave, 2001), vol. 3, pp. 121 *et seq.*

[150] See, recently, Ministry of Foreign Affairs, *Cabinet Committee on Security Reviews Operationalization of India's Nuclear Doctrine*, 4 January 2003.

[151] See, for instance, the intervention of Malaysia before the Security Council on 11 April 1995 (S/PV.3514, p. 14).

[152] In the preamble of Res. 984, in particular, the Security Council recognised the legitimate interest of non-nuclear weapons States parties to the TNP to receive security assurances.

[153] With regard to the *Nuclear Weapons case*, *supra* note 127, the British Government has categorically rejected that the conditions for individual self-defence may be different from those allowing collective self-defence. It stated: 'We do not believe that the Court intended to make a distinction between individual and collective self-defence. If it had, that would been contrary to Article 51 of the UN Charter and we would not accept it' (68 *BYIL* (1997) p. 638).

military alliance as well as bilateral or multilateral military security commitments.[154] In this regard it must be noted that security commitments are confined to the adoption of the measures – not necessarily of military nature – that the concerned State deems necessary to repel the armed attack. They do not imply any obligation to resort to armed force, let alone to threaten or use nuclear weapons.

Security assurances also embrace the pledge by nuclear weapons States not to use these weapons against non-nuclear weapons States (negative security assurances).[155] Again, the assurances have been linked to the participation in the NPT or other comparable international instruments.[156] Not surprisingly, the few nuclear weapons States that have not ratified the NPT insisted that negative security assurances must be universal and not restricted to State parties.[157]

States' practice on nuclear disarmament treaties and especially the network of negative and positive security assurances demonstrates that – under current international law – there is no absolute prohibition on using or threatening to use nuclear weapons. It has been observed that:

> the practice embodied in the policy of deterrence is based specifically on the right of individual or collective self-defence and so are the reservations to the guarantee of security. The State which support or which tolerate that policy and those reservations are aware of this. So was the Security Council when it adopted resolution 984 (1995). Therefore, the practice which finds expression in the policy of deterrence, in the reservations to the security guarantees and in their toleration, must be regarded as State practice in the legal sense.[158]

[154] See the declarations of the Russian Federation, the UK, the US and France, *supra* note 144.

[155] See A. Rosas, 'Negative Security Assurances and non-Use of Nuclear Weapons', 25 *GYIL* (1982) 199.

[156] See the declarations of the Russian Federation, the UK, the US, France and China, *supra* note 144. In the statement made on 5 May 2000 before the NTP Review Conference, Main Committee I, available at http:/cnsl.miis.edu/npt/npt_5/ussecas.htm, the US declared that by ratifying the NPT a State becomes 'eligible' for negative security assurances.

[157] See, for instance, the Statement of Pakistan on 'Conclusion of effective international arrangements to assure non-nuclear weapons against the threat or use of force', 7 November 1995, available at www.un.int/pakistan/0195117b.htm. The document also claims that the security assurances are 'inconsistent with the UN Charter which provides for unconditional and comprehensive security assurances to all States individually by Member States or collectively through action by the Security Council'.

[158] C. A. Fleishhauer, sep. op., p. 309. R. Higgins, diss. op., p. 591 observes that 'Nothing in relevant statements made suggests that those States giving nuclear weapons assurances or receiving them believed that they would be violating humanitarian law – but decided nonetheless to act in disregard of such violation'. According to S. Schwebel, diss. op., p. 317, 'Such affirmations by it – and their unanimous acceptance by the Security Council – demonstrate that nuclear Powers have asserted the legality and that the Security Council has accepted the possibility of the threat or use of nuclear weapons in certain circumstances'.

This conclusion is supported by the attitude of the General Assembly that, the rhetoric on disarmament notwithstanding, continues to

> call upon nuclear-weapons States, pending the achievement of the total elimination of nuclear weapons, to agree on an internationally and legally binding instrument on the joint undertaking not to be *first* to use nuclear weapons, and calls upon all States to conclude an internationally and legally binding instrument on security assurances of non-use and non-threat of use of nuclear weapons against non-nuclear-weapons States.[159]

Conditions and limits of the exercise of the right to self-defence with nuclear weapons

Once it is accepted that nuclear weapons could in exceptional circumstances be used in self-defence, it becomes unavoidable to discuss what circumstances may be considered as exceptional and to define the limits within which nuclear defensive action may be permitted. In order to emphasise the exceptional character of the use of nuclear weapons, the Court introduced the notion of State survival.[160] Resort to such a legally vague notion, which the Court did not hesitate to include among the fundamental rights of States, is at very best superfluous.[161]

The exceptional character of the circumstances in which nuclear weapons could be resorted to is not suitable for *a priori* legal definition. From the perspective of the *jus ad bellum* – which characterises this study – it is undisputed that defensive use of nuclear weapons must strictly satisfy the requirements of proportionality of necessity. It is precisely through the lenses of proportionality and necessity that the lawfulness of a nuclear defence action has to be ascertained on a case-by-case basis.

The proceedings before the ICJ in the *Nuclear Weapons case* disclosed a sharp division among States with regard to first requirement. Several States denied that these weapons could satisfy the requirement of proportionality and excluded their lawful resort in self-defence.[162] The opposite view was taken by a large group of

[159] Res. 56/24 R, adopted on 29 November 2001, para. 6 (italics supplied). Within the Conference on Disarmament, China has insistently urged that 'all nuclear-weapons States undertake not to be the first to use nuclear weapons at any time and under any circumstances, and that they unconditionally commit themselves never to use of threaten to use nuclear weapons against non-nuclear-weapons States. These undertakings should be codified into solemn, international legal instruments': see CD/PV.866, 15 February 2001, p. 12.

[160] For A. G. Koroma, diss. op., p. 571, 'State survival' is a concept invented by the Court.

[161] R. Ranjeva, declaration, p. 301, observes that the notion is 'not sufficient for the purpose of legal qualification'. According to M. Kohen, *supra* note 141, p. 313, 'the Court returned to the outdated idea of self-preservation'.

[162] See, in particular, the written statements of Mexico, p. 10; Egypt, p. 10; and the Solomon Islands, p. 65, available at the Court website. In literature, see in particular, E. L. Meyrowitz, 'The Law of War and Nuclear Weapons', 9 *BJIL* (1983) 227.

States, which included the United States, the United Kingdom, Russia and France.[163] The Court did not share the view that nuclear weapons are inherently disproportionate when it maintained that 'the principle of proportionality may . . . not in itself exclude the use of nuclear weapons in self-defence in all circumstances'.[164]

The defensive use of force involving nuclear weapons might be proportionate only if the consequences of the armed attack that have triggered it are so dramatic that they outweigh those expected from the nuclear reaction. Considering the devastating, irreversible and indiscriminate effects of nuclear weapons, the use weapons can be considered exclusively in the context of a massive armed attack. Such an assessment must be made on a case-by-case basis, taking into account all relevant factors.[165] *A contrario*, it may be argued that the use of nuclear weapons would be disproportionate if directed at repelling the military invasion of a portion of the territory of a State.

The recurrent refusal by some nuclear States to renounce first resort to nuclear weapons makes it premature to exclude that nuclear self-defence in response to a conventional, chemical or bacteriological attack[166] might be proportional.[167] Although the Court did not adequately address this question, its findings are compatible with this conclusion.

Finally, the proportionality requirement can hardly be satisfy by the so-called mini-nuclear weapons that the United States administration is currently developing.[168] The indiscriminate, irreversible and grave consequences that these weapons

[163] The US, for instance, declared: 'Whether an attack with nuclear weapons would be disproportionate depends entirely on the circumstances, including the nature of the enemy threat, the importance of destroying the objective, the character, size and likely effects of the device, and the magnitude of the risk to civilians. Nuclear weapons are not inherently disproportionate' (Written statement, *ibid.*, p. 23). See also the written statements of the UK, *ibid.*, p. 37; the Russian Federation, p. 10; France, p. 49 and the Netherlands, p. 12.

[164] *Nuclear Weapons case*, *supra* note 127, p. 245. The UK declared that 'Where what is at stake is the difference between national survival and subjection to conquest which may be of the most brutal and enslaving character, it is dangerously wrong to say that the use of nuclear weapons could never meet the criterion of proportionality' (CR 95/34, p. 45).

[165] A. C. Fleischhauer, sep. op., p. 310 notes that 'the present state of international law does not permit a more precise drawing of the border between lawfulness and unlawfulness of recourse to nuclear weapons'.

[166] See, for instance, Fleischhauer, sep. op., *Nuclear Weapons case*, *supra* note 127, p. 308. In the document referred to *supra* note 150, India stated that 'In the event of a major attack against India, or Indian forces anywhere, by biological or chemical weapons, India will retain the option of retaliating with nuclear weapons'.

[167] But see N. Singh, *Nuclear Weapons and International Law* (London: Stevens, 1959), pp. 132–3, according to whom 'the use of nuclear weapons to repel an attack with conventional weapons would appear to exceed the right (of self-defence), since the quantum of force would be out of proportion to the nature of the attack necessary to repel'.

[168] See the United States Nuclear Posture Review (excerpts at www.globalsecurity.org/wmd/library/policy/dod/npr.htm. See also the Assistant Secretary of Defense for International Security Policy, Special Briefing, 9 January 2002, at www.defenselink.mil/news/Jan2002/t01092002_t0109npr.html).

are bound to produce will never be proportionate to the defensive purposes they are trying to achieve.[169]

From the perspective of the requirement of necessity, 'the denial of the recourse to the threat or use of nuclear weapons as a legal option in any circumstance could amount to a denial of self-defence itself if such recourse was the *last available means* by way of which the victimized State could exercise its right under Article 51 of the Charter'.[170] In this sense, the bombings of Hiroshima and Nagasaki were clearly unnecessary – before than disproportionate – considering the imminent defeat of Japan.[171] It may also be argued that nuclear weapons could be resorted to in self-defence only when conventional weapons are ineffective.[172]

The question of the admissibility of anticipatory self-defence involving nuclear weapons is not a novelty. Advocates of the anticipatory nuclear self-defence often rely on the position taken in 1946 by the UN Atomic Energy Commission which admitted that a violation of a future treaty on the control of nuclear energy 'might be of so grave a character as to give rise to the inherent right of self-defence recognised in Art. 51'.[173] On closer scrutiny, however, the importance of the document might have been exaggerated. The United States proposed the inclusion in the future treaty on nuclear weapons control of a definition of 'armed attack' that would have included 'not simply the actual dropping of an atomic bomb, but also certain steps in themselves preliminary to such action'.[174] The Soviet Union complained about the initiative which it considered as an attempt to modify the Charter through an international treaty instead than through the procedure established under the Charter itself.[175] The attitude of the two superpowers demonstrates that at the time the proposed definition of 'armed attack' was perceived as being at variance with Art. 51.

[169] On the devastating effect that Earth-Penetrating Nuclear Weapons produce at the present stage of scientific development, see R. W. Nelson, 'Low-Yield Earth-Penetrating Nuclear Weapons', 10 *Science & Global Security* (2002) 1.

[170] C. A. Fleishhauer, sep. op., p. 307 (italics supplied).

[171] See R. Falk, 'Nuclear Weapons, International Law and the World Court: A Historic Encounter', 91 *AJIL* (1997) 64, p. 69. It was on this based that the bombings were considered unlawful in the *Shimoda case*, decided by the District Court of Tokyo on 7 December 1963. For a comment, see R. Falk, 'The *Shimoda* Case: A Legal Appraisal of the Atomic Attacks upon Hiroshima and Nagasaki', 59 *AJIL* (1965) 759.

[172] N. Singh, 'The Right of Self-Defence in Relation to the Use of Nuclear Weapons', 5 *Indian Yearbook Int. Affairs* (1956) 3, pp. 32–4.

[173] UN Doc. AEC/18/Rev. 1, p. 24. For D.W. Bowett, *supra* note IV-17, p. 189, 'the Commission clearly understood Art. 51 as permitting *anticipatory* self-defence'. C. H. M Waldock, *supra* note IV-51, p. 498, maintained that 'preparation for atomic warfare in breach of the Convention would in view of the appalling power of the weapons have to be treated as an armed attack within Article 51'.

[174] See the memorandum submitted on 12 July 1946, AECOR, 1st year, Special Supplement, Report to the Security Council, pp. 109 *et seq.*

[175] See P. C. Jessup, *A Modern Law of Nations* (New York: Macmillan, 1949), p. 167; P. Lamberti Zanardi, *supra* note IV-90, p. 235.

During the 1960s and 1970s, the main argument for anticipatory self-defence was based on the assumption that a nuclear attack would have been lethal for the victim State. Pre-emption was then considered as the only effective way to counter such an attack.[176] Following the acquisition of a 'second-strike' capability, however, the argument has lost most of its significance, especially in respect to the relationships between superpowers.[177]

The declarations containing the positive security assurances issued on the occasions of the extension of the NPT accurately distinguish the case in which there is a threat of use of nuclear weapons from that in which an armed attack is in progress. In the former case, the exclusive competence of the Security Council is preserved. It is only in the latter case that unilateral or joint use of nuclear force in self-defence may be permitted.[178]

In order to counter a nuclear armed attack lawfully, nonetheless, States do not have to wait until the weapons hit their targets but could intercept them as soon as the armed attack has been launched irreversibly. How difficult it is to establish, for the purpose of an interceptive action, when the last irrevocable act has been committed[179] has been summarised by the United States President during the Cuban Missile Crisis: 'nuclear weapons are so destructive and ballistic missiles are so swift that any substantially increased possibility of their use or any sudden change in their deployment may well be regarded as a definite threat to peace'.[180]

The difficulties in applying the concept of interceptive self-defence notwithstanding, it is clear that self-defence cannot be invoked when the nuclear attack is not absolutely impending,[181] let alone when it is only potential.

In the aftermath of the terrorist attacks and in the context of proliferation of weapons of mass destruction, the notion of pre-emptive self-defence has assumed a fundamental importance in the attitude of the United States with regard to the use of force in international law. The President unambiguously declared that:

> United States military force and appropriate civilian agencies must have the capability to defend against a weapons of mass destruction-armed adversary, including

[176] In this sense, see, for example, W. Friedmann, *The Changing Structure of International Law* (London: Stevens, 1964) pp. 259–60; L. Henkin, *How Nations Behave: Law and Foreign Policy*, 2nd ed. (New York: Columbia University Press, 1979), p. 141.

[177] I. Pogany, 'Nuclear Weapons and Self-defence in International Law', in I. Pogany (ed.), *Nuclear Weapons and International Law* (Aldershot: Avebury, 1987), pp. 63 *et seq*. Second-Strike capability has been described as 'A strategic concept which excludes preemptive actions before the onset of a war . . . In general nuclear war, this implies the ability to survive a surprise first strike and respond effectively' (J. M. Collins, *United States – Soviet Military Balance, 1980–1985* (Washington: Pergamon–Brassey's, 1985), p. 311).

[178] See *supra* text corresponding to notes 152 *et seq*.

[179] On the last irrevocable act, see N. Singh, *supra* note 172, pp. 25–6.

[180] Address by the US President, *The Soviet Threat to the Americas*, 47 *DSB* (1962) 715, p. 716.

[181] For A. A. D'Amato, 'Israeli's Air Strike upon the Iraqi Nuclear Reactor', 77 *AJIL* (1983) 584, p. 588, the only security against a war of nuclear annihilation is a clear legal rule prohibiting anticipatory self-defence. See also I. Brownlie, *supra* note I-59, p. 276.

in appropriate cases through pre-emptive measures. This requires capabilities to detect and destroy an adversary's weapons of mass destruction assets before there weapons are used. . . . The primary objective of a response is to disrupt an imminent attack or an attack in progress, and eliminate the threat of future attacks.[182]

The same argument was put forward in the preamble of the Congress authorisation of the use of force against Iraq:

> Whereas Iraq's demonstrated capability and willingness to use weapons of mass destruction, the high risk that the current Iraqi regime will either employ those weapons to launch a surprise attack against the United States or its Armed Forces or provide them to international terrorists who would do so, and the extreme magnitude of harm that would result to the United States and its citizens from such an attack, combine to justify action by the United States to defend itself.[183]

The claim to pre-emptive self-defence enjoys extremely limited support. In the Iraqi crisis, the United States itself, aware of the devastating effect of this notion, took great care not to rely exclusively upon it and invoked other legal grounds. It is equally significant that its most closest allies refrained from resorting to this notion; as underlined by the British Foreign Secretary:

> The issue of pre- or post-pre-emption in respect of Iraq, I do not quite see the relevance. The issue is that here you have a regime which is in clear breach of an endless number of Security Council Resolutions requiring them to do certain things under Chapter VII . . . the question of pre-emption does not arise.[184]

The overwhelming majority of States are staunchly opposed to the claim to pre-emptive self-defence lest it results in the abandonment of any collective control over the use of force and the return to the freedom to resort to military action.[185] The notion of pre-emptive self-defence remains utterly contrary to the principles upon which the Charter and customary international law are based: the renunciation to use of force unless necessary to counter or intercept hostile military activities and the submission to the international control of the use of force, especially when intended to tackle threats to international peace and security.

The introduction of the notion of pre-emptive self-defence would provoke the implosion of current legal regulation of force. Far from improving the effectiveness of the collective security system, it would sound its death knell by permitting the preventive use of force on the basis of the unilateral judgement of States,

[182] *National Strategy to Combat Weapons of Mass Destruction*, 17 September 2002, p. 3.

[183] *Supra* note III-108.

[184] Foreign Affairs Committee, Session 2002–03, *Second Report*, para 150. See also C. Gray, *supra* note 111–232, pp. 181 *et seq.*

[185] Furthermore, the UK Foreign Affairs Committee, Session 2002–03, *Second Report*, para. 154, concluded 'that should the United States, British and other governments seek to justify military action against Iraq for example, on an expanded doctrine of "pre-emptive self-defence", there is a serious risk that this will be taken as legitimising the aggressive use of force by other, less law-abiding States'.

substituting the collective judgement expressed through the Security Council. Pre-emptive self-defence is even more unacceptable when the Security Council is actively dealing with a given crisis. This was precisely the case in the recent showdown between Iraq and the United Nations, when the overwhelming majority of that organ's members and of the Organisation at large were still confident of the settlement of the crisis without a military intervention.

But even assuming that the Security Council is blocked by the opposition of one or more permanent members, pre-emptive self-defence would continue to be inadmissible becaus of the *erga omnes* obligation to refrain from threatening or using force existing under the Charter and customary international law. By 1945 at the latest, States definitely relinquished their right to use force in order to protect themselves against what they unilaterally perceived as a potential threat to their national security, while retaining the right to take defensive action to intercept or counter hostile military activities. The prohibition is based on the common interest of all States to outlaw the use of force and is not dependent upon the effective functioning of the collective security system.[186]

International obligations concerning weapons of mass destruction

A full analysis of the obligations regarding the possession, transfer and development of weapons of mass destruction goes beyond the purpose of this study.[187] Suffice it to note a few basic points. Not being prohibited under customary international law, the development of a nuclear weapons programme is subject only to conventional restrictions. States that have not ratified the NPT, accordingly, are not bound to refrain from building up nuclear capabilities.[188] The nuclear tests carried out in 1998 by India and Pakistan, albeit condemned from a political standpoint,[189] were not treated as violations of international law.[190] On the contrary, it is

[186] See *supra* pp. 124 *et seq*.

[187] In general, see G. Den Dekker, *The Law of Arms Control. International Supervision and Enforcement* (The Hague: Nijhoff, 2001), esp. pp. 62 *et seq*.).

[188] US Undersecretary for Arms Control and International Security J. Bolton has recently confirmed that 'There is unquestionably States that are not within existing treaty regimes that possess weapons of mass destruction legitimately', where 'weapons of mass destruction' is to be read as 'nuclear weapons' (posted at: http://tokyo.usembassy.gov/e/p/tp-se1642.htlm).

[189] See, in particular, the Statements issued by the President of the Security Council on 14 May 1998 (S/PRST/1998/12) and 29 May 1998 (S/PRST/1998/17), and Security Council Resolution 1172, adopted unanimously on 6 June 1998.

[190] The French Minister of Foreign Affairs, for instance, declared before the Parliament that 'on ne peut pas dire, pour être honnête, par rapport à l'Inde, que l'Inde viole des Traités, puisque ce sont des Traités que l'Inde n'a pas signé' (13 May 1998, in 44 *AFDI* (1998) 710).

generally admitted that the possession of chemical and biological weapons, and a *fortiori* their use, are not permitted under customary international law.[191]

This is without prejudice to the Security Council's power to impose disarmament obligations going beyond those already binding upon States under conventional or customary international law. The exercise of this power presupposes that the concerned State's behaviour poses a threat to international peace and security. A limited use of this power was made in 1991 with regard to Iraq. In Resolution 687 the Security Council compelled Iraq to destroy, remove or render harmless, under international supervision, (a) all chemical and biological weapons and all stocks of agents and all related subsystems and components and all research, development, support and manufacturing facilities thereto; (b) all ballistic missiles with a range greater than 150 kilometres and related major parts and repair and production facilities.[192] It also obliged Iraq not to acquire or develop nuclear weapons or nuclear-weapon-usable material or any related subsystem or component or any research, development, support or manufacturing facilities.[193]

In spite of the rather awkward expressions used in the resolution,[194] it is clear that Iraq was legally bound to implement the disarmament programme as defined by the Security Council. As far as nuclear weapons were concerned, Iraq had already renounced the acquisition or development of these weapons by ratifying the NPT. Resolution 687 reaffirmed Iraqi obligations under this treaty and noted that they were not limited by any reservations or conditions.[195] Accordingly, no additional obligations were imposed in this regard upon Iraq. The resolution, however, constituted an autonomous source of obligations so that the eventual withdrawal of Iraq from the NPT would have been deprived of any practical effect as long as the resolution was still in force.

The obligations concerning the prohibition and stockpiling of chemical weapons incumbent upon that State by virtue of the 1925 Geneva Protocol, in turn, were significantly extended by Resolution 687 in line with the legally non-binding Declaration accepted by Iraq in 1989. To the extent that the obligations

[191] See N. Ronzitti, 'Relations Between the Chemical Weapons Convention and Other Relevant International Norms', in D. Bardonnet (ed.), *The Convention on the Prohibition and Elimination of Chemical Weapons: A Breakthrough in Multilateral Disarmament* (Dordrecht: Nijhoff, 1995), pp. 167 *et seq.*, esp. pp. 184–5. See also L. Tabassi, 'Impact of the CWC: Progressive Development of Customary International Law and Evolution of the Customary Norm Against Chemical Weapons', in *CBW Conventions Bulletin*, March 2004, p. 1. See also International Committee of the Red Cross, *Use of Nuclear, Biological and Chemical Weapons: Current International Law and Policy Statements*, 4 March 2003, posted at www.icrc.org. Human Rights Watch, *Letter to Iraq Regarding Adherence to Laws of War*, 19 March 2003.

[192] Para. 8.

[193] Para. 12.

[194] In paras 8, 10 and 12, in particular, the Security Council decided that Iraq 'shall unconditionally accept, undertake or agree to' the disarmament programme.

[195] Iraq ratified, without reservations, the NTP on 29 October 1969.

were not covered by the 1925 Geneva Protocol, the resolution imposed on Iraq conduct to which it was so far committed only politically.[196]

Heavy limitations were finally imposed with regard to ballistic missiles. In this field, no conventional or customary international norm restricted Iraq's right to acquire and possess ballistic missiles. Yet, under Resolution 687 Iraq was obliged to destroy, remove or render harmless all ballistic missiles having a range greater than 150 kilometres.

It has been argued that the imposition of disarmament obligations may be based on Art. 39 of the Charter, according to which the Security Council takes the decisions it deems necessary to maintain and restore international peace.[197] It is more accurate to treat the imposition of new disarmament obligations as measures not involving the use of force decided by the Security Council in the exercise of its normative powers under Art. 41 of the Charter.[198]

Mechanisms of international enforcement of disarmament obligations not involving the use of force

The responsibility for verifying and ensuring compliance with the obligations stemming from the NPT and the CWC has been conferred by contracting States on the International Atomic Energy Agency (IAEA)[199] and the Organisation for the Prohibition of Chemical Weapons (OPCW).[200] No similar verification arrangements exist under the BWC.

The verification is composed of three phases: (a) the establishment of the facts, normally through on-site inspections and fact-finding missions; (b) the legal assessment of the evidence collected and the determination of violations of the

[196] No obligations concerning biological were imposed on Iraq. Here the Security Council limited itself to inviting it to ratify 1972 CBW. On 19 July 1991 Iraq ratified the Convention.

[197] See D. Fleck, *supra* note III- 25, p. 109.

[198] See *supra* pp. 15 *et seq*. See also J. A. Frowein and N, Kirsch, 'Art. 41', in B. Simma (ed.), *supra* note I-1, pp. 735 *et seq*, p. 742.

[199] According to Art. III of the NPT, in particular, each contracting Party accepted to negotiate and conclude with IAEA an agreement 'for the exclusive purpose of verification of the fulfilment of its obligations assumed under this Treaty'. See *The Structure and Content of Agreements Between the Agency and States Required in Connection with the Treaty on the Non-Proliferation of Nuclear Weapons*, INFCIRC/153 (Corrected); *Model Protocol Additional to the Agreement(s) Between State(s) and the Agency for the Application of Safeguards*, INFCIRC/540 (Corrected). IAEA has been established by the Agency's Statute which entered into force on 29 July 1957 (276 *UNTS* 4). On the verification activities of IAEA, see B. Monaham, 'Giving the Non-Proliferation Treaty Teeth: Strengthening the Special Inspection Procedures of the IAEA', 33 *VJIL* (1992) 161.

[200] Arts. VIII *et seq*. of the CWC.

disarmament obligations; and (c) the adoption of measures expected to ensure compliance.[201]

A typical sanctioning tool at the disposal of the IAEA and the OPCW is the restriction or suspension of the concerned State's rights and privileges of membership. Under Art. XIX of the IAEA Statute, the decision is taken in the event of persistent non-compliance by the General Conference acting by a two-thirds majority upon a recommendation by the Board of Governors.[202] Under Art. XII, para. 2 of the CWC, in turn, such a competence is reserved to the Conference that, on the basis of a recommendation of the Executive Council, sanctions a State that has failed to take the measures requested by the Executive Council to redress and remedy a situation which contravenes the provisions of the CWC. The Board of Governors of IAEA could also curtail or suspend the assistance provided by the Agency or by a Member State to the State regarded as in breach of its obligations and, alternatively or cumulatively, request the return of materials and equipments made available to the former by the Agency or a Member State.[203]

The Conference of the OPCW may also recommend Member States to take the collective measures deemed necessary to put an end to serious violations of the CWC, provided that these measures are in conformity with international law. The recommendation, which by definition has a hortatory character, produces neither a permissive nor a mandatory effect. Rather, it can be treated as the collective exercise of a right Member States could have exercised individually in response to the violation of the Convention. The advantage is that the reaction follows a collective – albeit not legally binding – determination of the violation and assessment of the situation and the remedies. Among States parties to the Convention, the recommendation produces, similar to the recommendation made by the UN General Assembly, the so-called effect of legality,[204] or at least a presumption of legality of the conduct conform to the recommendation coupled with the shifting of the burden of proof in the event of dispute.[205] This is without prejudice to the right of Member States individually or jointly to resort, outside the framework of the Convention, to the remedies permitted under international law. In any case, the collective measures cannot imply the use of force since the general ban established by Art. 2(4) of the Charter can be overcome exclusively by the Security Council acting under Chapter VII of the Charter.

More important for the purpose of the present study is the resort by the IAEA and OPCW to the Security Council and the General Assembly. Under Art. XII,

[201] S. Sur, *A Legal Approach to Verification in Disarmament and Arms Limitation* (New York: United Nations Publications, 1988); and *Vérification en matière de désarmement*, 273 *RdC* (1998) 9, esp. pp. 37 *et seq*.

[202] See also Art. XII, para. C.

[203] See Art. XII, paras. A.7 and C.

[204] On the effect of legality of UN General Assembly resolutions, see B. Conforti, *supra* note I-15, pp. 279–80.

[205] C. Schreuer, 'Recommendations and the Traditional Sources of International Law', 20 *GYIL* (1977) 103.

para. C of the IAEA Statute, the Board of Governors shall report non-compliance with the obligations imposed by the NPT to the two political organs of the United Nations.[206] According to Art. XII, para. 4 and Art. VIII, para. 36 of the CWC, respectively, the Conference and – in the event of particular gravity and urgency – the Executive Council shall bring to the attention of the above-mentioned organs particularly grave cases of non-compliance.[207] When the acting organ is one of restricted membership, it shall also inform all the Member States. It is then for the Security Council to assess whether the situation caused by the non-compliance threatens international peace and security and, ultimately, to consider what measures are necessary.

At the same time, in discharging its responsibilities in the collective security system, the Security Council is entitled to request the IAEA and the OPCW to give any information and assistance as may be required for the maintenance of international peace and security.[208] Alternatively or additionally, the Security Council could establish subsidiary organs charged with monitoring compliance with disarmament obligations, such as UNSCOM and UNMOVIC in the case of Iraq.

The recent case of Iraq is quite illustrative. In Resolution 687 the Security Council not only confirmed and imposed on Iraq the comprehensive disarmament obligations as defined in paras 8, 9 and 12; it also decided to ensure their respect through the monitoring and inspection activities to be carried out by IAEA and UNSCOM on Iraqi territory. The obligations concerning the possession and development of weapons of mass destruction were thus integrated with the obligations to allow the inspections and to co-operate with IAEA and UNSCOM in the performance of their mandate. Again, on the basis of Chapter VII of the Charter, the resolution permitted the overcoming of the sovereign barrier and the limit of domestic jurisdiction, thus making the consent of Iraq unnecessary.[209]

The UNSCOM mandate included: (a) as inspection and survey phase to gather the information necessary to make an informed assessment of Iraq's capabilities and facilities in the chemical, biological and ballistic missile fields; (b) the disposal of weapons of mass destruction, facilities and other related items through destruction, removal or rendering harmless and the destruction of ballistic

[206] See also Art. III, para. 2 of the Relationship Agreement. On 12 February 2003, for instance, the Board of Governors declared that North Korea was in further non-compliance with its safeguards agreement and decided to report the violation to the Security Council: see GOV/2003/14.

[207] See also Art. II, para. (a) of the Relationship Agreement.

[208] Art. IX and Art. II, para. 3 of the Relationship Agreements between the United Nations and IAEA, 30 October 1959 (281 *UNTS* 369), and between the United Nations and the OPCW, in A/55/283, Annex, 24 September 2001. The latter normally extends such co-operation to the General Assembly in accordance with its responsibilities under the Charter.

[209] In the case of the nuclear weapons, the Security Council resolution constituted an additional legal basis since IAEA could already undertake the controls accepted by Iraq through the conclusion of the safeguards agreement concluded on 29 February 1972: see INFCIRC/172.

missiles with a range greater than 150 km, including launchers, other items and repair and production facilities; (c) long-term monitoring to ensure ongoing verification of Iraq's compliance with its obligations under para. 10 of Resolution 687 – principally not to reacquire banned capabilities – in accordance with the plan prepared by the Special Commission and approved by the Security Council in its resolution 715 of 1991.

The IAEA, in turn, was charged with monitoring and verifying compliance with Iraq with its disarmament obligations concerning nuclear weapons, including mapping out and destroying, removing or rendering harmless the components of its nuclear weapons programme.

It was the responsibility of UNSCOM–UNMOVIC and IAEA to verify the implementation of Iraqi disarmament obligations and to report any violations to the Security Council.[210] Both of them were allowed to carry out their activities in the territory of Iraq only with the consent of the Baghdad Government or in accordance with the decision of the Security Council. Otherwise they would have amounted to violation of the sovereignty of Iraq and of the principle of non-intervention.

That the Security Council possesses the exclusive power to allow verification activities against the will of the sovereign State is confirmed by para. 7 of Resolution 1441. Here, the Security Council decided that UNMOVIC and IAEA must have unconditional and unrestricted access to all inspection sites, including those for which a special procedure had been established in Resolution 1154 following the conclusion on 23 February 1998 of the Memorandum of Understanding between Iraq and the UN Secretary General.[211] In so doing, the Security Council once again resorted to its normative powers and modified the obligations incumbent upon Iraq as previously defined through the agreement concluded with the Secretary General.

The collective use of force to impose the respect of disarmament obligations

When non-compliance with disarmament obligations threatens international peace and security, the Security Council could decide to resort to coercive measures and possibly to authorise member States or regional organisations to use military force. In the recent Iraqi crisis, the problem was precisely how to ensure the execution of the verification mission and how to react to the violations by the Baghdad government of the obligations imposed by Resolution 687.

[210] The plan for the verification activities was initially established by the Security Council with Res. 715, adopted on 11 October 1991, on the basis of the proposal submitted by IAEA (S/22872/Rev.1, 20 September 1991) and UNSCOM (S/22871/Rev. 1, 2 October 1991). Throughout the crisis, the mandates and powers of UNSCOM and IAEA had been revised and reinforced, as it occurred with Res. 1284 (17 December 1999).

[211] S/1998/166.

Throughout the crisis, Iraq's failure to comply with its disarmament obligation and to co-operate with the inspectors met the protest of the Security Council and the Member States of the United Nations. It prompted some States regularly to conduct limited air strikes in the context of the enforcement of the no-fly zones and on several occasions to resort to much more substantial use of military force, as occurred in 1993 and 1998 and, more importantly, in 2003.

The main feature of the crisis remains the debate over the choice between pursuing the co-operation of the Iraqi Government by peaceful means, or authorising Member States to resort to military force.[212] On several occasions, in particular, the Security Council considered how to react to non-compliance by Iraq, what action to take in order to obtain its co-operation, and how to assess its pledges. The members of the Security Council, including those having a permanent seat, held the same position on the existence of a threat to international peace and security the Security Council was bound to tackle; the unsatisfactory compliance by Iraq with its disarmament obligations; and the necessity that the IAEA and UNMOVIC fully and effectively perform their mandate.

The points of disagreement concerned the gravity and immediacy of the threat posed by Iraq, and consequently the means to resort to in order to neutralise it and compel Iraq to respect its disarmament obligations. Crucial in the assessment of the situation were the information gathered and analysis provided to the Security Council on a regular basis by the IAEA and UNMOVIC.

On the eve of the 2003 invasion, the IAEA and UNMOVIC admitted that Iraq had been failing to fully meet its obligations under the relevant Security Council resolutions. In spite of the degree of uncertainty inherent in any monitoring and verification mission, however, both of them maintained, on the one hand, that no conclusive evidence had been found on the existence and development of a programme of weapons of mass destruction; on the other hand, Iraq's more proactive attitude could eventually pave the way for effective inspections.

The IAEA Director General, in particular, affirmed:

> As of 17 March 2003, the Agency has found no evidence or plausible indication of the revival of a nuclear weapons programme in Iraq. However, the Agency did not have sufficient time to resolve completely the key question of whether Iraq's nuclear activities and capabilities has changed since December 1998. Provided that Iraq's co-operation had remained active, and barring unforeseen circumstances, the Agency would have been able to provide the Security Council, within an additional

[212] The report of the Panels established on 30 January 1999 by the Security Council (so-called Amorim Report) on this point reads: 'Rigorous implementation (of IAEA and UNSCOM mandates) is critically dependent upon the full exercise of the rights and full an free access set forth in relevant Security Council resolutions . . . the OMV (ongoing monitoring and verification) cannot be conceived as an enticement for Iraq to invite it into its territory . . . To be effective, any system has to be deployed on the ground, which is impossible without Iraqi acceptance. How this acceptance will be obtained is the fundamental question before the Security Council' (S/1999/356, 30 March 1999, paras 66–8).

two or three months of continuing verification activities, with credible assurance regarding the absence of the revival of Iraq's nuclear programme.[213]

The UNMOVIC Executive Director, in turn, stated:

So far, UNMOVIC has not found any such weapons, only a small number of empty chemical munitions, which should have been declared and destroyed. Another matter – and one of great significance – is that many proscribed weapons and items are not accounted for'.[214] 'It is only by the middle of January and thereafter that Iraq has taken a number of steps, which have the potential of resulting either in the presentation for destruction of stocks of items that are proscribed or the presentation of relevant evidence solving long-standing unresolved disarmament issues.[215]

Both IAEA and UNMOVIC not only refrained from envisaging the use of military force on the basis of the evidence available, but at the beginning of 2003 considered that the conditions existed to complete their respective mandates within a few months. Their conclusions are to be regarded as both authoritative and impartial. Nonetheless, they are not legally binding for the Security Council which remained free to judge the situation differently from the IAEA and UNMOVIC.

Among Member States, however, the behaviour of the Iraqi Government and the prospect of settling the crisis through peaceful means was assessed in different ways. A minority of States, led by the United States, believed that there was no alternative but to defuse the crisis by immediate military intervention. The majority of the Security Council membership and almost the whole international community, on the contrary, deemed that the disarmament of Iraq could still be achieved through measures not involving the use of force. It is important to stress that they did not rule out the military option: rather, they considered it premature, especially in the light of the pro-active attitude of Iraq and the concrete possibility of completing an accurate international control of the implementation of its disarmament in a matter of months.[216]

On 3 May 2003, in particular, Russia, Germany and France declared: 'Our common objective remains the full and effective disarmament of Iraq, in compliance with Resolution 1441. We consider that this objective can be achieved by the

[213] *Implementation of United Nations Security Council Resolutions Regarding Iraq, Report of the Director General*, 8 August 2003, GOV/2003/50 – GC (47) 10, para. 18. See also the reports submitted to and briefing of the Security Council as, for example, *Briefing of the Security Council*, 7 March 2003.

[214] UNMOVIC Executive Chairman, *Briefing of the Security Council*, 14 February 2003.

[215] *12th Quarterly Report of the Executive Chairman of UNMOVIC*, S/2003/232, 28 February 2003, para. 73.

[216] See, for instance, the position of the AIEA, *supra* note 213. Similarly, the UNMOVIC Executive Chairman declared that the verification process 'would not take years, nor weeks, but months': see *Oral Introduction of the 12th Quarterly Report*, posted at www.unmovic.org.

peaceful means of the inspections. We moreover observe that these inspections are producing increasingly encouraging results'.[217]

The process of control over Iraq's disarmament pursued the common interest of the whole United Nations membership to neutralise the threat to international peace posed by the weapons of mass destruction. Such a process cannot but be based on a collective assessment of the facts and a collective decision-making as to action to be taken, especially when the use of force is envisaged. The first phase of the process consisted of monitoring and verifying in the field the implementation of the disarmament programme, and was assigned to IAEA and UNSCOM–UNMOVIC. The second phase, namely the assessment of the threat to international peace and security posed by Iraq and adoption of the measures necessary to defuse it, falls within the exclusive competence of the Security Council.

In discharging its responsibilities under the Charter, the Security Council could have determined that the Iraqi Government, far from being genuinely committed to disarmament, represented a threat to international peace that needed to be countered militarily. Such a determination was complex as it concerned several delicate military and political questions, and in particular the potential offensive capabilities of Iraq, the progresses made in the monitoring and verification mission, the prospect of completing such a mission, the effectiveness of diplomatic pressure and measures not involving the use of force already in place or still available.

In Resolution 1441, the Security Council confirmed that Iraq continued to be in material breach of previous resolutions and, more crucially, that non-compliance threatened international peace and security. The two findings may be strictly related but must be kept distinct since they serve different purposes and produce different legal effects. The pronouncement on the material breach is neither necessary not sufficient for the resort to coercive means by the Security Council. It is the continuing existence of an international threat that entitled the Security Council to exercise the powers bestowed on it by Chapter VII of the Charter.

The determination of the existence of a threat to peace, however, is only the first leg of the decision-making process that could lead to the use of force by – or more probably authorised by – the Security Council. It is followed by the judgement on the necessity and effectiveness of the military measures.[218] In spite of the deficit of the organ's representativeness, such a judgement reflects the common will of the whole United Nations membership and renders lawful the use of force (permissive effect).

As seen above,[219] in the Iraqi crisis the Security Council never completed the decision-making process. At no time were there within the organ the conditions for authorising States to ensure Iraq's compliance with relevant resolutions militarily. No use of force was therefore authorised.

[217] Posted at www.un.int/france/documents_anglais/030305_mae_france_iraq.htm.

[218] See *supra* pp. 43 *et seq*.

[219] See *supra* pp. 78 *et seq*., p. 92 and p. 101.

As recently declared by the European Union – perhaps not as clearly as necessary – when peaceful measures fail 'coercive measures under Chapter VII of the Charter could be envisioned. The United Nations Security Council should play a central role'.[220] It further rightly insisted on the collective dimension of the decision concerning the means to obtain compliance with disarmament obligations and observed that 'the role of the Security Council, as the final arbiter on the consequences of non-compliance – as foreseen in multilateral regimes – needs to be effectively strengthened'.[221]

Unilateral or joint military measures to enforce disarmament obligations and to curb the trafficking of weapons of mass destruction

In addition to the collective measures taken within the framework of the international organisations involved in disarmament, States might compel recalcitrant States to comply with their obligations through the remedies available in international law. The peaceful remedies include positive sanctions,[222] acts of retortion, and economic countermeasures.[223]

Without prejudice to the exercise of the right to self-defence,[224] States are prevented from resorting, individually or jointly, to military measures in order to enforce compliance with disarmament obligations. The reaction to disarmament obligations cannot imply the violation of *erga omnes* obligations like those stemming from the prohibition on the use of force. The reacting State would otherwise breach its obligations under the Charter and customary international law with regard to all non-defaulting States.

The fact that the violation has been established by a competent international authority – as it might be by the IAEA – or condemned by the Security Council does not alter the picture. Even the qualification by the Security Council of the

[220] Council of the European Union, *Basic Principles for an European Union Strategy against Proliferation of Weapons of Mass Destruction*, 10 June 2003.

[221] *Ibid.*

[222] Positive measures were included in the Agreed framework, concluded on 21 September 1994 between North Korea and the US, see the excerpts of Testimony of the Secretary of State, 24 January 1995, in 89 *AJIL* (1995) 372. See also the *Common Strategy of the European Union on Russia*, adopted by the European Council on 4 June 1999, OJ L157, 24 June 1999, p. 1, and the Council Joint Action of 17 December 1999, *EU Cooperation Programme for Non-proliferation and Disarmament in the Russian Federation* (1999/878/CFSP), OJ L331, 23 December 1999, p. 11.

[223] As far as the unilateral economic sanctions imposed by the US are concerned, see, for instance, Executive Order 12938, Non-proliferation of Weapons of Mass Destruction, 14 November 1994; Executive Order 13094, Non-proliferation of Weapons of Mass Destruction, 28 July 1998; Iran Non-proliferation Act of 2000, Public Law 106–178, 14 September 2000; Syria Accountability Act, 14 November 2003.

[224] As observed by M. E. O'Connell, *supra* note 26, p. 11, the violation of a disarmament requirement may, but not necessarily does, amount to an armed attack.

situation brought about by the violation as threat to international peace for the purpose of Art. 39 is not enough: the use of force is permitted only when duly authorised by the Security Council.

Apart from the position of the United States in the Iraqi crisis, there is virtually no evidence of States claiming the right to take unilateral or joint military action to compel a State to comply with its disarmament obligations. In this sense, no derogation to the general ban on armed reprisals seems to have emerged with regard to breaches of disarmament obligations.

A fortiori, the perception of the situation as a threat to national security cannot justify the use of force. Such a claim has been advanced by the United States in the context of the recent crisis in Iraq. In authorising the President to use military force, the Congress acted to defend the national security against the threat posed by Iraq's refusal to disarm.[225]

The following elements, however, significantly reduce the relevance of this precedent. In the first place, the Congress also qualified the use of force as necessary to implement the relevant Security Council resolutions. In the second place, before the United Nations, the United States relied on other legal grounds – however unconvincing they might be.[226] In the third place, the national threat was not unrelated to the threat to international peace and security whose existence was determined unanimously by the Security Council and was not disputed among the members of the international community. Finally, and more importantly, the reference to the national threat remained confined to the United States. The right of a State to use force to face a situation that it considers as threatening its national security, but does not represent an immediate and concrete danger of armed attack, was firmly rejected by the rest of the international community. Even those States sharing the United States position on the necessity of the intervention refrained from basing the lawfulness of the use of force on the threat posed by Iraq to their national security.

Moving to the international efforts to curb the trafficking of weapons of mass destruction, the common interest to prevent the terrorist groups and the governments allegedly supporting or tolerating them in acquiring these weapons has prompted a group of Western States, led by the United States, to launch the Proliferation Security Initiative (PSI). The initiative is a political arrangement designed to develop 'partnerships of states working in concert, employing their national capabilities to develop a broad range of legal, diplomatic, economic, military and other tools to interdict threatening shipments of weapons of mass destruction and missile-related equipment and technologies'.[227]

[225] *Supra* note III-108.

[226] See *supra* pp. 78 *et seq.*

[227] Under-Secretary Bolton, *Testimony to the Committee on International Relations, U.S. House of Representatives*, 4 June 2003, at www.house.gov/international_relations/108/bolt0604.htm. He further maintained that the PSI envisage to set 'principles' that identify practical steps necessary to interdict shipments of weapons of mass destruction, their delivery systems, and related materials at sea, in the air, or on land, *Testimony*

Following a series of governmental meetings, these States adopted in September 2003 a 'Statement of interdiction principles' whereby they committed themselves to taking effective measures to interdict and intercept shipping of weapons of mass destruction through their internal waters, territorial waters and contiguous zones. The document is not legally binding and contains only political commitments. It remains to be seen, however, whether the enforcement of the interdiction in these areas may involve the use of force.

Although the Convention on the Law of the Sea is almost silent on the use of force,[228] the International Tribunal for the Law of the Sea has confirmed that coercive military measures may be resorted to arrest ships engaged in illicit activities. It was upheld in the *M/V Saiga case* that 'international law, which is applicable by virtue of article 293 of the Convention, requires that the use of force must be avoided as far as possible and, where force is unavoidable, it must not go beyond what is reasonable and necessary in the circumstances'.[229]

Assuming that the transport of weapons of mass destruction makes the passage offensive, the costal State might take coercive military measures that are strictly necessary and proportionate. Such a conclusion, however, is far from undisputed since Art. 19 does not include the transport of weapons of mass destruction among the activities incompatible with the right to innocent passage, whereas Art. 23 expressly grants such a right to ships carrying nuclear weapons.

The need to adapt the law of the sea, including the conditions for the exercise of the right to passage and the powers of coastal States, to the threats posed by terrorism and shipping of weapons of mass destruction is widely shared among States. The International Maritime Organisation is currently considering the need to amend the Suppression of Unlawful Acts at Sea Convention in order to make the transport of weapons of mass destruction, their delivery systems and related materials on commercial vessels an internationally recognised offence.[230]

The most serious legal problems are posed by the coercive military measures that States might envisage undertaking on the high seas against foreign vessels suspected of being engaged in illicit traffic of weapons of mass destruction. Under existing international law, no coercive military measures can be taken against a

Before the House International Relations Committee, Subcommittee on the Middle East and Central Asia, 16 September 2003, posted at www.house.gov/international_relations/108/bol091603.htm.

[228] See, in particular, B. Vukas, 'Peaceful Uses of the Sea, Denuclearization and Disarmament', in R. J. Dupuy and D. Vignes (eds.), *A Handbook on the New Law of the Sea* (Dordrecht: Nijhoff, 1995), pp. 1233 *et seq*.

[229] *The M/V Saiga case (No. 2)* (Saint Vincent and the Grenadines v. Guinea), Judgment, 1 July 1999, available at www.un.org/Dept/los/ITLOS/Judg_E.htm.

[230] The Legal Committee of the Organisation acknowledged that 'maritime interests are widely exposed to risks such as the use of ships as weapons and the transportation of material that might lead to the proliferation of weapons of mass destruction. The need to develop new Suppression of Unlawful Acts instruments seemed overdue on account of the dramatic change of circumstances since the adoption of the original treaties in 1988' (Summary of the 86th session, 28 April – 2 May 2003, posted at www.imo.org).

non-national vessel on the high seas, subject to some strictly tailored exceptions concerning ships without nationality[231] or ships engaged in piracy, the slave trade and unauthorised broadcasting.[232]

As a result, States cannot lawfully seize on the high seas a vessel transporting weapons of mass destruction.[233] On the occasion of the boarding and successive release of the North Korean cargo ship carrying missiles destined for Yemen, the United States conceded that it lacked the authority under international law to seize the vessel after Yemen had given assurances that the weapons would be used for defensive purposes.[234] This approach is in line with the longstanding attitude of the United States – shared by other nuclear weapons States – that 'any specific limitation on military activities would require the negotiation of detailed arms control agreements'.[235]

Bearing in mind the dynamic character of international law which enables it to meet the new needs of States through a process of claims and counter-claims, nothing prevents the development of the law of the sea in the sense of permitting States to resort to coercive measures to intercept foreign vessels suspected to be engaged in trafficking of weapons of mass destruction. Depending on the reaction of the generality of States, the process could lead, in due course, to the emergence of a new remarkable exception to the principle of freedom of navigation. Meanwhile, the action directed at curbing the trafficking of these weapons is to be conducted through the co-operation between States and in particular the conclusion of bilateral or multilateral agreements.[236]

The notion of self-defence does not need to be substantially reconsidered. On the one hand, there are no obstacles to the qualification of certain terrorist activities as armed attack for the purpose of Art. 51, especially if it is accepted that there is no threshold of gravity of hostile military activities below which defensive forceful reaction is not allowed. On the other hand, terrorist activities can be attributed to States in accordance with the general principles developed in international law. The debate on whether such an attribution depends on the existence of a relationship of control-dependence between the State and the terrorist groups (in terms of the *Nicaragua case* decided by the International Court of Justice) or at least an overall control of the former upon the later (in the sense of the *Tadic* case decided by the International Criminal Tribunal for the former Yugoslavia)

[231] In *United States* v. *Cortes*, 91 *ILR* (1993) 486, p. 491, the Court of Appeals, Fifth Circuit, affirmed that 'international law shelters only members of the international community of nations from unlawful boarding and searches on the high seas'.

[232] Arts. 99 to 107 and 109–110. Convention on the Law of the Sea.

[233] See Bipartisan Security Group, *The Proliferation Security Initiative: The Legal Challenge*, 4 September 2003.

[234] See F. L. Kirgis, 'Boarding of North Korean Vessel on the High Seas', *ASIL Insights*, 12 December 2002.

[235] 5 *UNCLOS* 111 (67th Plenary Meeting, para. 81).

[236] In this regard, see the treaty concluded between the US and Liberia on 11 February 2004, partly reproduced in 98 *AJIL* (2004) 355.

is largely an academic one. Most of the time, it may be overcome by assessing the behaviour of the State accused of supporting terrorism in its interaction with the other States and the Security Council. When a State cannot be held responsible for the terrorist activities originating from its territory, the other States could put an end to or neutralise these activities under the doctrine of state of necessity. On the contrary, it is clearly premature to recognise the admissibility of armed reprisals and preventive measures against potential terrorist threats. The second kind of measure, in particular, is staunchly resisted by the overwhelming majority of States for fear of provoking the collapse of the whole legal regulation on the use of force.

As to the lawfulness of the threat or use of nuclear weapons in self-defence, the question has proved rather intractable, as demonstrated by the opinion delivered by the ICJ in 1996. State practice, however, offers several elements that militate against their absolute prohibition, although the limits within which nuclear defensive measures can be taken remains rather controversial. What remains inadmissible, at any rate, is the unilateral action directed at preventing a potential – yet still not concrete and immediate – threat involving weapons of mass destruction from materialising.

There exist in international conventional and customary law effective remedies not involving the use of force against violations of the norms concerning weapons of mass destruction. Hence, the Iraqi crisis confirms that the decision-making process leading to the use of force in order to ensure compliance with disarmament obligations must be collective and that full use must be made of the Security Council's powers. Finally, new claims have been put forward by Western States as to the use of maritime coercive military measures directed at intercepting terrorist activities and curbing the trafficking in weapons of mass destruction. Depending on the reaction of the generality of States, a relaxation of the rules on the use of force on the high seas might be envisaged.

Concluding remarks

The expectations that arose at the end of the Cold War of revitalising the ambitious collective security system established under the Charter proved to be misplaced. On only one occasion, during the Somali crisis, did the United Nations directly take the military action necessary to maintain or restore international peace and security. Although carried out by the armed forces provided by some Member States through *ad hoc* agreements and put under the control of the Secretary General, the military involvement of the United Nations in Somalia conformed to both the letter and the spirit of the Charter. The failure of the intervention cannot be ascribed to alleged deficiencies of international law; it was caused by the incapacity of the Organisation to conduct coercive military operations and the lack of an adequate strategy. It meant the definitive abandonment of the idea of an authentic collective security system in the sense of Art. 42 of the Charter.

In most of the crises in which it has been involved since 1989, the Security Council merely authorised Member States to resort to military force. This practice was accepted by virtually all the members of the Organisation. It brought about, at once, the emergence of a customary norm allowing the use of force authorised by the Security Council, and the correspondent informal modification of the Charter. The authorisation of the use of force produces a permissive effect, thus rendering lawful conduct that would otherwise have been contrary to customary international law and to Art. 2(4) of the Charter. Reminiscent of the never-ratified 1924 Geneva Protocol, the authorisation practice represents a rather modest achievement from the standpoint of the collective security system. The role of the Security Council is limited to the initial assessment of the existence of one of the situations envisaged in Art. 39 of the Charter and on the need to take military action. Throughout the operations, the Security Council is usually unable to exercise effective control and otherwise to suspend or terminate the authorisation.

Even this minimalist version of the collective security system was subsequently challenged and defied on several occasions, most prominently during the Kosovo crisis and the recent intervention in Iraq. Individually taken, the instances of resort to force not authorised by the Security Council are unlawful under current international law. The impact they may have globally in terms of further evolution of the rules governing the use of force, however, has been analysed on the basis of the reaction of the international community.

The claim put forward by the intervening States that the Security Council authorisation was a matter of political convenience rather than a legal requirement manifestly failed to gather general acceptance. Quite to the contrary, it provoked firm protests and condemnations by the majority – overwhelming in the case of Iraq – of States. Although the wheels for change might have been put into motion through the manifestation of the *opinio necessitatis*, the law does not change as long as the claim is consistently and widely resisted.

If the claim eventually succeeds, it would not amount to a further downgrading of the collective security system; it would mean its abandonment altogether. The Security Council authorisation represents the minimum level of international control over the use of force. Below such a level there exists no collective security system at all.

Moving to individual or joint use of force, it has been submitted that the general prohibition on the use of force stands independently from the functioning of the collective security system. Since the prohibition exists under both customary international law and the Charter with no significant differences – a view corroborated in particular by the ICJ in the *Nicaragua case* – the argument that States have regained the right to resort to armed force to enforce their rights as a result of the malfunctioning of the collective security system cannot be shared.

This conclusion is without prejudice to the question of the evolution of the prohibition on the use of force, including the possibility of the (re-)emergence of exceptions other than self-defence, or even the obsolescence of the prohibition itself following persistent and generalised contrary practice. Yet, the rules on the use of force were not perpetually shaped in 1945. Not unlike any other rule of international law, they are exposed to the action of claims and counter-claims advanced by the subjects to which they are addressed. They constantly evolve through state practice and may occasionally found themselves in a state of flux[1] or legal incertitude. This is physiological in a horizontal system such as the international legal system.

Based on these premises, the research has explored the exceptions to the general prohibition on the use of force, starting with the most important one, namely self-defence. Self-defence has been defined as the military response to any armed attack perpetrated by a subject of international law. State practice is entirely inconsistent with the existence of a threshold of gravity or intensity below which the right of self-defence cannot be exercised. The position of the ICJ in the *Nicaragua case* notwithstanding, States regularly invoke self-defence to justify their forcible reactions to *any* such activities without meeting objections other than those based on the factual circumstances.

The notion of self-defence has proved sufficiently flexible to meet the evolving security needs of States. In particular, the generality of States considers as

[1] V. Lowe, *supra* note III-175.

admissible the so-called interceptive self-defence. States are allowed to counter hostile military activities in their initial phase of execution, without having to suffer from their effects. Interceptive self-defence must be kept separate from anticipatory self-defence, the latter intended as the military action aimed at preventing an imminent yet not irrevocably initiated armed attack from concretising. State practice is neither quantitatively nor qualitatively consistent enough to affirm the existence of a right to anticipatory self-defence, a development that would stretch beyond recognition the notion of self-defence itself.

The emergence of three further exceptions to the general prohibition on the use of force has been, and to a large extent still is, the subject of controversy. Firstly, State practice scarcely supports the admissibility of armed countermeasures. The overwhelming majority of States, on the contrary, remain committed to the obligation to settle their disputes through peaceful means, even if this could deprive them of an effective remedy and ultimately prevent them from enjoying their subjective rights.

Secondly, the picture is quite different as to the use of force to rescue nationals abroad. Numerous post-Cold War instances of limited military operations genuinely directed at extracting nationals trapped in situations threatening their lives did not attract any criticism or condemnation by the territorial or third States. The underlying claim seemed to have gained the general acceptance, or at least acquiescence, necessary to lead to the emergence of a new legal ground to resort to force.

Thirdly, the question of humanitarian intervention has proved rather intractable from the standpoint of international law. Beyond the highly politicised debate focusing on the swift progress of paradigm from legality to legitimacy, States remain sharply divided on the right to intervention on humanitarian grounds. Far from contributing to the emergence of such a right, the Kosovo crisis demonstrates that the claim put forward by a relatively small and homogeneous group of States – not without significant differences and reservations – continues to meet the strong opposition of the great majority of the international community.

As demonstrated in the last chapter, existing legal categories are flexible enough to meet the new threats to international peace and security. As far as terrorism is concerned, there are no reasons against the qualification of certain terrorist activities as armed attack for the purpose of self-defence, especially if it is accepted that there is no threshold of gravity below which defensive action is not allowed. An adjustment may nonetheless be imposed by the peculiar nature of the terrorist acts, which are often ordered as part of a larger military strategy. In this respect, the so-called cumulative events theory, while of little use for the purpose of assessing the proportionality of the reaction, is useful to qualify the terrorist acts as a continuous armed attack, allowing defensive military operations carried out in the periods between these single acts.

Furthermore, the dispute as to whether the attribution of the activities of terrorist to a State depends on the existence of a relationship of control-dependence between them or simply an overall control of the former upon the latter is largely doctrinal. The difficulties inherent in the attribution requirement can usually be overcome by assessing, in the light of the rules governing State responsibility, the behaviour of the State concerned towards the other States and the Security Council. In this sense, force may be used in self-defence to counter terrorist activities originating from the territory of a State that supports or tolerates them. In contrast, when the terrorist activities cannot be attributed to the State from which they originate, the use of force could be permitted under the state of necessity doctrine. The state of necessity completes the overall legal framework and ensures that a State can neutralise terrorist groups operating from the territory of another State when the latter is unable to obtain such a result by itself.

Moving to weapons of mass destruction, the threat or use of nuclear weapons in self-defence continues to be a rather controversial issue. State practice militates against an absolute prohibition. Pending a complete disarmament that still appears remote, the prominent problem is not to admit the use of nuclear weapons in self-defence, but rather to define and ensure the respect of the limits of proportionality, necessity and immediacy.

The most disturbing element concerning the use of force to tackle international terrorism and the proliferation and trafficking of weapons of mass destruction is certainly the (re-)emergence of a the notion of pre-emptive self-defence. A few States, led by the United States, have not hesitated unilaterally to resort to massive armed force in order to eliminate potential threats that were neither immediate nor concrete. This conduct is not dictated by the need to adapt the notion of self-defence to the new challenges. It is rather the negation of the notion itself and would provoke the implosion of the whole legal regulation on the use of force. The claim, however, has not only been poorly articulated in official documents; it has also been watered down by (unconvincing) additional legal arguments such as implied authorisation or reviviscence of previous Security Council resolutions.

Very few States are prepared to follow the United States in this direction. The overwhelming majority of the United Nations members are steadily committed to multilateralism. According to them, non-defensive use of force must continue to be conditional upon collective assessment and collective decision-making. It is therefore absolutely premature to certify the death of the prohibition on the use of force. The recent cases of non-defensive use of force must be treated as serious breaches of the basic rules upon which not only the United Nations but also the international community is built.

A constant feature of this study has been the international control over the use of force. Realistically, such control must be exercised principally by the Security Council. It cannot be denied that the organ suffers from a deficit of legitimacy and democracy and must be reformed.[2] However, no reform will cure all problems afflicting the collective security system. Whatever the composition and the voting

[2] For a sceptical look at the question of the Security Council reform, see B. Fassbender, 'All Illusions Shattered? Looking Back on a Decade of Failed Attempts to Reform the Security Council', 7 *MPYUNL* (2003) 183.

procedure, the crux of the matter remains the renunciation by States unilaterally to solve international controversies through military means and the commitment to the collective assessment and control over the use of force.[3] Incidentally, the so-called right to veto certainly permits a permanent member to frustrate the Security Council's activities. It nevertheless represents an effective guarantee against the abusive exercise by that organ of its extensive operative and normative powers.

The Security Council authority, which is based on the consent of all members of the United Nations, must be fully restored and respected. Otherwise, the goals painfully achieved in regulating the use of force would be lost. No differently from what happened in the past, States would unilaterally protect what they perceive as their legal rights through recourse to force. Hence, 'justice' would rest on the side of the most powerful State, which would ultimately be in a position to impose its own terms of settlement, regardless of the causes of the crisis and the underlying rights and obligations.[4]

[3] R. Y. Jennings, *General Course of Principles of International Law*, 121 *RdC* (1967–II) 323, p. 584, observes that 'the problem is not one of drafting legal precepts controlling the use of force but one of devising international institutions through which the use of force in international relationships can be legally ordered and controlled on an international instead of a sovereign basis'.

[4] A. Miele, *supra* note II-161, pp. 95 *et seq*. See also Historicus (Harcourt), *Letters by Historicus on Some Questions of International Law* (1863), reprinted in 1971, p. 41, according to whom in the relations between States what matters is the result of the military action, not its legality. He observed that 'in the case of intervention, as in that of revolution, its essence is illegality, and its justification is its success'.

Bibliography

Abi-Saab G., *The United Nations Operation in Congo*, Oxford: Oxford University Press, 1978.

Ago R., *Scienza giuridica e diritto internazionale*, Milano: Giuffrè, 1950.

Alexandrov S. A., *Self-Defense Against the Use of Force in International Law*, The Hague: Kluwer, 1996.

Antonopoulos C., *The Unilateral Use of Force by States in International Law*, Athens: A. N. Sakkoulas, 1997.

Anzilotti D., *Corso di diritto internazionale*, Roma: Athenaeum, 1915.

——, *Cours de droit international*, Paris: Sirey, 1929.

Arangio-Ruiz G., *Sulla dinamica della base sociale nel diritto internazionale*, Milano: Giuffrè, 1954.

——, *The United Nations Declaration on Friendly Relations and the System of the Sources of International Law*, Alpheen aan Rijn: Sijthoff & Noordhoff, 1979.

Arend, A. T. C. and R. J. Beck, *International Law and the Use of Force*, London: Routledge, 1993.

Bedjaoui M., *The New World Order and the Security Council. Testing the Legality of its Acts*, Dordrecht: Nijhoff, 1994.

Blum Y. Z., *Eroding the United Nations Charter*, Dordrecht: Nijhoff, 1993.

Bobbio N., *Una guerra giusta? Sul conflitto del Golfo*, Venezia: Marsilio, 1991.

Borchard E., *The Diplomatic Protection of Citizens Abroad*, New York: Banks Law Pub., 1915.

Bowett D. W., *Self Defense in International Law*, Manchester: Manchester University Press, 1957.

——, *United Nations Forces: A Legal Study of United Nations Practice*, London: Stevens, 1964.

Brierly J., *The Law of Nations*, 6th ed., Oxford: Clarendon Press, 1963.

Brownlie I., *The Use of Force by States in International Law*, Oxford: Clarendon Press, 1963.

——, *The Rule of Law in International Affairs*, The Hague: Nijhoff, 1998.

Butler W. E. (ed.), *The Non-Use of Force in International Law*, Dordrecht: Nijhoff, 1989.

Byers M., *Custom, Power and the Power of Rules*, Cambridge: Cambridge University Press, 1999.

Cannizzaro E., *Il principio della proporzionalità nell'ordinamento internazionale*, Milano: Giuffrè, 2000.

Castañeda J., *Legal Effects of United Nations Resolutions*, New York: Columbia University Press, 1969.

Cataldi G., *Il passaggio delle navi straniere nel mare territoriale*, Milano: Giuffrè, 1990.

Cellamare G., *Le operazioni di peace-keeping funzionale*, Torino: Giappichelli, 1999.

Chayes A., *The Cuban Missile Crisis*, Oxford: Oxford University Press, 1974.

Chesterman S., *Just War or Just Peace? Humanitarian Intervention and International Law*, Oxford: Oxford University Press, 2001.

Ciobanu D., *Preliminary Objections Relating to the Jurisdiction of the United Nations Political Organs*, The Hague: Nijhoff, 1975.

Collins J. M., *United States – Soviet Military Balance, 1980–1985*, Washington: Pergamon–Brassey's, 1985.

Combacau J., *Le pouvoir de sanction de l'ONU: étude théorique de la coercition non militaire*, Paris: Pédone, 1974.

Conforti B., *La funzione dell'accordo nel sistema della Nazioni Unite*, Padova: CEDAM, 1968.

——, *The Law and Practice of the United Nations*, 2nd ed., The Hague: Kluwer, 2000.

Constatinou A., *The Right of Self-Defence under Customary Law and Article 51 of the Charter*, Athens: A. N. Sakkoulas, 2000.

Crawford J., *The International Law Commission's Articles on State Responsibility*, Cambridge: Cambridge University Press, 2002.

D'Amato A. A., *The Concept of Custom in International Law*, Ithaca: Cornell University Press, 1970.

Danilenko G. M., *Law-Making in the International Community*, Dordrecht: Nijhoff, 1993.

De Visscher C., *Theory and Reality of Public International Law*, 2nd ed., Princeton: Princeton University Press, 1956.

Degan V. D., *Sources of International Law*, Dordrecht: Nijhoff, 1997.

Den Dekker G., *The Law of Arms Control. International Supervision and Enforcement*, The Hague: Nijhoff, 2001.

Dinstein Y., *War, Aggression and Self-Defence*, 3rd ed., Cambridge: Cambridge University Press, 2001.

Falk R., *The Vietnam War and International Law*, Princeton: Princeton University Press, 1968.

Fitzmaurice G., *The Law and Procedure of the International Court of Justice*, Cambridge: Grotius, 1986.

Forlati Picchio M. L., *La sanzione nel diritto internazionale*, Padova: CEDAM, 1974.

Franck T. M., *Nation against Nation*, New York: Oxford University Press, 1985.

——, *The Power of Legitimacy Among Nations*, New York: Oxford University Press, 1990.

——, *Fairness in International Law and Institutions*, Oxford: Clarendon Press, 1995.

——, *Recourse to Force. State Action Against Threat and Armed Attacks*, Cambridge: Cambridge University Press, 2002.

Friedmann W., *The Changing Structure of International Law*, London: Stevens, 1964.

Gianelli A., *Adempimenti preventivi all'adozione di contromisure internazionali*, Milano: Giuffrè, 1997.

Giuliano M., *La comunità internazionale e il diritto internazionale*, Padova: CEDAM, 1950.

Glennon M. J., *Limits of Law, Prerogatives of Power. Interventionism After Kosovo*, New York: Palgrave, 2001.

Goodrich L. M. and E. Hambro, *Charter of the United Nations*, 2nd ed., Boston: Peace Foundation, 1949.

Goodrich L. M. and A. Simons, *The United Nations and the Maintenance of International Peace and Security*, Washington: Brookings Institution, 1955.

Gowlland-Debbas V., *Collective Response to Illegal Acts in International Law: United Nations Action in the Question of Southern Rhodesia*, Dordrecht: Nijhoff, 1990.

Gray C., *International Law and the Use of Force*, 2nd ed. Oxford: Oxford University Press, 2004.

Greig D. W., *International Law*, 2nd ed., London: Butterworths, 1976.

Haas E. B., *When Knowledge is Power: Three Models of Change in International Organizations*, Berkeley: University of California Press, 1990.

Harris D. J., *Cases and Materials on International Law*, 5th ed., London: Sweet & Maxwell, 1998.

Henkin L., *How Nations Behave*, 2nd ed., New York: Columbia University Press, 1979.

Hershey A. S., *Essentials of International Public Law*, New York: Macmillan, 1912.

Higgins R., *The Development of International Law through the Political Organs of the United Nations*, London: Oxford University Press, 1963.

——, *The New United Nations: Appearance and Reality*, Hull: University of Hull Press, 1993.

——, *Problems and Process: International Law and how we use it*, Oxford: Clarendon Press, 1994.

Holland T. E., *Letters to 'The Times' upon War and Neutrality*, London: Longmans, 1921.

Iovane M., *La tutela dei valori fondamentali nel diritto internazionale*, Napoli: Ed. Scientifica, 2000.

Jessup P. C., *A Modern Law of Nations*, New York: Macmillan, 1949.

Jimenez De Arechaga E., *Derecho constitutional de la Naciones Unidas. Comentario teorico y pratico de la Carta*, Madrid: Escuela de funcionarios internationales, 1958.

Karl W., *Vertrag und spätere Praxis in Völkerrecht*, Berlin: Springer, 1983.

Kelsen H., *The Law of the United Nations*, London: Stevens, 1951.

——, *Principles of International Law*, New York: Rinehart & Company, 1952.

Kojanec G., *Trattati e Stati terzi*, Padova: CEDAM, 1961.

N. Kontou, *The Termination and Revision of Treaties in the Light of New Customary International Law*, Oxford: Clarendon Press, 1994.

Kopelmanas L., *L'Organisation des Nations Unies*, Paris: Sirey, 1949.

Krezdorn F. J., *Les Nations Unies et les accords régionaux*, Speyer am Rhein: Jägershe Buchdr, 1954.

Krutzsch W. and R. Trapp, *A Commentary on the Chemical Weapons Convention*, Dordrecht: Nijhoff, 1994.

Lamberti Zanardi P., *La legittima difesa nel diritto internazionale*, Milano: Giuffrè, 1972.

Lanfranchi M.-P. and T. Christakis, *La Licéité de l'emploi d'armes nucléaires devant la Cour internationale de justice*, Paris: Economica, 1997.

Lattanzi F., *Assistenza umanitaria e intervento di umanità*, Torino: Giappichelli, 1997.

Lauterpacht H., *Oppenheims's International Law*, 8th ed., London: Longman, 1955.

Malanczuk P., *Humanitarian Intervention and the Legitimacy of the Use of Force*, Amsterdam: Het Spihuis, 1993.

Malintoppi A., *Le raccomandazioni internazionali*, Milano, Giuffrè, 1958.

McCormack T. L. H., *Self-defense in International Law. The Israeli Raid on the Iraqi Nuclear Reactor*, New York: St Martin's Press, 1996.

McCoubrey H. and N. D. White, *International Law and Armed Conflict*, Aldershot: Dartmouth, 1992.
McDougal M. S. and F. Feliciano, *Law and Minimum World Public Order*, New Haven: Yale University Press, 1961.
McWhinney E., *The World Court and the Contemporary International Law-Making Process*, Alphen aan den Rijn: Sijthof & Noordhoff, 1979.
——, *Aerial Piracy and International Terrorism. Illegal Diversion of Aircraft and International Law*, Dordrecht: Nijhoff, 1987.
Miele A., *La guerra Irachena*, Padova: CEDAM, 1991.
——, *La comunità internazionale*, 3rd ed., Torino: Giappichelli, 2000.
Morelli G., *Nozioni di diritto internazionale*, 7th ed., Padova: CEDAM, 1967.
Murphy S. D., *Humanitarian Intervention. The United Nations in an Evolving World Order*, Philadelphia: University of Pennsylvania Press, 1996.
Nincic D., *The Problem of Sovereignty in the Charter and in the Practice of the United Nations*, The Hague: Nijhoff, 1970.
Österdahl I., *Threat to the Peace: an Interpretation by the Security Council of Article 39 of the Charter*, Uppsala: Iusus, 1998.
Park K. -G., *La protection de la souveraineté aérienne*, Paris: Pédone, 1991.
Phillimore W., *Commentaries upon International Law*, vol. III, London: Butterworths, 1885.
Pietrobon A., *Il sinallagma negli accordi internazionali*, Padova: CEDAM, 1999.
Pillitu A. P., *Lo stato di necessità nel diritto internazionale*, Perugia: Libreria Editrice Universitaria, 1981.
Pisillo-Mazzeschi R., *'Due Diligence' e responsabilità internazionale degli Stati*, Milano: Giuffrè, 1989.
Quadri R., Diritto internazionale pubblico, 6th ed., Napoli: Liguori, 1968.
Reisman M. W., *Nullity and Revision. The Review and Enforcement of International Judgments and Awards*, New Haven: Yale University Press, 1971.
Reuter P., *Introduction to the Law of Treaties*, London: Kegan Paul, 1995.
Ronzitti N., *Rescuing Nationals Abroad Through Military Coercion and Intervention on Ground of Humanity*, Dordrecht: Nijhoff, 1985.
Ross A., *The United Nations: Peace and Progress*, Totowa: Bedminster, 1966.
Sarooshi D., *The United Nations and the Development of Collective Security. The Delegation by the UN Security Council of its Chapter VII Powers*, Oxford: Oxford University Press, 1999.
Schachter O., *International Law in Theory and Practice*, Dordrecht: Nijhoff, 1991.
Schiffer W., *The Legal Community of Mankind*, New York: Columbia University Press, 1954.
Schwarzenberger G., *International Law as Applied and Interpreted by International Courts and Tribunals*, 3rd ed., London: Stevens, 1957.
——, *Power Politics*, 3rd ed., London: Stevens, 1964.
——, *The Inductive Approach to International Law*, London: Stevens, 1965.
——, *A Manual of International Law*, 5th ed., London: Stevens, 1967.
Sciso E., *Gli accordi configgenti nel diritto internazionale*, Bari: Cacucci, 1986.
Seyersted F., *United Nations Forces in the Law of Peace and War*, Leyden: Sijthoff, 1966.
Sicilianos A. L., *Les réactions décentralisées à l'illicite. Des contre-mesures à la légitime défense*, Paris: LGDJ, 1990.
Sico L. and L. Leanza, *La sovranità territoriale. Il mare*, Torino: Giappichelli, 2001.

Sinclair I., *The Vienna Convention on the Law of Treaties*, Manchester: Manchester University Press, 1973.

Singh N., *Nuclear Weapons and International Law*, London: Stevens, 1959.

Singh N. and E. McWhinney, *Nuclear Weapons and Contemporary International Law*, Dordrecht: Nijhoff, 1989.

Sohn L., *Rights in Conflict: The United Nations and South Africa*, New York: Transnational Publishers, 1994.

Stone J., *Aggression and World Order: A Critique of United Nations Theories of Aggression*, London: Stevens, 1958.

——, *Legal Controls of International Conflict*, London: Stevens, 1959.

Sur S., *A Legal Approach to Verification in Disarmament and Arms Limitation*, New York: United Nations Publications, 1988.

Tesauro G., *Il finanziamento delle organizzazioni internazionali*, Napoli: Jovene, 1967.

Teson F., *Humanitarian Intervention: An Inquiry into Law and Morality*, New York: Transnational Publishers, 1997.

Thirlway H., *International Customary Law and Codification: An examination of the Continuing Role of Custom in the Present Period of Codification in International Law*, Leiden: Sijthoff, 1972.

Triepel H., *L'egemonia*, trans. G. Battino, Firenze: Leonardo, 1949.

Tsagourias N. K., *Jurisprudence of International Law: The Humanitarian Dimension*, Manchester: Manchester University Press, 2001.

Tunkin G., *Theory of International Law*, London: Allen & Unwin, 1974.

Van Hoof G. J. H., *Rethinking the Sources of International Law*, Deventer: Kluwer, 1983.

Venturini G., *Necessità e proporzionalità nell'uso della forza militare in diritto internazionale*, Milano: Giuffrè, 1988.

Verdross A., *Völkerrecht*, Vienna: Springer, 1973.

Villani U., *Lezioni sull'ONU e la crisis del Golfo*, 2nd ed., Bari: Cacucci, 1995.

Villiger M. E., *Customary International Law and Treaties*, 2nd ed., The Hague: Kluwer, 1997.

Weisburd A. M., *Use of Force: The Practice of States Since World War II*, Pennsylvania: Pennsylvania State University, 1997.

White N. D., *The United Nations and the Maintenance of International Peace and Security*, Manchester: Manchester University Press, 1990.

——, *The Law of International Organisations*, Manchester: Manchester University Press, 1996.

——, *Keeping the Peace*, 2nd ed., Manchester: Manchester University Press, 1997.

Wolfke K., *Custom in Present International Law*, 2nd ed., Dordrecht: Nijhoff, 1993.

Zacklin R., *The Amendments of the Constitutive Instruments of the United Nations and Specialized Agencies*, Leyden: Sijthoff, 1968.

Zourek J., *La notion de légitime défense*, Leiden: Sijthoff, 1974.

Collected papers and essays

Al-Nauimi N. *et al.* (eds.), *International Legal Issues Arising under the United Nations Decade of International Law*, The Hague: Nijhoff, 1995.

Bardonnet D. (ed.), *The Adaptation of Structures and Methods at the United Nations*, Dordrecht: Nijhoff, 1986.

Boisson de Chazournes L. and P. Sands (eds.), *International Law, the International Court of Justice and Nuclear Weapons*, Cambridge: Cambridge University Press, 1999.

Bull H. (ed.), *Intervention in World Politics*, Oxford: Clarendon, 1984.

Cassese A. (ed.), *The Current Legal Regulation of the Use of Force*, Dordrecht: Nijhoff, 1986.

Cassese A. and J. H. H. Weiler (eds.), *Change and Stability in International Law-Making*, Berlin: W. De Gruyter, 1988.

Clarke W. and J. Herbst (eds.), *Learning from Somalia: Lesson of Armed Humanitarian Intervention*, Boulder: Westview, 1997.

Cot J. -P. and A. Pellet (eds.), *La Charte des Nations Unies*, Paris: Economica, 1991.

De Guttry A. and N. Ronzitti (eds.), *The Iran–Iraq War (1980–1988) and the Law of Naval Warfare*, Cambridge: Grotius, 1993.

Dekker I. F. and H. H. G. Post (eds.), *The Gulf War of 1980–1988: The Iran–Iraq War in International Legal Perspective*, Dordrecht: Nijhoff, 1992.

Delbrück J. (ed.), *The Future of International Law Enforcement: New Scenarios – New Law?*, Berlin: Duncker & Humblot, 1993.

Dewar J. (ed.), *Nuclear Weapons, the Peace Movement and the Law*, Basingstoke: Macmillan, 1986.

Dupuy R. -J. (ed.), *The Development of the Role of the Security Council*, Nijhoff: Dordrecht, 1993.

International Law at the Time of its Codification: Essays in Honour of Robert Ago, Milano: Giuffrè, 1987.

Fisler Damrosch L. and D. J. Scheffer (eds.), *Law and Force in the New International Order*, Boulder: Westview, 1993.

Fox H. (ed.), *The Changing Constitution of the United Nations*, London: BIICL, 1997.

Henkin L., *Right v. Might: International Law and the Use of Force* 2nd ed, New York: Council on Foreign Relations Press, 1991.

Higgins R. and M. Flory (eds.), *International Law and Terrorism*, London: Routledge, 1997.

Holzgrefe J. L. and R. O. Keohane (eds.), *Humanitarian Intervention. Ethical, Legal and Political Dilemmas*, Cambridge: Cambridge University Press, 2003.

Ku C. and H. K. Jacobson (eds.), *Democratic Accountability and the Use of Force in International Law*, Cambridge: Cambridge University Press, 2002.

Lattanzi F. and E. Sciso (eds.), *Dai tribunali penali internazionali* ad hoc *a una corte permanente*, Napoli: Ed. Scientifica, 1996.

Lillich R. B. (ed.), *Humanitarian Intervention and the United Nations*, Charlottesville: University Press of Virginia, 1973.

Luard E. (ed.), *The Evolution of International Organizations*, New York: Thames and Hudson, 1966.

Macdonald R. St. (ed.), *Essays in Honour of Wang Tieya*, Dordrecht: Nijhoff, 1993.

Macdonald R. St. and D. M. Johnston (eds.), *The Structure and Process of International Law: Essays in Legal Philosophy Doctrine and Theory*, The Hague: Nijhoff, 1983.

Makarczyk J. (ed.), *Essays in International Law in Honour of Judge Lachs*, The Hague: Nijhoff, 1984.

Muller A. S. *et al.* (eds.), *The International Court of Justice: Its Future Role after Fifty Years*, The Hague: Nijhoff, 1997.

Picone P. (ed.), *Interventi delle Nazioni Unite*, Padova: CEDAM, 1995.

Pogany I. (ed.), *Nuclear Weapons and International Law*, Aldershot: Avebury, 1987.

Rama-Montaldo M. (ed.), *International Law in an Evolving World, Liber Amicorum E. Jiménez de Arechaga*, Montevideo: Fundación de cultura universitaria, 1994.

Rodley N. (ed.), *To Loose the Bands of Wickedness*, London: Brassey's, 1992.

Schmidt G. (ed.), *A History of NATO . The First Fifty Years*, New York: Palgrave, 2001.

Schmitt M. N. and B. T. O'Donnell (eds.), *Computer Network Attacks and International Law*, Newport: Naval War College, 2002.

Sciso E. (ed.), *Intervento in Kosovo. Aspetti internazionalistici e interni*, Milano: Giuffrè, 2001.

Simma B. (ed.), *The Charter of the United Nations*, 2nd ed., Oxford: Oxford University Press, 2002.

SIOI, *L'O.N.U.: Cinquant'anni di attività e prospettive per il futuro*, Roma, Presidenza del Consiglio, 1996.

Storm Van Gravesonde J. W. E. and A. Van der Veen Vonk (eds.), *Air Worthy*, Deventer: Kluwer, 1985.

Swinarski C., *Studies and Essays on International Humanitarian Law and Red Cross Principles in Honour of J. Pictet*, Geneva: ICRC, 1984.

Tomuschat C. (ed.), *The United Nations at Age Fifty*, The Hague: Kluwer, 1995.

Walter C. *et al.* (eds.), *Terrorism as a Challenge for National and International Law: Security versus Liberty?*, Berlin: Springer, 2004.

Wellens K. (ed.), *International Law: Theory and Practice, Essays E. Suy*, The Hague: Nijhoff, 1998.

Yapko E. and T. Boumedra (eds.), *Liber Amicorum M. Bedjaoui*, The Hague: Kluwer, 1999.

Journal articles

Abi-Saab G., 'There is No Need to Reinvent the Law', posted at www.crimesofwar.org.

Ago R., 'Le délit international', 68 *RdC* (1939–II) 419.

——, 'Droit des traités à la lumière de la Convention de Vienne', 134 *RdC* (1971–III) 297.

Akande D., 'The International Court of Justice and the Security Council: Is there Room for Judicial Control of Decisions of Political Organs of the United Nations?', 46 *ICLQ* (1997) 331.

Akehurst M., 'Enforcement Action by Regional Agencies, with Special Reference to the Organisation of American States', 42 *BYIL* (1967) 175.

——, 'Custom as a Source of International Law', 47 *BYIL* (1974–5) 1.

——, 'The Hierarchy of the Sources of International Law', 47 *BYIL* (1974–5) 273.

——, 'The Use of Force to Protect Nationals Abroad', 5 *IR* (1977) 3.

Aldrich G., 'The Taliban, Al Qaeda, and the Determination of Illegal Combatants?', 96 *AJIL* (2002) 891.

Alessi G. P., 'L'evoluzione della prassi delle Nazioni Unite relativa al mantenimento della pace', 47 *RDI* (1964) 556.

Alvarez J. E., 'The Quest for Legitimacy: An Examination of The Power of Legitimacy by T. M. Franck', 24 *NYUJILP* (1991) 199.

——, 'Judging the Security Council', 90 *AJIL* (1996) 1.

Amerasinge C. F., 'Interpretation of Text of Open International Organizations', 65 *BYIL* (1994) 175.

Andrassy J., 'Uniting for Peace', 50 *AJIL* (1956) 563.

Antonopoulos C., 'The Turkish Military Operations in Northern Iraq of March–April 1995 and the International Law on the Use of Force', 1 *JACL* (1996) 33.

Anzilotti D., 'L'azione individuale contraria al diritto internazionale', in D. Anzilotti, *Scritti di diritto internazionale*, Padova: CEDAM, 1956, vol. I, p. 209.

Arangio-Ruiz G., 'L'individuo e il diritto internazionale', 54 *RDI* (1971) 561.

——, 'Consuetudine internazionale', in *Enciclopedia del diritto*, Milano: Giuffrè, 1988, vol. VIII, p. 1.

——, 'The "Federal Analogy" and UN Charter Interpretation: A crucial Issue', 8 *EJIL* (1997) 1.

——, 'Article 39 of the ILC First-Reading Draft Articles on State Responsibility', 83 *RDI* (2000) 747.

——, 'On the Security Council's "Law-Making"', 83 *RDI* (2000) 609.

Baby L., 'Interception d'un aéronef civil par un moyen militaire: Conséquences en matière de responsabilité', 55 *RFDAS* (2001) 400.

Badr G. M., 'The Exculpatory Effect of Self-Defence in State Responsibility', 10 *GJIL* (1980) 1.

Baxter R. R., 'Multilateral Treaties as Evidence of Customary International Law', 41 *BYIL* (1965–66) 275.

Blum Y. Z., 'State Response to Acts of Terrorism', 19 *GYIL* (1976) 223.

——, 'The Gulf of Sidra Incident', 80 *AJIL* (1986) 668.

Bolton J., 'Is there Really "Law" in International Affairs?', 10 *TLCP* (2000) 1.

Bourbonniere M. and L. Haeck, 'Military Aircraft and International Law: Chicago Opus 3', 66 *JALC* (2001) 885.

Bowett D. W., 'Reprisals involving Armed Force', 66 *AJIL* (1972) 1.

——, 'The Impact of Security Council Decisions on Dispute Settlement Procedures', 5 *EJIL* (1994) 89.

Briggs H. W., '*Nicaragua* v. *United States*. Jurisdiction and Admissibility', 79 *AJIL* (1985) 373.

Broms B., 'The Definition of Aggression', 154 *RdC* (1977–I) 299, p. 370.

Brownlie I., 'International Law at the Fiftieth Anniversary of the United Nations', 255 *RdC* (1995) 9.

——, 'Kosovo Crisis Inquiry: Memorandum on the International Law Aspects', 49 *ICLQ* (2000) 787.

Campbell L. M., 'Defending Against Terrorism: A Legal Analysis of the Decision to Strike Sudan and Afghanistan', 74 *Tulane LR* (2000) 1067.

Capotorti F., 'L'extinction et la suspension des traités', 134 *RdC* (1971–III) 417.

Caron D. D., 'The Legitimacy of the Collective Authority of the Security Council', 87 *AJIL* (1993) 552.

Cassese A., 'The International Community's "Legal" Response to Terrorism', 38 *ICLQ* (1989) 589.

——, 'Terrorism is also Disrupting Some Crucial Legal Categories of International Law', 12 *EJIL* (2001) 993.

Charney J. I., 'The Use of Force Against Terrorism and International Law', 95 *AJIL* (2001) 835.

Chayes A., 'Law and the Quarantine of Cuba', 41 *FA* (1963) 550.

Chinkin C., 'The Legality of NATO Action in the Former Republic of Yugoslavia (FRY) under International Law', 49 *ICLQ* (2000) 910.

Claude I., 'Collective Legitimization as a Political Function of the United Nations', 20

IO (1966) 370.

Condorelli L., 'L'imputation à l'Etat d'un fait internationalement illicite: solutions classiques et nouvelles tendances', 189 *RdC* (1984–VI) 19.

——, '*Consuetudine internazionale*', in *Digesto* Discipline Pubblicistiche, 4th ed., Torino: UTET, 1989, vol. III, 1989, p. 490.

——, 'A propos de l'attaque américaine contre l'Irak du 26 juin 1993: Lettre d'un professeur désemparé aux lecteurs du JEDI', 5 *EJIL* (1994) 134.

——, 'La Corte internazionale di giustizia e gli organi politici delle Nazioni Unite', 77 *RDI* (1994) 897.

——, 'Les attentats du 11 septembre et leur suites: où va le droit international?', 105 *RGDIP* (2001) 829.

Conforti B., 'Le rôle de l'accord dans le système des Nations Unies', 142 *RdC* (1974–II) 203.

Corten O. and F. Dubuisson, 'L'hypothèse d'une règle émergente fondant une intervention militaire sur une "autorisation implicite" du Conseil de sécurité', 104 *RGDIP* (2000) 873.

——, 'Opération "Liberté immuable": une extension abusive du concept de légitime défense', 105 *RGDIP* (2001) 51.

Cot J. P., 'La conduite subséquente des parties à un traité', 70 *RGDIP* (1966) 632.

Cuadra E., 'Air Defence Identification Zones: Creeping Jurisdiction on the Airspace', 18 *VJIL* (1978) 485.

D'Amato A. A., 'Israeli's Air Strike upon the Iraqi Nuclear Reactor', 77 *AJIL* (1983) 584.

——, 'Reply to Letter of Michael Akehurst', 80 *AJIL* (1986) 148.

Daems A., 'L'absence de la base juridique de l'Opération *Provide Comfort*', 25 *RBDI* (1992) 261.

De Hoogh A. J. J., 'Articles 4 and 8 of the 2001 ILC Articles on State Responsibility, the *Tadic* Case and Attribution of Acts of Bosnian Serb Authorities to the Federal Republic of Yugoslavia', 72 *BYIL* (2001) 255.

De Visscher P., 'Les conditions d'application des lois de la guerre aux opérations militaires des Nations Unies', 54 *AIDI* (1971) 39.

— —, 'Cours général de droit international public', 136 *RdC* (1972–II) 1.

Delbrück J., 'A Fresh Look at Humanitarian Intervention Under the Authority of the United Nations', 67 *ILJ* (1992) 887.

——, 'The Fight Against Global Terrorism: Self-defense or Collective Security as International Police Action? Some Comments on the International Legal Implications of the "War Against Terrorism"', 44 *GYIL* (2001) 9.

Dominicé C., 'La sécurité collective et la crise du Golfe', 2 *EJIL* (1991) 85.

Dopagne F., 'La responsabilité de l'Etat du fait des particuliers: les causes d'imputation revisitées par les articles sur la responsabilité de l'Etat pour fait internationalement illicite', 34 *RBDI* (2001) 492.

Engel S., 'The Changing Charter of the United Nations', 7 *YBWA* (1953) 71.

——, 'Procedures for the de facto Revision of the Charter', *ASIL Proceedings*, 1965, p. 108.

Eustathiades C. T., 'La définition de l'agression adoptée aux Nations Unies et la légitime défense', 28 *RHDI* (1975) 1.

Falk R., 'The *Shimoda* Case: A Legal Appraisal of the Atomic Attacks upon Hiroshima and Nagasaki', 59 *AJIL* (1965) 759.

——, 'The Beirut Raid and the International Law of Retaliation', 63 *AJIL* (1969) 415.

——, 'Questioning the UN mandate in the Gulf', IFDA Dossier (1991/2) 81.
——, 'Nuclear Weapons, International Law and the World Court: A Historic Encounter', 91 *AJIL* (1997) 64.
Farer T., 'The Bush Doctrine and the United Nations Charter Frame', 37 *IS* (2002) 91.
Fassbender B., 'All Illusions Shattered? Looking Back on a Decade of Failed Attempts to Reform the Security Council', 7 *MPYUNL* (2003) 183.
Fawcett J. E. S., 'Intervention in International Law. Study of Some Recent Cases', 103 *RdC* (1961–II) 343.
Feder M. N., 'Reading the UN Charter Connotatively: Toward a New Definition of Armed Attack', 19 *NYUJILP* (1986–87) 395.
Fenwick C. G., 'The Quarantine Against Cuba: Legal or Illegal', 55 *AJIL* (1963) 588.
——, 'When is There a Threat to Peace. Rhodesia', 61 *AJIL* (1967) 753.
Ferrari Bravo L., 'Méthodes de recherche de la coutume internationale dans la pratique des états', 192 *RdC* (1985–III) 237.
Fitzmaurice G., 'The Foundations of the Authority of International Law and the Problem of Enforcement', 19 *MLR* (1956) 1.
——, 'The General Principles of International Law', 92 *RdC* (1957–II) 1.
——, 'Some Problems Regarding the Formal Sources of International Law', in *Symbolae Verzijl* (The Hague: Nijhoff, 1958).
——, '*Vae Victis* or Woe to the Negotiators! Your Treaty or our "Interpretation" of it?', 65 *AJIL* (1971) 358.
Francioni F., 'The Gulf of Sirte Incident (United States and Libya) and International Law', 5 *IYIL* (1980–1) 85.
——, 'Of War, Humanity and Justice: International Law After Kosovo', 4 *MPYUNL* (2000) 107.
Franck T. M., 'Who Killed Art. 2(4) ? or: The Changing Norms Governing the Use of Force by States', 64 *AJIL* (1970) 809.
——, 'Of Gnats and Camels: Is There a Double Standard at the United Nations?', 78 *AJIL* (1984) 811.
——, 'The "Power of Appreciation": Who is the Ultimate Guardian of UN Legality?', 86 *AJIL* (1992) 519.
——, 'Fairness in the International Legal and Institutional System', 240 *RdC* (1993–III) 9.
——, 'Terrorism and the Right of Self-Defense', 95 *AJIL* (2001) 839.
Franck T. M. and F. Patel, 'UN Police Action in Lieu of War: "The Old Order Changeth"', 85 *AJIL* (1991) 63.
Freudenschuß H., 'Article 39 of the UN Charter Revisited: Threats to the Peace and the Recent Practice of the UN Security Council', 46 *AJPIL* (1993) 1.
——, 'Between Unilateralism and Collective Security: Authorizations of the Use of Force by the Security Council', 5 *EJIL* (1994) 492.
Frowein J. A., 'Reaction by Non-Directly Affected States to Breaches of Public International Law', 248 *RdC* (1994–IV) 349.
Gaja G., 'Il Consiglio di sicurezza di fronte all'occupazione del Kuwait: il significato di una autorizzazione', 74 *RDI* (1991) 696.
——, 'Réflexions sur le rôle du Conseil de Sécurité dans le nouvel ordre mondial. A propos des rapports entre maintien de la paix et crimes internationaux des Etats', 97 *RGDIP* (1993) 297.
Gardam J. G., 'Proportionality and Force in International Law', 87 *AJIL* (1993) 391.
——, 'Legal Restraint on Security Military Enforcement Action', 17 *MJIL* (1996) 285.

Gardner R. N., 'Neither Bush nor the "Jurisprude"', 97 *AJIL* (2003) 585.
Georgiev D., 'Letter to the Editor', 83 *AJIL* (1989) 554.
Gill T. D., 'Legal and Some Political Limitations on the Power of the UN Security Council to Exercise its Enforcement Power Under Chapter VII of the Charter', 26 *NYIL* (1995) 33.
Goodhart A. L., 'The North Atlantic Treaty of 1949', 79 *RdC* (1951–II) 183.
Gowlland-Debbas V., 'Security Council Enforcement Action and Issues of State Responsibility', 43 *ICLQ* (1994) 55.
——, 'The Relationship between the International Court of Justice and the Security Council in the Light of the Lockerbie Case', 88 *AJIL* (1994) 643.
Grado V., 'Il ristabilimento della democrazia in Sierra Leone', 83 *RDI* (2000) 360.
Graefrath B., 'Iraqi compensation and the Security Council', 55 *ZaöRV* (1995) 1.
Graham T. and J. Mendelsohn, 'NATO's Nuclear Weapons and the No-First-Use Option', 34 *IS* (1999) 5.
Gray C., 'The British Position in regard to the Gulf Conflict', 37 *ICLQ* (1988) 420 and 40 *ICLQ* (1992) 464.
——, 'After the Ceasefire: Iraq, the Security Council and the Use of Force', 65 *BYIL* (1994) 135.
Green L. C., 'Rescue at Entebbe. Legal Aspects', 6 *IYHR* (1976) 312.
Greenwood C., 'International Law and the "War against Terrorism"', 78 *IA* (2002) 301.
Greig D. W., 'Self-Defence and the Security Council: What does Article 51 Require?', 40 *ICLQ* (1991) 366.
Gross L., 'The Charter of the United Nations and the Lodge Reservation', 41 *AJIL* (1947) 531.
——, 'Expenses of the United Nations for Peace-Keeping Operations', 17 *IO* (1963) 11.
——, 'The United Nations and the Role of Law', 19 *IO* (1965) 537.
Haerr R. C., 'The Gulf of Sidra', 24 *SDLR* (1987) 751.
Haggenmacher P., 'La doctrine des deux éléments du droit coutumier dans la pratique de la Cour internationale', 90 *RGDIP* (1986) 5.
Halberstam M., 'The Right to Self-defence once the Security Council Takes Action', 17 *MJIL* (1996) 229.
Halderman J. W., 'Legal Basis for United Nations Armed Forces', 56 *AJIL* (1962) 971.
Hargrove J. L., 'The Nicaragua Judgment and the Future of the Law of Force and Self-Defense', 81 *AJIL* (1987) 135.
Harper K., 'Does the United Nations Security Council have the Competence to Act as Court and Legislature?', 27 *NUJILP* (1994) 103.
Heintschel von Heinegg, W. and H. R. Haltern, 'The Decision of the German Federal Constitutional Count of 12 July 1994 in *Re Deployment of the German Armed Forces Out of Areas*', 41 *NILR* (1994) 285.
Henkin L., 'The Reports of the Death of Article 2(4) Are Greatly Exaggerated', 65 *AJIL* (1971) 547.
——, 'General Course in Public International Law', 216 *RdC* (1989–IV) 10.
——, 'The Invasion of Panama under International Law: A Gross *Violation'*, 29 *CJTL* (1991) 293.
——, 'Conceptualizing Violence: Present and Future Developments in International Law', 60 *Albany LR* (1997) 571.
——, 'Kosovo and the Law of "Humanitarian Intervention"', 93 *AJIL* (1999) 824.

Higgins R., 'The Place of International Law in the Settlement of Dispute by the Security Council', 64 *AJIL* (1970) 1.

——, 'The Advisory Opinion on Namibia: Which UN Resolutions are Binding under Article 25 of the Charter?', 21 *ICLQ* (1972) 270.

——, 'The New United Nations and the Former Yugoslavia', 69 *IA* (1993) 465.

——, 'Peace and Security. Achievements and Failures', 6 *EJIL* (1995) 445.

Hugues E., 'La notion de terrorisme en droit international: en quête d'une définition juridique', 129 *JDI* (2002) 753.

Jennings R. Y., 'The *Caroline* and *McLeod* Cases', 32 *AJIL* (1938) 82.

——, 'The Progressive Development of International Law and its Codification', 24 *BYIL* (1947) 301.

——, 'The United Nations and the Congo', in *The Listener*, 19 October 1961, p. 612.

——, 'General Course of Principles of International Law', 121 *RdC* (1967–II) 323.

Jiménez De Arechaga E., 'International Law in the Past Third of a Century', 159 *RdC* (1978–I) 1.

Joyner C. C. and M. A. Grimaldi, 'The United States and Nicaragua: Reflections on the Lawfulness of Contemporary Intervention', 25 *VJIL* (1984) 621.

Kahn S. G., 'Private Armed Groups and World Order', 1 *NYIL* (1970) 32.

Kaikobad K., 'Self-Defence, Enforcement and the Gulf Wars, 1980–88 and 1990–91', 63 *BYIL* (1992) 300.

Kelsen H., 'Théorie du droit international coutumier', 13 *RIDT* (1939) 253.

——, 'Sanctions in International Law under the Charter of the United Nations', 31 *Iowa LR* (1946) 499.

——, 'Collective Security and Collective Self-Defense under the Charter of the United Nations', 42 *AJIL* (1948) 783.

——, 'Collective Security under International Law', 49 *ILS* (1954) p. 27.

Kido M., 'The Korean Airlines Incident on September 1, 1983 and Some Measures Following It', 62 *JALC* (1997) 1049.

Kirgis F. L., 'The Security Council's First Fifty Years', 89 *AJIL* (1995) 506.

——, 'Security Council Resolution 1441 on Iraq's Final Opportunity to Comply with Disarmament Obligations', *ASIL Insights*, November 2002.

——, 'Boarding of North Korean Vessel on the High Seas', *ASIL Insights*, December 2002.

Kissinger H., 'America at the Apex: Empire of Leader', *Nat. Int.* (2001) 9.

— —, 'Beyond Baghdad, *New York Post*, 11 August 2002, 24.

Kress C., 'L'organe *de facto* en droit international public. Réflexions sur l'imputation à l'Etat de l'acte d'un particulier à la lumière des développements récents', 105 *RGDIP* (2001) 93.

Kristiotis D., 'The Legality of the 1993 US Missile Strike on Iraq and the Right of Self-defence in International Law', 45 *ICLQ* (1996) 162.

Kunz J., 'L'article 11 du Pacte de la Société des Nations', 39 *RdC* (1932) 683.

——, 'Individual and Collective Self-Defense in Article 51 of the Charter of the United Nations', 41 *AJIL* (1947) 872.

——, 'Revolutionary Creation of Norms of International Law', 41 *AJIL* (1947) 121.

——, '*Bellum Justum* and *Bellum Legale*', 45 *AJIL* (1951) 528.

——, 'General International Law and the Law of International Organizations', 47 *AJIL* (1953) 456.

——, 'La crise et les transformations du droit des gens', 88 *RdC* (1955–II) 9.

——, 'Sanctions in International Law', 54 *AJIL* (1960) 324.

Lachs M., 'General Course in Public International Law', 169 *RdC* (1980–IV) 9.
Lauterpacht H., 'Sovereignty over Submarine Areas', 27 *BYIL* (1950) 376.
Liang Y.L., 'Abstention or Absence of a Permanent Member', 44 *AJIL* (1950) 694.
Lillich R., 'Forcible Self Help to Protect Human Rights', 53 *Iowa LR* (1967) 325.
——, 'Forcible Protection of Nationals Abroad: The Liberian "Incident" of 1990', 35 *GYIL* (1992) 205.
——, 'Humanitarian Intervention through the United Nations: Towards the Development of Criteria', 53 *ZaöRV* (1993) 557.
Lillich R. B. and J. M. Paxman, 'State Responsibility for Injuries to Aliens Occasioned by Terrorists' Activities', 26 *AULR* (1977) 217.
Lissitzy O. J., 'Some Legal Implications of the U-2 and RB 47 Incidents', 56 *AJIL* (1962) 135.
Lorenz F. M., 'Rules of Engagement in Somalia: Were They Effective?', 42 *Naval LR* (1995) 62.
Lowe V. A., 'International Legal Issues Arising in the Kosovo Crisis', 49 *ICLQ* (2000) 934.
——, 'The Iraq Crisis: What Now?', 52 *ICLQ* (2003) 859.
MacDougall M., 'United Nations Operations: Who Should be in Charge?', 33 *RDMDG* (1994) 21.
Majid A. A., 'Treaty Amendment Inspired by the Korean Plane Tragedy: Custom Clarified or Confused?', 29 *GYIL* (1986) 190.
Malanczuk P., 'The Kurdish Crisis and allied Intervention in the Aftermath of the Second Gulf War', 2 *EJIL* (1991) 114.
Marston G., 'Armed Intervention in the 1956 Suez Canal Crisis: The Legal Advice Tendered to the British Government', 37 *ICLQ* (1988) 773.
Martenczuk B., 'The Security Council, the International Court and Judicial Review: What Lesson from Lockerbie?', 10 *EJIL* (1999) 517.
McDougal M. S., 'The Hydrogen Bomb Tests and the International Law of the Sea', 49 *AJIL* (1955) 353.
——, 'The Soviet-Cuban Quarantine and Self-Defence', 57 *AJIL* (1963) 597.
——, 'Authority to Use Force on the High Seas', 20 *NWCR* (1967) 19.
McDougal M. S. and M. W. Reisman, 'Rhodesia and the United Nations: The Lawfulness of International Concern', 62 *AJIL* (1968) 11.
McNair A. D., 'The Legal Meaning of War, and the Relation of War with Reprisals', 9 *GS* (1926) 7.
Meeker L. C., 'Defensive Quarantine and the Law', 55 *AJIL* (1963) 515.
Mendelson M. H., 'The Formation of Customary International Law', 272 *RdC* (1998) 155.
Meron T., 'Classification of Armed Conflicts in the Former Yugoslavia: Nicaragua's Fallout', 92 *AJIL* (1998) 326.
Meyrowitz E. L., 'The Law of War and Nuclear Weapons', 9 *BJIL (*1983) 227.
Meyrowitz H., 'Le débat sur le non-recours en premier aux armes nucléaires et la déclaration soviétique du 15 juin 1982', 28 *AFDI* (1982) 147.
Miller A. S., 'Universal Soldiers: U.N. Standing Armies and the Legal Alternatives', 81 *Georgetown LJ* (1993) 773.
Mindua A., 'Intervention armée de la CEDEAO au Liberia: illégalité ou avancée juridique?', 7 *AJICL* (1995) 257.
Monaham, B., 'Giving the Non-Proliferation Treaty Teeth: Strengthening the Special Inspection Procedures of the IAEA', 33 *VJIL* (1992) 161.
Morelli G., 'A proposito di norme internazionali cogenti', 51 *RDI* (1968) 108.

Morgenthau H., 'Positivism, Functionalism and International Law', 34 *AJIL* (1949) 260.

Morth T. A., 'Considering Our Position: Viewing Informational Warfare as a Use of Force Prohibited by Art. 2(4) of the UN Charter', 30 *Cal. Western ILJ* (1998) 567.

Murphy S. D., 'The Security Council, Legitimacy, and the Concept of Collective Security After the Cold War', 32 *CJTL* (1994) 201.

——, 'Terrorism and the Concept of "Armed Attack" in Article 51 of the U.N. Charter', 43 *HJIL* (2002) 41.

——, 'Terrorist Attacks on World Trade Center and Pentagon', 96 *AJIL* (2002) 237.

Myjer E. P. J. and N. D. White, 'The Twin Towers Attack: An Unlimited Right to Self-Defence?', 7 *JCSL* (2002) 5.

Nagan W. P., 'Rethinking Bosnia and Herzegovina's Right of Self-Defence: A Comment', 52 *RICJ* (1994) 34.

Nelson R. W., 'Low-Yield Earth-Penetrating Nuclear Weapons', 10 *Science & Global Security* (2002) 1.

Nollkaemper A., 'Concurrence between Individual Responsibility and State Responsibility in International Law', 52 *ICLQ* (2003) 615.

Nowrot K. and E. W. Schabacker, 'The Use of force to Restore Democracy: International Legal Implications of the Ecowas Intervention in Sierra Leone', 14 *AUILR* (1998) 373.

Nussbaum A., 'Just War: A Legal Concept?', 42 *Mich. LR* (1043) 453.

O'Connell D. P., 'International Law and Contemporary Naval Operations', 44 *BYIL* (1970) 19.

O'Connell M. E., 'Evidence of Terror', 7 *JCSL* (2002) 19.

——, 'The Myth of Preemptive Self-Defence', *ASIL*, August 2002, p. 7.

O'Hanlon M. E., S. E. Rice, Steinberg J. B., 'The New National Strategy and Preemption', at www.brook.edu/comm/policybriefs/pb113.htm.

Osieke E., 'The Legal Validity of *Ultra Vires* Decisions of International Organizations', 77 *AJIL* (1983) 239.

Palchetti P., 'L'uso della forza contro l'Iraq: la ris. 678 (1990) legittima ancora l'azione militare degli Stati?', 81 *RDI* (1998) 471.

Panzera A. F., '*Raids* e protezione dei cittadini all'estero', 61 *RDI* (1978) 759.

Paust J., 'Entebbe and Self Help: The Israeli Response to Terrorism', 2 *FA* (1978) 86.

——, 'Use of Armed Force against Terrorists in Afghanistan, Iraq and Beyond', 35 *CILJ* (2002) 533.

Pellet A., 'La formation du droit international dans le cadre des Nations Unies', 6 *EJIL* (1995) 401.

Perl R. and R. O'Rourke, 'Terrorist Attack on USS Cole: Background and Issues for Congress', CRS Report for Congress, 30 January 2001.

Picone P., 'Valori fondamentali della comunità internazionale e Nazioni Unite', 50 *CI* (1995) 439.

——, 'La "guerra del Kosovo" e il diritto internazionale generale', 83 *RDI* (2000) 309.

Picone P., 'La guerra contro l'Iraq e le degenerazioni dell'unilateralismo', 86 *RDI* (2003) 329.

Pisillo-Mazzeschi R., 'The "Due Diligence" Rule and the Nature of the International Responsibility of States', 35 *GYIL* (1992) 9.

Pogany I., 'Book Review of Dinstein's War Aggression and Self-Defence, 1st ed.', 38 *ICLQ* (1989) 435.

Puoti P., 'Limiti giuridici all'azione del Consiglio di sicurezza delle Nazioni Unite nel settore del mantenimento della pace', 108 *Studi Senesi* (1996) 287.

Quigley J., 'The United States and the United Nations in the Persian Gulf War: New Order or Disorder?', 25 *CILJ* (1992) 1.
——, 'The "Privatization" of Security Council Enforcement Action: A Threat to Multilateralism', 17 *MJIL* (1996) 249.
Rama-Montaldo M., 'International Legal Personality and Implied Powers of International Organizations', 44 *BYIL* (1970) 111.
Rambaud P., 'La définition d'agression par l'Organisation des Nations Unies', 80 *RGDIP* (1976) 835.
Ratner S. R., 'The Gulf of Sidra Incident of 1981', 10 *YJIL* (1984) 59.
Redgwood R., 'NATO's Campaign in Yugoslavia', 93 *AJIL* (1999) 828.
Reicher H., 'The Uniting for Peace Resolution on the Thirtieth Anniversary of its Passage', 20 *CJTL* (1981) 1.
Reisman M. W., 'International Lawmaking: A Process of Communication', 75 *ASIL Proceedings* (1983) 101.
——, 'Article 2 (4): The Use of Force in Contemporary International Law', 78 *ASIL* (1984) 74.
——, 'The Constitutional Crisis in the United Nations', 87 *AJIL* (1993) 83.
——, 'The Raid on Baghdad: Some Reflections on its Lawfulness and Implications', 5 *EJIL* (1994) 120.
——, 'Assessing the Claims to Revise the Laws of War', 97 *AJIL* (2003) 80.
Roberts A., 'NATO's Humanitarian War', 41 *Survival* (1999) 102.
Ronzitti N., 'Sommergibili non identificati, pretese baie storiche e contromisure dello Stato costiero', 66 *RDI* (1983) 5.
——, 'La Corte internazionale di giustizia e la questione della liceità della minaccia o dell'uso delle armi nucleari', 79 *RDI* (1996) 861.
——, '*Raids* aerei contro la Repubblica federale di Iugoslavia e Carta delle Nazioni Unite', 82 *RDI* (1999) 476.
Rosas A., 'Negative Security Assurances and Non-Use of Nuclear Weapons', 25 *GYIL* (1982) 199.
Rostow E., 'The Legality of the International Use of Force by and from States', 10 *YJIL* (1985) 286.
——, 'The International Use of Force after the Cold War', 32 *HJIL* (1991) 411.
——, 'Until What? Enforcement Action or Collective Self-Defence?', 85 *AJIL* (1993) 506.
Roucounas E., 'Engagements parallèles et contradictoires', 206 *RdC* (1987–VI) 9.
Rougier A., 'La théorie de l'intervention d'humanité', 17 *RGDIP* (1910) 468.
Sadurska R., 'Foreign Submarines in Swedish Waters: The Erosion of an International Norm', 10 *YJIL* (1984–5) 34.
Sadurska R., 'Threats to Force', 82 *AJIL* (1988) 239.
Salter L. M., 'Commando Coup at Entebbe: Humanitarian Intervention or Barbaric Aggression?', 11 *IL* (1977) 331.
Scelle G., 'Règles générales du droit de la paix', 46 *RdC* (1933–IV) 327.
Schachter O., 'The Enforcement of International Judicial and Arbitral Decisions', 54 *AJIL* (1960) 1.
——, 'Legal Issues at the United Nations', *Annual Review of the UN Affairs*, 1960–1, p. 142.
——, 'The Right of States to Use Armed Force', 82 *MLR* (1984) 1620.
——, 'In Defense of International Rules on the Use of Force', 53 *UCLR* (1986) 113.
——, 'The Lawful Use of Force by a State against Terrorists in Another Country', 19 *IYHR* (1989) 209.

——, 'United Nations in the Gulf Conflict', 85 *AJIL* (1991) 452.
Schmitt M. N., 'Computer Network Attack and the Use of Force in International Law: Thoughts on a Normative Framework', 37 *CJTL* (1999) 885.
——, 'Preemptive Strategies in International Law', 24 *MJIL* (2003) 513.
Schreuer C., 'Recommendations and the Traditional Sources of International Law', 20 *GYIL* (1977) 103.
Schwarzenberger G., 'The Fundamental Principles of International Law', 87 *RdC* (1955–I) 191.
——, 'Problems of a United Nations Force', 12 *CLP* (1959) 247.
——, 'The Problem of an International Criminal Law', 13 *CLP* (1960) 263.
Schwebel S. M., 'Aggression, Intervention and Self-Defense', 136 *RdC* (1972–II) 411.
Sciso E., 'L'aggressione indiretta nella definizione dell'Assemblea Generale delle Nazioni Unite', 66 *RDI* (1983) 253.
——, 'Legittima difesa ed aggressione indiretta secondo la Corte internazionale di giustizia, 70 *RDI* (1987) 627.
——, 'On Article 103 of the Charter of the United Nations in the Light of the Vienna Convention on the Law of Treaties', 38 *ÖZöRV* (1987) 161.
Scott J. B., 'Interpretation of Article X of the Covenant of the League of Nations', 18 *AJIL* (1924) 108.
Seyersted F., 'United Nations Forces: Some Legal Problems', 36 *BYIL* (1961) 351.
Shapira A., 'The Six Days War and the Right of Self-Defence', 6 *Isr. LR* (1971) 65.
Sicilianos A. L., 'L'autorisation par le Conseil de sécurité de recourir à la force: une tentative d'évaluation', 105 *RGDIP* (2001) 5.
Simma B., 'NATO, the UN and the Use of Force: Legal Aspects', 10 *EJIL* (1999) 1.
Singh N., 'The Right of Self-Defence in Relation to the Use of Nuclear Weapons', 5 *Indian Yearbook Int. Affairs* (1956) 3.
Skubiszewski K., 'Definition of Terrorism', 19 *IYHR* (1989) 39.
Slaughter A-M. and W. Burke-White, 'An International Constitutional Moment', 43 *HILJ* (2002) 1.
Sofaer A., 'Terrorism, the Law and the National Defense', 126 *Mil. LR* (1989) 89.
——, 'On the Necessity of Pre-emption', 14 *EJIL* (2003) 209.
Sohn L., 'The Authority of the United Nations to Establish and Maintain a Permanent Force', 52 *AJIL* (1958) 229.
——, 'The Missile Attack on Baghdad and its Justifications', *ASIL Newsletter*, Jun.–Aug. 1993, p. 4.
Spatafora M., 'L'intervento militare delle Nazioni Unite in Congo', 51 *RDI* (1968) 517.
Stahn C., 'International Law at a Crossroad?', 62 *ZaöRV* (2002) 183.
Starace V., 'Uso della forza nell'ordinamento internazionale', in 32 *EG* (1994) 1.
Stavropoulos C. A., 'The Practice of Voluntary Abstention by Permanent Members of the Security Council under Article 27, Paragraph 3, of the Charter of the United Nations', 61 *AJIL* (1967) 737.
Stein T. L., 'Contempt, Crisis, and the Court: The World Court and the Hostage Rescue Attempt', 76 *AJIL* (1982) 499.
Stephens D., 'Rules of Engagement and the Concept of Unit Self-defence', 45 *NLR* (1998) 126.
Stone J., 'Book Review of I. Brownlie, *International Law and the Use of Force by States*', 59 *AJIL* (1965) 396.
Sundeberg J., 'Legitimate Responses to Aerial Intruders: The View from a Neutral State',

10 *AASL* (1985) 251.
Sur S., 'Vérification en matière de désarmement', 273 *RdC* (1998) 9.
Szasz P. C., 'The Security Council Starts Legislating', 96 *AJIL* (2002) 901
Taft IV W. H., 'Self-Defense and the *Oil Platforms* Decision', 29 *YJIL* (2004) 295.
Tammes A. J. P., 'Decisions of International Organs as a Source of International Law', 94 *RdC* (1958–II) 265.
Tharoor S., 'The Changing Face of Peace-Keeping and Peace-Enforcement', 19 *FILJ* (1995) 408.
Thirlway H., 'The Law and Procedure of the International Court of Justice, 1960–1989, Part Three', 62 *BYIL* (1991) 1.
Tomuschat C., 'Obligations Arising for Member States Without or Against their Will', 241 *RdC* (1993–IV) 195.
——, 'Der 11 September und seine rechtlichen Konsequenzen', 28 *EuGRZ* (2001) 535.
Tucker R. W., 'The Interpretation of War under Present International Law', 4 *ILQ* (1951) 11.
Tunkin G., 'Is General International Law Customary Only?', 4 *EJIL* (1993) 534.
Vagts D. F., 'Hegemonic International Law', 95 *AJIL* (2001) 843.
Verhoeven J., 'Etats alliés ou Nations Unies? L'O.N.U. face au conflit entre l'Iraq et le Koweït', 36 *AFDI* (1990) 145.
Villani U., 'Sul ruolo quasi giudiziario del Consiglio di sicurezza', 51 *CI* (1996) 25.
——, 'La nuova crisi del Golfo e l'uso della forza contro l'Iraq', 82 *RDI* (1999) 451.
——, 'The Security Council's Authorization of Enforcement Action by Regional Organizations', 6 *MPYUNL* (2002) 535.
Von Elbe J., 'The Evolution of the Concept of Just War in International Law', 33 *AJIL* (1939) 786.
Walden R., 'Customary International Law: A Jurisprudential Analysis', 13 *Isr. LR* (1978) 86.
Waldock C. H. M, 'The Regulation of the Use of Force by Individual States in International Law', 81 *RdC* (1951–I) 455.
——, 'General Course on Public International Law', 106 *RdC* (1962–II) 1.
Walter C., 'Security Council Control over Regional Action', 1 *MPYUNL* (1997) 129.
Warbrick C., 'The Invasion of Kuwait by Iraq', 40 *ICLQ* (1990) 965.
Watson G. R., 'Constitutionalism, Judicial Review, and the World Court', 34 *HILJ* (1993) 1.
Wedgwood R., 'Responding to Terrorism: The Strikes Against Bin Laden', 24 *YJIL* (1999) 559.
Weil P., 'Towards Relative Normativity in International Law?', 77 *AJIL* (1983) 413.
Weisburd M., 'Customary International Law: The Problem of Treaties', 21 *VJTL* (1988) 1.
Weller M., 'The Kuwait Crisis: Survey of Some Legal Issues', 3 *AJICL* (1991) 1.
——, 'The Lockerbie Case: a Premature End of the "New World Order"', 3 *AJICL* (1992) 319.
——, 'Peace-Keeping and Peace-Enforcement in the Republic of Bosnia and Herzegovina', 56 *ZaöRV* (1996) 70.
Weston B. H., 'Security Council Resolution 678 and Persian Gulf Decision Making: Precarious Legitimacy', 85 *AJIL* (1991) 516.
White N. D., 'The Legality of Bombing in the Name of Humanity', 5 *JCSL* (2000) 27.
——, 'The Will and Authority of the Security Council after Iraq', 17 *LJIL* (2004) 1.
White N. D. and Cryer R., 'Unilateral Enforcement of Resolution 678: A Threat too Far?', 29 *Cal. Western ILJ* (1999) 243.

White N. D. and Ö. Ülgen, 'The Security Council and the Decentralised Military Option: Constitutionality and Function', 44 *NILR* (1997) 378.

Wolfrum R., 'The Attack of September 11 2001, the Wars against the Taliban and Iraq: Is There a Need to Reconsider International Law on the Recourse of Force and the Rules on Armed Conflict?', 7 *MPYUNL* (2003) 1.

Wood M. C., 'The Interpretation of Security Council Resolutions', 2 *MPYUNL* (1998) 73.

Wright Q., 'Changes in the Conception of War', 18 *AJIL* (1924) 755.

——, 'The Outlawry of War', 19 *AJIL* (1925) 76.

——, 'Permissive Sanctions Against Aggression', 37 *AJIL* (1942) 103.

——, 'The Prevention of Aggression', 50 *AJIL* (1956) 514.

——, 'Legal Aspects of the U-2 Incident', 54 *AJIL* (1960) 836.

——, 'The Cuban Quarantine', 55 *AJIL* (1963) 546.

Yasseen M. K., 'L'interprétation des traités d'après la Convention de Vienne sur le droit des traités', 151 *RdC* (1976–III) 1.

Yokaris A. and G. Kyriakopoulos, 'La juridiction de l'Etat côtier sur l'espace aérien national et international. A propos de l'affaire de CESSNA abattus par la chasse cubaine', 101 *RGDIP* (1997) 493.

Yoxall T., 'Iraq and Article 51: A Correct Use of Limited Authority', 25 *IL* (1991) 967.

Zoller E., 'The "Corporate Will" of the United Nations and the Rights of the Minority', 81 *AJIL* (1987) 610.

Articles in collected essays

Ago R., 'Le quarantième anniversaire des Nations Unies', in D. Bardonnet (ed.), *The Adaptation of Structures and Methods at the United Nations*, Dordrecht: Nijhoff, 1986, pp. 25 *et seq*.

Akehurst M., 'Humanitarian Intervention', in H. Bull (ed.), *Intervention in World Politics*, Oxford: Clarendon Press, 1984, pp. 106 *et seq*.

Angelet N., 'Protest against Security Council Decisions', in K. Wellens (ed.), *International Law: Theory and Practice, Essays E. Suy*, The Hague: Nijhoff, 1998, pp. 277 *et seq*.

Arangio-Ruiz G., 'The Establishment of the International Criminal Tribunal for the Former Territory of Yugoslavia and the Doctrine of Implied Powers of the United Nations', in F. Lattanzi and E. Sciso (eds.), *Dai tribunali penali internazionali* ad hoc *a una corte permanente*, Napoli: Ed. Scientifica, 1996, pp. 31 *et seq*.

Barsotti R., 'Armed Reprisals', in A. Cassese (ed.), *The Current Legal Regulation of the Use of Force*, Dordrecht: Nijhoff, 1986, pp. 79 *et seq*.

Bernhardt R., 'Article 103', in B. Simma (ed.), *The Charter of the United Nations*, 2nd ed., Oxford: Oxford University Press, 2002, pp. 1292 *et seq*.

Bothe M., 'Les limites des pouvoirs du Conseil de Sécurité', in R. -J. Dupuy (ed.), *The Development of the Role of the Security Council*, Nijhoff: Dordrecht, 1993, pp. 67 *et seq*.

Bowett D. W., 'Collective Security and Collective Self-Defence: The Errors and Risks in Identification', in M. Rama-Montaldo (ed.), *International Law in an Evolving World, Liber Amicorum E. Jiménez de Arechaga*, Montevideo: Fundación de cultura universitaria, 1994, pp. 425 *et seq*.

——, 'Judicial and Political Functions of the Security Council and the International Court of Justice', in H. Fox (ed.), *The Changing Constitution of the United Nations*, London: BIICL, 1997, pp. 73 *et seq*.

Brownlie I., 'Thoughts on Kind-Hearted Gunman', in R. B. Lillich (ed.), *Humanitarian Intervention and the United Nations*, Charlottesville: University Press of Virginia, 1973, pp. 139 *et seq.*

——, 'The Decisions of the Political Organs of the United Nations and the Rule of Law', in S. St Macdonald (ed.), *Essays in Honour of Wang Tieya*, Dordrecht: Nijhoff, 1993, pp. 91 *et seq.*

Caflish L., 'Is the International Court Entitled to Review Security Council Decisions adopted under Chapter VII of the United Nations Charter?', in N. Al-Nauimi *et al.* (eds.), *International Legal Issues Arising under the United Nations Decade of International Law*, The Hague: Nijhoff, 1995, pp. 633 *et seq.*

Capotorti F., 'Sul valore della prassi applicativa dei trattati secondo la Convenzione di Vienna', in *Essays Ago, International Law at the Time of its Codification*, Milano: Giuffrè, 1987, pp. 197 *et seq.*

Cassese A., 'Return to Westphalia? Considerations on the Gradual Erosion of the Charter System', in A. Cassese (ed.), *The Current Legal Regulation of the Use of Force*, Dordrecht: Nijhoff, 1986, pp. 505 *et seq.*

——, 'Article 51', in J. P. Cot and A. Pellet (eds.), *La Charte des Nations Unies*, Paris: Economica, 1991, pp. 771 *et seq.*

Chayes A., 'The Use of Force in the Persian Gulf', in L. Fisler Damrosch and D. J. Scheffer (eds.), *Law and Force in the New International Order*, Boulder: Westview, 1993, pp. 3 *et seq.*

Cheng B., 'The Destruction of KAL Flight KE 007 and Art 3 bis of the Chicago Convention', in J. W. E. Storm Van Gravesonde and A. Van der Veen Vonk (eds.), *Air Worthy*, Deventer: Kluwer, 1985, pp. 49 *et seq.*

Claude I. L., 'The Security Council', in E. Luard (ed.), *The Evolution of International Organizations*, New York: Thames and Hudson, 1966, pp. 68 *et seq.*

Cohen-Jonathan G., 'Article 39', in J. P. Cot and A. Pellet (eds.), *La Charte des Nations Unies*, Paris: Economica, 1991, pp. 648 *et seq.*

Combacau J., 'The Exception of Self-Defence in U.N. Practice', in A. Cassese (ed.), *The Current Legal Regulation of the Use of Force*, Dordrecht: Nijhoff, 1986, pp. 9 *et seq.*

Condorelli L., 'Discussion', in A. Cassese and J. H. H. Weiler (eds.), *Change and Stability in International Law-Making*, Berlin: W. De Gruyter, 1988, pp. 117 *et seq.*

Condorelli L. and L. Boisson de Chazournes, 'Quelques remarques à propos de l'obligation des Etats de "respecter et faire respecter" le droit humanitaire "en toutes circonstances"', in C. Swinarski, *Studies and Essays on international Humanitarian Law and Red Cross Principles in Honour of J. Pictet*, Geneva: ICRC, 1984, pp. 17 *et seq.*

Conforti B., 'Le pouvoir discrétionnaire du Conseil de sécurité en matière de constatation d'une menace contre la paix, d'une rupture ou d'un acte d'agression', in R. J. Dupuy (ed.), *The Development of the Role of the Security Council*, Nijhoff: Dordrecht, 1993, pp. 51 *et seq.*

Cottereau G., 'Obligation de négocier et de conclure?', in SFDI, *Le droit international des armes nucléaires*, Paris: Pédone, 1998, pp. 163 *et seq.*

Cremasco M., 'Il caso Somalia', in N. Ronzitti (ed.), *Comando e controllo nelle forze di pace e nelle coalizioni militari*, Milano: Angeli, 1999, pp. 173 *et seq.*

Delbrück J., 'Article 24', in B. Simma (ed.), *The Charter of the United Nations*, 2nd ed., Oxford: Oxford University Press, 2002, pp. 442 *et seq.*

Dinstein Y., 'Computer Network Attacks and Self-Defence', in M. N. Schmitt and B. T.

O'Donnell (eds.), *Computer Network Attacks and International Law*, Newport: Naval War College Press, 2002, pp. 163 *et seq*.

Dominicé C., 'L'Article 103 de la Charte des Nations Unies et le droit international humanitaire', in L. Condorelli, A. M. La Rosa and S. Scherrer (eds.), *The United Nations and International Humanitarian Law*, Paris: Pédone, 1996, pp. 177 *et seq*.

Elaraby N., 'The Office of the Secretary-General and the Maintenance of International Peace and Security', in UNITAR, *The United Nations and the Maintenance of International Peace and Security*, Dordrecht: Nijhoff, 1987, pp. 177 *et seq*.

Flory T., 'Article 103', in J. P. Cot and A. Pellet (eds.), *La Charte des Nations Unies*, Paris: Economica, 1991, pp. 1381 *et seq*.

Forlati Picchio M. L., 'Introduzione', in M. L. Forlati Picchio (ed.), *Le Nazioni Unite*, Torino: Giappichelli, 1998, pp. 7 *et seq*.

Franck T. M., 'The Relation of Justice to Legitimacy in the International System', in *Humanité et droit international. Mélanges R-J. Dupuy*, Paris: Pédone, 1991, pp. 159 *et seq*.

Frowein J. A. and N. Krisch, 'Article 39', in B. Simma (ed.), *The Charter of the United Nations*, 2nd ed., Oxford: Oxford University Press, 2002, pp. 717 *et seq*.

Gaja G., 'Use of Force Made or Authorized by the United Nations', in C. Tomuschat (ed.), *The United Nations at Age Fifty*, The Hague: Kluwer, 1995, pp. 41 *et seq*.

——, 'Problemi attuali concernenti l'uso della forza nel sistema delle Nazioni Unite', in SIOI, *L'O.N.U.: Cinquant'anni di attività e prospettive per il futuro*, Roma: Presidenza del Consiglio, 1996, pp. 416 *et seq*.

Gioia A., 'The Chemical Weapons Convention and its Application in Time of Armed Conflict', in M. Bothe, N. Ronzitti and A. Rosas (eds.), *The New Chemical Weapons Convention. Implementation and Prospects*, The Hague: Kluwer, 1998, pp. 379 *et seq*.

Giraud E., 'Le droit positif, ses rapports avec la philosophie et la politique', in *Hommage d'une génération de juristes au Président Basdevant*, Paris: Pédone, 1960, pp. 210 *et seq*.

Henkin L., 'Use of Force: Law and United States Policy', in L. Henkin, *Right* v. *Might: International Law and the Use of Force* 2nd ed, New York: Council on Foreign Relations Press, 1991, pp. 37 *et seq*.

Higgins R., 'The Attitude of Western States Towards Legal Aspects of the Use of Force', in A. Cassese (ed.), *The Current Legal Regulation of the Use of Force*, Dordrecht: Nijhoff, 1986, pp. 435 *et seq*.

——, 'Introduction', in R. Higgins and M. Flory (eds.), *International Law and Terrorism*, London: Routledge, 1997, pp. 13 *et seq*.

Jennings R. Y., 'International Force and the International Court of Justice', in A. Cassese (ed.), *The Current Legal Regulation of the Use of Force*, Dordrecht: Nijhoff, 1986, pp. 323 *et seq*.

Kohen M., 'The notion of "State survival" in International Law', in L. Boisson de Chazournes and P. Sands (eds.), *International Law, the International Court of Justice and Nuclear Weapons*, Cambridge: Cambridge University Press, 1999, pp. 293 *et seq*.

Koojimans P. H., 'The Enlargement of the Concept Threat to Peace', in R. J. Dupuy (ed.), *The Development of the Role of the Security Council*, Nijhoff: Dordrecht, 1993, pp. 111 *et seq*.

Ku C. and H. K. Jacobson, 'Toward a Mixed System of Democratic Accountability', in C. Ku and H. K. Jacobson (eds.), *Democratic Accountability and the Use of Force in International Law*, Cambridge: Cambridge University Press, 2002, pp. 349 *et seq*.

Lamb S., 'Legal Limits to United Nations Security Council Powers', in S. G. Goodwin-Gill and S. Talmon (eds.), *The Reality of International Law. Essays Brownlie*, Oxford: Clarendon Press, 1999, pp. 361 *et seq.*

Lamberti Zanardi P., 'Indirect Military Aggression', in A. Cassese (ed.), *The Current Legal Regulation of the Use of Force*, Dordrecht: Nijhoff, 1986, pp. 111 *et seq.*

Lattanzi F., 'Consiglio di sicurezza ed emergenza umanitaria', SIOI, *L'O.N.U.: Cinquant'anni di attività e prospettive per il futuro*, Roma: Presidenza del Consiglio, 1996, pp. 503 *et seq.*

Lauterpacht E., 'The Legal Effects of Illegal Acts of International Organizations', in R. Y. Jennings *et al.* (eds.), *Cambridge Essays in International Law*, London: Stevens, 1956, pp. 88 *et seq.*

Lowe V. A., 'Self-Defence at Sea', in W. E. Butler, (ed.), *The Non-Use of Force in International Law*, Dordrecht: Nijhoff, 1989, pp. 185 *et seq.*

Marchisio S., 'La teoria dei due cerchi', in E. Sciso (ed.), *Intervento in Kosovo. Aspetti internazionalistici e interni*, Milano: Giuffrè, 2001, pp. 21 *et seq.*

Mendelson M. H., 'The *Nicaragua* Case and Customary International Law', in W. E. Butler (ed.), *The Non-Use of Force in International Law*, Dordrecht: Nijhoff, 1998, pp. 85 *et seq.*

Müller J. P. and R. Kolb, 'Article 2(2)', in B. Simma (ed.), *The Charter of the United Nations*, 2nd ed., Oxford: Oxford University Press, 2002, pp. 91 *et seq.*

Picone P., 'Interventi delle Nazioni Unite e obblighi *erga omnes*', in P. Picone (ed.), *Interventi delle Nazioni Unite*, Padova: CEDAM, 1995, pp. 552 *et seq.*

Pogany I., 'Nuclear Weapons and Self-defence in International Law', in I. Pogany (ed.), *Nuclear Weapons and International Law*, Aldershot: Avebury, 1987, pp. 63 *et seq.*

Reisman M. W. and M. S. McDougal, 'Humanitarian Intervention to Protect the Ibos?', in R. B. Lillich (ed.), *Humanitarian Intervention and the United Nations*, Charlottesville: University Press of Virginia, pp. 167 *et seq.*

Reuter P., 'Organisations internationales et évolution du droit', in *L'évolution du droit public. Etudes offertes à Achille Mestre*, Paris: Sirey, 1956, pp. 447 *et seq.*

Rivkin D. B., 'Commentary on Aggression and Self-Defense', in L. Fisler Damrosch and D. J. Scheffer (eds.), *Law and Force in the New International Order*, Boulder: Westview Press, 1993, pp. 54 *et seq.*

Roberts A., 'The Relevance of the Laws of War in the Nuclear Age', in J. Dewar (ed.), *Nuclear Weapons, the Peace Movement and the Law*, Basingstoke: Macmillan, 1986, pp. 25 *et seq.*

Rodley N., 'Collective Intervention to Protect Human Rights and Civilian Populations: The Legal Framework', in N. Rodley (ed.), *To Loose the Bands of Wickedness*, London: Brassey's, 1992, pp. 33 *et seq.*

Ronzitti N., 'Relations Between the Chemical Weapons Convention and Other Relevant International Norms', in D. Bardonnet (ed.), *The Convention on the Prohibition and Elimination of Chemical Weapons: A Breakthrough in Multilateral Disarmament*, Dordrecht: Nijhoff, 1995, pp. 167 *et seq.*

Rosas A., 'Reaction in the Event of Breach', in D. Bardonnet (ed.), *The Convention on the Prohibition and Elimination of Chemical Weapons: A Breakthrough in Multilateral Disarmament*, Dordrecht: Nijhoff, 1995, pp. 555 *et seq.*

Sciso E., 'L'intervento in Kosovo. L'improbabile passaggio dal principio del divieto a quello dell'uso della forza armata', in E. Sciso (ed.), *Intervento in Kosovo. Aspetti internazionalistici e interni*, Milano: Giuffrè, 2001, pp. 47 *et seq.*

Shaw M. N., 'The Security Council and the International Court of Justice', in A. S. Muller *et al.* (eds.), *The International Court of Justice. Its Future Role after Fifty Years*, The Hague: Nijhoff, 1997, pp. 219 *et seq*.

Simma B., 'Does the UN Charter Provide an Adequate Legal Basis for Individual or Collective Responses to violations of International Obligations *erga omnes*?', in J. Delbrück (ed.), *The Future of International Law Enforcement. New Scenarios – New Law?*, Berlin: Duncker & Humblot, 1993, pp. 125 *et seq*.

Skubiszewski K., 'Implied Powers of International Organizations', in Y. Dinstein (ed.), *International Law at a Time of Perplexity, Essays Rosenne*, Dordrecht: Nijhoff, 1989, pp. 855 *et seq*.

Sorel J. -M., 'L'élargissement de la notion de menace contre la paix', in SFDI, *Le Chapitre VII de la Charte des Nations Unies*, Paris: Pédone, 1996, pp. 3 *et seq*.

Stromseth J., 'Rethinking Humanitarian Intervention: the Case of Incremental Change', in J. L. Holzgrefe and R. O. Keohane (eds.), *Humanitarian Intervention. Ethical, Legal and Political Dilemmas*, Cambridge: Cambridge University Press, 2003, pp. 232 *et seq*.

Virally M., 'Article 2 Paragraph 4', in J. P. Cot and A. Pellet (eds.), *La Charte des Nations Unies*, Paris: Economica, 1991, pp. 115 *et seq*.

Vukas B., 'Peaceful Uses of the Sea, Denuclearization and Disarmament', in R. -J. Dupuy and D. Vignes (eds.), *A Handbook on the New Law of the Sea*, Dordrecht: Nijhoff, 1995, pp. 1233 *et seq*.

Walter C., 'Defining Terrorism in National and International Law', in C. Walter *et al*. (eds.), *Terrorism as a Challenge for National and International Law: Security versus Liberty?*, Berlin: Springer, 2004, pp. 23 *et seq*.

Wheeler M. O., 'NATO Nuclear Strategy, 1949–90', in G. Schmidt (ed.), *A History of NATO . The First Fifty Years*, New York: Palgrave, 2001, vol. 3, pp. 121 *et seq*.

Zemanek K., 'Majority Rule and Consensus Technique in Law-Making Diplomacy', in R. St Macdonald and D. M. Johnston (eds.), *The Structure and Process of International Law: Essays in Legal Philosophy Doctrine and Theory*, The Hague: Nijhoff, 1983, pp. 857 *et seq*.

——, 'Is the Security Council the Sole Judge of its own Legality?', in Yapko E. and Boumedra T. (eds.), *Liber Amicorum Judge M. Bedjaoui*, The Hague: Kluwer, 1999, pp. 629 *et seq*.

Index